Managing TV Brands with Social Media

Jennifer Berz

Managing TV Brands with Social Media

An Empirical Analysis of Television Series Brands

 Springer VS

Jennifer Berz
Mainz, Deutschland

Die vorliegende Arbeit wurde vom Fachbereich 02 - Sozialwissenschaften, Medien und Sport der Johannes Gutenberg-Universität Mainz im Jahr 2015 als Dissertation zur Erlangung des akademischen Grades eines Doktors der Philosophie (Dr. phil.) angenommen.

ISBN 978-3-658-14293-3   ISBN 978-3-658-14294-0 (eBook)
DOI 10.1007/978-3-658-14294-0

Library of Congress Control Number: 2016940116

Springer VS
© Springer Fachmedien Wiesbaden 2016

Printed on acid-free paper

This Springer VS imprint is published by Springer Nature
The registered company is Springer Fachmedien Wiesbaden GmbH

Vorwort

Als die Idee für diese Arbeit entstand, hatte ich eine Forschungsfrage im Kopf, aber noch keine Ahnung, wie ich sie jemals zu dem umfangreichen Projekt machen sollte, das letztendlich aus ihr geworden ist. Ich möchte deshalb all denjenigen danken, die es mir ermöglicht haben, mich an dieses Forschungsprojekt heranzuwagen und mich auf dem Weg, meine Dissertation fertigzustellen, begleitet haben.

Zunächst möchte ich Professor Heinz-Werner Nienstedt für die Begleitung und Betreuung meiner Promotion danken. Dank Ihrer kritischen Anmerkungen habe ich den roten Faden nie aus den Augen verloren und meine Arbeit immer wieder hinterfragen und verbessern können.

Vielen Dank an Professor Christian Schemer für die Übernahme des Koreferats.

Einige Kollegen an der Uni Mainz haben meine Promotion durch wertvolle Anmerkungen, bereitwilliges Diskutieren oder auch ein offenes Ohr bereichert. Insbesondere danken möchte ich Tanja Eiff, Yasin Gülsahin und Jana Mitreuter.

Die vorliegende Arbeit mag meine Leistung sein, aber jede Promovendin ist nur so gut wie das Team, das hinter ihr steht. Ganz besonders danken möchte ich deshalb Paula Helbig, die gegen Ende immer genau das richtige Maß an Ungeduld aufbrachte, und Jannik Berz. Dein motivierender Zettel hing fast drei Jahre lang über meinem Schreibtisch. Christiane Helbig-Berz und Helmut Berz, für mehr als ich hier aufzählen könnte. Und ganz besonders Nicola Berz.

Table of Contents

List of Figures

List of Tables

List of Abbreviations

AGF	Arbeitsgemeinschaft Fernsehforschung
ALM	Arbeitsgemeinschaft der Landesmedienanstalten
AMOS	Analysis of Moment Structures
AVE	average variance extracted
BARP	brand as relationship partner
BRQ	brand relationship quality
ed.	editor
eds.	editors
EUR	Euro
eWOM	electronic word-of-mouth
f.	and the following page
ff.	and the following pages
GfK	Gesellschaft für Konsumforschung
GNTM	Germany's Next Topmodel
LISREL	Linear Structural Relationship
MMORPG	massively multiplayer online role-playing game
OECD	Organisation for Economic Co-operation and Development
p.	page
pp.	pages
PLS	Partial Least Squares
SEM	structural equation modelling
SNS	social networking site(s)
TV	television
TVoG	The Voice of Germany
UGC	user generated content
UK	United Kingdom of Great Britain and Northern Ireland
US	United States (of America)
VIF	variance inflation factor
WOM	word-of-mouth

List of Construct Abbreviations

BL	Brand loyalty
CBR	Consumer-brand relationship
SMP	Attitude toward the social media programme for the serialised TV brand
SME	Engagement in the social media programme for the serialised TV brand
GOS	Gratifications obtained from the social media programme
GO	Gratifications obtained from the serialised TV brand
PCR	Perceived critics' response to the serialised TV brand
PWR	Perceived WOM response to the serialised TV brand

1 Introduction

The television industry in Germany has adopted principles of branding and brand management in recent years. While branding has been common practice and an essential marketing tool for fast-moving consumer goods for decades, media brands tend to lag behind. Whereas print media can provide some evidence of a tradition of branding, TV and radio brands, due to strict regulation in these markets, were for a long time not necessary. Only after deregulation of broadcasting in the mid 1980s did commercial television and radio start to introduce consistent brand concepts (Wirtz 2006, p. 106). To sharpen channel profiles despite the rising number of available channels, the development of television brands has become increasingly relevant in order to establish strong images in consumers' minds (Chan-Olmsted 2011). However, media brands have to a wide extent evolved gradually and without dedicated planning or management effort behind them (Siegert 2001, p. 97f.).

Branding means "endowing products and services with the power of a brand" (Kotler & Keller 2007, p. 136). The American Marketing Association (2014) defines a brand as a "name, term, design, symbol, or any other feature that identifies one seller's good or service as distinct from those of other sellers" (cf. section 2.1). Thus, companies try to distinguish their products or services from those of other companies.

This study explores the employment of social media tools for brand management purposes with regard to serialised television brands and investigates the impact of social media strategies on users' loyalty toward these brands. The aim of this study is to develop a model framework that assumes brand loyalty as the key television specific success indicator and that investigates the hypothesized causal relationships between social media related constructs, television related constructs, as well as brand related constructs. The model is then empirically tested for three German television brands.

This chapter provides an introduction to the study: The relevance of the topic from a media management perspective is identified, followed by a specification of the research focus and objectives of the study. The orientation of the study in science theory is explained, and the last section provides an outline of the structure of this study.

1.1 Relevance of the topic from a media management perspective

Commercial television makes use of a two-phase business model addressing two distinct target groups, namely audiences and advertisers, and therefore operates on three markets: the markets for audiences, advertisers, and content. While audience-based strategies focus on the general public as potential viewers, advertiser-based strategies are aimed at business decision-makers (McDowell 2006a, p. 3). The underlying business model of commercial television is to sell audiences to advertisers or, in the case of pay television, direct payments received from subscribers.[1] This, in a first step, requires the production and/or broadcasting of content that attracts and retains audiences.

Commercial television faces three distinct factors influencing the success of its core business model, i.e. the generation of advertising revenue: firstly, the economic development in general, which impacts advertising spending; secondly, the development of the share of television advertising with regard to the advertising market as a whole; and thirdly, the broadcaster's own share with regard to the television advertising market (Weil 2011, p. 20).

The general economic development cannot be influenced by the television company and therefore has to be taken as a given. Similarly, the development of the share of television advertising with regard to the advertising market as a whole is difficult to influence. Currently, despite ongoing technological change and the alternative choices and subsequent change in media consumption it entails, television still holds a strong position with both consumers and advertisers. According to the 2010 ARD/ZDF-Langzeitstudie Massenkommunikation, a longitudinal study on mass media and their consumption in Germany, television was the most important medium consumers used every day (Zubayr & Gerhard 2011, p. 126). In 2010, the average viewing time of the German population across all age groups starting at age three increased from 212 minutes per day in 2009 to 223 minutes per day (ibid., p. 127). Although television usage decreased to 222 minutes per day in 2012, television remained the most frequently used medium (ALM 2013, p. 54).

As a result, television is the most important advertising medium in Germany (cf. Figure 1-1). In 2013, net advertising spending totalled EUR 15.3 billion, EUR 4.1 billion of which

---

[1] In Germany, due to the dual broadcasting system ("Duales Rundfunksystem"), commercial television exists alongside public service television. While the business model for commercial television is based on advertising or subscription revenue, public service television is funded by licence fees.

accounted for television, an increase of 2.2 percent as opposed to 2012 (ZAW 2014). This positive development can be monitored since 2010 (Möbus & Heffler 2011; Heffler & Möbus 2014; ZAW 2014). Hence, despite competition from other media, especially the internet, television is still able to generate considerable advertising revenue. While 27.1 percent of net advertising revenue was generated by television in 2013, only 7.6 percent were generated by online and mobile (ZAW 2014; cf. Figure 1-1).

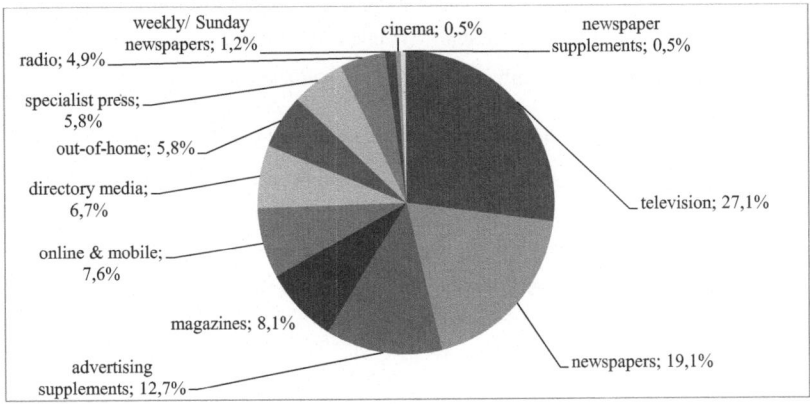

Figure 1-1: Net advertising revenues of advertising media in Germany in 2013

Source: Own design based on data provided by ZAW (2014)

In the long run, however, the distribution of advertising revenues between media types is difficult to foresee and can hardly be influenced by a television company. In contrast, the company's own share of the television advertising market can be managed, an objective for which attraction and retention of audience attention are a crucial success factor.

Branding strategies support this managerial objective, but need to take into account the changes in the environment such as digitisation and subsequent technological change and convergence, cultural and economic globalisation, as well as ongoing privatisation and concentration (Siegert 2002, p. 178). These changes have led to both fiercer competition in the media industries and to changes in consumer behaviour such as an increase in individualisation, value pluralism and a focus on experience orientation.

With regard to *competition,* new technological standards, especially digital television, have enabled a rise in the number of channels available for consumers. Competition, therefore, has increased among television channels, but also between media types. The emergence of new technologies has not led to a replacement of established ones, but rather to a coexistence. With regard to Dimmick's theory of the niche (Dimmick & Rothenbuhler 1984; Dimmick, Kline, & Stafford 2000), these types of media provide different gratifications (cf. section 2.4.2 for an overview of social media gratifications and sections 3.1.5 and 3.1.6 for conceptualisations of social media and television gratifications with regard to this study); i.e. there is no complete competitive displacement of traditional media. For television, especially the internet is a competitor for both consumer attention and advertising spending, which calls for distinct branding objectives to offer distinguishable gratifications.

Also, ongoing *media convergence* blurs the boundaries between media. Online extensions of content are no longer an additional offering, but essential to survive, which challenges brand boundaries and demands transferability of brands from one medium to the next. Media convergence is also increasingly reflected in corporate structures of media companies. Large media corporations control diversified portfolios, which necessitates a clear brand architecture.

With television sets having a plethora of features, among them recording, and with channels offering their content online after broadcasting, *timeshifted television consumption* continues to increase. While market penetration of these technologies is expected to take significantly more time than that of other technological innovations due to the fact that television sets are replaced in longer intervals than mobile phones or computers (Schmidt 2011), consumers already make active use of the internet and their computers in order to watch video content. On-demand television and mobile TV are also on the rise. This blurring of boundaries between television and online experiences makes it crucial to develop extensions of television brands for digital environments. Television programmes and other video content is consumed online, but to a considerable extent also on illegal streaming and file sharing websites: A study by the European Commision found that 56 percent of viewers are already streaming video content free of charge (European Commission 2014). One reason for this is that many viewers show a high degree of commitment towards their favourite TV programmes. However, this loyalty does not always translate into loyalty toward the branded content available through official channels. A 2012 study conducted by GfK found that almost 30 percent of respondents could not agree to the statement that the current legal possibilities to buy or use films and series/serials online were sufficient, and over 50 percent could not agree to the statement that the current possibilities were perfectly suitable for their needs (GfK 2013, p. 9). Especially fans of serialised entertainment are increasingly less willing to wait for the German broadcasting of content already available in other countries. Through online channels, they receive information about release dates and programme planning, both in Germany and abroad. In the multi-channel and multi-device environment brought about by technological change, consumers are able to act out their preferences and will seek other ways to receive the content they desire if it is not (yet) available via traditional outlets. In addition, the ability of many viewers to watch content in English language also decreases dependence on German language broadcasts and significantly changes the way audiences interact with serialised content.

Consumer habits and behaviour are changing rapidly. With regard to television consumption, consumers are increasingly indifferent to where they find content. In 2013, in the United States, 43 percent of people aged 18-36 had subscribed to Netflix, as compared to 46 percent to cable TV (Richter 2013). Hence, the quality and the accessibility of content are relevant to consumers, while it no longer matters how that content is delivered to them. Media companies have begun to embrace changes in consumer behaviour. ProSiebenSat.1, for instance, is further developing their online video platform MyVideo. While part of the content is re-used television content, other programmes are developed for online streaming only. To promote the platform, some content is made available on MyVideo earlier than on television (ALM 2013, p. 74).

Also, ***modes of interaction*** have changed. A Nielsen study (2013) shows that television ratings in the United States have a statistically significant impact on related Twitter conversations among 48 percent of programme episodes aired, and that the volume of Twitter messages causes statistically significant changes in television ratings for 29 percent of these episodes. As a result, Nielsen Twitter TV Ratings provide media companies and advertisers with data on Twitter conversations for television programmes aired, thereby measuring the total activity and reach of TV related messages on Twitter (SocialGuide 2014). GfK and Twitter have recently announced a comparable partnership for Germany, Austria and the Netherlands (GfK 2014).

Branding hence takes place in an environment where consumers have more power than ever while historically, companies were in control if their brands. Social media, which allow for encounters between consumers and their brands, have made consumers part of the brand building process. In fact, social media strategies are already widely used in a television branding context (cf. section 2.5). It is therefore of particular academic and managerial relevance to investigate the management of serialised television brands with supporting social media strategies and how social media impact brand loyalty and the consumer-brand relationship.

1.2 Specification of the research focus and objectives of the study

Drawing upon existing literature, a conceptual model is developed that assumes loyalty as the key television specific success indicator and investigates the hypothesized causal relationships between social media related constructs, television related constructs, constructs referring to the social environment as well as brand related constructs.

1.2.1 Brand loyalty as key outcome variable of this study

In the light of the above mentioned developments in media consumption and consumer behaviour, audience retention can no longer only be described as regular watching of linear television, and no longer translates into ratings only. It is therefore necessary to regard a television programme as a concept that is extended into online and mobile environments, and that offers consumers consistent product quality. This study therefore uses the concept of television programmes as brands (cf. 2.1 for an overview on branding theory and 2.2 for television branding as a reference point of this study).

Brand loyalty is a "deeply held commitment to rebuy or repatronize a preferred product/service consistently in the future" (Oliver 1999, p. 34; cf. 3.1.1), which makes it a desirable outcome of brand management. It is used as key television specific success indicator in this study because, in contrast to other industries or product categories, the goal of branding objectives for television is not purchase, but consumer attention and retention.

This is due to the fact that although today's technology enables channels to restrict access to television content, commercial television is still largely free of charge, a circumstance that is unlikely to change. Firstly, the business model has proven successful so far (cf. 1.1). Secondly, in the dual broadcasting system, channels have to compete with free public service television. The German pay television market has therefore traditionally been struggling with the competition from public service broadcasting and the high number of free-to-air programmes (Karstens & Schütte 2010; Kiefer 2002), but has very recently started to undergo a positive development (ALM 2014, p. 79). Thirdly, a learned price of zero, a resulting high tolerance for advertising as well as institutional inertia and unwillingness to change on the part of media companies make it difficult to introduce paid content (Picot, Kooths, Kruse, & Dewenter 2009).

Hence, brand loyalty is the most suitable brand related outcome variable for this study because it combines attitudinal and behavioural components and can draw upon a rich theoretical background (e.g. Berry & Parasuraman 1991; Chaudhuri & Holbrook 2001; Day 1969; Dick & Basu 1994; Jacoby & Chestnut 1978; Morgan & Hunt 1994; Oliver 1999). Since the brand management paradigm this study uses as its framework is identity-based brand management as put forward by Aaker (1996), Kapferer (1992), and Meffert and Burmann (1996; 2005), the consumer-brand relationship construct, which relies heavily on the research conducted by Fournier (1994, 1998), is also part of the model, but is hypothesized to be an antecedent of brand loyalty (cf. 2.1.2.3 and 3.1.2).

Other constructs are not suitable because they lack the behavioural component brand loyalty provides. Brand knowledge, for instance, is defined as consisting of brand image and brand awareness, which in turn consists of brand recall and recognition (Keller 1993), all of which are cognitive variables.

It was also decided against the construct brand equity, which is "the 'added value' with which a brand endows a product" (Farquhar 1989, p. 24). Various perspectives on the construct have been formulated (for a financial perspective on brand equity, cf. Farquhar (1989) and Simon & Sullivan (1993); for a value-added perspective on brand equity, cf. Aaker & Biel (1993); for customer-based brand equity, cf. Keller (1993)) and both consumer level outcomes and firm level outcomes need to be addressed (Ailawadi, Lehmann, & Neslin 2003). In addition, measures of brand equity are diverse (e.g. Agarwal & Rao 1996; Ailawadi et al. 2003; Simon & Sullivan 1993). Since this study focuses on television brands as an audience construct, brand loyalty was chosen as the more suitable and straightforward construct.

1.2.2   Serialised television brands as the object of this study

Serialised television content exists in various forms, such as sports programmes, shows, or fictional content. Since sports programmes largely depend on events, such as the Olympics or national and international football matches, and brands are not managed by television channels, but by associated institutions, they are excluded from this study.

Various sections in chapter 2 provide examples and, if available, a theoretical background on serialised television brands in the form of fictional content and shows. Investigating brand loyalty in this context is particularly relevant for serialised television content. Since re-using of a product, i.e. re-buying it or continually consuming it, is part of the definition of brand loyalty, serialised content is better described by the loyalty construct than stand-alone branded media products.

In fact, loyalty and serialty are closely connected concepts (cf. 2.2.3 for a more detailed discussion of serialised television brands). On the one hand, viewers of serialised television content are very likely to pursue the content independently of platform or device. Firstly, they will wish to continue a series or serial they have started but not finished and therefore be more keen on accessing the content than consumers interested in stand-alone video content. Secondly, consumers of serialised content have previously assessed the quality of the content and will know what to expect, therefore being more loyal consumers.

Despite the obvious connection between loyalty and seriality, German television channels have struggled to convert it into audience retention (ALM 2014, p. 50). Programmes that had been successful in the previous year, such as the second season of the European production *Borgia* in autumn 2013 or the German broadcasting of *Downton Abbey* in December 2013, both on ZDF, failed to meet expectations in their second seasons. It is therefore particularly interesting to investigate new strategies to positively impact loyalty, such as social media.

In the course of model building, gratifications obtained (Katz, Blumler, & Gurevitch 1974; Palmgreen, Wenner, & Rayburn 1980; 1981) from television content are revisited (Cha & Chan-Olmsted 2012; Dehm & Storll 2003; Dehm, Storll, & Beeske 2005; Haridakis 2002; Haridakis & Hanson 2009; Kim & Rubin 1997; Logan 2011; Palmgreen & Lawrence 1991; Papacharissi & Mendelson 2007). It will be shown that gratifications obtained from the serialised TV brand directly impact brand loyalty in this study.

1.2.3 The social media programme as a branding tool

Social media refer to "a group of Internet-based applications that build on the ideological foundations of Web 2.0, and that allow the creation and exchange of User Generated Content" (Kaplan & Haenlein 2010, p. 61; cf. 2.4). In this study, all communicative messages dispersed via channel-owned social media tools aiming at viewer retention and acquisition are defined as the social media programme for the serialised TV brand (cf. 2.5).

It is due to the nature of social media, which require a certain level of activity on the side of the user, that targeted respondents of a social media branding study have to be users of social media content specifically produced for the brand under investigation. This implies that respondents are already aware of the brand, and need to have entered a basic relationship with it in order to be users of the social media offerings. Like seriality, social media are therefore particularly suitable to manage loyalty.

The sections on social media related input variables mainly explore attitude towards (Eagly & Chaiken 1998; Fazio & Olson 2003; Fishbein & Ajzen 1975; Petty & Cacioppo 1981; 1983; Rosenberg & Hovland 1960) and engagement in social media (Calder, Malthouse, & Schaedel 2009; Laurel 1993; O'Brien & Toms 2008; 2010; Zaichkowsky 1986; 1994). Gratifications users obtain from social media are revisited (Brandtzæg, Lüders, & Skjetne 2010; Busemann, Fisch, & Frees 2012; Foregger 2008; Park, Kee, & Valenzuela 2009; Quan-Haase & Young 2010; Raacke & Bonds-Raacke 2008) and electronic-word-of-mouth as a concept is examined (Godes & Mayzlin 2004; 2009; Hennig-Thurau, Gwinner, Walsh, & Gremler 2004; Kozinets, de Valck, Wojnicki, & Wilner 2010; Romaniuk 2007; Trusov, Bucklin, & Pauwels 2009).

It will be shown that attitude toward the social media programme has a strong positive impact on engagement in the social media programme, i.e. usage and involvement. Usage intensity in turn influences the key outcome variables, the consumer-brand relationship and brand loyalty. It will also be shown that gratifications obtained from the social media programme indirectly impact brand loyalty.

1.2.4 Objectives of the study

By investigating social media branding for serialised television brands, it is the intention of this study to contribute to the national and international state of the art in media branding research. It will be a valuable contribution to television brand management as well as to media and brand management literature.

Despite focusing on the German television market, it is inevitable to approach the topic from an international perspective. Many television series and serials broadcast in Germany are American productions. Since branding does not start at the stage of the broadcaster, but operates along the whole value chain, international examples of application will be examined as well.

Although the relevance of social media for branding has been recognized and large media companies have begun to exploit the potential of social media to help them reach a subscribed audience and deepen relationships with them (Carter 2009a; 2009b), the phenomenon has not been explored in depth in academic research so far, in particular not applied to television branding. Instead, most available research about television branding examines the uses and effects of network websites as a form of brand extension (e.g., Ha & Chan-Olmsted 2004; Lin & Peña 2011, p. 17).

1.2.5 Research questions and outlook on the findings

With regard to the research deficits in the field of social media branding for serialised television brands, the key question this study aims at answering is:

Q. How does accompanying social media content support successful management of a serialised television brand?

Hence, four research questions can be formulated for this study:

1. Which drivers – social media related, TV related, and/or related to the social environment – are most important for a consumer's relationship with the serialised television brand?
2. How do social media influence the image of the serialised television brand?
3. Which conditions drive social media usage as well as attitude toward the social media programme for the serialised television brand?
4. Which aspects of the social media programme for the serialised television brand are particularly important for users?

To the knowledge of the author, thus far, no comprehensive theoretical adaptation of social media branding for serialised television brands has been developed. However, many of the neighbouring fields of study have a very rich tradition of research and theoretical background at their disposal. This study draws on established findings from branding and communication research, which are transferred to the research questions to allow for an understanding of the drivers of consumer loyalty toward a serialised television brand.

Findings of this study will provide evidence that the television programme is the decisive driver for the consumer-brand relationship. Social media support and drive TV usage: Attitude toward the social media programme for the serialised television brand directly positively affects brand loyalty, while engagement in the social media programme impacts brand loyalty via its positive influence on the consumer-brand relationship. Features of the social media programme are crucial to generate these positive effects. These features are mostly television brand related content, not possibilities to interact with other users.

1.3 Methodology: Orientation of the study in science theory

This section goes into detail with the epistemological and paradigmatic orientation of the study. Theory development can be approached by two different ways: deductive theory testing and inductive theory building (Bonoma 1985, p. 199). As can be seen in Table 1-1, deduction and induction belong to different scientific paradigms, deduction representing the positivist paradigm, induction representing the phenomenological paradigm (Easterby-Smith, Thorpe, & Lowe 1991, p. 24). The phenomenological paradigm can be separated into critical theory, constructivism and realism (Perry 1998, p. 186).

Paradigm		Deduction/ induction	Dimension Objective/subjective	Commensurable/ incommensurable
Positivist paradigm		Deduction	Objective	Commensurable
Phenomenological paradigm	Critical Theory	Induction	Subjective	Commensurable
	Constructivism	Induction	Subjective	Incommensurable
	Realism	Induction	Objective	Commensurable

Table 1-1: An overview of scientific paradigms

Source: Own design, adapted from Perry (1998, p. 786)

In addition to its paradigmatic classification, research can also be examined by three perspectives (Kumar 2011, p. 9): the application of the findings of the research study, the objectives in undertaking the research, and the inquiry mode that is employed.

The application of the findings of the research study refers to research being either pure or applied (ibid., p. 10). Pure research adds to the existing body of knowledge by developing new research methods or techniques that can then be applied to particular phenomena. Thus, most social science research, like this study, is applied research.

Concerning the objectives undertaken, research can be classified as descriptive, correlational, explanatory or exploratory (ibid., pp. 10ff.). While a descriptive study aims at systematically describing a situation, problem, or phenomenon, a correlational study attempts to uncover the existence of a relationship. Explanatory research deals with the reasons for a relationship, while exploratory research explores a not yet well known research area. This study contains correlational and exploratory objectives: While the first part seeks to explore theoretical underpinnings of social media marketing and branding for the media type of a TV format, the second part is correlational since it analyses the relationship between the use of social media and the loyalty towards a TV brand.

With reference to the inquiry mode, research can be quantitative or qualitative. While qualitative research employs "a more reflective or exploratory approach", quantitative research methods use "the traditions of science" (Davies 2007, p. 25). This study is quantitative in nature since it draws upon the findings of a survey.

The aim of this study is to develop a model framework that displays the interdependencies between a social media branding strategy and the brand loyalty towards a serialised television brand. In order to develop this model, literature research is conducted. This approach makes it possible to firstly draw upon existing research in order to build a model. After that, the model is tested. Literature research is generally considered deductive and falls under the positivist paradigm. Model testing is also deductive in nature and falls under the positivist paradigm. Comparing own findings with the general trends as identified in the literature is a first step to triangulate findings.

Since the focus of this study is the relationship between the brand and the consumer, it does not focus on direct economic outcomes, but is concerned with consumer behaviour. Being part of consumer research, it follows the tradition of behavioural science (Trommsdorff 2009, p. 18).

1.4   Structure of the study

The aim of this study is to develop a conceptual model that displays the interdependencies between a social media branding strategy and brand loyalty towards a serialised television brand. Drawing upon existing literature, a model is developed that assumes loyalty as the key television specific success indicator. The model is subsequently tested by a survey and evaluated by investigating causal relations using Partial Least Squares (PLS) analysis, a variance-based structural equation modelling technique.

This chapter has outlined the objectives of the study by introducing the research area, by addressing the managerial relevance of the study and by providing specifications of the research focus. Orientation of the study in science theory has been provided and research questions have been formulated.

Figure 1-2 displays the structure of the study. As can be seen, chapter 2, which outlines concepts of brand management, media branding and social media research provides a general theoretical foundation, precedes conceptualisation and model development. While the brand related output variables – brand loyalty and the consumer-brand relationship – have a rich theoretical background, some of the input variables are rather exploratory in nature and for conceptualisation rely on examples and use cases rather than theory. By giving a broad overview of the topics in chapter 2, gaps in existing research are identified so that model building and conceptualisation in chapter 3 can draw upon the theoretical background provided in chapter 2.

Section 2.1 goes into detail with branding theory and brand management. The orientation of the study in branding theory and management is introduced and relevant terms are defined. Section 2.2 applies branding theory to media brands in general and television brands in particular and explores serialised television content. Section 2.3 introduces relevant concepts for brand related communication, thus paving the way for and addressing the relevance of the sections on social media research. Section 2.4 provides a literature overview of social media research, while section 2.5 contains examples of application that support hypothesis building.

Chapter 3 outlines model development and conceptualisation. Hypotheses regarding the building of brand loyalty toward a serialised television brand with social media strategies are derived from theoretical considerations and transferred into a conceptual model.

Chapter 4 goes into detail with the specifications of the model. Operationalisation of the constructs is explained and research design and methods are introduced.

Chapter 5 covers empirical model validation and the testing of hypotheses. The outcomes are presented and interpreted.

The study closes with a summary and conclusion in chapter 6 and discusses limitations and suggestions for further research.

2 Theoretical foundation in relevant fields of research

BRANDING

2.1 Literature review:
Branding and brand
management theory

TELEVISION

2.2 Media branding as
reference point of this study

SOCIAL MEDIA

2.4 Literature review: Social
media research

2.5 Using social media for
brand related communication
in a television context

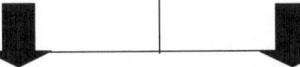

2.3 Relevant concepts in brand related communication

3 Model development (conceptualisation)

3.1 Conceptualisation and derivation of hypotheses by constructs

3.2 Finalisation of the causal model and summary of hypotheses

4 Specifications of model development

4.1 Choice of method and 4.2 Survey

4.3 Structural equation modelling with PLS and 4.4 Operationalisation

5 Empirical model evaluation and hypothesis testing

Evaluation of the measurement model / Evaluation of the structural model /
Moderating effects / Further insights by exploratory data analysis

6 Conclusion

Results and findings

Managerial implications

Figure 1-2: Structure of this study

Source: Own design

2 Theoretical foundation in relevant fields of research

This chapter provides the theoretical foundation in relevant fields of research. Due to the fact that part of this study is exploratory and because it combines findings from brand research, media research and social media research, it is necessary to expand on the theoretical foundation of all fields. Chapter 3 will draw upon this theoretical foundation and concretises it when necessary.

The chapter presents a literature review as well as application examples for the research fields of brand management, television branding, as well as social media and relevant neighbouring fields of study. Section 2.1 provides an overview of branding theory. The orientation of the study in brand theory and management is introduced and relevant terms are defined. The identity-based brand management approach, which serves as a theoretical framework for this study, is outlined. Section 2.2 applies branding theory to media brands in general in section 2.2.1 and to television brands in particular in section 2.2.2. It concludes with section 2.2.3, which puts emphasis on serialised television content as the product category this study investigates. Section 2.3 introduces concepts of brand related communication. It focuses on concepts that are relevant for social media communication or that can be considered related concepts. Section 2.4 provides a literature overview of social media research. It concludes by proposing a categorization scheme for social media that takes into account the tools' relevance for brand communication and suggests ways of application in a television branding context.

At the end of this chapter, the reader will have a comprehensive overview of branding and brand management theory. Media branding will have been introduced with particular focus on television branding in serialised formats. Relevant concepts in brand related communication will have been introduced and will have provided an overview of interactive marketing and brand communication, brand communities, user innovation, user generated content and word-of-mouth communication. Section 2.5 transfers the findings gathered in the previous sections into real-life application examples with regard to serialised television content and attempts to bring the concepts brand, social media and television together.

2.1 Literature review: Branding and brand management theory

In their meta-study on media brands and media branding that analyses articles published in the *International Journal on Media Management*, the *Journal of Media Business Studies*, and the *Journal of Media Economics*, Malmelin and Moisander (2014) find that "the research on brands and media brands draws on the basic concepts and models that have been introduced in the literature on marketing and marketing communication" (e.g. Aaker 1991; 1996; Keller 1993). Also, the research on media brands lacks theoretical coherence (Malmelin & Moisander 2014) and an empirically tested taxonomy for media brands (Förster 2011, p. 15). Therefore, this section investigates brands in general first, before section 2.2 applies branding theory to media brands.

This section outlines the development of branding and the changing understanding of what a brand is, from signalling function to a managerial concept. The identity-based brand management approach is introduced as theoretical foundation of this study, and the consumer-brand relationship as the key concept within the framework is described.

2.1.1   Orientation in brand management theory

German brand companies' sales of branded products and services add up to a gross value of about EUR 900 billion per year (Markenverband 2011; 2013). Due to the fact that brands add significant value to a firm's assets, brand management is considered an important task in both business-to-business and business-to-consumer markets (Kapferer 2008, p. 2). However, over time, both the definition of what a brand is and of how it should be managed has undergone profound changes. The development of the resource-based view of the firm in the 1980s and of brand equity research, in combination with significant changes in market dynamics and structures, led to "a reconfiguration of managerial and academic perceptions on the role and importance of brands in strategy formation" (Joao Louro & Vieira Cunha 2001, p. 849).

The central purpose of a brand is to make a distinction. Historically, brands were created to identify the owner or the source of a product (Kapferer 2008, pp. 10-11). The brand served as a physical sign that informed the consumer about the origin of a product, about who had produced it, and it guaranteed stable or improved quality of the product (Esch 2005, p. 18). In the middle ages, guilds used symbols similar to today's brands to identify the creator of a product (Leitherer 2001, p. 62). During the Renaissance, brands were used to support the new trade routes that were no longer regional, where a branded product raised trust, not yet in the brand, but in the firm the brand identified (Leitherer 2001, p. 64). The concept of a branded product as a manufacturer's brand evolved no sooner than the 19th century and after industrialisation had led to a loss of personal relationships between producers and buyers due to greater regional distance (Leitherer 2001, p. 57). At that time, brand management was nevertheless not yet a managerial concept aiming at contributing to the firm's success (Meffert & Burmann 2005, p. 22).

Dedicated brand management arose in the early 20th century and focused on product orientation, interpreting the brand as a set of features determining the defining characteristics of a product (Meffert & Burmann 2005, p. 23). For consumers, such manufacturer-branded products were clearly identifiable, which facilitated re-purchase if the product had been satisfactory or avoidance if it had not (Low & Fullerton 1994, p. 176). The approach to managing a brand was instrumental in nature and focused predominantly on naming, packaging, and traditional advertising (Meffert & Burmann 2005, p. 23). Many brands were only locally or regionally distributed; however, improvements in transportation and communication as well as in production processes gradually allowed for a wider distribution (Low & Fullerton 1994, p. 175).

Starting in the middle of the 20th century, brands were increasingly conceptualised as focal platforms for articulating and implementing a firm's strategic intent. Brand management, at that time, was "enacted through the creation, development and communication of a coherent brand identity" (Joao Louro & Vieira Cunha 2001, p. 860). Although this supply-oriented approach to brand management succeeded in stressing the importance of the concept of the brand as more than the sum of its parts, it over-emphasizes the firm's input in brand marketing activities as the exclusive determinants of brand meaning, since the role of consumers as active co-creators of brand significance is largely ignored (de Chernatony & Dall'Olmo Riley 1998, p. 421).

From the mid-1970s on, brand management became more demand and consumer oriented. Many markets were experiencing saturation tendencies, consumers became increasingly price-sensitive, technological innovations were quickly imitated, and consumers were facing information overload due to the number of brands on the market (Meffert & Burmann 2005, p. 25). The then evolving view on brand management emphasized consumer response to brands as crucial and regarded the consumer as central to the construction of brand meaning (Joao Louro & Vieira Cunha 2001, p. 864). The firm's input activities were managed using feedback from consumers by analysing the brand image in order to change identity, making thorough market research crucial (de Chernatony & Dall'Olmo Riley 1998, p. 426).

On this basis, the identity-based brand management approach evolved in the 1990s. It balances brand identity and brand image so that brand value and meaning are created through collaboration between organisations and consumers (Joao Louro & Vieira Cunha 2001, p. 865).

Source	Definition
Ogilvy 1951	The brand is the consumer's idea of a product.
Aaker 1991, p. 7	A brand is a name and/or symbol (such as a logo, trademark, or package design) intended to identify the goods or services of either one seller or a group of sellers, and to differentiate those goods or services from those of competitors. A brand thus signals to the customer the source of the product, and protects both the customer and the producer from competitors who would attempt to provide products that appear to be identical.
Kotler 1991, p. 442 as cited in Keller 1993, p. 2	A brand is "a name, term, sign, symbol, or design, or combination of them which is intended to identify the goods and services of one seller or group of sellers and to differentiate them from those of competitors".
Burmann, Blinda, & Nitschke 2003, p. 3	A brand is a bundle of benefits with specific features that, in the eyes of relevant target groups, permanently differentiate it from other bundles of benefits that satisfy the same basic needs.[2]
Kapferer 2008, p. 11	"[A] brand is a name that influences buyers, becoming a purchase criterion."
Keller 2008, p. 5	"A brand is […] more than a product, because it can have dimensions that differentiate it in some way from other products designed to satisfy the same need."

Table 2-1: Brand definitions

Source: Own design

Table 2-1 shows a selection of modern definitions of what a brand is. Conceptualisations of brands and brand management evolved from the one-dimensional approach, which focused on the role of brands as legal instruments or as visual identification and differentiation, towards "multidimensional views emphasizing holistic conceptions of brands comprising functional, emotional, relational and strategic dimensions"; in particular, it was the emergence of the resource-based view that provided the conceptual foundations "for linking brands and brand

---

[2] Translated from German. Original definition: "Die Marke ist ein Nutzenbündel mit spezifischen Merkmalen, die dafür sorgen, dass sich dieses Nutzenbündel gegenüber anderen Nutzenbündeln, welche dieselben Basisbedürfnisse erfüllen, aus Sicht relevanter Zielgruppen nachhaltig differenziert."

management to the development of sustained competitive advantage" (Joao Louro & Vieira Cunha 2001, p. 851).

This study follows the definition by Burmann et al. (2003) and defines a brand as a bundle of benefits with specific features that, in the eyes of relevant target groups, permanently differentiate it from other bundles of benefits that satisfy the same basic needs.

2.1.2   The identity-based brand management approach

The identity-based brand management approach was developed in the 1990s, the most important contributions being the works by Kapferer (1992), Aaker (1996), and Meffert and Burmann (1996) (Burmann, Blinda, & Nitschke 2003, p. 1).

Joao Louro and Vieira Cunha (2001) describe identity-based brand management as falling under a relational paradigm of brand management. A paradigm, as defined by Deshpandé (1983, p. 101) with reference to Kuhn (1962), "is a set of linked assumptions about the world which is shared by a community of scientists investigating that world".

In contrast to older brand management approaches, the identity-based brand management approach aims at a comprehensive integration of supply and demand oriented perspectives by relying on two dominant strategic management paradigms: the market-based view, and the resource-based view of the firm (Barney 1991; Burmann & Meffert 2005a, pp. 38ff.; Porter 1996; 1998).

Hence, identity-based brand management exceeds the one-dimensional outside-in focus of the perception of the brand by the consumer (brand image), and attributes equal importance to the inside-out perspective, i.e. the self-image of the brand, or brand identity (de Chernatony 1999; Burmann & Meffert 2005a, p. 51; Burmann, Meffert, & Feddersen 2007, p. 4; Burmann, Meffert, & Koers 2005, p. 8). This is consistent with one of the fundamental demands of strategic management according to which a sustainable, successful strategy requires a combination and integration of both market and resource orientation (Burmann & Stolle 2007, pp. 5f.).

Brand image approaches start their analyses with the recipient side of the brand and investigate how external stakeholders perceive the brand; in contrast, brand identity approaches focus on the sender of brand communication (Kapferer 2008, p. 174). Brand identity is the way in which a company aims to position itself or its products, while brand image is the way the consumer perceives the outcomes of this attempt (Kotler, Keller, Brady, Goodman, & Hansen 2009, p. 426). While brand identity represents the internal self-perception of the brand ("Selbstbild"), brand image stands for the external perception of others ("Fremdbild") (Burmann & Meffert 2005a, p. 44). Hence, brand image is both the result and the interpretation of brand identity; brand identity precedes and therefore represents the basis for brand image (Kapferer 2008, p. 174).

2.1.2.1 Brand identity

Brand identity expresses the defining characteristics of a brand from a self-image perspective. Burmann and Zeplin state that, "like a person, a brand needs to have a credible identity in order to be trusted" (2005, p. 280). The dimensions of brand identity have been conceptualised in a number of ways (cf. Table 2-2).

Aaker 1996, p. 79	de Chernatony 1999, p. 166	Kapferer 2008, p. 183
brand identity system	dimensions of brand identity	brand identity prism
brand as product	brand vision	physique
brand as organisation	brand culture	personality
brand as person	brand positioning	culture
brand as symbol	brand personality	self-image
	brand relationship	reflection
	brand presentation	relationship

Table 2-2: Dimensions of brand identity

Source: Own design, adapted from Burmann & Zeplin (2005, p. 280)

This study follows the conceptualisation of brand identity as put forward by Burmann and Meffert. Their identity-based brand management approach focuses on the six dimensions of brand heritage, brand management competences, brand values, personality, vision and performance (Burmann et al. 2003, pp. 18ff.; Burmann & Meffert 2005a, pp. 58-64; Burmann et al. 2007). The six dimensions of brand identity can be described in detail as follows:

1. **Brand heritage** is the basis of brand identity and makes use of the brand's history. It provides authenticity and credibility for all other activities and comprises geographic, cultural, and institutional facets.

2. **Brand management competences** comprise the organisational capabilities to efficiently manage the brand.

3. **Brand values** reflect the general convictions of management and staff and embody emotional components of brand identity.

4. **Brand personality** is "the set of human characteristics associated with a brand" (Aaker 1997, p. 347). Gilmore's theory of animism (1919) suggests that in order to facilitate interaction with objects, humans tend to anthromorphize those objects, i.e. to assign human character traits to them. The theory of animism can be transferred to branded objects (Aaker 1997; Fournier 1998) and is particularly relevant for social media communication, which per se makes the brand more approachable due to interactivity.

5. **Brand vision** refers to the long-term development of the brand and serves as motivational factor for internal target groups.

6. **Brand performance** is "the total of activities displaying functional and symbolic consumer benefits in order to position the brand" (Arnhold 2010, p. 36). The fundamental quality of brand performance determines in which way a brand can be used by the consumer and which functional benefits it will have (Burmann & Meffert 2005a, p. 60).

Brand identity as a management concept serves two purposes: Firstly, brand identity allows for a positioning of the brand with regard to external target groups (Meffert, Burmann, & Kirchgeorg 2008, p. 372). Secondly, since consumer-brand interaction takes place at all consumer-brand touchpoints, many of which are determined by employees from all corporate departments, the positioning against the backdrop of the internal perspective is of utmost importance (Burmann & Zeplin 2005, p. 281).

2.1.2.2   Brand image

Brand image is a multidimensional attitude construct (Trommsdorff 2009, p. 155) which represents the individual, subjective brand associations in the minds of relevant consumers. It therefore is the result of individual perception and decoding of all signals coming from the brand (Burmann & Meffert 2005a, p. 52). While brand identity can be actively shaped by brand management processes, brand image develops in the minds of external target groups with a time lag and over a longer period of time. Brand image, therefore, represents a market response model (Burmann et al. 2007, p. 5).

A precondition for the development of brand image is brand awareness (Burmann & Meffert 2005a, p. 53). Brand awareness is the ability of a potential customer to recall a brand, i.e. retrieve it from memory when given the product category, or to recognize it, i.e. to confirm prior exposure to the brand when presented with it (Aaker 1991, p. 61; Keller 1993, p. 3; Keller 2008, p. 54). According to the identity-based brand management approach, brand image consists of three components (Meffert et al. 2008, pp. 365ff.; Burmann & Stolle 2007, pp. 82ff.):

1. **Brand attributes** represent all descriptive elements a consumer associates with a brand, like price or origin, but also the perception of typical users or buyers of the brand.
2. **Brand personality associations** represent the personality traits consumers associate with the brand.
3. **Brand benefit associations**, both symbolic and functional, are the result of brand attributes and brand personality associations. Functional brand benefit associations comprise all physical or functional features of a brand, while symbolic brand benefit associations address all additional benefits that go beyond the functional level. Brand benefit associations, hence, are of highest relevance for purchase behaviour.

Brand managers can neither directly access nor control the image of the brand. Also, part of the definition of brand image, namely subjectivity, prevents the construct from being directly controlled by the corporation (Burmann & Stolle 2007, p. 3). This implies that active management of the brand is only possible through the management of brand identity, which in turn influences brand image. Ultimately, therefore, "the power of a brand lies in the minds of customers" (Keller 2009, p. 143).

2.1.2.3 Consumer-brand relationship as a link of brand identity and image

The two concepts of brand identity and brand image are not completely independent, but interact with each other. While the specific characteristics of the brand identity dimensions brand vision, brand personality and brand values primarily determine the symbolic brand benefit associations, brand performance primarily determines the functional brand benefit associations (Burmann & Meffert 2005a, p. 65). Figure 2-1 illustrates that the consumer-brand relationship links the two concepts of brand identity and brand image and therefore represents a crucial success factor in the framework of identity-based brand management (Burmann & Meffert 2005b, p. 75; Meffert et al. 2008, pp. 367f.).

Brand identity (management concept)   **Brand image (market response concept)**

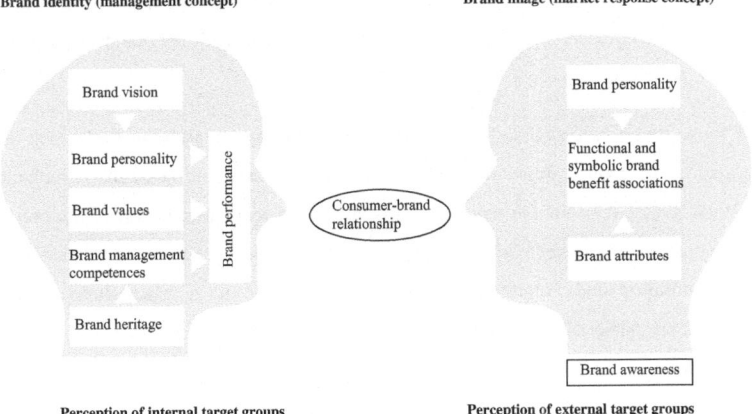

Figure 2-1: Identity-based brand management
Source: Own design based on Arnhold (2010, p. 39); Meffert et al. (2008, pp. 359, 361, 364)

According to Fournier (1998, p. 344), brands "can and do serve as viable relationship partners", so that the relationship between consumer and brand forms the basis for the economic value of a brand (Burmann 2005, p. 256). Drawing upon Fournier's conceptualisation (1994, p. 29), a relationship can be described as consisting of three basic elements: interdependence, temporality, and "some form of emotional or substantive bond". Two concepts that are crucial to understanding relationships are relationship commitment and trust. Relationship commitment refers to an exchange partner's desire and effort to maintain a relationship (Moorman et al. 1992, p. 316; Morgan & Hunt 1994, p. 23). Trust is a major determinant of both relationship commitment and relationship quality (Moorman et al. 1992, p. 315; Morgan & Hunt 1994, p. 24).

According to Fournier's conceptualisation, brand relationship quality (BRQ) is a property of the relationship between a person and a brand, not a characteristic of either the person or the brand. It is dynamic, changes over time, and is not defined as an objective characteristic, but as perceived by the individual (Fournier 1994, p. 125). BRQ evolves through interaction between the brand and the consumer, who are both considered to be relationship partners.

Fournier therefore introduces the concept of the brand as a "relationship partner" (BARP), in which the brand is seen as personified, as a member of a relationship dyad, i.e. as part of a one-to-one relationship, and as an active contributor to the relationship, which means that marketing actions are considered as behaviours executed on the part of the "brand-as-partner" (Fournier 1994, pp. 14ff.).

As part of those brand behaviours, Fournier identifies traditional marketing tools such as television advertising, sponsorships and sales, but also service calls and customer complaint handling (1994, p. 21). It is notable that social media communication on behalf of the brand seems even more suitable as behaviour executed by the brand as a relationship partner than traditional promotional and communicative strategies because it is more direct, more interactive and more personal, thereby appearing even more strongly like behaviours on the part of the brand.

Consumer-brand relationships, thus, are two-dimensional concepts emphasizing the active role of the consumer. The identity-based brand management approach therefore seems particularly suitable for research on branding with social media, where brand communication enters a direct and measurable feedback loop with consumer reactions, leading to responses and traceable changes in the way consumers interact with brands. The consumer-brand relationship construct therefore, in addition to brand loyalty, serves as a key brand-related construct in the conceptual model. It will further be elaborated on in section 3.1.2, where it will be conceptualised with regard to this study.

2.2   Media branding as reference point of this study

Having introduced the relevant concepts in branding theory, this section outlines media branding in general (2.2.1), television branding in particular (2.2.2), and concludes with a section on serialised television content as object of investigation of this study (2.2.3).

2.2.1   Literature review: Media branding

Media brands are omnipresent today. In the 2014 Interbrand *Best Global Brands* ranking, four of them are among the 100 most valuable brands: Disney (#13), Facebook, which is counted as a technology brand (#29), Thomson Reuters (#57), Discovery (#67), and MTV (#80) (Interbrand 2014). Hence, Disney is more valuable than Amazon (#15) or Nike (#22), and all of them but MTV are more valuable than Tiffany & Co. (#71), Burberry (#73), or Starbucks (#76). In Germany, the market and media study *best 4 planning* now includes a section on media brands, where it ranks the most used media brands independent of carrier medium, i.e. print, online, and mobile combined (Schröder 2014).

Despite media brands' presence in the media landscape, media branding has only relatively recently been applied to media products on a strategic basis. No sooner than the 1990s did media companies begin to seriously consider managing media products as brands (Habann, Nienstedt, & Reinelt 2008, p. 25), or did radio and television broadcasters develop a profound interest in brand management (McDowell 2006a, p. 42). Before, competition on media markets had been very weak, also because media products based on different technologies were marketed and sold on separated markets (Chan-Olmsted 2006, p. 59), which is changing with "partitions separating one medium from another" disappearing (McDowell 2006b).

Hence, lacking a strategic approach, media brands have to a wide extent evolved gradually and without dedicated planning or management effort behind them. Due to their role of structuring consumers' lives and supporting orientation and identification, media content has, however, in many cases been institutionalised as a brand by the consumers and without management strategy (Siegert 2013, p. 215). Brands like the German news programme *Tagesschau*, for instance, have resided in the minds of consumers before they were deliberately planned as such (Siegert 2001, pp. 97f.).

Today, media markets face harsh within and between media competition due to a large supply of content that is distributed via media that cannibalize each other (cf. 1.1; McDowell 2006b).

While consumers' attention is scarce, that of available content is not. Media companies can no longer rely on dominant brands and have to compete for an audience's attention (Stipp 2012, p. 109).

These changes have also sparked academic interest and led to an increase in media brand research that does, however, still require further strengthening of the theoretical foundations, a focusing on the strategic nature of media brands, and "empirically well-grounded and theoretical sophisticated studies on the challenges of brand management in the media field" (Malmelin & Moisander 2014, p. 17).

2.2.1.1 Definition and unique characteristics of media branding

A brand has been defined as a bundle of benefits with specific features that, in the eyes of relevant target groups, permanently differentiate it from other bundles of benefits that satisfy the same basic needs. (cf. 2.1.1). Media brands "offer value propositions about what their customers can expect in terms of type of content, interactivity, and user experience" (Ots 2008, p. 3). Siegert (2013, p. 215) defines a media brand as media organisations, media products, or media offerings such as programmes, broadcasts, or titles that are implicitly or explicitly managed according to branding objectives. Media brand management can hence be regarded as "a strategic management process to maximize the long-term value of a brand" (Chan-Olmsted 2006, p. 59). According to the identity-based brand management approach as introduced in section 2.1.2, successful media brand management leads to broad consistency between brand identity as mapped out by the media company and brand image as perceived by the consumer. Hence, all brand communication should be aimed at convergence between media brand identity and media brand image.

2.2.1.2 Brand functions in media management

Media brands are appropriate to position a media company both on the market for content and on the market for consumers, as well as to differentiate itself from the competition (Siegert 2002, p. 192). Independent of the ultimate choice of branding strategy and target, brands have several functions. De Chernatony and Dall'Olmo Riley (1998, p. 426) identify twelve functions of a brand: the brand as a legal instrument that signals ownership, as a logo, as a company with recognisable corporate name and image, as a memory shortcut, as a risk reducer that gives customers confidence that their expectations will be fulfilled, as an identity-system, as an image in the consumers' minds, as a value system, as a personality, as a relationship, as adding value in the form of non-functional extras, and as an evolving entity which undergoes an evolutionary change process, gradually shifting its meaning from the firm to the consumer. Media brands fulfil the same functions as consumer brands, but since their relevance is strongly referring to the unique characteristics of media products, their functions need to be discussed against the background of media management.

For consumers, media brands perform a signalling function in various ways: Since media products are experience or credence goods (Siegert 2013, p. 215; Wirtz 2006, pp. 31f.), consumers encounter difficulty assessing their quality prior to purchase and encounter relatively high risk during the decision making and purchasing process. One of the key functions of media brands therefore is to compensate for intangibility, to help consumers identify the source of a product, and to decrease uncertainty about the quality of the product (Chan-Olmsted 2006, p. 58; Siegert 2001, p. 121). The brand therefore performs a signalling function for the consumers and other stakeholders (Kotler et al. 2009, pp. 428f; Siegert 2013, p. 215). Media brands perform structuring and orientation functions and facilitate and accelerate consumer decision making by creating mental short-cuts, thus reducing cognitive effort for consumers (McDowell 2006b; Siegert 2013). Media brands support consumers in remembering what distinguishes one media brand's offering from that of a competitor (Ots 2008, p. 2), thereby providing orientation and allowing consumers to identify "the brands that are compatible with their needs and expectations" (Chan-Olmsted 2011, p. 4) despite abundant choice.

For media companies, brands allow for differentiation of an intangible product that is easy to imitate despite harsh competition, empowerment of audiences and abundant choice (Chan-Olmsted 2006; McDowell 2006b; Siegert 2013). A lot of media products being continuous production products, i.e. serialised content, branding them is crucial to realize decreases in marketing spendings since "these products tend to require lower marketing and sales costs because they are able to create habitual use patterns" once established (Picard 2005, p. 62). In addition, a branded media product is more likely to be part of consumers' relevant set (Chan-Olmsted 2006, p. 67), increases consumer satisfaction and loyalty (Ots 2008, p. 2), and allows companies to charge a premium price (Chan-Olmsted 2006, p. 67).

For advertisers, media provide an environment in which they present their own brands and want to reach consumers (Calder & Malthouse 2008). Media brands serve as a familiar, credible symbol for advertisers and can allow for positive brand image transfer from the media brand to the advertised brand.

2.2.1.3 Branding strategies in media management

Since media brand architectures are becoming more complex in a digitised, multi-channel world and because brand management serves more detailed purposes, it is crucial to define and differentiate the levels on which media brands operate. Kotler et al. (2009, p. 436) provide an overview of brand architecture strategies applicable to brands in general:

1. Individual names: many individually named brands within a company's portfolio;
2. Blanket corporate, family, or house name: corporate, family, or house brand is used across a range of products or services;
3. Separate family or house names: different brand names target different consumer segments or parts of the company's product portfolio;
4. Corporate name in combination with individual product name: image transfer from the corporate brand name to the individual product names is attempted.

Due to the fact that there is no separate empirically tested taxonomy for media brands (Förster 2011, p. 15), these brand architecture strategies can be transferred and applied to media branding. Table 2-3 gives an overview of brand architecture strategies; in reality, mixed approaches can often be detected.

With regard to television, in addition to the umbrella brand (channel), there are sub-brands like genre brands (e.g. access prime time crime serials on *Das Erste*), programme brands (e.g. *Tatort, Game of Thrones*), but also personal brands of actors, presenters, or hosts (Förster 2011, p. 15). These brands frequently co-exist and are of equal importance, but have different aims.

Brand architecture strategy	Individual names	Blanket corporate, family, or house name	Separate family or house names	Corporate + individual product name
General branding	Procter & Gamble owns the brands Gillette, Pampers, Wella, etc.	Apple and IBM use their corporate name for all products.	Beiersdorf owns the Nivea and tesa brand families, both of which comprise a full product range.	Adidas uses brand names adidas Originals, adidas NEO, etc.
Media branding	ProSiebenSat.1 owns free TV brands SAT.1, ProSieben, kabel eins, sixx, and other brands.	The VOGUE brand is used consistently internationally – all international editions are branded equally.	Gruner+Jahr owns several brand families, e.g. GEO or stern.	ZDF uses the house brand as well as brand extensions such as ZDFneo or ZDFmediathek.

Table 2-3: Branding strategies, general and media

Source: Own design, partly adapted from Kotler et al. (2009, p. 436)

Branding media products can be achieved by dedicated naming, logo, design and brand development efforts, but also by merchandising products, as well as by celebrity endorsers.

2.2.1.4 Relevant concepts in media brand research

In their meta-study, Malmelin and Moisander (2014) identify five different approaches to conceptualizing brands and branding in the context of media management: brand as product, brand as extension, brand as identity, brand as differentiation, and brand as equity. Due to the focus of this study, a sixth approach is added, i.e. brand as part of social media communication.

Brand as product

This approach regards the brand as a branded product or service, as studies by Nienstedt, Huber, and Seelmann (2012, p. 4) or Chan-Olmsted and Cha (2008, p. 41) have conceptualized it (Malmelin & Moisander 2014, p. 13). Another view on brands as product is research in ingredient branding (Lis & Post 2013).

Brand as extension

Media companies can stretch their brands "across media channels and delivery formats", by "windowing, modifying, and re-issuing content in order to increase lifespan", and by "creating new revenues by turning content into products and services" (Ots 2008, p. 4). A number of studies have investigated media brand extensions (Chang & Chan-Olmsted 2010; Chan-Olmsted & Cha 2008; Doyle 2006; Habann, Nienstedt, & Reinelt 2008).

Völckner and Sattler (2006, p. 18) define brand extensions as the "use of established brand names to launch new products". They serve as "an attempt to leverage the equity of an established brand by *extending* the brand name to a new product" (McDowell 2006b, p. 235; italics in original).

Prior research has found the perceived similarity or fit between the parent brand and the brand extension and the perceived quality of the parent brand to be key determinants of brand extension success (Völckner, Sattler, Hennig-Thurau, & Ringle 2010). Successful brand extensions are competitive assets and help reduce consumers' perception of risk (McDowell 2006b, pp.230; 235).

Well-known examples for media brand extensions are *Der Spiegel* with its various brand extensions, including further print magazines such as *Spiegel WISSEN* or *Spiegel GESCHICHTE*, as well as *Spiegel Online*, *Spiegel TV*, and the iPad App. An example from television is the BBC with its brand extensions operating on a global basis. Apart from its various TV and radio channels and online offerings produced for the UK market, the brand has been extended and applied to international markets and adapted to local tastes, for instance by employing native presenters.

Brand as identity

This perspective "refers to the distinctive characteristics and outward expression of a brand" and is closely related to brand personality (Malmelin & Moisander 2014, p. 14). Siegert, Gerth, and Rademacher (2011) put forward a comprehensive model with media brand identity at its core (cf. Figure 2-2).

The MBAC model conceptualises the role of media brands for "media managers within the constraints of rather complex environment" and consists of structures, external and internal actors, and their behaviours (Siegert et al. 2011, p. 55). Drivers are identified on the basis of the structure-conduct-performance (SCP) model (Bain 1959) and new, media brand specific drivers have been added. Since an elaboration on the model would go beyond the scope of this study, the reader should refer to Siegert et al. (2011) for details.

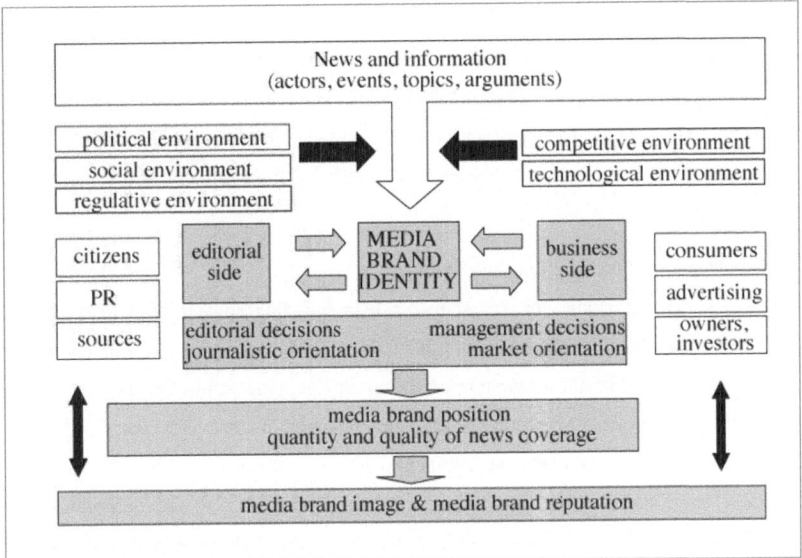

Figure 2-2: The media, brands, actors, and communication (MBAC) model
Source: Own design, adapted from Siegert et al. (2011, p. 56)

For media brands, the brand identity approach has been pursued via a focus on brand personality. This has been investigated by Nienstedt, Huber, and Seelmann (2012), who examined congruence between consumers' perception of their own personality and their perception of brand personality and detected positive effects of congruence on the brand relationship and brand loyalty. Chan-Olmsted and Cha (2008) investigated factors that shape the brand personality of a television network news product and found that its perceived brand personality contributes to consumers' attitude, usage, and loyalty of the news brand.

Brand as differentiation

It has been stated in 2.2.1.2 that brands allow for differentiation of media products that are mostly intangible, thereby allowing for consumer attention despite harsh competition and abundant choice (Chan-Olmsted 2006; McDowell 2006b; Siegert 2013). This perspective hence understands branding as a "strategic practice of eliciting positive consumer attitudes toward the brand, increasing consumption, and strengthening brand loyalty" (Malmelin & Moisander 2014, p. 15).

Brand as equity

Brand equity has been defined above as the added value of a brand (Farquhar 1989, p. 24). Media brand specific studies have been conducted (e.g. McDowell & Sutherland 2000; Ots & Wolff 2008; Oyedeji 2007). This approach regards the brand "in terms of a specific asset" and "describes the relationship between brand and consumer" (Malmelin & Moisander 2014, p. 15).

Brand as part of social media communication

Although a number of studies on social media in a branding context exist to date (e.g. Arnhold 2010; Laroche, Habibi, & Richard 2012; cf. 2.3.4 for a literature overview on user generated content; cf. 2.3.5 for a literature overview on electronic word-of-mouth; cf. 2.5 for an overview on social media for brand related communication in a television context), studies on media branding in a social media environment (e.g. Chan-Olmsted 2011; Lis & Berz 2011) are still scarce. Social media and web 2.0 technologies (cf. 2.4 for definitions and classification) have altered branding efforts in the media industries and make brand management more complex (Chan-Olmsted 2011, p. 3). Consumers' empowerment and control necessitate even stronger branding activities in order for brands to be consistent through all channels and consumer touchpoints and to not lose their distinctive features when in contact with consumers.

To add to the current state of research on media branding and social media is one aim of this study. The following section therefore investigates serialised television brands in more detail, before relevant concepts in brand related communication and social media are examined in detail.

2.2.2   Literature review: Television branding

Television brands are a sub-category of media brands. The following section goes into detail with television brands in particular and investigates branding strategies applied to this distinct case. With "increasing program choices, the distinctiveness of a media brand, the ability to clearly state what the viewer can expect to find at any time of day, and viewers' feelings that the network is designed for their needs", branding has become a strong asset for television companies (Stipp 2012, p. 116).

Traditionally, viewers used to only be able to "communicate" with broadcasters via ratings, which can be regarded as the currency that measures the value of a given format (Plake 2004,

p. 36). Today, it has become easier to gain customer feedback via channels such as social media, which allow broadcasters to directly communicate with their audience. Nevertheless, measuring the success of a programme has become more difficult. Due to technological change, viewers can watch programmes online, record content and watch it later, use a multitude of devices and increasingly escape programme scheduling by watching content on DVD or Blu-ray, by subscribing to services that enable access to a wide range of content, such as Netflix or Hulu, or by purchasing content online and downloading it directly to their devices.

While the supply of media content increases constantly, the demand side, i.e. the audience, is limited. However, because imitation is limited by copyright, there is monopolistic competition and oligopolistic market structure, which allows broadcasters to profit from economies of scale (Radtke 2010, p. 41). Media products are characterised by high first copy costs: While their production underlies high fixed costs, i.e. producing the original is very expensive, the costs for all copies are comparatively low (Siegert 2002, p. 182). Despite the fact that consumers can today produce their own content cheaply or free of charge online, television content is better protected from competition by non-professional producers than, for instance, the publishing industry, because producing a high-quality programme entails higher costs and hence barriers to entry than self-publishing a novel.

Also, television companies can generate economies of scope and engage in fixed cost degression by using the same content several times. Branding is an important way of labelling formats that are repeated later: It provides orientation for viewers and makes it easy to communicate and market a format in a consistent way that attracts the target audience. Since television consumption is characterised by non-rivalry, i.e. there are almost no marginal costs of an additional viewer, branding and promotion activities can prove highly economically viable: If communication strategies work, they are particularly cost-efficient since a bigger audience brings higher revenue, but is associated with almost no additional costs (Heinrich 2010, p. 515), as long as the increase in audience size has not yet been accounted for in the costs for advertising.

In this highly competitive environment, it is crucial for media companies to determine a distinct brand identity and to transform it into a corresponding brand image, which communicates unique selling propositions (USP). Differentiation in this case is the key for success: If consumers do not perceive differences in products, they are more likely to switch between them. Consumers with a high parity perception tend to be less loyal than consumers with a low parity perception (Iyer & Muncy 2005, p. 223).

This section investigates television brands and television branding. 2.2.2.1 outlines relevant literature on business dynamics within which television brands operate, 2.2.2.2 gives a brief overview of branding strategies, and 2.2.2.3 will then provide a cursory outline of studies focusing on television brands.

2.2.2.1 Framework und business models

Commercial television operates on a two-sided market. Broadcasters need to deliver engaging content in order to reach relevant target groups, and then sell this target group's attention to advertisers. A mutual dependence evolves between advertiser-supported television and advertisers, resulting in content not being the primary business model, but only a means to an end (cf. 1.1).

Since this study focuses on the German market, this section will pay particular attention to television branding in Germany. The most important public service broadcasters in Germany are ARD and ZDF, the market leaders in commercial television are RTL, Sat.1 and ProSieben (Hein 2014; cf. Figure 2-3).

An elaborate overview of the television landscape in Germany and, for comparison, other countries such as the US, where many imported programmes broadcast in Germany are produced, goes beyond the scope of this study and would add to the object under investigation to a limited extent only. Also, since the television market has been undergoing profound changes in the last decade, the discussion of markets, competition, regulation, strategy, and innovation is a research topic in its own right. Therefore, the reader should refer to other comprehensive sources for a profound elaboration on these topics (e.g. Karstens & Schütte 2010; Plake 2004; Radtke 2010; Weil 2011).

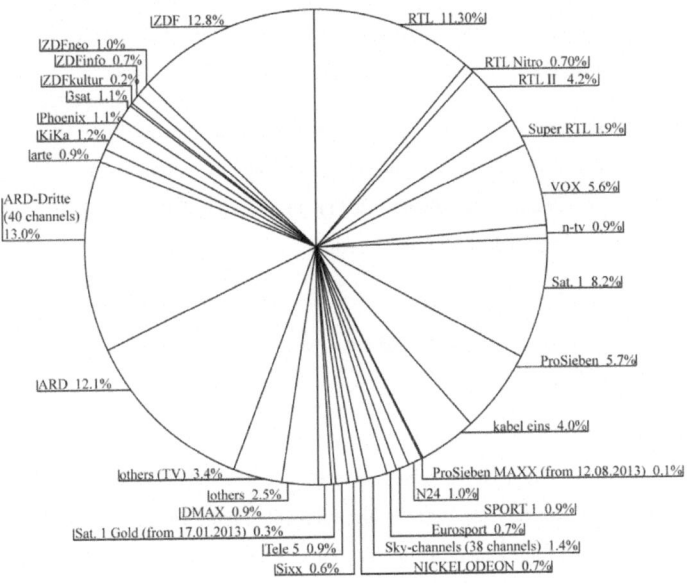

Figure 2-3: Market shares of German channels, daily average 2013

Based on all viewers and all channels, Monday-Sunday, 03:00-03:00, overall viewing: 221 minutes

Source: Own design, based on AGF/GfK (2014)

For detailed elaborations on and examples of current television branding and programming for selected German channels, refer to Hirsch and Förster (2011) with regard to ZDF, to Aumüller (2011) and Weil (2011) with regard to RTL, and to Hofstätter (2011) and Weil (2011) with regard to ProSieben.

The US television market is also of relevance when investigating television in Germany because of the popularity of American films and television programmes in Germany. Stipp (2012) provides a historical analysis of television branding in the United States. Blumenthal and Goodenough (2006) provide a comprehensive overview of regulation, history, the market landscape and the competitive environment in the United States, as do McDowell (2006a) and Chan-Olmsted (2006, esp. pp. 76-105). Chan-Olmsted, Cha, and Oba (2008) investigate the export of video media products like film and television programmes from a US perspective and determine host country factors affecting export volumes. De Bens and de Smaele (2001) investigate this phenomenon from a European perspective, finding that while American series and serials are nevertheless less popular than domestic ones, American films are predominant in prime time over European productions. This finding should, however, be challenged nowadays, American serialised content being very popular (cf. 2.2.3).

Bignell (2004) provides an overview of television studies from a UK perspective. Mark and Swann (2011) provide a brief outline of the regulatory and competitive framework in which British television operates. Swann and Förster (2011) analyse the BBC in detail, with emphasis on the BBC as a brand, and Mark (2011) outlines brand management of the British channel ITV.

The following sections refer to television management and television brands in a German context, if not otherwise indicated.

2.2.2.2 Branding strategies for television brands

Branding strategies for media content have been developed and applied at a broader scale in recent years. One example for this tendency with reference to television brands is the increased formatting of programmes in order to position content with regard to the target audience (Siegert 2002, p. 193). For instance, in 2008, ZDF combined all its Sunday evening documentary brands, which are now broadcast under the *Terra X* umbrella brand, one of the most successful documentary series on German television (Hesse 2008).

Programme planning and communication policy function as the positioning strategies a channel uses to communicate the intended brand identity to the consumer in order to create the desired unique image (Förster 2011, p. 26). Television content is repeated a lot, which reduces the number of individual formats and supports positioning of the remaining formats through higher broadcast frequency.

Programme planning

The most important instruments of programme planning are the programme profile, the programme scheme and the programme portfolio (Förster 2011, pp. 15ff.).

The programme profile refers to the composition of the entire programme, i.e. the amount of time dedicated to individual categories such as entertainment, information, and the diversity of the programme. A channel's programme planning mirrors its strategy and positioning (Swann & Förster 2011, p. 82).

The programme scheme describes the organisational composition of the programme and can be described as a timetable that includes all scheduled programmes (Karstens & Schütte 2010, p. 129). The success of a programme scheme is determined by two factors – timing/day parting[3] and positioning[4] (cf. Förster 2011, pp. 17-19; Karstens & Schütte 2010, pp. 134ff.; Verspohl 2008, pp. 78-82).

With regard to the programme portfolio Förster (2011, p. 20) suggests that common portfolio analyses are not suitable for television brands and instead proposes three criteria for the assessment of a channel's profitability: the success of the programme, measured by ratings; the proportion of own and third-party productions the programme contains (Förster suggests that own productions are better suited for developing brand image); and the time span over which a programme has been running, which is supposed to allow for conclusions concerning willingness to innovate or readiness to assume risk.

Communication policy

In addition to programme planning, channels attempt to support their brand and product policy by a strategic communication policy (Heinrich 2010, p. 509). Park (2004, p. 94) points out that promotion can be aimed at advertisers (sales promotion) or viewers (audience promotion). This study focuses on audience promotion, because the research question is concerned with audience retention and ultimately, attracting an audience is a requirement to attract advertisers. Key tools are identified by Förster (2011, p. 21) as corporate design, on-air as well as off-air communication.

Corporate design is a complex concept ensuring recognition and representation of the brand promise and can therefore be regarded as equally important as a channel's programme portfolio (Karstens & Schütte 2010, p. 224). It communicates the logo, the colours and the claim of a channel or programme brand, which enhances recognition value. While programmes are running, the channel logo is displayed in one of the corners of the TV screen, which connects the logo and the programme in the consumer's mind (Förster 2011, p. 22).

---

[3] Vertical programming takes account of the daytime, i.e. programmes that appeal to the same target group are broadcast after one another to optimize audience flow and prevent viewers from switching channels. Horizontal programming takes account of the course of the week and aims at conditioning viewers until they are used to watching specific programmes at a specific time every day.
[4] Consumer oriented programme planning strategies like lead-in, lead-off, and lead-out; programme oriented programme planning strategies focusing on the position of a programme in relation to other programmes; competition oriented planning strategies focusing on the programme schedule of the competition.

On-air communication addresses a channel's target audience within the medium in which the content is presented (Park 2004, p. 94). On-air communication is a retentive strategy which targets existing viewers and aims at creating loyalty (Eick 2007, p. 157). Tools include programme trailers, image trailers, as well as teasers.[5] On-air communication is a viable strategy to promote individual programmes, but less suitable to strengthen the channel brand.

Off-air communication is a communicative effort in other media, while cross-promotion is communication in other media of the same network (Park 2004, p. 94). It is an acquisitive strategy aimed at new audiences, which usually makes use of other media such as print media like magazines or newspapers, radio, billboards and teletext, but also cinema and merchandising, in order to reach those audiences (Eick 2007, p. 157; Förster 2011, p. 24). Off-air communication includes all online and social media measures, which will be discussed in section 2.5 in more elaborate detail. It is notable that this study investigates how social media, i.e. an off-air strategy which, according to this categorization, is assumed to be an acquisitive strategy, does in fact work as an audience retention strategy.

With regard to identity-based brand management, programme planning and communication policy serve as connecting elements between sender and recipient, thereby bringing brand identity and brand image together (Förster 2011, p. 26). They can hence be regarded as shaping the consumer-brand relationship, which is the connecting factor between brand image and brand identity in identity-based brand management (cf. 2.1.2). This is in line with Fournier's view on marketing and communication actions as brand behaviours executed by the brand as a relationship partner (Fournier 1994; cf. 2.1.2.3).

2.2.2.3 Literature review of research on television branding

While "the main focus of brand research has clearly been on television" (Malmelin & Moisander 2014, p. 14), there is, to the knowledge of the author, no separate meta-study on the field of television branding. This section will therefore outline relevant literature on business dynamics within which television brands operate. Table 2-4 provides an overview of studies on television branding. The overview is not a systematic meta-study, but a selection of research applicable to this study. Studies included in this overview were identified by own literature research or, if indicated, adapted from the overview provided by Malmelin and Moisander (2014).

---

[5] For a detailed description, refer to Eick (2005, pp. 158-162) and Park (2004, p. 131).

Article	Research focus and, if applicable, key findings
Chang & Chan-Olmsted 2010	Investigation of variables affecting viewers' attitudes toward cable network brand extensions. Parent brand attitude, brand portfolio quality variance, perceived number of previous brand extensions, perceived fit, and innovativeness were found to significantly affect attitude toward brand extensions.
Chang & Ki 2005*	Classification and development of predictors of box office performance for theatrical movies. Brand-related variables were found to be not as important as expected, neither brand power of actors nor directors being strong enough to affect the box office success of theatrical movies.
Chang, Bae, & Lee 2004*	Examination of factors influencing the evaluation of brand extensions of the Discovery network. Perceived fit between the original Discovery channel and extended channels, evaluation of the original Discovery channel, and perceived quality variance of the Discovery channels were found to be predictors of brand extension success.
Chan-Olmsted 2011	Outline of challenges and opportunities for media branding in a web 2.0 environment with particular focus on television brands.
Chan-Olmsted & Cha 2007	Investigation of the perceived differences among television news brands by adopting the construct of brand personality. Broadcast network news was perceived to be more traditional and liberal than cable network news.
Chan-Olmsted & Cha 2008	Investigation of antecedents and effects of brand images for television news. Findings suggest that an audience's attitude toward an affiliated television network, perceived importance of anchors, and use of television as a news source support building the personality of a network news brand. Perceived brand personality was found to contribute to viewers' attitude, usage, and loyalty of the news brand.
Chan-Olmsted & Jung 2001*	Examination of U.S. television networks' strategies in an environment of digitization, focusing, among other factors, on television brands.
Chan-Olmsted & Kim 2002	Investigation of viewers' perceptions of public television in comparison to competing cable networks. Findings suggest that public television holds a positive brand image and the popularity of comparable cable networks does not dilute the brand perception of public television.
Coffey & Cleary 2011*	Comparative content analysis of new and traditional news spaces, i.e. the ticker space and the screen space. It was found that, proportionally, more promotional content occurs within the traditional video content space than in the ticker space.
Förster 2011	Analysis of television brands, e.g. brand personality, brand promise, programme planning and communication policy.

Ha & Chan-Olmsted 2004	Investigation of internet users' usage of cable television website features. Findings suggest that increased usage positively predicts viewer and subscriber loyalty.
Lis & Post 2013	Analysis of television show consumption. Findings provide evidence that brand image is the driving for viewers' motivation to consume specific television content.
Nysveen, Thorbjørnsen, & Pedersen 2005*	Investigation of the influence of additional online television content on brand knowledge, brand satisfaction, direct relationship investments, and indirect relationship investments. Findings provide evidence that online channel additions positively impact all four brand relationship dimensions.
Stipp 2012	Historical analysis of branding of television networks in the United States.
Sung & Park 2011*	Development of a theoretical framework for cable network personality dimensions and a scale to measure them. Results suggest that audiences perceive cable networks to have five distinct brand personality dimensions, i.e. excitement, warmness, intelligence, controversy, and ruggedness.

Table 2-4: Literature overview of research on television branding

Source: Own design, if indicated (*) partly adapted from Malmelin & Moisander (2014)

Table 2-4 shows that research on branding in a television context covers a variety of topics, from historical and descriptive analyses of branding to studies on brand personality, brand image and other brand related constructs. Most noteworthy for this study, however, are the findings on brand extensions (Chang & Chan-Olmsted 2010; Chang, Bae, & Lee 2004) and, in particular, websites and online content as an extension of a television brand (Ha & Chan-Olmsted 2004; Nysveen, Thorbjørnsen, & Pedersen 2005). Ha and Chan-Olmsted (2004) find evidence that increased usage of website features positively predicts viewer and subscriber loyalty to the television brand, and Nysveen et al. (2005) provide evidence that additional online television content positively impacts brand knowledge, brand satisfaction, direct relationship investments, and indirect relationship investments. These findings will be revisited for the derivation of hypotheses in chapter 3.

Having outlined television branding and brand management, the next section goes into detail with serialised television content, which is the object of investigation of this study.

2.2.3 Serialised television content as object of investigation of this study

In recent years, television has been discovered to be a sophisticated narrative medium. At the latest since serials like *Mad Men* or *Homeland* have received critical acclaim, serialised formats are increasingly regarded as highbrow entertainment.

From a branding perspective, seriality facilitates creating loyalty toward the branded product because viewers who are curious about the succession of the plot are more likely to watch again. As pointed out in section 1.2.2, loyalty and seriality are closely connected concepts. Firstly, viewers of serialised television content are very likely to further pursue the content because they will wish to solve the riddles presented during the plot. Secondly, having previously assessed the quality of the content and knowing what to expect, all episodes of a series or serial after the first are no longer mere experience products. Thirdly, seriality facilitates the building of a routine because episodes can usually be watched at the same point in time every day or week. Fourthly, by encountering the same characters over and over again increases the likelihood of viewers building parasocial relationships, i.e. one-sided relationships between media users and the media consumed or media figures (Ballantine & Martin 2005; Gardner & Knowles 2008). Arguably, viewers are even more likely to be loyal to a serialised television brand if the content is complex and sophisticated. The following sections will therefore deal with modern serialised content, how it has evolved and how it is consumed.

The emergence of "quality TV" started with more sophisticated programming in the 1980s and 1990s (Jahn-Sudmann & Kelleter 2012, p. 205; Thompson 1996, p. 12).[6] The innovations made in storytelling in the 1980s were used as a basis by the programmes of the 1990s and the new kinds of serialised formats established after the millennium, which further expanded the role of plotlines that stretched across episodes and seasons (Mittell 2006, p. 33; Mittell 2010).

This led to an increased awareness by critics and academia and spiked interest that had previously been reserved to literature (Kelleter 2012a). Narratively complex quality TV, as well as the emergence of other sophisticated serialised publishing products, such as graphic novels, has led to increased interest in seriality and serialisation (Denson 2011).

These changes in serialised formats entail changes in consumer behaviour and lead to a more participatory culture among viewers of programmes. Kelleter (2012b, p. 14) argues that popular seriality is often public in nature: Although viewers watch the programme alone, a virtual community develops and individuals sharing an interest in a certain programme tend to

---

[6] For a detailed account of the emergence of quality TV during that age, as well as a comprehensive description of what elements quality TV is composed of, refer to Thompson (1996).

feel belonging. This is facilitated by the internet. While *Twin Peaks* fans were avid users of Usenet boards as early as the 1990s (Jenkins 1995, as cited by Mittell 2010), social media have given rise to even more active participation and interaction.

Narratively complex television hence "encourages, and even at times necessitates, a new mode of viewer engagement" (Mittell 2006, p. 38): With regard to the fact that modern quality TV applies high standards to both content and form, viewers do no longer only have the narrative universe as subject-matter, but increasingly also the decoding process. This demands both increased media literacy and awareness with regard to narratology from viewers (ibid., p. 39).

What distinguishes serialised media products from finished works is the fact that recipients often try to – and in fact do – influence the story. This has been the case with serialised novels or book series (e.g. Sherlock Holmes), and is not different for television serials. Nowadays, tools like social media enable viewers to directly interact with producers and writers, which allows for instant feedback as well as for the expression of wishes and expectations concerning future plot developments. Viewers are encouraged to communicate about the complex narrative environments long-running serials are often set in and that loyal viewers have invested time and effort into (Kelleter 2011, p. 74; Kelleter 2012b, p. 24). This entails that serials and series, by per se engaging viewers, are well-suited to create loyalty with channels, as well as to address target groups and retain audiences, thereby serving advertisers (Weber & Junklewitz 2008, p. 13).

Non-narrative serialised content profits from this as well. Viewers of formats such as *Germany's Next Topmodel* or *The Voice of Germany* can discuss their favourite candidates, comment on episodes and criticize developments not anticipated or liked. In the case of *The Voice of Germany*, where the audience can actually vote for the candidates, they can also try to influence other viewers' voting behaviour. Viewers of magazine programmes such as the German format *Galileo* can communicate their interests, comment on their favourite topics, and engage in community behaviour with other viewers with whom they have shared interests.

2.2.3.1 Definition: Series and serials

The focus of this study is on brands in the context of serialised television content. Although channel brands are not completely neglected, the research focuses on format brands, in particular on the recurring format of television series and serials.

In general, a series or a serial can be regarded as an established frame within the programme scheme (Hickethier 1992, p. 13). Apart from this similarity, television series and serials have to be distinguished from each other. In contrast to a series, which lacks an overarching storyline and consists of self-contained episodes, a serial is similar to a serialised novel: A new episode continues where the previous one ended (Plake 2004, p. 146). Williams (2003, p. 57) points out that for a series, the continuity "is not of an action but of one or more characters."[7]

Since many examples for series and serials named in this study are of American origin, but the study itself focuses on Germany, it seems worthwhile to clarify terminology in both German and English languages. Kelleter (2012b, p. 26) points out that for the English terms "mini-series", "series" and "serial", the German conventional terms "Mehrteiler", "Serie" and "Sendereihe" have been coined by Mikos (1992). Today, series and serials are usually both referred to with the German term "Serie".[8]

However, this clear distinction is increasingly being abandoned: Many modern programmes are serials insofar as part of the plot is continued without interruption between episodes, and series insofar as they consist of recurring situations repeating or alluding to one another, thereby combining elements of both (Jahn-Sudmann & Kelleter 2012, p. 215; Mittell 2006, p. 33). On *Grey's Anatomy*, for instance, which possesses more features of a series, episodes contain self-enclosed storylines referring to patients, supplemented by overarching storylines for the doctors. Conversely, serials like *Six Feet Under* frequently contain elements of a series, such as every episode's introductory scene in *Six Feet Under* that prominently features the "casualty of the week".

---

[7] For a thorough discussion of the properties of a series, cf. Weber & Junklewitz (2008).
[8] For an overview of terminology and examples in both German and English (USA), refer to Bock (2013, p. 33).

2.2.3.2   Narrative complexity

From a production perspective, innovative narrative forms and complex storytelling are directly related to the realities of television programming and broadcasting, shifts in the television industry having reinforced strategies of complexity (Mittell 2006, p. 31). Kelleter (2012a) argues that the emergence and success of complex programmes categorized as quality TV is directly related to them being produced by American cable and pay television channels: Cable serials often run for 12 to 13 episodes of almost one hour length, not interrupted by commercial breaks, while traditional network serials usually run for about 23 episodes of one hour length with a net airtime of 39 to 42 minutes due to commercial breaks. Traditional formats therefore often need two internal cliff-hangers (Seiler 2008, p. 6), leading to fragmented story arcs, where innovative cable serials enable sophisticated storytelling and consistent plotlines.

This narrative complexity in modern quality TV, which is defined by Mittell (2006, p. 32) as "a redefinition of episodic forms under the influence of serial narration", improves conventional formats by putting more emphasis on narration instead of episodic storytelling. Mittell mentions programmes like *The X-Files, Buffy the Vampire Slayer, Angel,* and *The Sopranos* as examples for complex programmes that "oscillate between long-term arc storytelling and stand-alone episodes" (ibid., p. 33). Another example is the mystery format *Supernatural,* where about three self-enclosed episodes are usually followed by a so-called mythology episode expanding on the story arcs of the main characters. With this format, producers hope to allow casual viewers to be able to watch most of the episodes without being too familiar with the mythology (Sullivan 2007).

However, narrative complexity is not restricted to complex drama programmes but can also enrich formats like sitcoms, which belong to the earliest serialised formats on television (Kelleter 2012c, p. 204). Elements of narrative complexity can also be detected in non-fictional formats that make use of the loyalty-building features of serials.

Serialised content such as magazine programmes, (talent) shows and reality television in the form of formats such as *Germany's Next Topmodel* or *The Voice of Germany* follow the dramaturgy of fictional serials insofar as they run for seasons of a limited amount of episodes. There is an overarching storyline within the seasons – viewers know that one candidate will win the respective contest eventually. Conflicts between and developments of candidates are carefully set in scene, thereby increasing suspense as the season advances and creating cliff-hangers for the episodes to follow. This can be used to create emotion and positively impact the consumer-brand relationship.

2.2.3.3 New strategies: Rewatchability and narrowcasting

Two managerial strategies are associated with American innovative cable channels such as HBO: "rewatchability" and "narrowcasting" (Kelleter 2012a). Due to subscription revenue, the dependence of (American) cable channels on ratings is less pronounced than that of the networks, so that they can "narrowcast", i.e. address distinct target groups more directly (ibid.). While in traditional broadcasting models, seriality required regular and consistent viewing of a programme and rewatching was limited to reruns (ibid.), "rewatchability" refers to the fact that serialised content is increasingly produced with the deliberate objective to re-distribute the content in the form of DVD boxes or downloads after the first airing, thus enhancing quality and complexity (Kelleter 2012a; Mittell 2010).

While television serials differed from other publishing products such as magazines or books with regard to their intangibility, the possibilities for collecting and archiving programmes have made serialised television content a product that can stand on the bookshelf next to other representative publishing products (Jahn-Sudmann & Kelleter 2012, p. 211).[9] This also challenges branding strategies: Holistic brand designs need to be developed that operate along the whole value chain of the content.

In addition, DVD boxes have led to profound changes and viewing behaviour. Viewers can consume the content on their own terms, rather than be dependent on schedules and programming decisions of broadcasters (Kompare 2006, p. 336). Firstly, viewers control the time they take to watch single episodes by making interruptions, fast-forward and rewind. Secondly, viewers can choose how to watch. When consumed independently of the television schedule, episodes can be watched in much shorter intervals ("binge watching"). These developments in viewer behaviour have started to affect television programming. Especially for sophisticated American quality TV programmes not appealing to the masses, traditional airing strategies of German translations often have only limited success because the viewers

---

[9] For a thorough analysis of the changing relationship between television and home video brought about by the DVD box set, refer to Kompare (2006).

they target tend to order foreign DVD boxes or watch the programmes online (Hein 2012a). When the critically acclaimed HBO serial *Game of Thrones* was broadcast by RTL2 in March 2012, the channel therefore chose an event programming strategy and aired the complete first season, consisting of 10 episodes of one hour length, in only three days. Being a daring programming strategy, it proved successful: The channel received above-average ratings for *Game of Thrones* (Hein 2012b), and repeated the schedule with the second season in March 2013.

Serialised content such as magazine programmes, (talent) shows and reality television are only affected by these developments to a limited extent. They are usually not purchased and watched on DVD, and not re-watched. However, viewers of formats such as *Germany's Next Topmodel* or *The Voice of Germany* who miss episodes can watch content online, or consume additional content. This requires awareness: Availability of content in different formats needs to be communicated and branding strategies need to be extended to these formats.

2.2.3.4 Innovation, brand identity, and outbidding

For serialised programmes to get re-ordered by channels or networks, they need to constantly innovate. However, in order to create novelty, they have to make surprising changes, while they cannot change too profoundly in order to not damage brand identity (Jahn-Sudmann & Kelleter 2012, p. 207; Kelleter 2011, p. 73).

In order to succeed in this process, serialised formats have to keep telling the same again, but differently. In theory running eternally, serials need to suggest that they strive towards a conclusion, which they then repeatedly withhold in order to retain audiences (Kelleter 2012b, p. 27). To not lead to fatigue, serials often revert to strategies Jahn-Sudmann and Kelleter (2012, pp. 215ff.) call "outbidding": intraserial outbidding refers to a serial's attempt to outperform itself, interserial outbidding means that innovative concepts are developed in order to outperform the competition. However, the latter are usually quickly imitated by competitive formats, so that a new cycle of outbidding is unavoidable.

With regard to serialised magazine programmes, such as the German information magazine *Galileo*, which is broadcast daily, strategies such as outbidding do not refer to narrative content and storytelling, but to the stories presented on the programme. In order to retain audiences, content needs to fit into a closely defined framework and not differ too much. At the same time, content needs to have an aspect of novelty about it.

What lies at the core of this is the fact that serialised television content as a media product with commercial objectives does not only compete with alternative options, but also with itself. Quality standards need to be upheld or excelled in order to stay in consumers' relevant sets.

2.3   Relevant concepts in brand related communication

After concepts of branding have been introduced, concepts of brand related communication relevant for social media brand communication will be outlined. Mangold and Faulds (2009) identify two key roles of social media in the corporate context. Firstly, brands can use social media to communicate with consumers. Secondly, social media enable consumers to communicate with one another and can therefore be used by companies and brands to monitor and influence customer communication. In this respect, social media are a "technological extension of traditional word-of-mouth both marketer influenced and organic" (Myers 2012, pp. 51f.). However, in contrast to traditional processes in which messages were spread, users are now able to reach a far bigger audience, as are companies. Using social media, they can share information with thousands of users at a time.

This chapter opens with an introduction to interactive marketing and brand communication. In the sections that follow, brand communities, user innovation, user generated content, and electronic word-of-mouth are discussed. Although the realm of digital branding touches on a plethora of additional concepts, the chapter decidedly focuses on concepts that are related to social media communication, or that are crucial to understanding the dynamics of social media interaction from a branding perspective. In order to not go beyond the scope of this study, only the mentioned concepts, which are relevant for the theoretical background against which the conceptual model will be built, are included.[10]

2.3.1   Interactive marketing and brand communication

Interactive marketing can be described as part of relationship marketing. Regardless of the employment of technology, relationship marketing can be regarded as an exchange system, while interactive marketing reflects the potential of participatory media such as social media for customer dialogue and interaction (Arnhold 2010, p. 51).

Relationship marketing, which acknowledges the active role of the brand as well as that of the consumer, has been suggested to be the marketing strategy of the future (Casaló, Flavián, & Guinalíu 2008, p. 19; Andersen 2005). Berry and Parasuraman (1991, p. 133) suggest that "relationship marketing concerns attracting, developing, and retaining customer relationships", while Evans and Laskin (1994, p. 440) define relationship marketing in a

---

[10] For a comprehensive overview of related concepts, cf. Arnhold (2010, pp. 64ff.).

similar way as "a customer-centered approach whereby a firm seeks long-term business relationships with prospective and existing customers".

Associated positive outcomes of relationship marketing for the firm are assumed to include greater profitability, increased consumer loyalty, and long-term alliances with customers, all of which are supposed to result in competitive advantage (Grossman 1998, p. 27; Evans & Laskin 1994, p. 440). However, consumers can equally benefit from the development of a relationship, for instance through more simplified buying associated with less risk as well as through rewards or loyalty programmes (Grossman 1998, p. 36).

The relationship between a customer and a brand refers to both the processes of personal and social identification that customers associate with the core values signalled by the brand, as well as "the associated reduction of uncertainty and trust benefits of sticking to a particular brand" (Andersen 2005, p. 47). Morgan and Hunt (1994, p. 21) identify ten discrete forms of relationship marketing:

1. relational exchanges between manufacturers and suppliers;
2. relational exchanges between service suppliers;
3. strategic alliances between firms and their competitors;
4. alliances between firms and non-profit organisations;
5. partnerships for joint research and development;
6. long-term exchanges between firms and customers;
7. relational exchanges of working partnerships, e.g. channels of distribution;
8. exchanges involving functional departments;
9. exchanges between firms and their employees;
10. within-firm relational exchanges involving business units.

The plethora of relationship forms this list comprises indicates that the definitions for relationship marketing provided above are insufficient. They all focus on the partners being a firm and a customer of some sort, and therefore come short of exchange relationships where the distinction between buyer and seller is not clear-cut. The list above shows that relationships do not necessarily evolve between the firm and a customer, but between partners in the business process. In addition, Olsen (1993, p. 578) argues that by purchasing brands, customers renew the relationships they have with those products as well as the relationships they have with the people who introduced those products to them. Relationship marketing should therefore rather be described in more general terms as the establishment, development, and maintenance of successful relational exchanges (Andersen 2005, p. 41; Morgan & Hunt 1994, p. 22).

Due to the interactivity it provides, the internet is widely regarded as a suitable medium to build and manage consumer-brand relationships (Thorbjørnsen, Supphellen, Nysveen, & Pedersen 2002, p. 18). Interactivity has been described in various ways. Bezjian-Avery, Calder, and Iacobucci (1998, p. 23) define interactive marketing as "the immediately iterative process by which customer needs and desires are uncovered, met, modified, and satisfied by the providing firm", and Deighton (1996, p. 151) sees interactivity as "a tool that allows good marketing to become good conversation". Based on these approaches to interactive marketing, Thorbjørnsen et al. (2002, p. 19) put forward the definition of interactive marketing as being "an iterative dialogue where individual consumers' needs and desires are uncovered, modified and satisfied to the degree possible". Bezjian-Avery et al. (1998, p. 24) further point out that the fundamental difference between traditional and interactive marketing lies in the role of the consumer: While traditional marketing leaves the consumer in a passive state, interactive marketing grants the consumer an active role in the processing of and reacting to information.

A relationship approach to marketing is a crucial step in identity-based brand management. Not only do both the company's and the consumer's perspective play important roles in managing the brand, but also does the consumer-brand relationship lie at the core of connecting both concepts. Interactivity allows for direct communication between the two, facilitating the harmonisation of brand image and brand identity as intended by management, as well as the swift reaction to deviations in the brand image.

To investigate how social media can be used for interactive brand communication, six of the twelve brand functions identified by de Chernatony and Dall'Olmo Riley (1998, p. 426) serve as a suitable framework.[11] The selected brand functions play a decisive role in consumer-brand communication and can particularly easily be achieved via social media branding strategies.

---

[11] Brand functions identified in section 2.2.1.2 referred to the brand as a legal instrument, a logo, a company with recognizable corporate name and image, a memory shortcut, a risk reducer, an identity-system, an image in the consumers' minds, a value system, a personality, a relationship, as adding value in the form of non-functional extras, and as an evolving entity (De Chernatony & Dall'Olmo Riley 1998, p. 426).

1. **The brand as a risk reducer:** Social media offerings related to a brand reduce perceived risk for potential consumers because they can interactively engage with it prior to the actual purchase or usage decision, thereby getting a first impression as to whether the product will meet expectations. While the brand promise itself reduces risk, the supporting social media strategy makes this promise more credible and comprehensible. This is particularly meaningful for media brands as experience products. With regard to serialised television brands, social media can help reduce perceived risk prior to watching a first episode. Later, once a consumer has started watching and knows what to expect with regard to product quality, social media can support reassurance that the product is actually worth consuming.

2. **The brand as an identity system:** According to identity-based brand management, brand identity consists of six dimensions: brand heritage, brand management competences, brand values, personality, vision and performance (Burmann & Meffert 2005a, pp. 58-64; Burmann et al. 2007). Brand heritage makes use of the brand's history. Social media can be used to communicate and display important steps in the evolution of the brand, making use of multimedia options via various channels. With regard to serialised television brands, this might also refer to the evolution of content and what the brand stood for throughout the lifetime of the serialised content. Brand management competences address the capability of the organisation to efficiently manage the brand. Depending on a brand's aspirations, management techniques need to reflect those claims: A technology-savvy, high-end brand has to communicate correspondingly. Brand values reflect the general convictions of management and staff and embody emotional components of brand identity. With regard to this internal dimension of identity-based brand management, the degree of brand commitment is important (Burmann et al. 2005, p. 10). Social media facilitate commitment and active participation in the brand management process. Brand vision refers to the long-term development of the brand. Due to their importance, the remaining two dimensions, brand performance and brand personality, are discussed as separate brand functions.

3. **The brand as a personality:** Brand personality is "the set of human characteristics associated with a brand" (Aaker 1997, p. 347). Social media tools open up possibilities for two-way communication companies can use to complement advertising in broadcast style. This can help to identify and exploit new customer segments that are

hard to reach by traditional advertising. Social media strategies support brand communication in an unobtrusive way consumers may not at once identify as advertising. This helps build a brand personality and makes the brand more approachable for customers. With regard to serialised television brands, social media can be used to not only promote brand personality for the television brand itself, but also to enable consumers to engage with actors or character fan pages, which makes the brand more approachable and adds human facets to it.

4. **The brand as an image in the consumers' minds:** According to the identity-based brand management approach, brand image develops in the minds of external target groups and represents the individual, subjective brand associations in the minds of relevant consumers. A prerequisite for brand image to evolve is brand awareness (Burmann & Meffert 2005a, p. 53). Social media, with their ability to stimulate brand related conversations and to promote the creation of brand related user generated content, blur the boundaries of the outside-in and the inside-out perspective and move the brand towards a desirable state of convergence between brand identity and brand image. They also increase brand awareness, for instance for new serialised content, since being mentioned on social networks leads to more conversations about the brand and to more links to the corporate or brand website. For instance, this might lead to viewers having heard about a foreign programme on social media before it is available on the German market, which facilitates and accelerates the building of brand image.

5. **The brand as a relationship:** While communication becomes more customer initiated, exploiting the two-way communication opportunities offered by social media tools means that feedback channels can be incorporated into brand communication more easily. Brand controlling is facilitated by those feedback channels since reactions to brands can be detected more easily. The relationship dimension this opens up is a crucial success factor because the consumer-brand relationship links the two concepts of brand identity and brand image. With regard to serialised television content, this might even mean that viewers' reactions to episodes are taken into account when deciding how to continue the plot and to position the brand.

6. **The brand as adding value in the form of non-functional extras:** This brand function refers to the brand identity dimension of brand performance. Brand performance determines in which way a brand can be used by the consumer and which functional benefits it will have (Burmann & Meffert 2005a, p. 60). Brands can play a

part in defining identity if customers transfer attributes of a brand to their own identity, and support the expression of group membership. Social media serve the formation of individual and group identity by providing transparency about a person's preferences or activities. Being part of the online conversation about a brand supports belonging and puts the individual in touch with like-minded others. As mentioned in section 2.2.3, serialised television content is increasingly consumed in a participatory, public way. Viewers still watch the programme alone, but discuss it afterwards in a virtual community that shares an interest in a certain programme.

The following sections provide insights into concepts that are related to both interactive marketing and brand communication, as well as social media communication.

2.3.2 Brand communities

A brand community is a group of individuals who can be described as fans of a particular brand and who voluntarily relate to each other on behalf of their interest in that brand (Andersen 2005, p. 40; Casaló, Flavián, & Guinalíu 2008, p. 21; Muniz & O'Guinn 2001, p. 412).

Traditionally, research into customer-brand relationships has focused on a "customer-brand dyad" (McAlexander, Schouten, & Koenig 2002, p. 38). Muniz and O'Guinn (2001) established a new approach to brand community research by extending and transforming this model into a "customer-customer-brand triad". Within their model, the existence and meaningfulness of the community are inherent in the customer experience, not in the brand around which that experience revolves (McAlexander et al. 2002, p. 39). Also, in Muniz' and O'Guinn's model, "community is no longer restricted to geographic co-presence of members", but depends on the presence of three attributes of community, namely shared consciousness, rituals and traditions, and a sense of moral responsibility (2001, p. 412). A brand community, in their view, can be defined as a "specialized, non-geographically bound community, based on a structured set of social relationships among admirers of a brand" (ibid.). The situational framework in which these communities operate centres around the consumption of a brand, i.e. a good or a service, while the elements building the community include its members, their relationships and "the sharing of essential resources either emotional or material" (Laroche, Habibi, & Richard 2013, p. 77).

Due to the fact that brand communities are not restricted by geographic boundaries, the development of the internet served as "an infrastructure for communication and information exchange", thereby providing an impetus for overcoming space and time constraints (Andersen 2005, p. 40). Brand communities have traditionally been called virtual brand communities (Casaló et al. 2008, p. 20). Today, most brand communities are online communities, predominantly based on or closely connected to social media offerings.[12] Therefore, with regard to "the motivations for joining social media and brand communities for both people and brand managers, the concepts of social media and brand communities have become closer to each other" (Laroche et al. 2013, p. 77).

The reasons why consumers join online communities – internet self-efficacy, collective self-esteem, and need to belong (Gangadharbatla 2008) – are discussed in section 2.4.1.4 with regard to social networking sites.[13] The benefits of brand communities from a brand or corporate point of view is that they allow for the "creation and negotiation of meaning" (McAlexander et al. 2002, p. 38), as well as for facilitated information sharing, the perpetuation of history and culture of the brand, and that they provide assistance to consumers (Muniz & O'Guinn 2001, p. 427). Hence, communities are of great relevance for marketers and brand managers for a variety of reasons:

1. Casaló et al. (2008) find that participation in a virtual community has a general positive influence on consumer commitment to the brand around which the community is centred. Active participation in virtual brand communities may lead to higher levels of individuals' loyalty to the brand (Andersen 2005, p. 41). In addition, they find trust in a virtual community to have a positive and significant effect on members' participation in the virtual community activities.

2. In their ethnographic study, McAlexander et al. (2002, p. 50) find data strongly indicating "a long-term, lasting impact of relationship-building efforts". They conclude that for some customers, the expectation of developing relationships motivates initial product acquisition: They purchase a branded product with the support of other community members who "serve as brand missionaries, carrying the marketing message into other communities" (ibid., p. 51).

---

[12] This notion will be referred to again in section 2.5, when the use of social media for brand related communication in a television context is discussed, and in sections 3.1.3 and 3.1.4, where hypotheses with regard to the social media programme are derived.

[13] For a comprehensive review of the social media and brand community literature on consumers' incentives to join brand communities, also refer to Laroche et al. (2013, p. 77).

3. Muniz and O'Guinn (2001, p. 427) suggest that brand communities affect brand equity. Following Aaker's conceptualisation of brand equity as consisting of the four components perceived quality, brand loyalty, brand awareness, and brand associations (Aaker 1991; Keller 1993), they state that brand communities directly affect all four of these components.

4. The rise of brand communities is consistent with the tendency towards a more relationship-oriented approach to marketing and branding (Muniz & O'Guinn 2001, p. 427). Brand communities are in line with the broadening definitions of brand loyalty and the rise of the concept of brand relationship (ibid.; Fournier 1998; Olsen 1993).

5. Laroche et al. (2013, p. 81) find that brand communities based on social media strengthen the consumer-brand relationship and enhance brand loyalty by providing benefits to their members, by facilitating information sharing and by enhancing customers' bonds with one another.

Despite the positive implications, community research highlights obstacles as well. Thorbjørnsen et al. (2002) find that online communities are particularly effective in building a consumer-brand relationship for consumers who consider themselves inexperienced with regard to the internet, but less so for experienced users. Hence, brand communities are not equally suitable for all consumer groups and their employment for branding purposes needs to be assessed with regard to the consumers the community is supposed to target.

Also, membership in a brand community might not always be deliberate, or even conscious. Brands used in very specific circumstances, which elicit high involvement with their particular group of users, might seem to inspire strong communities, when it is actually the usage situation that does. For instance, owners of *Polar* or *Garmin* sports watches often wear the watches in everyday situations, signalling their self-conception as athletes and their implicit membership in the athletic community, not their membership in a *Polar* or *Garmin* brand community.

Moreover, reaching and maintaining a critical mass of users is a general problem for all communities (Becker, Clement, & Schaedel 2010, p. 166). In order to be beneficial for existing users, newly established communities need to quickly attract and retain new users. Communities set up by brands or companies themselves hence need to be managed actively in order to grow. This is more difficult for brand communities operated entirely by fans or consumers, which forces them to convince users due to their relevance.

2.3.3 User innovation

Although not a direct part of brand management, user innovation does provide insights into consumers' preferences and needs. Also, it offers the opportunity to integrate consumers into the brand or product creation process, thereby strengthening involvement and loyalty. This "affects the prospects of establishing positive market relationships" because devoted users engage in "consumption-related activities and share their knowledge with others" (Andersen 2005, p. 39).

Innovation can be defined in various ways, depending on the lens through which it is investigated. Definitions of innovation may focus on the novelty of the product or service, on the first-time use or application of the idea, on new process management and other aspects.[14] According to Schumpeter, innovation is characterised by a process of "creative destruction" (1942), where the development of new products leads to the replacement of traditional offerings. Innovation can therefore be regarded as the market launch of a product that is either new or significantly improved and that cannot coexist with the established product, but replaces it on the market.

According to Roberts' (1987, p. 3) market oriented definition, innovation equals invention plus exploitation. Dosi (1988, p. 222) describes innovation as "the search for, and the discovery, experimentation, development, imitation, and adoption of new products, new production processes and new organisational set-ups". This search takes place under uncertainty, which is due to insufficient information, but also unknown solution procedures to technological and economic problems, as well as unknown consequences of the innovative approach (ibid.). Innovations can be incremental or radical (Habann 2003, p. 19): While incremental innovations refer to the improvement of existing products or of processes for existing target groups, radical innovations mean the launching of a new product that targets new markets.

Freeman (1988, p. 6) points out that innovation cannot be defined solely on the basis of resources and knowledge of the company: Environmental influences as well as economic

---

[14] For a sound overview of definitions of and approaches to innovation, refer to Hauschildt and Salomo (2001, pp. 6f.).

circumstances affect the innovation process as well. Similarly, Chesbrough (2003) argues that focusing on closed innovation, an approach that relies solely on corporate R&D capabilities, is no longer a viable option. Instead, open innovation, (or user innovation, in von Hippel's (1986) nomenclature) is a model in which "firms commercialize external (as well as internal) ideas", and which makes them more successful (Chesbrough 2003, p. 36).

Quite frequently, innovation happens in online communities, similar to brand communities, in which users have the opportunity to contribute their ideas and sometimes even see them implemented (von Hippel 2001). A current example is Haribo, which lets consumers vote for their favourite additions to the traditional package of their *Gold-Bear Gummi candy,* called *GOLDBÄREN FAN-edition* (Gummi Bear fan edition). On an especially designed website[15] or on Haribo's Facebook page[16], consumers could choose between two new flavours every week for six weeks in the spring of 2014. The winning flavour of every week was then added to the special edition, for sale in July 2014.

Von Hippel argues that most innovations developed by users are created by what he calls "lead users" (1986). Lead users are members of the user population who have two distinguishing characteristics. Firstly, they recognize important market trends or develop new needs early, thereby experiencing needs that many users will experience at a later point in time. Secondly, they "anticipate relatively high benefits from obtaining a solution to their needs", which gives them an incentive to innovate (ibid., p. 22). With reference to an online social network, Goldenberg, Han, Lehmann, and Hong (2009) found that there are actually two different types of lead users, which they call "hubs": innovative hubs, who have a greater impact on the speed of the adoption process, and follower hubs, who have a greater impact on the total number of adoptions. This implies that if the different kinds of lead users can be identified, they can be addressed for either innovation or marketing communication purposes.

User innovation as a concept is similar to what is meant by the buzzword "crowdsourcing". Christodoulides, Jevons, and Blackshaw (2011, p. 103) define crowdsourcing as "the ability to tap the positive creativity of enthusiastic amateurs in problem solving". They also suggest that being involved in the production process enhances consumers' likelihood of engaging with the brand (ibid., p. 106), which is underpinned by the Haribo example.

---

[15] https://goldbaeren-fan-edition.de
[16] http://www.facebook.com/haribo

Marketing and brand managers need to understand these motivations, consequences, as well as the user structure in order to make use of user innovation and user generated content. In order to satisfy users' needs for a sense of community, it appears useful to embed innovation into brand communities.

2.3.4   User generated content

What unites all concepts introduced above is that they require consumer co-creation. Interactive marketing and brand communication would not be interactive without a response reaction from consumers.

Brand communities have been described above as fans of a particular brand related to each other on behalf of their interest in that brand, implying that by engaging with or communicating about that brand, community members create content. User innovation explicitly demands the contribution of ideas and content as well as knowledge sharing.

In accordance with the OECD (2007) definition, Christodoulides et al. (2011, p. 101) define user generated content (UGC) as "consumers creating content that is made available through publicly accessible transmission media such as the Internet, reflects some degree of creative effort, and is created for free outside professional routines and practices". Daugherty, Eastin, and Bright (2008, p.16) describe user generated content as media content created by the general public. Hence, three basic requirements for UGC can be postulated:

- public accessibility and publication;
- "some degree of creative effort" (Christodoulides et al. 2011, p. 105);
- creation in a non-professional environment and/or for non-professional reasons.

It is notable that these definitions do not explicitly refer to UGC in a branding context. Although UGC can be created for any reasons, a number of studies have shown its effectiveness with regard to branding purposes. Christodoulides, Jevons, and Bonhomme (2012) show that UGC has an effect on consumer-based brand equity via involvement, which, in a circular feedback loop, subsequently affects consumers' co-creation efforts. Boyle (2007) developed a process model of brand co-creation highlighting the impact of brand co-creation on brand loyalty. Muniz and Schau (2007, p. 35) review the literature on consumer co-creation and enumerate terms such as "homebrew ads", "folk ads", "open source branding", and "vigilante marketing" for brand-related UGC, all of which they view as "unpaid advertising and marketing efforts, including one-to-one, one-to-many, and many-to-many commercially oriented communications, undertaken by brand loyalists on behalf of the brand". Christodoulides et al. (2012, p. 54) add the terms brand-related UGC, consumer generated media (CGM), and consumer generated content (CGC) to the list of expressions used for UGC that is created with a brand focus.

Arnhold (2010, p. 33) defines brand related UGC, which she calls user generated branding (UGB), as "the representation of the voluntary creation and public distribution of personal brand meaning undertaken by non-marketers outside the branding routines and enabled by multimedia technology". She then proceeds (ibid., pp. 127ff.) to distinguish between sponsored and non-sponsored UGB, where non-sponsored UGB refers to "the management of naturally occurring unprompted brand related UGC", while sponsored UGB means "the management of prompted or stimulated brand related UGC". This distinction is in line with the concept of owned, earned and bought media, where owned media are communication outlets such as corporate websites owned by the company or brand, paid media is paid-for advertising, and earned media refers to coverage on news outlets and includes online discussions or social media engagement.

With regard to branding, UGC leads to a loss of control, because consumers can interact with brands and by contributing content alter meaning. Brand managers' tasks need to encompass that loss of control: In order to not lose their defining characteristics when in touch with consumers and UGC, brands need an even stronger foundation.

Becker et al. (2010, p. 168) note that users' motivation to "engage in value creation is especially remarkable from an economic perspective, as most user-generated Web features can be considered as public goods". In fact, Daugherty et al. (2008) found out that ego-defensive sources (i.e. the pursuit to minimise self-doubts) and social functional sources (i.e. users wanting to spend time with others and experience a sense of community) predominantly motivate users to create UGC.

Christodoulides et al. (2012, p. 56) provide an extensive overview of studies tapping into the research area of motivating factors for creating brand-related UGC. Table 2-5 displays an extract from their findings. In their study, Christodoulides et al. (2012) provide evidence that consumers' perceptions of co-creation, community, and self-concept have a positive impact on their involvement with UGC, which in turn has a positive impact on consumer-based brand equity.

While the aforementioned distinction between sponsored and non-sponsored UGC seems noteworthy in order to clearly distinguish between possible forms of UGC, it is difficult to investigate the effects of both separately. Firstly, it cannot be assumed that users can always clearly distinguish between the two. While it might be clear that UGC is sponsored, i.e. prompted, if it is created on the Facebook page of a company, this is not the case if content is forwarded to and presented on private blogs.

Factor	Authors	Description
Co-creation	Burmann & Arnhold (2008) Christodoulides (2009) Daugherty, Eastin, & Bright (2008) Kozinets, de Valck, Wojnicki, & Wilner (2010) Kristensson, Matthing, & Johansson, (2008) Muniz & Schau (2007) OECD (2007) Prahalad & Ramaswamy (2004) Smith (2009) Trusov, Bucklin, & Pauwels (2009) Uncles, East, & Lomax (2010)	• Social benefit function • Risk reduction
Empower-ment	Berthon, Pitt, & Campbell (2008) Burmann & Arnhold (2008) Dhar & Chang (2009) Grégoire, Tripp, & Legoux (2009) Muniz & Schau (2007) OECD (2007)	• Change perceptions • Influence others • Feelings of power and control • Engage online • Reveal personal information • Complement traditional media • Request greater choice
Community	Burmann & Arnhold (2008) Christodoulides (2009) Daugherty, Eastin, & Bright (2008) Gangadharbatla (2008) Kozinets, de Valck, Wojnicki, & Wilner (2010) Krishnamurthy & Dou (2008) Muniz & Schau (2007) OECD (2007) Smith (2009) Uncles, East, & Lomax (2010) von Hippel (2001)	• Knowledge-sharing • Advocacy • Social connections • Wanting to be heard • Interaction • Collaboration • Social networking
Self-concept	Berthon, Pitt, & Campbell (2008) Burmann & Arnhold (2008) Daugherty, Eastin, & Bright (2008) Kozinets, de Valck, Wojnicki, & Wilner (2010) Krishnamurthy & Dou (2008) Muniz & Schau (2007) OECD (2007) Smith (2009) von Hippel (2001)	• Personal documentation • Self-expression • Creativity • Social function • Self promotion • Identity shaping • Ego defensive function

Table 2-5: Motivating factors for creating brand-related UGC

Source: Own design, based on Christodoulides et al. (2012, p. 56)

Secondly, it is difficult to define what exactly is a prompt. Is it only a clearly addressed message, asking consumers to participate, or also a commercial that leads to the production of UGC, even if that was not its original purpose?

Thirdly, for a lot of content, it is not even clear if it is of corporate origin. Author blogs, for instance, are frequently run by authors without support of media companies or publishing houses, but despite their individual and private look-and-feel, they do have distinct professional purposes. Also, if actors promote themselves and the films or serials they participate in on their own social media channels, this serves a marketing purpose, but it can partly be regarded as private conversation, too. Hence, due to the blurring of the boundary between corporate and private communication and assuming that viral effects and electronic word-of-mouth (eWOM) processes make the sponsored/non-sponsored distinction a problematic one, it is not explicitly made in this study.

Having outlined concepts interactive marketing as well as brand communication and UGC as the outcome of consumer co-creation, the last section of this chapter deals with electronic word-of-mouth, which can be regarded as a particular form of consumer co-creation focusing on information processing and sharing.

2.3.5   Electronic word-of-mouth (eWOM)

Word-of-mouth (WOM) can be described as "the process of conveying information from person to person" (Jansen, Zhang, Sobel, & Chowdury 2009, p. 2169). Word-of-mouth (WOM) communication has always been an important part of consumer communication and behaviour because people seek advice and recommendations from others if they lack information or if they perceive high involvement or high (financial) risk when making their purchase decision.

Word-of-mouth advertising has been part of marketing research for a long time as well (e.g. Dichter 1966; Sheth 1971). With the rise of the internet, this form of communication has started to also take place in the online environment, online or electronic word-of-mouth (eWOM) becoming an increasingly important influence of consumer opinion. From a brand perspective, the most important difference between WOM and eWOM is the fact that online reviews or recommendations are accessible to a larger number of users, which affects consumer opinion and in its wake product performance much more strongly.

Hennig-Thurau, Gwinner, Walsh, and Gremler (2004, p. 28) define eWOM communication as "any positive or negative statement made by potential, actual, or former customers about a product or company, which is made available to a multitude of people and institutions via the Internet." Word-of-mouth processes can be used for marketing and branding purposes; marketing by eWOM is often called viral marketing. Motives for participation in viral marketing campaigns can be extrinsic or intrinsic in nature, where the former refer to incentive programmes such as vouchers, and the latter mean motives of impression management, such as increasing one's own personal network or self-presentation (Schulz, Mau, & Löffler 2007, pp. 7f.).

Social media tools are a powerful means to spread eWOM; Twitter in particular is well-known for its capability to quickly and efficiently spread information (cf. section 2.4.1.5 for Twitter with reference to social media brand communication). Especially the retweeting function allows messages to "cascade down from one user's follower network to another's", thereby transforming it from information to word-of-mouth (Kaplan & Haenlein 2011, p. 107).

In the last decade, eWOM has been extensively researched (e.g. Brown, Broderick, & Lee 2007; Burton & Khammash 2010; Dellarocas 2003; Godes & Mayzlin 2004; Godes & Mayzlin 2009; Hennig-Thurau et al. 2004; Trusov et al. 2009), partly with a direct focus on the consumer reaction or on the impact eWOM has on sales (e.g. Chevalier & Mayzlin 2006; Kozinets et al. 2010), and a plethora of findings have shed light on how eWOM affects consumer decision making.

The former group of studies focuses on definitions, antecedents, and the measurement of WOM and eWOM, as well as consumers' motivations to engage in it. For instance, in a study concerning eWOM on Usenet for new television shows during the 1999-2000 season, Godes and Mayzlin (2004) found that online conversations are "an easy and cost-effective opportunity to measure word of mouth" (p. 545). Motivations to engage in eWOM communication include "consumers' desire for social interaction, desire for economic incentives, their concern for other consumers, and the potential to enhance their own self-worth" (Hennig-Thurau et al. 2004, p. 37). Chu and Kim (2011) developed a conceptual framework identifying social relationship factors and their relations with eWOM on social networking sites. Their study indicates that trust, normative influence, tie strength and informational influence are all positively associated with a social networking site's users' overall eWOM behaviour on their favourite site.

The latter group covers various aspects with regard to the concepts of WOM, eWOM and consumer behaviour. Chevalier and Mayzlin (2006) investigated customer reviews on Amazon.com and Barnesandnoble.com. They found that customer reviews tend to be positive and that the relative sales numbers of books are related to the number of reviews the books have received. Kozinets et al. (2010) show that eWOM "does not simply increase or amplify marketing messages; rather, marketing messages and meanings are systematically altered in the process of embedding them" (p. 71). This shows that consumers make active use of informational or promotional content instead of being mere transmitters of these messages. In a study on WOM communication referring to television programmes, Romaniuk (2007) found the effect of WOM to be asymmetrical: Positive WOM was four times more common than negative WOM and was found to have a positive impact on those it reached. By comparison, the effects of negative WOM were not only small, but also insignificant. In contrast, Anderson (1998), who researched the relationship between customer satisfaction and word-of-mouth, found evidence that highly dissatisfied customers engage more than highly satisfied customers, making crisis management and immediate response to complaints and problems vital – especially on the internet, where word spreads much more quickly. This is in line with the results of another study that found brand crises to change consumer perceptions not only of the brand immediately affected, but of the entire product category (Dahlén & Lange 2006). Brands are hence becoming increasingly vulnerable and require swift and determined reactions to negative consumer responses.

Cheung, Luo, Sia, and Chen (2009) investigated the role of credibility for eWOM processes. They found that both informationally and normatively based determinants affect perceived eWOM credibility, which in turn "is found to have a significant impact on subsequent adoption" (p. 33). Winning consumers' trust is crucial for product adoption, meaning that brands need to be credible themselves, and have credible brand ambassadors in order to be trusted.

Although eWOM seems to be a viable alternative to other forms of communication and a powerful tool to encourage consumers to buy a brand, there are also problems and risks attached to it. Fitzsimons and Lehmann (2004) found that recommendations do not always lead to positive reactions. If advice goes contrary to individual choice tendencies, it can lead to the activation of a reactant state and the refusal of the recommendation. Also, companies must not assume that their marketing messages run through eWOM processes unaffected. As Kozinets et al. (2010) found out, consumers may alter messages. Also, eWOM cannot solely be regarded as an indicator or forecasting tool for future performance. Being endogenous in nature, i.e. frequently an outcome of past behaviour, not of planned or future actions, high eWOM activity may be a sign of high sales in the past, not in the future (Godes & Mayzlin 2004, p. 546). Godes and Mayzlin (2004) stress this dual nature of eWOM by arguing that it is both a driver and an outcome of consumer behaviour.

Having introduced concepts of brand related communication relevant for social media brand communication, the next section deals with social media research. After an outline of types of social media offerings and an overview of usage motivations and gratifications, social media offerings will be categorized with regard to brand management purposes in section 2.4.3. The concepts introduced in this section will be revisited in this context and connected to social media research.

2.4   Literature review: Social media research

This section explores the field of social media research. To revisit research results in this field is crucial because firstly, practitioners' knowledge and recommendations about social media marketing and branding seem abundant. A systematic, research oriented view on the field therefore seems necessary. Secondly, for the development of the model, gratifications obtained from using social media accompanying serialised television content need to be identified. This section therefore starts with a cursory outline of the types of social media offerings that exist to date, derives usage motivations and gratifications from the literature and concludes with an attempt to categorize social media offerings with regard to brand management purposes.

Kaplan and Haenlein (2010, p. 61) name web 2.0 as the technological and ideological foundation of social media. The term web 2.0 refers to websites providing content that gets richer as the number of people using the website increases, thereby exploiting the power of user contribution, collective intelligence, as well as of network effects (Ganley & Lampe 2009, p. 266). While web 2.0 can be perceived as a technological precondition for social media, UGC is the result of people's interaction with social media. Social media can hence be defined as "a group of Internet-based applications that build on the ideological foundations of Web 2.0, and that allow the creation and exchange of User Generated Content" (Kaplan & Haenlein 2010, p. 61).

The success of social media platforms depends on the size and growth of the networks. Positive network externalities are a crucial factor in enhancing the value of the network for all users, because the value of joining a network, real or virtual, depends on the number of others already in that network (Shapiro & Varian 1999, pp. 174, 183). Although the functionality of a network is independent of real-life connections between the members of the virtual network, research has shown that loyalty to the network does depend on real-life ties: Users who are invited by people with whom they share pre-existing social relationships tend to stay longer and be more active in the network (Lento, Welser, Smith, & Gu 2006).

In practice, the term "social media" refers to a plethora of tools and types of websites, each of which serves a distinct purpose and operates according to specific rules and terms of usage. Although Facebook, Flickr, YouTube, Twitter and Tumblr can clearly all be described as social media of some sort, they differ significantly in the functionality they offer and in the way they are made use of. Kaplan and Haenlein (2010) propose a classification scheme for social media that allows for a systematic categorization of social media tools. Since an investigation into social media touches on both dimensions, they categorize alongside media research and social processes.

With regard to the media research dimension, Kaplan and Haenlein rely on social presence theory and media richness theory. According to social presence theory (Short, Williams, & Christie 1976), media differ in their degree of social presence, which is the acoustic, visual, and physical contact between the communication partners.[17] The higher the social presence, the stronger the social influence the communication partners have on each other's behaviour (Kaplan & Haenlein 2010, p. 61). For the second part of the media dimension, Kaplan and Haenlein refer to media richness theory (Daft & Lengel 1986), according to which media differ in the degree of richness they possess. This means that the amount of information that can be transmitted in a given time interval differs between media types.

The social processes dimension of the classification scheme is self-presentation/self-disclosure. Self-presentation refers to people's desire to present themselves and control others' impressions of them, while self-disclosure is "the conscious or unconscious revelation of personal information" (Kaplan & Haenlein 2010, p. 62). For instance, the main reason why people create a personal webpage, which can be regarded as the predecessor to the personal profile on a social media network, is the wish to present themselves (Schau & Gilly 2003).[18] This kind of self-presentation can be achieved through self-disclosure, which is the aptitude an individual has for revealing personal information to others (Collins & Miller 1994).

Combining the two dimensions of "social presence/media richness" and "self-presentation/self-disclosure" results in a categorization as visualized below.

---

[17] Social presence is influenced by the intimacy (ranging from interpersonal to mediated) and the immediacy (ranging from asynchronous to synchronous) of a medium, meaning that mediated (e.g. telephone conversation) and asynchronous communication (e.g. e-mail) exhibits a lower degree of social presence than interpersonal (e.g., face-to-face discussion) and synchronous (e.g., messenger apps) communication.

[18] Consumers use self-presentation strategies to construct digital collages representing the self (Schau & Gilly 2003, p. 390). This aims at controlling the impressions of others, at repressing personal information or replacing it with modified and more desirable information that is more congruent with the ideal self, but it also aims at creating an image of oneself that is consistent with one's personal identity (Kaplan & Haenlein 2010, p. 62; Schau & Gilly 2003, p. 387).

		Social presence/ Media richness		
		Low	Medium	High
Self-presentation/ Self-disclosure	High	Blogs	Social networking sites (e.g. Facebook)	Virtual social networks (e.g. Second Life)
	Low	Collaborative projects (e.g. Wikipedia)	Content communities (e.g. YouTube)	Virtual Game worlds (e.g. World of Warcraft)

Figure 2-4: Categorization of social media

Source: Own design, adapted from Kaplan & Haenlein (2010, p. 62)

With respect to the dimension of social presence/media richness, applications such as collaborative projects and blogs score lowest, since they are usually text-based and therefore allow for only a relatively simple exchange of information. However, blogs score higher on the dimension self-presentation/self-disclosure because collaborative projects are usually content driven, while blogs can also be personal diaries, or serve purely private purposes.

Social networking sites such as Facebook and Google+, but also professional networks such as LinkedIn or Xing, as well as content communities like the video platform YouTube or the photo platform Flickr, score higher on the dimension social presence/media richness because they make use of a combination of text, pictures, and videos. While content communities usually show rather low levels of self-disclosure, social networking sites are often explicitly used to disclose information about oneself.

The highest level of social presence/media richness is achieved by virtual games and social worlds, such as World of Warcraft or Second Life. Second Life, created and operated by Linden Lab, has existed since June 2003 (Linden Lab 2013) and claims to be the most popular virtual world on the internet (Linden Lab 2014). World of Warcraft is the world's most subscribed to massively multiplayer online role-playing game (MMORPG), with approximately 10 million subscribers in 2013 (Business Wire 2013). Both types of platforms require a very high level of social presence/media richness, but while virtual social worlds also score high on the dimension self-presentation/self-disclosure, virtual games do not, since they are structured by the rules of the game, thereby controlling users' behaviour.

The following sections attempt to provide an overview of the various forms of applications, organised by the categorization scheme provided by Kaplan and Haenlein (2010), and revisits relevant research about them. Virtual social networks and virtual game worlds will be excluded from the analysis because they are of only marginal relevance for branding communication. Microblogging will be added as a category that does not fit into any of the other categories.

2.4.1   Investigating social media tools

2.4.1.1   Collective/collaborative projects

Collaborative projects allow many users to participate in the simultaneous creation of content. One kind of such collaborative projects are wikis, the most well-known of which is the online encyclopaedia Wikipedia. A wiki is a web-based software that allows all users of a page to change its content by editing the page online in a browser (Ebersbach, Glaser, Heigl, & Dueck 2006, p. 12). This makes wikis a simple and easy-to-use platform for collaborative work. Wikis consist of a loosely structured set of pages that are linked to one another and to external internet resources in multiple ways (Godwin-Jones 2003, p. 15).

The word "wiki" derives from the Hawaiian "wiki wiki" which translates into "to hurry" and alludes to the tools' quick and easy editing process (Wheeler, Yeomans, & Wheeler 2008, p. 989). Wikis can be used by anybody to publish content or share knowledge, including text, images, and hyperlinks. Existing content can be edited at any time, and since wikis provide a page history, it is possible to view any prior changes to the page and, if necessary, revert to an earlier version.

There are two different purposes wikis can serve. Firstly, they may be used as tools in a closed work group, where only selected members have access. Secondly, they can be made accessible and usable for potentially everybody. Wikis can be utilized as knowledge management tools, for open, web-based content management, or as project-oriented collaboration platforms.

In his research on *Lostpedia*, a wiki platform dedicated to the television serial *Lost*, Mittell attempted to analyse how a the wiki "functions as a place for the aggregation of fan creativity, what limits and boundaries are placed on that fan-generated content, and what rationales underlie those policies and preferences" (2009, [no page]). He concludes that *Lostpedia's* core purpose is that of a shared archive performing the dual function of on the one hand being a catalogue of canon and on the other hand a site of original creativity for fans, thereby overcoming and blurring the boundaries between "fiction and truth, canon and fanon" (ibid.).

Other forms of collaborative projects are social bookmarking sites, such as Delicious, Diigo, or StumpleUpon, which allow for the storage and sharing of web bookmarks. Users can bookmark their favourite web pages, tag them, and make their lists of bookmarks public.

Although collective or collaborative projects are highly convenient tools for users of all kinds and preferences, they are hard to utilize for brand communication. However, the technological foundation, i.e. wikis and similar platforms, can be used to encourage consumers to participate in a creative effort aimed at further developing and enhancing the brand experience, and they might be suitable for user innovation processes.

2.4.1.2   Content communities

Content communities enable the sharing of content between users. In content communities, the focus is on the content a user contributes, not on the users themselves. Therefore, users do usually not create a detailed individualized personal profile page. There are content communities for a variety of media types, among them text (e.g. BookRix for self-published books), photos (e.g. Flickr), videos (e.g. YouTube), or even presentation slides (e.g. Slideshare).

Founded in February 2005 (YouTube 2014a), YouTube is arguably one of the most important and widely used content communities with more than 1 billion unique users visiting each month (YouTube 2014b). It allows any internet user to watch and registered account holders to also share originally created videos. Companies can use YouTube to upload promotional videos or employ it for viral campaigns. Especially for media companies, YouTube bears the risk of being used as a platform for the illegal sharing of copyright-protected materials: Recent episodes of popular television programmes are often uploaded to YouTube shortly after they have been aired. On the one hand, this creates the challenge for networks to put an end to copyright infringing behaviour. On the other hand, the sharing of and commenting on YouTube videos strengthens the ties of communities centring around the television content, thereby providing a powerful tool for brand relationship management.

With regard to the Uses and Gratification approach, Haridakis and Hanson (2009) analysed the motives users have to watch videos on YouTube and to share them afterwards on other social networking sites. Just as for television, the main motives to watch YouTube videos are information and entertainment. Taking into account that a lot of the content posted to YouTube is original TV content, this is hardly surprising (ARD-Forschungsdienst 2011, p.

117). What distinguishes media consumption on YouTube from watching classic, linear television is the fact that YouTube provides the opportunity to share and discuss the content, and to recommend it on other platforms.

2.4.1.3 Blogs

On blogs (originally called weblogs), individuals and organisations can present content to a broader audience and in antichronological order. The latest addition (or post) is usually presented on the top of the page. What distinguishes blogs from static websites is that they contain elements of social networks: Users can usually subscribe to them via RSS or e-mail alerts, and entries can be shared, commented on, or reblogged.

Blog entries can contain text, images, and video. The content presented can be purely private, but often, blogs are used to present creative ideas or expert knowledge. To date, there are many different blogging platforms, most of which are free of charge in their basic versions. Wordpress, for instance, offers a free version with restricted functionality, which is popular with private users. There is also a premium version available, with the possibility to choose domain names, and a software solution with enhanced features that requires users to host the blog or website themselves. Other well-known services that are free of charge are Blogger, Blogspot, or Tumblr. Tumblr, which was launched in March 2007 (Milstein, Chowdhury, Hochmuth, Lorica, & Magoulas 2008, p. 26), is a blogging service that encourages comparatively short posts and uses a follower model similar to Twitter's. There are no user profiles, meaning that members of the network do not have to disclose personal information to become part of the network. On their blogs, users can post text, pictures, or video content. The content, which can also be created on other sites and then included into Tumblr, can be spread and referenced to ("reblogged") within the network by other users who have subscribed to the account providing it.

While blogs used to be clearly distinguishable from other social media tools in the early days of web 2.0, it is becoming increasingly difficult to differentiate them from content communities. While the difference between a text-based private journal and a YouTube channel is still clear cut, it is difficult to draw the line between blog and content community for Tumblr, where users upload or link to photo or video content originally uploaded to Flickr or YouTube, sometimes making the creative effort to make changes to the original content, sometimes just sharing something they like and want to show their followers. Another tool that blurs the boundary between blog and content community is Pinterest. Pinterest is a pinboard-styled social photo sharing website that allows users to create and manage theme-based image collections. The boards, which are sets of pins grouped into a specific topic, can be filled with images found online using the "Pin It" button, or uploaded from users' computer. The service, which allows for sharing, "liking" and reproducing the content, combines features of blogging platforms as well as that of common content communities.

According to Nardi, Schiano, Gumbrecht, and Swartz (2004), there are five major motivations why people blog: documenting one's own life, providing commentary and opinions, expressing emotions, articulating ideas through writing, and forming and maintaining community forums. Huang, Shen, Lin, and Chang (2007) separate blogging into an interaction and a content gathering function and find interaction to be motivated by users' desire for self-expression and documenting their own lives, as well as by commenting, while motivating factors for content gathering are commenting, forum participation, and information seeking. These motivations can be adapted to blogs run by companies and by groups. Corporate and brand blogs facilitate customer support or participation, while blogs run by brand supporters or fan groups are used for interaction with likeminded individuals or to engage in a shared creative effort. In their study with corporate blogs, Hsu and Tsou (2011) found out that information credibility has a significant positive association with customer experiences, which means that the credibility of information on a blog is critical in online environments. Customer experiences, in turn, were found to have a significant and positive association with purchase intention.

Engaging with customers via blogs can be a powerful way of influencing consumer behaviour. Interactivity creates the impression of a one-to-one relationship with the individual or brand behind the blog, which positively influences attitude toward the website and might ultimately enhance attitude towards the brand (Thorson & Rogers 2006). Yet, this strategy does not come without risks. Firstly, disappointed customers might use the blog as a space to post their complaints. Secondly, once companies encourage their employees to be active on blogs, it becomes harder to control communication and to ensure compliance (Kaplan & Haenlein 2010, p. 63).

2.4.1.4 Social networking sites

Social networking sites (SNS) are websites that connect participating users by linking their profile pages. Networks such as Facebook or Google+ are primarily used for private communication, while LinkedIn or Xing are specifically designed to develop and maintain business contacts. In accordance with Boyd and Ellison (2007), SNS are defined as web-based services that allow individual users to (1) construct a public or semi-public profile within a bounded system, (2) establish a list of other users with whom they share a connection, and (3) view connections made by others within the system.

The usage of social networking sites is rapidly increasing across all age groups. By 2010, 40 percent of all German internet users had a profile on at least one social networking site (Frees & Fisch 2011, p. 154); by 2013, it were 46 percent (ARD/ZDF-Onlinestudie 2013a). However, teenagers and young adults between 14 and 29 are significantly more active: In 2010, 71 percent of them had an account on an SNS (Frees & Fisch 2011, p. 154), while in 2013, 87 percent of those aged 14-19 and 80 percent of those aged 20-29 had (ARD/ZDF-Onlinestudie 2013a). Teenagers join SNS for a variety of reasons, such as to stay in touch with friends met frequently as well as with friends rarely seen in person, to make plans with friends, to make new friends, as well as to flirt (Lenhart & Madden 2007). Valkenburg, Peter, and Schouten (2006) found that the frequency with which the young age group uses SNS influences their social self-esteem and well-being. Applying the Uses and Gratifications approach to friend-networking sites, Raacke and Bonds-Raacke (2008) found that the vast majority of college students are using friend-networking sites for reasons such as making new friends and locating old friends.

For SNS users in general, existing literature names various factors that influence the adoption of SNS. An empirical study by Sledgianowski and Kulviwat (2009) showed that an individual's perceptions of playfulness, critical mass of other users, normative pressure, his or her trust in the site, its usefulness, and ease of use significantly affect the intention to use an SNS. Gangadharbatla (2008) found that internet self-efficacy, collective self-esteem, and need to belong all have positive effects on attitudes towards SNS. *Internet self-efficacy,* also referred to as internet confidence, describes people's confidence in their own ability to "successfully understand, navigate, and evaluate content" (Daugherty, Eastin, & Gangadharbatla 2005, p. 71). Thus, the more competent and confident a user feels with regard to handling the technology, the more likely he is to become an active member of an online social network.[19] *Collective self-esteem* is described as the aspect of an individual's self-concept that derives from that individual's interaction with others and the social groups that the individual is a member of (Crocker & Luhtanen 1990). *Need to belong* refers to people's endeavours with regard to the contact with other people and their striving for social acceptance and the love of others (Gangadharbatla 2008, p. 8).[20] SNS, which enable conversations and information sharing, the expression of opinions as well as the possibility to gain social approval, address this need to belong. Also, they provide a platform to influence other users. However, Trusov, Bodapati, and Bucklin (2010) found that although users typically have numerous connections to other site members of a network, only a fraction of those contacts actually influences a user's site usage: On average, approximately one fifth of a user's contacts actually have an impact on his or her activity level on the network.

One of the most widely used social networks is Facebook. Launched in February 2004 (Facebook 2014), Facebook is a web-based service that allows people to create profiles and build connections with other members of the network. Those profiles may contain photos, status updates, links to other websites, as well as lists of contacts and personal interests. Users can add others to their personal network by invitation, which makes the two users "friends". By 31 December 2012, Facebook had 1.06 billion monthly active users (618 million daily active users on average in December 2012), as compared to 845 million monthly active users on 31 December 2011 (483 million daily active users on average in December 2011) (Facebook 2013, p. 5). In 2010, the average Facebook user had 130 friends (Facebook 2010).

On Facebook, communication with friends and other users is possible through private messages, public messages on each others' profile pages, or by a chat tool. Users can create interest groups or join groups created by others, as well as play games, which are usually integrated into the platform by external service providers. In addition to the personal profiles, Facebook also hosts "groups" and "pages". Facebook groups provide a place for smaller groups of private users to share common interests, discuss issues, express opinions, and post photos (Chu 2011, p. 31). The four primary reasons for participating in groups within Facebook are socializing, entertainment, self-status seeking, and information seeking (Park,

---

[19] This corresponds to the notion of "ease of use" in the study by Sledgianowski and Kulviwat (2009).
[20] This corresponds to the critical mass of other users, as well as normative pressure as mentioned by Sledgianowski and Kulviwat (2009).

Kee, & Valenzuela 2009). In addition to groups founded for private matters, groups can also be brand or product related and open to anybody who wants to join. This opens up new opportunities to build consumer-brand relationships and viral advertising platforms, as well as to positively influence brand perceptions and purchasing decisions (Chu 2011, p. 30). However, public profiles of companies, brands, celebrities or NGOs (non-governmental organisations) usually use Facebook pages to communicate with consumers.

Facebook pages differ from Facebook groups in that they are official profiles of organisations, interest groups, clubs, or brands. As of 31 December 2012, there were more than 50 million pages with ten or more "likes" (Facebook 2013, p. 5). Page owners can post updates, ask and answer questions and receive general feedback from their users. If users want to connect with a page, they can "like" it and Facebook pushes stories published by the page owner to the subscriber's news feed. On other networks such as Google+, there are similar structures in place that allow for the creation of profiles that are not those of private users. Users can also "like" individual posts, comment on posts, or share the content found on the page with their friends, which increases the page's exposure on the SNS.

Facebook has become the biggest relationship-marketing provider for many brands (Neff 2010). Like other industries, large media companies have recognized the potential of SNS like Facebook to help them reach their audience and deepen relationships (Carter 2009b). However, while Facebook pages work very similar to traditional owned media like corporate websites and the migration from websites to Facebook pages provides advantages to managing the consumer-brand relationship, pages are in fact owned by Facebook.

Advertising on Facebook is highly attractive for marketing purposes because it provides very clearly defined target groups, thereby guaranteeing advertisers to reach the relevant target groups. Advertisements can be placed on Facebook via a cost-per-click model, and Facebook Insights provides statistics and analytics, such as user growth and demographics, consumption of content, click-through rates and average costs per click.

What makes this form of advertising more attractive than traditional forms is that SNS users not only embrace advertising-related content, but actively promote it if they find it engaging (Taylor, Lewin, & Strutton 2011). In their study on the popularity of brand posts on brand pages, de Vries, Gensler, and Leeflang (2012) found evidence that brand posts with interactive characteristics such as video content receive higher numbers of "likes", while posts with interactive characteristics such as a question receive more comments. However, Lipsman, Mud, Rich, and Bruich (2012) highlight the importance of evaluating the individual importance of the pages' fans, because mere counts of the number of engagements fail to address the potential as well as scope of social media brand impressions[21] (p. 52).

While SNS aim at boosting their advertising revenues, they "encounter the severe risk that members will feel exploited if the sites suddenly appear overrun with ads" (Zeng, Huang, & Dou 2009, p. 1). While personal profiles are public in that they are broadly accessible, they are also private in presenting the personal identity (Schau & Gilly 2003, p. 390). Therefore, consumers may develop a negative attitude toward social media advertising and abandon SNS because of what they perceive as excessive advertising (Taylor, Lewin, & Strutton 2011). Whether SNS users accept the amount of advertising on the network or perceive it as an intrusion into their private sphere depends on a number of factors, one of which is the social identity of the community members: The stronger their social identity, the more likely they seem to be to develop group intentions to accept advertising in online communities (Zeng, Huang, & Dou 2009, p. 9). However, despite increasing scepticism in the face of the ongoing commercialisation of social networks, to date, users have not started to abandon networks such as Facebook because of data protection issues or excessive advertising.

Another issue marketers need to consider is that users explicitly take into account that what they disclose about themselves is openly visible to other users, and present themselves according to the specific audiences they want to address, such as friends, family, or even potential employers (Schau & Gilly 2003, p. 390). Hence, the users targeted are people consciously communicating their personality, if not even actively marketing themselves (Casteleyn, Mottart, & Rutten 2009, p. 440).

2.4.1.5 Microblogging

Microblogging tools, usually associated with Twitter, are a mixture of a blogging platform and a social networking site. Since Twitter is in fact the only noteworthy example of the category, this section focuses on Twitter only. Despite the fact that Twitter, compared to other social media tools, plays an only marginal role in Germany, findings are relevant because in the US, Twitter is widely used for marketing and branding purposes (see below). Also,

---

[21] Social-media brand impressions are defined as a unit of branded content (Lipsman et al. 2012, p. 41).

Twitter usage in Germany has been increasing over the last years, from 3 percent of German online users in 2010 to 7 percent in 2013 (ARD/ZDF-Onlinestudie 2013b). Also, possibly due to the fact that data on Twitter is easily available, a lot of social media studies focus on Twitter. Since it can be assumed that findings can at least partly be transferred to social media in general, investigating Twitter seems worthwhile.

Twitter was launched as a private beta version in March 2006, as a public beta version in August 2006 (Milstein et al. 2008, p. 3), and incorporated in April 2007 (Twitter 2014). The service enables users to create and read posts called "tweets". Tweets are displayed on their author's main Twitter home page and contain up to 140 characters. This makes a standard microblog post the approximate length of a newspaper headline and subhead (Milstein et al. 2008, p. 10), which results in a message that is "asynchronous", "noninvasive" as well as "easy to both produce and consume" (Jansen, Zhang, Sobel, & Chowdhury 2009, p. 2170). The linguistic study conducted by Jansen et al. for tweets containing brand related content found that tweets share more characteristics of natural language sentences than of shorter forms of expression like web search queries (2009, p. 2180).

A user's tweets can be subscribed to by other users, which is called "following". When users follow another account, Twitter pushes tweets posted by that account onto the user's main home page. Hashtags, which are words or phrases prefixed with "#", enable grouping posts together by topic or type. To mention, address, or reply to a specific user, his username can be prefixed by "@".

Users can access Twitter via the website or by external application clients, both for computers and mobile devices. This makes it difficult to assess the actual number of users or of tweets sent. According to Twitter (2014), there are 241 million monthly active users, 76 percent of active users use the mobile version, and 500 million tweets are sent per day.

McFedries (2007) suggests that one goal for users of microblogging services is enhancing one's online presence. In fact, users' motives on Twitter can be roughly categorized into information sharing, information seeking, and friendship-wise relationships, the main intentions being daily chatter conversations, sharing information or URLs and reporting news (Java, Song, Finin, & Tseng 2007).

While Twitter was initially predominantly used for private purposes, it became more professional at a later stage of its development (Milstein et al. 2008). When incorporating links and retweets, Twitter becomes increasingly similar to an RSS feed or a news content aggregator, which makes it attractive for uses other than purely personal status updates. Twitter paid justice to this development in 2009: In the early years, Twitter used to prompt user comments with the question "What are you doing?", which users mostly answered with personal status updates. On 19 November 2009, to react to the fact that people, organisations, and businesses had started to ignore the original question, but were posting all kinds of content, Twitter changed the prompt to "What's happening?" (Twitter 2009).

This change in user behaviour differentiates Twitter from social networking sites. While Facebook has for many users remained a largely personal and private sphere, Twitter users connect with people they have never met in person and share observations on their surroundings, information, or opinions regarding certain topics (Kwon & Sung 2011, p. 4; Milstein et al. 2008). The more loosely connected way in which Twitter works is due to the fact that any user can follow any other user's tweets without permission – the default of all Twitter messages is public, which means that they can not only be read, but also commented on by everybody. Also, since Twitter users usually do not provide a detailed personal profile, the network remains more anonymous.

Not only do users extend their social networks to people they will never actually meet, but also do they willingly connect with brand managers and marketers. For companies, the interconnectedness of Twitter users "provides a distinctive channel for marketing communication" (Carter 2009a; Kwon & Sung 2011, p. 6). The interactive features of Twitter, which allow for conversations and exchange within a loosely connected network of likeminded consumers, also makes Twitter a touchpoint between marketers and consumers that a traditional corporate website cannot provide. This enables managers to use Twitter from pre-purchase activities such as marketing research, to purchase related communications such as brand-reinforcing messages or sales promotions, and to post-purchase contacts, such as customer services (Kaplan & Haenlein 2011, pp. 108ff.).

Microblogging is a new form of eWOM[22] (Jansen et al. 2009, p. 2170) and thereby provides a viable alternative for companies to explore as part of their overall branding strategy (ibid., p.

---

[22] See section 2.3.5 for an in-depth description of electronic word-of-mouth (eWOM).

2186). In fact, over a third of all Twitter users are 35 years and older, with an above- average annual household income (Kaplan & Haenlein 2011, p. 106). Obviously, this target group is highly interesting for marketers, which adds another reason to why companies use Twitter for part of their marketing and branding strategies. In their study on the use of Twitter for eWOM as a means for brand communication, Jansen et al. (2009, p. 2184) found out that of all tweets analysed, almost 20% mentioned a corporate or product brand. Of those, about 20 percent expressed a sentiment or an opinion concerning that brand, 80 percent did mention a brand but did not express any emotions towards it. This suggests that Twitter is also used to seek information, as well as to ask and answer questions about brands.

A study conducted by Kwon and Sung (2011, p. 5; cf. 2.1.2.1) suggests that Twitter also enhances brand personality perceptions due to the fact that it allows for brand anthropomorphism, which refers to the association of the brand with human characteristics. This means that due to company-customer interactions with a human voice, long-term and personal relationships may be encouraged and consumers' attachment to the brand strengthened. The study found out that of all brands analysed, about half had human representatives, meaning that global brands make use of Twitter to initiate and maintain relationships with consumers and to post emotionally loaded content. In contrast, although brand names were regularly mentioned in tweets and tweets often contained embedded links, product or company related information was posted less frequently (Kwon & Sung 2011, p. 13). If provided at all, informational cues were more common in original tweets, while more anthropomorphism variables occurred in replies and in retweets, which suggests that if consumers engage in conversation, brand managers make an effort to give the brand a human voice.

To date, there has not been much research on how television networks and channels make use of Twitter for their brand communication (cf. 2.5). In practice, however, large television companies have already recognized the potential of Twitter in their brand relationship activities (Carter 2009b).

2.4.2   Gratifications obtained from using social media

Having reviewed relevant social media tools, this section provides an overview of usage motivations against the theoretical backdrop of Uses & Gratifications (U&G) research.

According to Katz, Blumler, and Gurevitch (1974, p. 20), U&G research is concerned with "(1) the social and psychological origins of (2) needs, which generate (3) expectations of (4) the mass media or other sources which lead to (5) differential patterns of media exposure (or engagement in other activities), resulting in (6) need gratifications and (7) other consequences, perhaps mostly unintended ones". As an expansion of the concept of gratifications, Palmgreen, Wenner, and Rayburn (1981) elaborate on the evidence that suggests gratifications sought and gratifications obtained need to be treated separately. They argue that gratifications sought can be viewed as "the seeking of a valued outcome mediated by the expectancy of obtaining that outcome, while a gratification obtained may be viewed as the perceived outcome of engaging in a particular behavior" (p. 473). Table 2-6 displays social media gratifications for different types of social media investigated by other studies. Interestingly, complemented by social interaction functions particular to social media, these gratifications resemble gratifications that prior studies have identified as being obtained from television. For television and video content, a plethora of studies that deal with gratifications users obtain exist to date, many of them naming entertainment and information seeking as core gratifications (e.g. Cha & Chan-Olmsted 2012; Haridakis 2002; Haridakis & Hanson 2009; Kim & Rubin 1997; Logan 2011; Palmgreen & Lawrence 1991; Papacharissi & Mendelson 2007).

Gratifications	Type of social media	Source
shared archive catalogue of canon site of original creativity for fans	Collective/collaborative projects (study on *Lostpedia*, a wiki platform dedicated to the television serial *Lost*)	Mittell (2009)
→ information organisation, content creation		
information entertainment (identified by factor analysis: convenient entertainment, interpersonal connection, convenient information seeking, escape, co-viewing, social interaction)	content communities (U&G study on users' motives to watch videos on YouTube and to share them on other SNS)	Haridakis & Hanson (2009)
→ entertainment and information seeking, interpersonal connection		
motivations for interaction: users' desire for self-expression, documenting of their own lives, and commenting; motivations for content gathering: commenting, forum participation, and information seeking	blogging	Huang, Shen, Lin, & Chang (2007)
motivations: documenting one's own life, providing commentary and opinions, expressing emotions, articulating ideas through writing, forming and maintaining community forums	blogging	Nardi, Schiano, Gumbrecht, & Swartz (2004)
→ social interaction function		
interacting with friends (young users) checking up on children (older users)	SNS (Facebook)	Brandtzæg, Lüders, & Skjetne (2010)
belonging networking/keeping in touch information management (being up to date)	SNS	Busemann, Fisch, & Frees (2012)
pastime connection sexual attraction utilities and upkeep establish/maintain old ties accumulation social comparison channel use networking	SNS (exploratory factor analysis of gratifications obtained from Facebook)	Foregger (2008)

socializing entertainment self-status seeking information	SNS (factor analysis of needs for participating in Facebook groups)	Park, Kee, & Valenzuela (2009)
pastime affection fashion share problems sociability social information	SNS (factor analysis of gratifications obtained from Facebook)	Quan-Haase & Young (2010)
making new friends locating old friends	SNS (Facebook)	Raacke & Bonds-Raacke (2008)
→ **mainly social interaction function, also entertainment and information seeking**		
motives: information sharing, information seeking, and friendship-wise relationships main intentions: daily chatter and conversations, sharing information or URLs, and reporting news	microblogging (Twitter)	Java, Song, Finin, & Tseng (2007)
enhance one's online presence	microblogging	McFedries (2007)
→ **socializing & information seeking**		

Table 2-6: Overview of social media gratifications

Source: Own design

For German viewers, Dehm and Storll (2003) identify five central experience factors that form the basis of viewers' expectations of a positive viewing experience. These are emotionality, orientation, balance, pastime, as well as social experience.[23] In a later study, Dehm, Storll, and Beeske (2006) confirmed these experience factors for internet usage, arguing that having become a common and mainstream media option, expectations toward the television experience can be transferred to internet usage experiences. Other studies have also found no significant differences in motives for media use between users of television and online streaming video (Haridakis & Hanson 2009; Logan 2011), suggesting that gratifications users obtain from television and social media are in fact very similar.

2.4.3   Categorizing social media

To conclude the section on social media, a categorization scheme will be provided in order to classify social media with regard to their brand management related relevance. Having reviewed social media tools above, it is obvious that the categorization scheme for social

---

[23] Original terminology is German (Emotionalität, Orientierung, Ausgleich, Zeitvertreib, Soziales Erleben).

media as put forward by Kaplan and Haenlein (2010) is not fully suitable for the tools existing today and that a new scheme is needed. This is due to a number of reasons.

Firstly, microblogging tools like Twitter do not fit into the schedule. Although they carry the term "blog" in their name, these applications are a mixture of blogs and social networking sites and need their own category. The existing scheme does not allow for this. Secondly, the assumption that blogs score low on the media richness dimension seems outdated. Most of today's blogs make use of pictures, videos and sound, either to add to the text or even as the main form of expression. Some blogging platforms, e.g. Tumblr, blur the boundaries of blogs, content communities, and social networking sites. Thirdly, and crucially for this study, the categorization by Kaplan and Haenlein does not include any reference to the potential application of any of the social media tools with regard to branding purposes.

Arnhold (2010, pp. 65ff.) provides an overview of phenomena related to social media and ranks them according to the brand focus they provide (Figure 2-5). In her framework, users who innovate, collaborate, or spread the word can, at a more brand-centred stage, become users who join networks, who create content and eventually generate brand related content.

Her framework seems more suitable to incorporate a wider range of social media tools and the usage situations that apply. It also puts the phenomena that take place in a social media environment into perspective and includes the brand as a reference point. However, it lacks a clear differentiation between the levels on which those phenomena operate, i.e. it falls short of clearly distinguishing between input factors and their corresponding outcomes: According to the definition provided above, web 2.0 can be described as the ideological and technological precondition for social media to exist and be made use of, while user generated content is the result of people's interaction with social media. While user innovation, eWOM or community building are communication processes developing as a result of the opportunities social media tools provide users with, UGC and UGB are results of the interaction via those opportunities of communication and should therefore not be placed on the same scale.

Brand focus					
low → high					
User innovation	**Collective intelligence**	**Word-of-mouth**	**Communities**	**User Generated Content (UGC)**	**User Generated Branding (UGB)**
Prosumers Lead users Open Source	Wisdom of crowds	WOM eWOM	Brand related online communities		
users as creators and innovators	users as collaborators	users disperse information	user networks	users generating content	users generating brand related content

Figure 2-5: Social media applications for branding purposes

Source: Own design, adapted from Arnhold (2010, p. 65)

As a consequence of the fact that both categorization schemes seem helpful but not entirely fitting for the purposes of this research, an extended combination of both seems appropriate. Figure 2-6 attempts to merge all aspects required to analyse social media against the backdrop of branding purposes. It includes the social presence/media richness and self-presentation/self-disclosure dimensions as suggested by Kaplan and Haenlein (2010), and expands the categorization by an assessment of social media tools' potential for brand related application and forms in which this may occur. It adds the relevant concepts in brand related communication introduced in section 2.3, thereby arriving at a comprehensive categorization.

Being tools based on the foundations of web 2.0, all of the social media tools enable user generated content production (cf. 2.3.4).

In this design, collaborative projects score low on both the social presence/media richness and the self-presentation/self-disclosure dimensions. As noted in section 2.4.1.2, their potential for brand related application is low. With regard to usage in branding context, they are restricted to a user innovation context (cf. 2.3.3).

	Collective/ collaborative projects	Microblogging	Blogs	Content communities	Social Networking Sites
Examples	Wikipedia	Twitter	Blogs	YouTube Flickr	Facebook LinkedIn MySpace
Social presence/ Media richness	low	either / or			high
Self-presentation/ Self-disclosure	low	either / or			high
Potential for brand related application	low	medium			high
Usage in branding context	UGC user innovation	UGC user innovation	UGC user innovation	UGC user innovation	UGC user innovation
		brand communication	brand communication	brand communication	brand communication
			brand community	brand community	brand community
		eWOM			eWOM

Figure 2-6: Categorization of social media applications for branding purposes

Source: Own design

Microblogging, namely Twitter, provides possibilities to score either high or low on both the social presence/media richness and the self-presentation/self-disclosure dimensions, depending on the media options embedded and the kind of information dispersed. Twitter has a medium potential for brand related application. On the one hand, it might to a limited extent also be used for user innovation in the form of market research and for eWOM purposes (cf. 2.3.5). It can be used for brand communication (cf. 2.3.1), but hardly for brand community building (cf. 2.3.2).

Blogging and content communities also provide possibilities to score either high or low on both the social presence/media richness and the self-presentation/self-disclosure dimensions, depending on the media options embedded and the kind of information dispersed. Blogs and content communities have a medium potential for brand related application. On the one hand, they can be used for user innovation, brand communication and also brand community building (cf. 2.3.3, 2.3.1, 2.3.2). On the other hand, it is difficult to initiate eWOM processes (cf. 2.3.5). While users can display opinions and review products, these tools are not as well-suited as Twitter to spread these opinions.

SNS score high on both the social presence/ media richness and the self-presentation/ self-disclosure dimensions. As noted in section 2.4.1.4, their potential for brand related application is high. They are useful tools for all forms of concepts in brand related social media communication, i.e. UGC, user innovation, brand communication, brand community, and eWOM. This is one of the reasons why for this study, a focus on SNS seemed particularly suitable. As will be elaborated on in chapter 4, the empirical analysis presented in this study particularly focuses on Facebook.

Having discussed brand related communication, the use of social media, and having combined them in a new, comprehensive framework, the following section attempts to bring brand, social media and television together before chapter 3 unites these topics in a model framework.

2.5   Using social media for brand related communication in a television context

Previous sections have defined the thematic scope of this study. Section 2.2 has dealt with media brands in general and television brands in particular. The dynamics of seriality have been discussed and it has been outlined why and how seriality and loyalty are two concepts that closely relate to each other. Section 2.3 has introduced relevant concepts in brand related communication that touch on or are inherent to social media brand communication. Section 2.4 has introduced social media tools and provided a literature review on social media research. It has concluded with a categorization scheme classifying social media with regard to their brand management related relevance, thereby attempting to combine all relevant aspects of sections 2.3 and 2.4 (cf. 2.4.3).

This section attempts to bring brand, social media and serialised television content together. Chan-Olmsted (2011) emphasizes the importance of media branding in a web 2.0 environment with particular focus on television brands and discusses both challenges and opportunities. However, to the knowledge of the author, to date, no comprehensive empirical study investigating the overlap of media brand research, social media research and serialised television brands exists.

The following sections – 2.5.1, 2.5.2, 2.5.3, and 2.5.4 – will therefore approach this niche of using social media for brand related communication in a television context from a rather practical vantage point.

It will be shown how social media are already used by television companies for branding purposes. A plethora of examples exist of how social media tools have been employed in the context of television, most of which focus on Facebook, Twitter, and YouTube as the most widely used. Before engaging in them, it is crucial to strategically identify ways in which social media campaigns can serve branding purposes, because brand campaigns such as groups and interactive experiences on social networking sites "should be a means to an end rather than an end in itself" (Christodoulides et al. 2011, p. 105).

In this study, all communicative messages dispersed via channel-owned social media tools aiming at viewer retention and acquisition have been defined as the social media programme for the serialised TV brand. The following sections will therefore not focus on pure UGC, but will, if applicable, include examples where social media are employed not directly by the television company, but by relevant brand ambassadors such as actors.

To support branding of serialised television content, social media can be used in four different ways: As a channel for advertising on-air programmes, to strengthen the consumer-brand relationship, as a way of viewer interaction during the programme, or as a medium to harness the creative power of audiences. Each of these strategic targets will shortly be outlined below.

This section will conclude with a specification of the research gap in 2.5.5, resulting from the divergence of how social media are already used for branding purposes as shown in sections 2.5.1, 2.5.2, 2.5.3, and 2.5.4, and the apparent lack of research in that field.

2.5.1   Advertising on-air programmes to create brand awareness

Advertising of on-air programmes aims at creating awareness for a television brand. In order to create loyalty in a final step, viewers need to be made aware that a serialised programme brand exists and subsequently be reminded to watch it again or to pick it up once more after it has been interrupted by the end of a season.

There are plenty of examples for the advertising of on-air programmes. For instance, German networks ProSieben, RTL and Sat.1 all have a Twitter channel via which they regularly promote the programme for the evening. Another example is the Facebook page of ZDF, http://www.facebook.com/ZDF. There, the broadcaster informs users where to find content that they missed when it was aired via links to its "Mediathek", or it gives programme updates and promotes shows, films, serials or any other content that is about to be broadcast.

A study conducted by Lin and Peña (2011) found that currently, television companies employ Twitter predominantly to publicize their on-air programmes and to "optimize relationships with their consumers by using distinct relational messages" (2011, p. 24). Their content analysis of 1,350 individual tweets posted by nine networks' official programme accounts in three genres (e.g. @TrueBloodHBO, for the drama series *True Blood* which was at the time aired on HBO) came to the following conclusions: Firstly, television companies post more task-oriented than socio-emotional tweets. They use Twitter to promote their programmes, escalate viewership, and increase popularity among viewers. The second, and hardly surprising finding is that television companies post more positive than negative socio-emotional tweets. As a result, it can be noted that television brands strategically make use of

Twitter to "inform their viewers, direct their attention to upcoming shows and events, and generate buzz about specific televised events" (Lin & Peña 2011, p. 26). Thus television companies seem to develop a strategic and tactical approach towards Twitter with regard to their brands, akin to consumer goods brands.

2.5.2 Strengthening the consumer-brand relationship

Once viewers were aware of the serialised television brand and have started watching it, another important task of social media campaigns is to strengthen the consumer-brand relationship.

The study by Lin and Peña (2011) also found that in the sample of tweets used, socio-emotional messages got retweeted more often than task-oriented communication. If retweeting is accepted as an indicator for popularity and influence, this suggests that socio-emotional messages are considered more important by followers.

To achieve an emotional response, it is often tried to engage audiences. One example is the American premium cable television company HBO and its communication strategy around the critically acclaimed television serial *True Blood* as well as the medieval fantasy serial *Game of Thrones*. For *True Blood*, HBO operated a Twitter account named @TrueBloodHBO, which was used to promote upcoming seasons of the serial, to announce DVD releases, but also to retweet, reply to and comment on users' tweets concerning the serial. HBO also posts favourite quotes as well as information concerning the cast and the shooting of new material. On Facebook, they operated an official *True Blood* Facebook page[24] which they used to post promotional pictures, to ask users questions and create polls, and to spread information about the serial. On YouTube, they operated a channel dedicated solely to *True Blood* related material such as promotional trailers, previews and short videos of selected *True Blood* scenes, all presented in an official, HBO and *True Blood* branded environment.[25] The official website[26] offered screen savers and wallpapers for download, merchandise for purchase and special scenes not aired during the programme. Also, HBO created websites with community pages for the "American Vampire League" as well as the "Fellowship of the Sun", two fictitious rivalling organisations playing a major part in the

---

[24] http://www.facebook.com/TrueBlood
[25] http://www.youtube.com/trueblood
[26] http://www.hbo.com/true-blood

story, for the season in which they occurred.[27] For *Game of Thrones*, HBO offered similar content, including an official website,[28] a Facebook page, a Google+ page, a YouTube channel,[29] a Twitter as well as a Tumblr account.[30] During the months of the year when no new episodes were aired (*True Blood* seasons consisted of ten to twelve episodes aired between June and August; *Game of Thrones* seasons consisted of ten episodes aired between March/April and June), HBO is able to keep in touch with its audience and thus succeeded in nurturing the consumer-brand relationship.

Another example for the use of social media to improve the consumer-brand relationship is the American drama television serial *The Vampire Diaries*, which was broadcast on The CW Television Network. A typical network serial, *The Vampire Diaries* seasons consisted of 22 to 23 episodes, broadcast between September/October and May. For new episodes, producers and cast created buzz, mainly on Twitter, which led to very active interaction with the audience, both related to the serial and to general conversations about the shooting, the actors and other topics. Instead of working against users who infringed copyright, executive producer Julie Plec frequently shared links to videos on YouTube that included footage used by fans to create their own versions of scenes and storylines. Other examples include general interaction between the cast and the fans. On 9 November 2011, 4:37 p.m. MET, actor Paul Wesley tweeted "Hi everybody".[31] At 5:25 p.m., he tweeted "Wait did me just saying hi incite a trending topic?" in response to the many reactions following his tweet. [32] At 5:54 p.m., Wesley tweeted "Still trending!!?? (is this a glitch?)", due to the fact that "Hi Paul" was still a worldwide trending topic on Twitter.[33] The fact that those phrases trended worldwide indicates that the community of fans of the serial is not restricted to American viewers. Many viewers from other countries partake in the conversation; the German community tends to both engage in conversations with the American cast and crew, as well as in discussions referring to the German adaptation.

When ProSieben announced on 25 August 2011 via Twitter that, due to disappointing ratings for the first episodes of the second season, *The Vampire Diaries* would be transferred to

---

[27] www.americanvampireleague.com; www.fellowshipofthesun.org; now redirect to www.hbo.com/ true-blood

[28] www.hbo.com/game-of-thrones

[29] Facebook: www.facebook.com/GameOfThrones; Google+: http://plus.google.com/+gameofthrones; YouTube: www.youtube.com/GameofThrones

[30] Twitter: @GameOfThrones; Tumblr: http://gameofthrones.tumblr.com

[31] https://twitter.com/paulwesley/status/134293440119836672

[32] https://twitter.com/paulwesley/status/134306574117249024

[33] https://twitter.com/paulwesley/status/134312869285208066

Sixx,[34] incomprehension and harsh complaints by viewers followed.[35] Possibly due to the complaints, when the serial's third season started in March 2012, it was aired both on Sixx and ProSieben.[36]

Social media strategies for television brands can hence be used for interactive brand communication (cf. 2.3.1) and serve many of the purposes brand communities (cf. 2.3.2) do. Social media make the brand as well as cast, crew, and also fictitious characters approachable and support relationship building.

2.5.3 Viewer interaction

According to Tony Wang, former General Manager of Twitter UK, 80 percent of viewers already use a second screen like a laptop, a smartphone or a tablet while watching TV, and 72 percent of them communicate on social media channels about the programme currently running, frequently encouraging other users to switch on a programme they would not have been interested in otherwise (Majica, Mielke, & Wirth 2012). Another study comes to the conclusion that slightly more than half of German television viewers make use of a second screen (36th WWW-Benutzer-Analyse W3B[37] as cited by Schwegler 2013). Second screen usage decreases channel hopping (Paperlein 2013), but it remains unclear how attentive viewers actually are when using it. Schwegler (2013) states that in their study, only about 10 percent were using the second screen for something related to the programme they were watching, the rest was using other features like browsing, e-mail, or games on their device. Research needs to examine consumers' motivations for second screen usage contrast findings to media companies' assertions as to how and how much viewers use a second screen.[38]

However, to provoke viewer interaction during the programme, television companies want viewers to be engaged by the second screen, not distracted by it. The reality talent show *The Voice of Germany* provides an example of how this can be achieved. The television channels ProSieben and Sat.1 aired the first season of *The Voice of Germany* from November 2011 to

---

[34] https://twitter.com/ProSieben/status/106727786206605312
[35] For instance https://twitter.com/ProSieben/status/107375817063018496
[36] https://www.facebook.com/ProSieben/posts/140007396115946; http://www.vampirediaries-news.de/index.php /vampire-diaries-staffel-3-ab-15-marz-auf-sixx-und-ab-19-marz-auf-prosieben-in-deutschland/
[37] 69,282 respondents representative for German internet users
[38] An unpublished MA thesis found social interaction, exerting influence and information as key usage motives (Wirdemann, J. (2014). *Erfolgsdeterminanten von Second-Screen-Angeboten auf mobilen Endgeräten* [Success factors of second screen offerings on mobile devices] (Unpublished MA thesis). Johannes Gutenberg-Universität, Mainz.

February 2012. There was an integrated online campaign surrounding the show: It had its own website with information and promotional material as well as social media plug-ins that led to the Facebook page of the show and the individual Facebook profiles of all contestants. Only two weeks into the season, 180,000 users liked *The Voice of Germany* on Facebook, with 56,600 talking about it, and some of the candidates had more than 1,000 fans (Weber 2011). To accompany the online content, viewers could download an app for iOS as well as for Android to use mobile versions of the website and access additional content.[39] Users of the apps could communicate with friends who were also watching the show, play games and take part in the votes, which made the experience a very social one. The music presented during the shows was downloadable from iTunes while the show was still running, and later into the season, music sales counted towards the contestants' scores for the finals. [40] The channels operated an official Twitter account called @TheVoiceGermany and had at an early stage established the hashtag "#voice" (later changed to "#TVOG"), which accompanied all messages posted about the show. During airtime, viewers were asked questions or encouraged to discuss on Twitter, using the hashtag. The answers to those questions, or also general comments posted by viewers – who their favourite candidates were, which songs they preferred, how much they liked the show – were then superimposed on the screen and seen on TV. The presenters frequently referred to the messages or included viewers' questions while interviewing the candidates, giving them the impression of being an active part of the show, not a passive audience.

Similar activities of interaction have also been used by ARD and ZDF. The *Tatort* episode *Der Wald steht schwarz und schweiget*, aired on 13 May 2012 on Das Erste, did not present the viewers with a complete solution, but they had to find the murderer themselves online.[41] With *Wer rettet Dina Foxx?*, ZDF pursued a similar approach, showing a film where a character was innocently arrested and the viewers had to find the real murderer online.[42]

Campaigns like these blur the boundaries between on-air and off-air communication, because they can start with either and merge into the other at any time. Social media actually enable viewers to participate and engage with their brands, thereby improving the consumer-brand relationship as well.

---

[39] http://www.the-voice-of-germany.de/apps
[40] http://www.the-voice-of-germany.de/musik-downloads
[41] http://www.daserste.de/unterhaltung/krimi/tatort/specials/tatort-plus-100.html
[42] http://www.zdf.de/das-kleine-fernsehspiel/wer-rettet-dina-foxx-13099690.html

2.5.4   Harnessing the creative power of audiences

The fourth way to use social media for television is to harness the creative power of audiences by engaging in collaboration between the audience and the producers. It can be described as a method of user innovation (cf. 2.3.3) and includes the viewer at a much earlier stage of the brand management process than the other strategies.

However, according to Carter (2009b), this method is only rarely used because copyright issues might result and because producers prefer having control over their content. In the case of serialised content, audiences are included indirectly in the development of the series/serial if the story arcs and the characters are adapted to the audience's preferences or if plot developments embrace feedback from the audience (cf. 2.2.3; 2.3.5).

Since this strategy is negligible in a television branding context, it will not be further elaborated on at this point.

2.5.5   Specification of the research gap

As a result, it can be stated that social media strategies are already widely used in a television context for a number of reasons, including branding objectives. However, many strategies still have a rather experimental status: Although it seems to be common knowledge that social media strategies "do some good", it remains largely unknown which particular positive outcomes can be expected and achieved.

Partly, this is due to the fact that the usage of supporting social media tools has not been sufficiently researched, as illustrated by the fact that knowledge about how much and in what manner television viewers make use of a second screen is still relatively scarce and differs greatly with regard to the source claiming the numbers.

Also, as shown above, when taking a closer look at effects on the brand, it is not always possible to clearly separate the levels on which brands operate in the television context (for the notion of ingredient branding in a television context, cf. e.g. Lis & Post 2013). Social media strategies might positively affect the programme brand, the channel brand, or other brands involved such as that of the producers, directors, or actors. It therefore seems necessary to develop a comprehensive explanatory model that incorporates branding related constructs, social media related constructs, as well as television related constructs. The model should aim at addressing a universal success factor.

As stated above, to the knowledge of the author, no empirical study examining the phenomenon of managing serialised television brands with social media strategies exists to date. A number of studies on social media in a branding context exist to date (e.g. Arnhold 2010; Boyle 2007; Christodoulides et al. 2012; Laroche et al. 2012; Muniz & Schau 2007), but studies on media branding in a social media environment (e.g. Chan-Olmsted 2011; Lis & Berz 2011) are still scarce.

To add to the current state of research on media branding and social media is one aim of this study. It will take a first step towards closing that research gap by identifying how social media branding strategies affect brand loyalty, and how relevant that influence is in comparison to other potential influencing factors. As noted before, brand loyalty for the television brand is chosen as the success factor because price and willingness to purchase are not viable outcome variables in a model designed for free commercial television. This allows for the focusing on usage and choice related factors, such as continued viewing of a programme.

The key research questions were defined as:

1. Which drivers – social media related, TV related, and/or related to the social environment – are most important for a consumer's relationship with the serialised television brand?
2. How do social media influence the image of the serialised television brand?
3. Which conditions drive social media usage as well as attitude toward the social media programme for the serialised television brand?
4. Which aspects of the social media programme for the serialised television brand are particularly important for users?

To answer the research questions, chapter 3 deals with the development of the conceptual model. The conceptualisation of the constructs as well as the derivation of hypotheses are presented by construct. Section 3.2 presents the final model and an overview of hypotheses.

Chapter 4 will then provide a specification of the model, and in chapter 5, results will be presented.

3 Model development (conceptualisation)

Chapter 2 provided the theoretical background for the development of the conceptual model. In this chapter, firstly, the constructs relevant for the model are conceptualised, and secondly, hypotheses regarding the relationships between those constructs are derived from theoretical considerations.

Within the developed model framework, the identity-based brand management approach as put forward by Meffert and Burmann (2005) serves as a paradigmatic framework for branding related theory development. In the tradition of Fishbeins and Ajzens theory of reasoned action (1975), behavioural intention, which is part of the brand loyalty construct, is conceptualised as a consequence of attitude toward the social media programme (section 3.1.3). A positive impact of attitude toward the social media programme on the consumer-brand relationship (cf. 3.1.2), as well as on brand loyalty (cf. 3.1.1), has already been accounted for by Arnhold (2010) for consumer goods. This approach, which follows brand relationship research in the tradition of Fournier (1994, 1998), is extended by approaches specific to media research, i.e. Uses & Gratifications research, agenda-setting as well as the influence effect with regard to critics' opinions and reviews (sections 3.1.5, 3.1.6, 3.1.7). The model is completed by incorporating hypotheses from neighbouring research fields like brand community research and WOM research (sections 3.1.4, 3.1.8).

The chapter deals with the constructs one at a time and one section each, the final section providing an overview of the causal relationships in a path diagram, as well as a table listing all hypotheses.

3.1 Conceptualisation and derivation of hypotheses by constructs

3.1.1 Brand loyalty

It has been noted (cf. 1.2.1, 2.5.5) that brand loyalty serves as the key outcome variable in this model because price and willingness to purchase are not viable outcome variables in a model designed for free commercial television; in contrast, the goal of branding objectives for free commercial television is not purchase, but consumer attention and retention.

Brand loyalty has been discussed in the marketing literature and its importance recognized for several decades (Aaker 1991, p. 39; Howard & Sheth 1969, pp. 232ff.). According to Jacoby and Chestnut (1978, p. 80), brand loyalty refers to a "biased (i.e. non-random) behavioral response (i.e. purchase) expressed over time by some decision-making unit with respect to one or more alternative brands out of a set of such brands".

This has two consequences. Firstly, brand loyal consumers may be willing to pay a price premium for a brand because they perceive unique value in the brand that competitors cannot provide (Chaudhuri & Holbrook 2001, p. 81; Pessemier 1959). For instance, less brand loyal customers might switch brands at a low increase in price, while more loyal customers tolerate such increases.

Secondly, brand loyalty can lead to greater market shares as opposed to the competition if, in line with the theory of double jeopardy (Dekimpe, Steenkamp, Mellens, & Abeele 1997, p. 414; Uncles, Ehrenberg, & Hammond 1995, p. G73), loyal consumers repeatedly purchase the same brand or if they buy more of the brand because they identify with its image (Baldinger, Blair, & Echambadi 2002, p. 13; Chaudhuri & Holbrook 2001, p. 81; Upshaw 1995, pp. 34ff.). Hence, Aaker (1991, p. 39) regards brand loyalty as "the core of a brand's equity" that bears several marketing advantages, such as reduced marketing costs, greater trade leverage (i.e. more shelf space), as well as the attraction of new customers (1991, pp. 46-48).

It is crucial to distinguish "true" loyalty from "spurious" loyalty (Day 1969, p. 30; Dick & Basu 1994, pp. 101ff.; Bloemer & Kasper 1995). While true loyalty signifies a favourable attitude towards the brand as well as high repeat purchase, spuriously loyal customers' repeat purchase rate is high, while their attitude towards the brand is low. This results in a behavioural pattern similar to inertia: As long as the customer feels sufficiently satisfied with the brand, there is no incentive to switch brands, but customers can be captured at any time by another brand if it offers a preferable deal. This might be the case for low-involvement categories where the customer perceives little differentiation between the brands. In this case, satisfaction only weakly translates into loyalty (Iyer & Muncy 2005, p. 226).

In addition, Dick and Basu (1994, p. 101) identify a form of loyalty which they call "latent loyalty". Latent loyalty signifies a high relative attitude compared to the competition, accompanied by low repeat purchase rates. This might be the result of a marketplace environment where "non-attitudinal influences such as subjective norms and situational effects are at least equally if not more influential than attitudes" in determining repeat purchase behaviour (Dick & Basu 1994, p. 102). For example, instead of watching their favourite television programmes alone and enforcing individual preferences, individuals often conform to group preferences of friends, family, or flatmates.

Day (1969, p. 30) stresses that as a consequence of these different kinds of loyalty, brand loyalty should be evaluated with both attitudinal and behavioural criteria. Dick and Basu (1994, p. 100) highlight that both a favourable attitude in comparison to competitors as well as repeat purchase are required for brand loyalty to exist.

In accordance with this view, Oliver (1999, p. 34) defines loyalty as a "deeply held commitment to rebuy or repatronize a preferred product/service consistently in the future, thereby causing repetitive same-brand or same brand-set purchasing, *despite* situational influences and marketing efforts having the potential to cause switching behavior" (italics in original). This definition emphasizes the two different aspects of brand loyalty – behavioural and attitudinal – that have also been identified in other works (Chaudhuri & Holbrook 2001; Day 1969; Jacoby & Chestnut 1978; Tucker 1964).

Within this concept, behavioural loyalty means repeat purchase of the brand, whereas attitudinal loyalty refers to "a degree of dispositional commitment in terms of some unique value associated with the brand" (Chaudhuri & Holbrook 2001, p. 82). This definition of attitudinal brand loyalty is in line with the theory of reasoned action (Ha 1998, p. 53), which states that an individual's behavioural intention depends on that individual's attitude about the behaviour and subjective norms (Fishbein & Ajzen 1975, pp. 301ff.). When acknowledging the importance of attitude for the definition of true loyalty, brand loyalty becomes increasingly similar to the conceptualisation of commitment in so far as it might be conceptualised as the commitment to a certain brand (Assael 1998; Morgan & Hunt 1994).

As an implication of the emerging research on brand relationship marketing (Fournier 1998; Moorman, Zaltman, & Deshpandé 1992; Morgan & Hunt 1994), Chaudhuri and Holbrook (2001) suggest that both behavioural and attitudinal loyalty are related to both brand trust and brand affect.

Interpersonal trust is defined as "an expectancy held by an individual or a group that the word, promise, verbal or written statement of another individual or group can be relied upon" (Rotter 1967, p. 651). Hence, trust requires two parties, at least one of which is the trusting party. With regard to brands, trust is defined as "the willingness of the average consumer to rely on the ability of the brand to perform its stated function" (Chaudhuri & Holbrook 2001, p. 82). Brand trust can be assumed to lead to brand loyalty because by fostering exchange relationships, it leads to the building of a foundation for mutual commitment of the parties involved (Berry & Parasuraman 1991, p. 139; Chaudhuri & Holbrook 2001, p. 83).

Brand affect is defined as the potential of a brand to "elicit a positive emotional response in the average consumer as a result of its use" (Chaudhuri & Holbrook 2001, p. 82). Dick and Basu (1994, p. 104) suggest that affective components positively impact brand loyalty, and others argue that affective attachment is a part of commitment (Allen & Meyer 1990, p. 2; Gundlach, Achrol, & Mentzer 1995, p. 79).

In line with this, Fournier and Yao (1997, p. 453) criticize investigations of loyalty that focus primarily on cognitive psychology, "with theories of attitude formation guiding most of the work" (e.g. Dick & Basu 1994). They emphasize that approaches need to embrace the fact that brand loyalty is not a static, but a dynamic construct and that it does not suffice to restrict the dynamic aspect of the construct to the investigation of intergenerational patterns of brand preferences (Olsen 1993). In contrast, approaches should also draw upon the dynamic aspects of brand loyalty, and include theories of consumer behaviour as well as of cultural anthropology and consumer-brand interaction (McCracken 1993; Schouten & McAlexander 1995), or consumer socialization (Muniz & O'Guinn 2001).

Brand loyalty, as described, refers to a commitment to repurchase or reuse a preferred product despite situational influences, thereby emphasizing both behavioural and attitudinal loyalty (Chaudhuri & Holbrook, 2001; Day 1969; Jacoby & Chestnut 1978; Oliver 1999; Tucker 1964). Relational aspects of consumer-brand interaction are not specifically discussed in this context. To incorporate these in the model, the consumer-brand relationship is treated as a separate construct in addition to brand loyalty in this study, with its own implications and antecedents.

3.1.2   Consumer-brand relationship

Since the 1990s, there has been a shift in marketing research from a transaction focus to a relationship focus (Webster 1992, p. 14). Modern marketing science, as derived from other fields of social science theory (Deshpandé 1983, p. 102), viewed the customer and the firm as separate from each other, the customer being the recipient of the firm's internal value creation. However, in recent years, value creation is increasingly regarded as involving the customer (Schau, Muniz, & Arnould 2009, p. 30), both with regard to collaboration in developing competitive strategy and to the company's innovation process (von Hippel 2006). According to Blackston (1992, p. 80), in order to create long-lasting, strategic brand equity, a brand's relationships need to be managed rather than just the brand personality alone and the brand needs to be regarded as both the object of consumers' attitudes and as a subject with its "own" set of attitudes.

It has been argued in chapter 2.1 that the consumer-brand relationship links the two concepts of brand identity and brand image and therefore represents a crucial success factor in the framework of identity-based brand management (Burmann & Meffert 2005b, p. 75). Traditionally, brand loyalty has been an established framework for measuring and conceptualising long-term, committed consumer-brand relationships (Dick & Basu 1994; Oliver 1999; Thorbjørnsen et al. 2002, p. 20). However, Fournier (1994; 1998) argues that brand loyalty research frequently fails to address why and in which ways consumers engage in and value relationships with brands. She therefore introduced the concept of brand relationship quality (BRQ) as an alternative to brand loyalty when conceptualising and evaluating the relationship between consumers and the brands they use.

BRQ, which is a higher-order construct, is regarded as an underlying multi-faceted latent variable influencing performance of six interrelated relationship dimensions, each capturing some of the aspects determining the strength and richness of consumer-brand relationships (Fournier 1994, p. 127). Table 3-1 provides an outline of those facets.

BRQ dimension		Description
socioemotive attachment	love and passion	Intensity and depth of the emotional bond between the consumer and the brand. Characterised by attraction and affection toward the brand.
	self-connection	Degree to which the brand delivers on important identity concerns or themes, thereby referring to the consumer's self.
behavioural ties	interdependence	Degree and frequency of brand interactions, scope and diversity of brand-related activities, and intensity of individual interaction events.
	commitment	Intention to behave in a manner supportive of relationship longevity.
supportive cognitive beliefs	intimacy	Degree of closeness, mutual understanding, and openness between relationship partners.
	brand partner quality	Consumer's evaluation of the brand's performance in its partnership role.

Table 3-1: The six BRQ dimensions as conceptualised by Fournier (1994; 1998)

Source: Own design, based on Fournier (1998, p. 363); Thorbjørnsen et al. (2002, p. 21)

As results of BRQ, Fournier identifies nine pre-economic consumer response variables, seven of which are behavioural variables and two of which are cognitive structure variables (Fournier 1994, pp. 160ff.):

A. Behavioural variables

1. frequency of use as an indicator of relationship depth;

2. share of uses;

3. repeat purchase intention as an indicator for relationship durability and stability;

4. relationship duration;

5. resistance to competitive threat;

6. insulation from competitive activities;

7. supportive customer responses, including

    a. willingness to try brand extensions;

    b. willingness to testify on behalf of the brand in an advertising setting;

    c. willingness to pay a significant price premium for the brand;

    d. willingness to recommend the brand to a friend.

B. Cognitive structure variables

8. top-of-mind saliency;
9. consideration set size, with a smaller set reflecting higher cognitive insulation from the competition and vice versa.

Fournier's empirical results suggest that while BRQ levels only play a marginal role in affecting the cognitive structure variables, a high impact on supportive customer response outcomes was proven as well as a significant positive impact on indicators such as repeat purchase and share of use, which are both indicators for stability and loyalty, as well as on usage frequency (1994, pp. 171ff.).

The pre-economic consumer response variables to the consumer-brand relationship which Fournier (1994, pp. 160ff.) identifies correspond to the conceptualisation of brand loyalty as put forward by a majority of studies, especially repeat purchase behaviour and supportive customer responses. It can hence be argued that effective relationship management leads to enhanced customer loyalty (Evans & Laskin 1994, p. 440), i.e., it is possible to conceptualise brand loyalty as an outcome of the consumer-brand relationship (instead of as an alternative to it). This has been proven in many empirical studies; for instance, Arnhold (2010) and Stichnoth (2008) found evidence for the suggested direction of influence in their studies referring to user generated content and brand communities, respectively, which are two fields of research closely related to social media branding.

#	Hypothesis
1	The consumer-brand relationship positively influences brand loyalty.

3.1.3   Attitude toward the social media programme for the serialised TV brand

Brand loyalty and the consumer-brand relationship being outcome variables, input variables favourably affecting the desired outcomes have to be defined. Social media being the object of investigation in this study, social media related input factors need to be identified and set into context with brand loyalty and the consumer-brand relationship.

One social media related input factor is attitude toward the social media programme. The social media programme for the serialised TV brand has been defined as communicative messages dispersed via sponsored, i.e. channel-owned, social media tools aiming at viewer retention and acquisition. It is a part of interactive marketing and brand communication (cf. 2.3.1) and supports community building for the television brand (cf. 2.3.2) by allowing for the incorporation of UGC (cf. 2.3.4) and the fostering of eWOM processes (cf. 2.3.5).

While the concept of the social media programme has been easy to identify, the concept of attitude is more complicated to grasp. Being central to consumer behaviour research, attitude has been widely investigated, as has the question of "how consumers' evaluations of issues, candidates, and products are affected by media advertisements" (Petty, Cacioppo, & Schumann 1983, p. 135). Eagly and Chaiken define attitude as "a psychological tendency that is expressed by evaluating a particular entity with some degree of favor or disfavor" (1998, p. 269). This implies that attitude encompasses not only a notion of opinion, but also of evaluation of a person, situation, product, etc.

Assumptions about attitude formation have changed over the years. According to the traditional tripartite model, attitude is based on cognitive, affective, and conative components, i.e. beliefs, emotions, and behavioural intentions (Rosenberg & Hovland 1960). Attitude was hence regarded as "an unobservable construct which can manifest itself in relevant beliefs, feelings, and behavioral components" (Fazio & Olson 2003, p. 140). This view has since been frequently criticized, mainly because it implies that attitude always has to manifest in all three ways and that the three components – since they depend on the same underlying construct – must be consistent with each other (ibid.). Other theories therefore pursue more flexible approaches to attitude formation and change.

One example is the Elaboration Likelihood Model (ELM) developed by Petty and Cacioppo, which differentiates between two distinct routes to attitude change (1981; 1983). Via the central route to persuasion, changes in attitude result "from a person's diligent consideration of information" and lead to rather enduring changes in attitude that are "predictive of behavior" (Petty et al. 1983, p. 135). Changes in attitude occurring via the peripheral route to persuasion are based on a person's association of the object under consideration with positive or negative signals; the person "makes a simple inference about the merits of the advocated position based on various simple cues in the persuasion context" (Petty & Cacioppo 1984, p. 70). Consumers finding themselves in a high-involvement situation are more likely to be persuaded by advertising messages via the central route, while in low-involvement situations, the peripheral route might be more effective (Petty et al. 1983, p. 138).

Another shortcoming of the tripartite model is that it postulates an assumption of "attitude-behavior consistency" (Fazio & Olson 2003, p. 140); however, it is problematic to assume that "attitudes always guide behaviour" (ibid.). The theory of reasoned action (Fishbein & Ajzen 1975) resolves this by linking the attitude concept to behavioural intention instead of behaviour. According to the theory of reasoned action, an individual's behavioural intention depends on that individual's attitude about the behaviour and subjective norms (ibid., pp. 301ff.).

It has been stated above that in this study, behavioural intention is regarded as part of brand loyalty. With regard to Fishbein's and Ajzen's (1975) theory of reasoned action according to which behavioural intention, which is part of brand loyalty, is an outcome of attitude, a direct influence of attitude on brand loyalty can be assumed.

The assumption that attitude toward the social media programme for the serialised television brand positively affects loyalty toward the brand itself originates in findings from research on media brand extensions (Chang & Chan-Olmsted 2010; Chan-Olmsted & Cha 2008; Doyle 2006; Habann et al. 2008; cf. 2.2.1 and 2.2.2). The social media programme is in this context regarded as an extension of the serialised television brand.

Brand extensions have been defined as the "use of established brand names to launch new products" (Völckner & Sattler 2006, p. 18). Media brands can be extended across channels and formats, by modification and re-issuing, and by turning content into products and services (Ots 2008, p. 4).

A number of studies on brand extensions for television exist (Chang & Chan-Olmsted 2010; Chang et al. 2004), with a particular focus on online content as an extension of a television brand (Ha & Chan-Olmsted 2004; Nysveen et al. 2005). In section 2.2.2.3, it has been stated that increased usage of website features positively predicts viewer and subscriber loyalty toward the television brand (Ha & Chan-Olmsted 2004), and that additional online television content positively impacts brand knowledge, brand satisfaction, direct relationship investments, and indirect relationship investments (Nysveen et al. 2005).

Considering these positive implications of brand extensions with regard to loyalty and relational aspects, it seems legitimate to hypothesize that attitude toward the social media programme for the serialised television brand positively affects loyalty toward the brand itself.

#	Hypothesis
2	Attitude toward the social media programme for the serialised TV brand positively affects brand loyalty.

It has been stated above (cf. 2.1.2.3) that marketing actions can be considered as behaviours executed on the part of the brand as active contributions to the consumer-brand relationship (Fournier 1994, pp. 14ff.). While Fournier identifies traditional marketing tools such as television advertising, sponsorships and sales, but also service calls and customer complaint handling (1994, p. 21) as part of those brand behaviours, social media communication on behalf of the brand has been stated to seem even more suitable to be regarded as brand behaviour than traditional promotional and communicative strategies since it is more direct, more interactive and more personal (cf. 2.1.2.3).

Since social media programmes can be interpreted as brand behaviours, it is hypothesized that attitude toward the social media programme for the serialised TV brand positively affects the consumer-brand relationship. A comparable hypothesis could be confirmed in Arnhold's dissertation (2010) with regard to consumer goods.

#	Hypothesis
3	Attitude toward the social media programme for the serialised TV brand positively affects the consumer-brand relationship.

3.1.4   Engagement in the social media programme for the serialised TV brand

The discussions of interactive marketing, brand communities (cf. 2.3.2) and in particular user generated content (cf. 2.3.4) have emphasized the role of the consumer when marketing and branding employ social media strategies. Therefore, while it may be sufficient to only incorporate an attitude construct in models dealing with classic forms of advertising, this is not the case for a study where the impact of social media strategies is to be investigated. In order to do justice to the importance of the user within the causal model, engagement in the social media programme for the serialised TV brand is incorporated as well.

Engagement, or brand engagement, is a buzzword in contemporary marketing. It is used in various contexts and for a wide variety of situations. It is sometimes referred to as something very similar to the consumer-brand relationship, sometimes it simply stands for how-to lists that advise brands on how to "engage" with consumers. It is used in contexts dealing with touchpoints, or with regard to consumers picking up on brand related communicative messages. It can, however, also be defined with regard to technology, which is closer to the concept used in this study that refers to social media engagement, not brand engagement.

Besides the plethora of hands-on definitions, engagement has in recent years also received academic attention by researchers of various areas who come to different conclusions about how to define the concept, and which and how many dimensions are to be taken into account (e.g. Calder et al. 2009; Laurel 1993; O'Brien & Toms 2008; 2010; Pagani & Mirabello 2011). In a general sense, engagement can be described as "a desirable – even essential – human response to computer-mediated activities" (Laurel 1993, p. 112). Engagement, therefore, can be regarded as a user response to social media offerings, which are also computer-mediated activities. O'Brien and Toms define engagement as "a quality of user experiences with technology that is characterised by challenge, aesthetic and sensory appeal, feedback, novelty, interactivity, perceived control and time, awareness, motivation, interest, and affect" (O'Brien & Toms 2008, p. 949). This definition goes beyond the idea of engagement as a form of behavioural reaction und incorporates emotional factors, i.e.

awareness, interest, or affect. This study attempts a definition of engagement that alludes to both its close relation to usage intensity and to involvement.

Involvement has been thoroughly researched in the last decades. Zaichkowsky (1986) provides an overview of involvement with regard to advertising and points out that involvement is determined by "inherent person factors, different physical characteristics or situational factors". Zaichkowsky (1994) identifies both affective and cognitive relevance and subsequently defines involvement as "a person's perceived relevance of the advertisement based on inherent needs, values, and interests" (ibid, p. 61).

With regard to these definitions, engagement in the social media programme for the serialised TV brand is defined as the personal involvement with and usage intensity of the social media programme for the serialised TV brand, i.e. communicative messages dispersed via channel-owned social media tools aiming at viewer retention and acquisition.

A study conducted by Christodoulides et al. (2012) found that user generated content, which can be assumed to be an outcome of engagement with regard to social media, has a positive impact on consumer-based brand equity, part of which is brand loyalty. Active participation in virtual brand communities may lead to higher levels of individuals' loyalty toward the brand (Andersen 2005, p. 41; Casaló et al. 2008), and brand community integration increases brand loyalty (McAlexander, Kim, & Roberts 2003). Laroche et al. (2013) found particular evidence that "a brand community based on social media [...] cements the customers' relationships with the brand" (p. 81), resulting in brand loyalty.

That these results are transferrable to social media engagement seems to be a sound conclusion, because taking part in social media based brand communities requires a certain level of engagement with both the brand and the technology. In addition, based on the assumption that the social media programme for the serialised television brand can be regarded as a brand extension (cf. 3.1.3 for a sound deduction), it can be hypothesized that engagement with the social media programme for the serialised television brand affects loyalty toward the brand itself.

#	Hypothesis
4	Engagement in the social media programme for the serialised TV brand positively affects brand loyalty.

Fournier (1994, 1998) states that brand behaviours positively affect the consumer-brand relationship. Since social media programmes can be interpreted as brand behaviours, engagement with them is active dialogue with the brand. It can hence be assumed that engaging in the social media programme for the serialised TV brand positively affects the consumer-brand relationship.

#	Hypothesis
5	Engagement in the social media programme for the serialised TV brand positively affects the consumer-brand relationship.

With regard to the theory of reasoned action, behavioural intention results from attitude. It can therefore be theorised that attitude toward the social media programme influences the engagement in that programme, which is a consumer response and hence behaviour.

#	Hypothesis
6	Attitude toward the social media programme for the serialised TV brand positively affects engagement in the social media programme for the serialised TV brand.

3.1.5   Gratifications obtained from the social media programme

In addition to the hypothesized impact of users' attitude toward and engagement with the social media programme, it can be argued that gratifications they obtain from the social media programme are crucial as well.

The development of the construct gratifications obtained from the social media programme for the serialised TV brand is based on Uses & Gratifications (U&G) research. Gratifications obtained, in this study, are closely connected to the notion of functional congruity. According to Kressmann, Sirgy, Herrmann, Huber, Huber, and Lee (2006, p. 955), functional congruity "refers to the match between consumers' ideal expectations of utilitarian product features and their perceptions of how the brand is perceived along the same features". Gratifications obtained from the social media programme for the serialised TV brand are therefore defined as the meeting of defined experience factors by the social media programme for the serialised TV brand.

In section 2.4.2, gratifications obtained from social media usage have been outlined. It has been shown that expectations toward the television experience can be transferred to internet usage experiences (Dehm et al. 2006; Haridakis & Hanson 2009; Logan 2011), suggesting that gratifications users obtain from television and social media are in fact very similar. For television and video content, prior research has extensively identified entertainment and information seeking as core gratifications (e.g. Cha & Chan-Olmsted 2012; Haridakis 2002; Kim & Rubin 1997; Palmgreen & Lawrence 1991; Papacharissi & Mendelson 2007). For German viewers, Dehm and Storll (2003; Dehm, Storll, & Beeske 2005) identify emotionality, orientation, balance, pastime, as well as social experience[43] as central experience factors forming the basis of viewers' expectations of a positive viewing experience and later confirm these experience factors for internet usage (Dehm et al. 2006).

In addition to gratifications comparable to television consumption, a plethora of studies on gratifications obtained from social media consumption mention a social interaction function to be at least part of consumers' experience (e.g. Brandtzæg at al. 2010; Busemann et al. 2012; Foregger 2008; Huang et al. 2007; Java et al. 2007; Mittell 2009; Nardi et al. 2004; Park et al. 2009; Quan-Haase & Young 2010; Raacke & Bonds-Raacke 2008).

Therefore, for the social media gratifications construct, an index is designed and further elaborated on in section 4.4.5 that incorporates television experience factors as well as an extension with regard to social media. Index construction is based on

- gratifications such as entertainment and information as identified by research on television and video content gratifications (Haridakis 2002; Kim & Rubin 1997; Palmgreen & Lawrence 1991; Papacharissi & Mendelson 2007);
- TV experience factors emotionality, orientation, balance, pastime, and social experience particularly identified for a German viewership (Dehm & Storll 2003; Dehm, Storll, & Beeske 2005);
- interaction-focus added to account for social media specifics (e.g. Busemann et al. 2012; Foregger 2008; Nardi et al. 2004; Park et al. 2009; Quan-Haase & Young 2010; Raacke & Bonds-Raacke 2008).

Since gratifications obtained refer to the functional congruity a TV serial or series offers, with regard to the studies by Sirgy, Johar, Samli, and Claiborne (1991) and Kressman et al. (2006), it can be argued that functional congruence and hence gratifications obtained positively affect

---

[43] Original terminology is German (Emotionalität, Orientierung, Ausgleich, Zeitvertreib, Soziales Erleben).

brand loyalty. Nienstedt, Huber, and Seelmann (2012) detected positive effects of functional congruence on the brand relationship and brand loyalty. Due to the fact that gratifications obtained from the social media programme do not refer to the actual functional congruity of the brand under investigation, but to that of a tool assumed to support the consumer-brand relationship, the link between gratifications obtained and brand loyalty is only assumed for gratifications obtained from *the serialised TV brand* (cf. the following section, 3.1.6), while gratifications obtained *from the social media programme* are assumed to positively affect the consumer-brand relationship only.

#	Hypothesis
7	Gratifications obtained from the social media programme for the serialised TV brand positively affect the consumer-brand relationship.

This leads to the conclusion that the consumer-brand relationship must be a mediator for the relationship between gratifications obtained from the social media programme for the serialised TV brand and brand loyalty. According to Baron and Kenny (1986, p. 1176) a variable can be "said to function as a mediator to the extent that it accounts for the relation between the predictor and the criterion." Hence, a hypotheses of mediation can be stated.

#	Hypothesis
7_m	The impact of gratifications obtained from the social media programme for the serialised TV brand on brand loyalty is mediated by the consumer-brand relationship.

It can also be assumed that the more the social media programme meets expectations, the more likely are intensive usage and interaction.

#	Hypothesis
8	Gratifications obtained from the social media programme for the serialised TV brand positively affect engagement in the social media programme for the serial brand.

In addition, the more the social media programme meets expectations, the more positive the attitude towards it should be.

#	Hypothesis
9	Gratifications obtained from the social media programme for the serialised TV brand positively affect attitude toward the social media programme for the serialised TV brand.

3.1.6   Gratifications obtained from the serialised TV brand

In accordance with the elaborations on gratifications obtained from the social media programme, gratifications obtained from the TV brand itself are defined as the meeting of defined experience factors by the TV brand.

The aforementioned TV experience factors (Dehm & Storll 2003; Dehm, Storll, & Beeske 2005) are again used for index construction, which is further elaborated on in section 4.4.6. In accordance with the social media gratifications construct, the index incorporates

- gratifications such as entertainment and information as identified by research on television and video content gratifications (Haridakis 2002; Kim & Rubin 1997; Palmgreen & Lawrence 1991; Papacharissi & Mendelson 2007);
- TV experience factors emotionality, orientation, balance, pastime, and social experience particularly identified for a German viewership (Dehm & Storll 2003; Dehm, Storll, & Beeske 2005).

Since gratifications obtained from the serialised TV brand do in fact refer to the actual functional congruity of the brand under investigation, the aforementioned link between gratifications obtained and brand loyalty, which is based on the studies by Sirgy et al. (1991) and Kressman et al. (2006), leads to the hypothesis that gratifications obtained from the serialised TV brand positively affect brand loyalty.

#	Hypothesis
10	Gratifications obtained from the serialised TV brand positively affect brand loyalty.

In addition, it can be assumed that gratifications obtained from the serialised TV brand also impact the consumer-brand relationship.

#	Hypothesis
11	Gratifications obtained from the serialised TV brand positively affect the consumer-brand relationship.

3.1.7   Perceived critics' response to the serialised TV brand

Television programmes are hedonic products, i.e. their consumption "designates those facets of consumer behavior that relate to the multi sensory, fantasy and emotive aspects" of consumers' experience with the products (Hirschman & Holbrook 1982, p. 92). Since they are also media products, they are credence products for which quality can generally not be assessed. Therefore, uncertainty when choosing them needs to be reduced for consumers in order to bring about purchase or, in the case of commercial television, usage.

To reduce that uncertainty, promotional communicative messages alone are not sufficient. Hence, in a conceptual model focusing on television content and comprising brand and social media related constructs, limiting the view on brand behaviours to promotional, i.e. channel-sponsored, social media messages is not adequate, but has to be expanded by concepts stemming from general media research. This refers mainly to media effects research, i.e. agenda-setting, priming, and framing (Iyengar & Kinder 1987; Iyengar & Simon 1993), as well as the effects of critics and gatekeeping effects (Lewin 1943; White 1950).

Agenda-setting is defined as "the ability of the news media to define the significant issues of the day" (Iyengar & Simon 1993, p. 366; Kepplinger 2009), i.e. the impact news coverage has on the importance attributed to an issue by media consumers. Priming, on the other hand, "refers to the ability of news programs to affect the criteria by which political leaders are judged" (Iyengar & Simon 1993, p. 368). This touches on the relevance an issue obtains for decision making (Iyengar & Kinder 1987). Framing, in contrast, refers to how qualitative features of news messages affect public opinion (Iyengar & Simon 1993, p. 366). Gitlin (1980, p. 7) describes media frames, "largely unspoken and unacknowledged", as "persistent patterns of cognition, interpretation, and presentation, of selection, emphasis, and exclusion" which help journalists and to some extent consumers of news content to organise information.

Gatekeeping can be described as "the process by which [...] potential news messages are winnowed, shaped, and prodded into those few that are actually transmitted by the news media" (Shoemaker, Eichholz, Kim, & Wrigley 2001, p. 233). White (1950) therefore points out that news transmission depends on subjective rather than systematic selection processes.

In fact, according to the two-step flow of communication hypothesis, mass media like television influence opinion leaders first, who then pass on their opinions to other media users, i.e. opinion followers (Jäckel 2011, pp. 144 ff.; Kepplinger 2009; Lazarsfeld, Berelson, & Gaudet 1948;). Clement, Proppe, and Rott (2007, p. 84) point out that journalists, critics, and experts represent opinion leaders, which makes them important reference points for media users. Therefore, the aforementioned concepts which mostly apply to media effects, news selection and the spreading of news with regard to news media, not entertainment media, can to a certain extent be transferred to television programmes and the role of critics.

Most media products are reviewed by critics on a regular basis. National newspapers contain reviews of books, films, or music, and television programme magazines, websites, or the radio also review television content. In this study, perceived critics' response refers to critics' reactions or reviews with regard to the serialised TV brand, as perceived by the consumers. This approach was chosen because measuring actual critics' response is very complex, and because for this study, how users perceive critics' response, i.e. how they perceive the responses they were actually informed about, is important – not so much how critics in general did in fact review the programmes.

Critics' choices and opinions are crucial in the decision making process related to films. Eliashberg, Elberse, and Leenders (2006, p. 641) state that moviegoers are "heavily influenced by others' opinions and choices" and highlight the fact that this can refer to friends and acquaintances, but also critics and other opinion leaders, as well as to "the market as a whole". For another media product, Chevalier and Mayzlin (2006) found evidence that critics' opinions in the form of customer reviews can increase sales of books through word-of-mouth effects.

The role of critics in influencing consumer behaviour has been analysed from an influencer as well as from a predictor perspective. From the influencer perspective, a critic is an opinion leader influencing subsequent product adoption, while from the predictor perspective, the critic is a good representative of the target group and therefore a leading indicator without any significant influence (Eliashberg & Shugan 1997; Reinstein & Snyder 2005).[44] In a study on the impact of movie critics' reviews on box office revenues, empirical findings put forward by Eliashberg and Shugan (1997) suggest a statistically insignificant relationship between reviews and revenues. They found that the percentage of positive reviews was only marginally significant during the first four weeks following the review, from which they conclude that an influencer effect does not take place. In another study, Reinstein and Snyder (2005) have been able to refute this result. They find a significant influence effect for some types of movies, and weak evidence of an influence effect in their complete sample. Elberse and Eliashberg (2003, p. 350) add to that by stating that advertising support is a predictor of a film's opening weekend performance, while word-of-mouth communication is a predictor of performance in subsequent weeks. It is also notable that reviews do not only affect consumer response when they are positive. In their study, Clement et al. (2007) found that the success of books reviewed for the German television show *Das Literarische Quartett* did not solely depend on favourable reviews, but were in fact more likely to be impactful if critics either disagreed about quality and expressed extreme judgments, or if those judgments were negative.

Thus, in accordance with research on critics' influence on product success and media effects research, critics' response can be regarded as an extension of brand communication and behaviours. It can therefore be hypothesized that perceived critics' response influences the consumer-brand relationship.

#	Hypothesis
12	Perceived critics' response to the serialised TV brand positively affects the consumer-brand relationship.

In addition, a critic can be regarded as an opinion leader influencing subsequent product adoption (Eliashberg & Shugan 1997; Reinstein & Snyder 2005) as well as expectations consumers associate with the brand. It might therefore also be hypothesized that perceived critics' response positively affects gratifications obtained from TV brand.

---

[44] For a detailed description of both perspectives, refer to Eliashberg and Shugan (1997, pp. 71f.).

#	Hypothesis
13	Perceived critics' response positively affects gratifications obtained from the serialised TV brand.

3.1.8   Perceived WOM response to the serialised TV brand

Electronic word-of-mouth communication has been defined in section 2.3.5 as "any positive or negative statement made by potential, actual, or former customers about a product or company, which is made available to a multitude of people and institutions via the Internet" (Hennig-Thurau et al. 2004, p. 28).

Since the research design does not allow for an actual measurement and evaluation of WOM processes regarding the examined brand, perceived WOM response is measured instead. Perceived word-of-mouth (WOM) response is defined as the perceived reactions from users' online and offline social network toward the serialised TV brand, i.e. recommendations and positive comments. Since users' perception of WOM response is, in fact, more important for this study than actual general WOM, this is an appropriate approach.

In section 2.3.5, it has been shown that eWOM has been extensively researched, partly with a direct focus on consumer reactions to it or on the impact eWOM has on sales (e.g. Brown, Broderick, & Lee 2007; Burton & Khammash 2010; Chevalier & Mayzlin 2006; Dellarocas 2003; Godes & Mayzlin 2004; Godes & Mayzlin 2009; Hennig-Thurau et al. 2004; Kozinets et al. 2010; Trusov et al. 2009). Motivations to engage in eWOM communication have been identified as including social interaction and economic incentives, among others (e.g. Chu & Kim 2011; Hennig-Thurau et al. 2004). EWOM in the form of customer reviews impacts sales (Chevalier & Mayzlin 2006), and consumers make active use of informational or promotional content in the form of eWOM instead of merely passing messages along (Kozinets et al. 2010).

In a study on referring to television programmes, Romaniuk (2007) found the effect of positive WOM to positively impact future viewing. Therefore, perceived WOM response can be hypothesized to positively affect the consumer-brand relationship because it can, like perceived critics' response, be interpreted as a form of brand communicative behaviours talked about, hence influencing the consumer-brand relationship.

#	Hypothesis
14	Perceived WOM response to the serialised TV brand positively affects the consumer-brand relationship.

With regard to the direct impact of perceived critics' response on gratifications obtained from the serialised TV brand and the fact that consumers are influenced by opinion leaders' assertions about television programmes, it can also be hypothesized that perceived WOM response positively affects gratifications obtained from the serialised TV brand.

#	Hypothesis
15	Perceived WOM response to the serialised TV brand positively affects gratifications obtained from the serialised TV brand.

3.2 Finalisation of the causal model and summary of hypotheses

In addition to direct causal effects, moderating and mediating effects are hypothesized for the model. According to Jaccard and Turrisi (2003, p. 1), six types of relationships can occur within causal models:

1. direct causal relationships where an independent variable X directly causes a dependent variable Y;
2. indirect causal relationships (also called mediating effects) where the independent variable X impacts the dependent variable Y via a third variable Z;
3. spurious causal relationships where a relation between X and Y can be traced back to a common cause Z;
4. bidirectional causal relationships where X and Y influence each other;
5. unanalysed causal relationships where X and Y are related, but the source is unspecified;
6. moderated causal relationships where the relationship between X and Y is influenced by a moderator variable Z.

Spurious, bidirectional and unanalysed relationships shall not be investigated. Mediating hypotheses, with the exception of $H7_m$, have not expressly been stated. Many of the constructs are assumed to impact other constructs via various paths, so that mediating effects might be present and will be further investigated during model testing.

Moderating effects are triggered by variables "whose variation influences the strength or the direction of a relationship between an exogenous and an endogenous variable". (Henseler & Fassott 2010, p. 713). Baron and Kenny (1986, p. 1174) define a moderator as a "qualitative (e.g., sex, race, class) or quantitative (e.g., level of reward) variable that affects the direction and/or strength of relation between an independent or predictor variable and a dependent or criterion variable." Hence, it is assumed that the moderating effect influences the relationship between two variables.

Social media research being exploratory in nature, the deduction of sound hypotheses about moderating effects seems difficult. There is, for instance, no reason to assume that viewers of different television programmes of the same or a similar genre (e.g. entertainment) show differing patterns with regard to social media influencing their attitude and behaviour towards the TV brand. The basic assumptions for direction and intensity of causality being derived from more general theories of behaviour and media usage, it is therefore hypothesized that within the same genre, TV programme choice has no moderating effect on the basic hypotheses.

#	Hypothesis
16	TV programme choice has no moderating effect on the causal model.

Similarly, it seems hardly reasonable to state moderating hypotheses with regard to demographic factors such as age or gender. Concerning the latter, social media usage does not seem to be determined by gender. Table 3-2 shows that usage of different applications is quite similar for males and females, usage of private networks, i.e. tools like Facebook, which are most widely used in the television context, are equally used.

	Female	Male
Wikipedia	73%	75%
video communities, e.g. YouTube	56%	64%
private networks & communities	46%	46%
photo collections, communities	22%	30%
professional networks & communities	8%	12%
Weblogs	16%	16%
Twitter	6%	8%

Table 3-2: Usage of Web 2.0 applications across gender 2013

Casual usage, based on German speaking internet users age 14 and up (2013: n=1,389)

Source: Own design, adapted from ARD/ZDF-Onlinestudie 2013 (2013a)

It is therefore hypothesized that gender has no moderating effect on the other hypotheses.

#	Hypothesis
17	Gender has no moderating effect on the causal model.

Due to the research area being relatively new, it is difficult to deduce a sound moderation hypothesis for age. On the one hand, younger people might be more familiar with social media in general than older users. On the other hand, with this study actually investigating social media for TV users' reaction to brand behaviours, there is no reason to assume a difference in strength and direction of assumed causality within the model. With regard to constructs like perceived critics' and WOM response, one might state that younger people are easier to influence than older people. On the other hand, having grown up with social media, younger people might also be more sceptical about eWOM, and critics might not be an issue for them at all. It is therefore hypothesized that age has no moderating effect on the other hypotheses.

#	Hypothesis
18	Age has no moderating effect on the causal model.

Table 3-3 lists all hypotheses, and Figure 3-1 shows the full structural model.

#	Hypothesis
1	The consumer-brand relationship positively influences brand loyalty.
2	Attitude toward the social media programme for the serialised TV brand positively affects brand loyalty.
3	Attitude toward the social media programme for the serialised TV brand positively affects the consumer-brand relationship.
4	Engagement in the social media programme for the serialised TV brand positively affects brand loyalty.
5	Engagement in the social media programme for the serialised TV brand positively affects the consumer-brand relationship.
6	Attitude toward the social media programme for the serialised TV brand positively affects engagement in the social media programme for the serialised TV brand.
7	Gratifications obtained from the social media programme for the serialised TV brand positively affect the consumer-brand relationship.
7_m	The impact of gratifications obtained from the social media programme for the serialised TV brand on brand loyalty is mediated by the consumer-brand relationship.
8	Gratifications obtained from the social media programme for the serialised TV brand positively affect engagement in the social media programme for the serialised TV brand.
9	Gratifications obtained from the social media programme for the serialised TV brand positively affect attitude toward the social media programme for the serialised TV brand.
10	Gratifications obtained from the serialised TV brand positively affect brand loyalty.
11	Gratifications obtained from the serialised TV brand positively affect the consumer-brand relationship.
12	Perceived critics' response to the serialised TV brand positively affects the consumer-brand relationship.
13	Perceived critics' response positively affects gratifications obtained from the serialised TV brand.
14	Perceived WOM response to the serialised TV brand positively affects the consumer-brand relationship.
15	Perceived WOM response to the serialised TV brand positively affects gratifications obtained from the serialised TV brand.

Hypotheses of moderation:

16	TV programme choice has no moderating effect on the causal model.
17	Gender has no moderating effect on the causal model.
18	Age has no moderating effect on the causal model.

Table 3-3: Complete overview of model hypotheses

Source: Own design

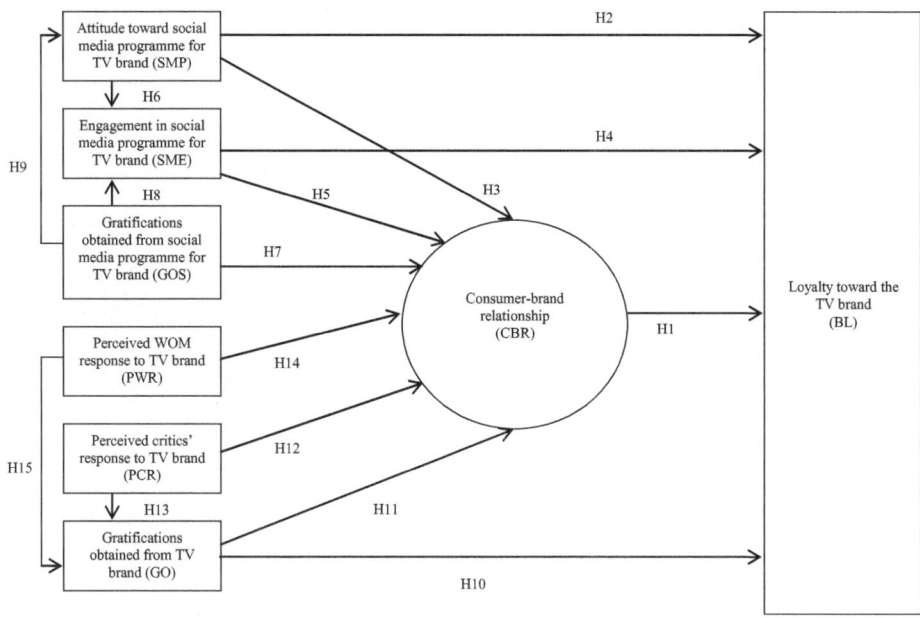

Figure 3-1: Full structural model

Source: Own design

4 Specifications of model development

Chapter 4 goes into detail with the specifications of the model and model validation. Why Partial Least Squares (PLS), a structural equation modelling approach, is chosen as the method for model testing is explained in section 4.1, while 4.2 describes the survey conducted to collect data for model testing. Section 4.3 goes into detail with the PLS approach, its theoretical background and its application to the research question, before section 4.4 outlines the necessary operationalisation of the constructs introduced in chapter 3. Empirical model validation and hypothesis testing follow in chapter 5.

4.1 Choice of method

Partial Least Squares (PLS) is a structural equation modelling approach used to investigate causal relationships between variables. Structural equation modelling (SEM) allows for the simultaneous modelling of "relationships among multiple independent and dependent constructs" (Haenlein & Kaplan 2004, p. 285). The assumed causal relationships need to be defined within a scientifically and logically sound system of hypotheses, because the model does not actually measure causality, but covariance or variance (Homburg & Pflesser 1999, p. 635).

An important advantage of the method is "its ability to bring together psychometric and econometric analyses in such a way that some of the best features of both can be exploited" (Fornell & Larcker 1981, p. 39). Path or structural equation modelling overcomes the limitations of other methods by explicitly including model measurement error in the estimation procedure as well as unobservable latent variables (Haenlein & Kaplan 2004, pp. 284f.). Each of these latent variables can be indirectly observed by a block of underlying items also called manifest variables or observed measures (e.g. Christophersen & Grape 2007, p. 103; Fornell & Cha 1994, p. 55; Haenlein & Kaplan 2004, p. 285). The model distinguishes between endogenous variables, which are explained by the model, and exogenous variables, which are not explained.

To estimate the model, different approaches can be used. Covariance-based approaches like LISREL or AMOS estimate model parameters by attempting to reproduce the covariance matrix of the observed measures, i.e. the difference between the sample covariances and those predicted by the theoretical model are minimised (Huber, Herrmann, Meyer, Vogel, &

Vollhardt 2007, p. 6). The direction of causality is hypothesized to be from the latent variable to the indicators, i.e. the correlation between indicators is caused by the influence of the latent variable, thus the measures are referred to as "reflective" (Jarvis, Mackenzie, & Podsakoff 2003, p. 200; Ringle 2004a, p. 12).

PLS, in contrast, also allows for formative indicators, which means that the indicators are not caused by, but have an impact on, or cause, the underlying construct (Jarvis et al. 2003, p. 201). PLS is a variance-based approach that makes use of a regression-based technique, which aims at "maximizing the variance of the dependent variables explained by the independent ones instead of reproducing the empirical covariance matrix" (Haenlein & Kaplan 2004, p. 290). Dependent variables, in this context, are the endogenous variables of the structural model, as well as those latent variables with formative indicators, and the reflective manifest variables (Huber et al. 2007, p. 6). PLS divides the set of model parameters into subsets and estimates them each at once by ordinary multiple regression while the values of parameters in other subsets are regarded as given. An iterative process (iteration cycle) "provides successive approximations for the estimates, subset by subset, of loadings and structural parameters" (Fornell & Cha 1994, p. 62).

The central difference in model development between covariance-based SEM approaches and PLS is the operationalisation of the constructs: Covariance-based SEM allows for reflective indicators only, which bears the risk of measurement model misspecification if due to causal relationships, the direction of causality is in fact from the measure to the construct, so that formative operationalisation is required (Jarvis et al. 2003). In marketing theory, covariance-based approaches have been prevalent, while PLS has been used to a limited extent only. This might be due to learning and lock-in effects such as available software (Diamantopoulos & Winklhofer 2001, p. 274; Fornell & Cha 1994, pp. 52; 73). However, there are a number of circumstances that suggest using PLS over covariance-based SEM approaches. Covariance-based approaches are particularly useful in cases where a sound and theory-backed system of research hypotheses is investigated and the focus is on the constructs and the hypotheses connecting them (Huber et al. 2007, p. 13). The level of theoretical knowledge required to develop the model is a major precondition for the use of covariance-based procedures, the main objective being to obtain optimum parameter accuracy (Chin & Newsted 1999, p. 335).

However, research might also focus on explanations for changes in one or several variables, for instance with regard to management oriented research questions where the identification of key determinants is more interesting than a theory-based explanatory model. In those cases, the use of a variance-based approach like PLS is more useful (Huber et al. 2007, p. 14). Another advantage of PLS is that it imposes no distribution restrictions (Fornell & Cha 1994, pp. 52; 55) and can be used for small sample sizes (Haenlein & Kaplan 2004, p. 295; Huber et al. 2007, p. 14). Also, PLS "involves no assumptions about the population or scale of measurement" (Fornell & Bookstein 1982, p. 443); it can be used for nominal, ordinal, and interval scaled variables (Haenlein & Kaplan 2004, p. 291).

Chin and Newsted (1999, p. 337) recommend making use of the PLS approach if all, or a selection of, the following applies:[45]

1. The objective of the research is prediction.
2. The phenomenon that is to be investigated is relatively new or changing, and the theoretical model or the measures are not yet well formed.
3. The model is relatively complex and comprises a large number of latent and/or manifest variables.
4. The relationship between the latent variables and the indicators requires both formative and reflective measures.
5. The data conditions for normal distribution, independence, and/or sample size are not met.

Hence, PLS should be used for models where relationships between constructs, but also between indicators and constructs, are not completely known or not well researched. PLS allows for the identification of connections, even if theoretical knowledge in the area is scarce and model relationships are based on plausibility considerations; i.e. the model can also be used in a predictive or exploratory sense (Chin & Newsted 1999, p. 330; Huber et al. 2007, p. 14). Due to the fact that PLS tends to underestimate the correlations between the latent variables, an exploratory use of PLS is, in contrast to covariance-based approaches, not problematic because the risk of drawing premature conclusions on the basis of incorrect connections between constructs is practically non-existent (Haenlein & Kaplan 2004, p. 292; Huber et al. 2007, p. 14).

---

[45] For an extensive comparison of both PLS and covariance-based approaches, see Ringle (2004a, p. 34).

On the basis of the above-mentioned properties, PLS seems an appropriate approach for this study. Firstly, the research focus is relatively new and findings on social media branding, especially for serialised television brands, are scarce. It is therefore impossible to rely on the existing literature to provide a sound system of hypotheses. Secondly, the research question is of managerial interest and focuses on practical implications rather than on underlying theory. Thirdly, some of the constructs involved, e.g. "Gratifications obtained from the serialised TV brand" as well as "Gratifications obtained from the social media programme for the serialised TV brand", require formative indicators. PLS will therefore be used in this analysis, and following sections will focus on PLS only.

4.2 Survey

To answer the research questions, a survey was designed that could be accessed online in July 2013. A question at the beginning worked as a filter so that only users of social media offerings for television brands were presented with the full questionnaire. Respondents indicating they did not use social media for television related content were redirected to an alternative questionnaire that asked them for the reasons they did not make use of such offerings. The following sections describe sampling for the survey, the questionnaire, as well as data collection. Results and interpretations are presented in chapter 5.

4.2.1 Sampling

Since this study investigates social media, it did not seem appropriate to recruit a representative sample of the population since social media usage differs strongly across age groups. For instance, according to ARD/ZDF-Onlinestudie 2013 (2013a), private networks and communities were used by 41 percent of German speaking internet users age 14 and up (see Table 4-2), but by 87 percent and 16 percent of users aged 14-19 and 60-69, respectively (see Table 4-1). Therefore, it seemed appropriate to address the questionnaire at current users of social media offerings.

	all	Gender		Age							Education		
		F	M	14-19	20-29	30-39	40-49	50-59	60-69	70+	elementary school	secondary school, A-levels	university
Wikipedia	74	73	75	95	93	81	77	61	47	32	51	83	88
video communities	60	56	64	91	87	71	62	43	25	13	49	64	70
private networks & communities	46	46	46	87	80	55	38	21	16	6	36	52	46
photo collections & communities	27	22	30	28	38	37	26	16	17	13	20	27	36
professional networks & communities	10	8	12	5	14	19	13	4	2	0	3	9	25
Weblogs	16	16	16	18	31	19	17	7	3	5	8	16	29
Twitter	7	6	8	22	10	7	5	3	4	0	4	8	11

Table 4-1: Usage of Web 2.0 applications across gender, age and education 2013

Casual usage, in %

Based on German speaking internet users age 14 and up (2013: n=1,389)

Source: Own design, adapted from ARD/ZDF-Onlinestudie 2013 (2013a)

Web 2.0 applications	2012	2013
Wikipedia	30	32
video communities, e.g. YouTube	32	32
private networks & communities	36**	41**
photo collections, communities	3*	4*
professional networks & communities	2	4
Weblogs	2	2
Twitter	30	32

Table 4-2: Usage of Web 2.0 applications 2012 and 2013

Usage at least once every week, in %

*   networks accessed with own personal profile

**   most accessed network

Based on German speaking internet users age 14 and up (2012: n=1,366; 2013: n=1,389)

Source: Own design, adapted from ARD/ZDF-Onlinestudie 2013 (2013c)

In order to investigate the effect of the social media programme for serialised television brands, respondents also had to be users of social media content specifically produced for television management purposes. As a result, respondents needed to already be aware of the brand and have entered a basic relationship with it; otherwise, they would not have been using the social media programme (cf. 1.2.3). Since this study aims at investigating the impact of social media on brand loyalty and the consumer-brand relationship, it is necessary to recruit respondents who are already associated with the social media offerings for the TV brands under investigation. This makes it impossible to recruit respondents who have no previous attachment to the brand.

Nevertheless, the direct targeting of specific users of selected programmes seems to be an appropriate group. Three programmes were selected for the survey: *The Voice of Germany*, *Germany's Next Topmodel* and *Galileo,* and users of the Facebook pages for the three programmes were defined as the key target group. These three programmes were chosen for various reasons.

One of them was that ProSiebenSat.1 Digital GmbH, a subsidiary of ProSiebenSat.1 Media AG that is responsible for online and video business and manages websites and social media sites for all TV stations of the group, manages the Facebook pages and they are hence in managerial control of ProSiebenSat.1. In contrast, for other programmes that are, for instance, of American origin, social media offerings are usually managed by the American television channels and cannot be controlled by ProSiebenSat.1. It would therefore not have been useful to have analysed these from a German channel's perspective.

Another reason for the choice of programmes was that they are all entertainment programmes that have similar slots in the programme scheme and very similar social media offerings. While this limits the transferability of the findings of this study to other programmes and social media offerings (cf. 6.3), it also provides the necessary comparability and allows for their treatment in the same sample.

While *The Voice of Germany* and *Germany's Next Topmodel* have a seasonal schedule, i.e. they run for a certain number of episodes before not being broadcast for the remainder of the year, *Galileo* runs for seven days a week throughout the whole year. It is also the longest running programme of the three, having been launched in 1998. *The Voice of Germany* and *Germany's Next Topmodel* were launched in 2011 and 2006, respectively. Table 4-3 gives an overview of the three programme brands investigated with regard to both the television programme as well as the accompanying Facebook page.

Social media objectives for the Facebook pages of the three programmes differ. The Facebook page for *The Voice of Germany* accompanies the programme, supports discussions with and among fans and provides them with bonus material and background information. The strategic significance of the Facebook page is underpinned by its launch date: It is the only of the three examined pages to be launched *before* the TV programme. The Facebook page for *Germany's Next Topmodel,* on the other hand, was launched after the programme had been running for four seasons. While it is used to post links to the programme's website and to inform about the TV schedule, it also supplements television and online content by additional content. It focuses on the participants and on fashion. The Facebook page for *Galileo* developed similarly, having started out as a provider of information about the TV programme and now providing its own magazine content.

		The Voice of Germany	*Germany's Next Topmodel*	*Galileo*
TV	**launch**	24 November 2011	25 January 2006	30 November 1998
	current schedule	yearly seasons running for 16-17 biweekly episodes; Thursday 20:15, Friday 20:15	yearly seasons running for 10-16 weekly episodes; Thursday 20:15	continuous schedule; Monday - Sunday 19:05
	genre	entertainment, music	entertainment	information / magazine programme
	network	ProSieben (Thursdays) and Sat.1 (Fridays)	ProSieben	ProSieben
	target group	people aged 14-49	women aged 14-49	people aged 14-49
Facebook page	**launch**	20 August 2011	2 January 2010	January 2009
	number of fans as of 01/2014	1 million	700,000	1.8 million

Table 4-3: Description of TV programme brands investigated

Sources: Own design based on www.the-voice-of-germany.de; www.facebook.com/TheVoiceOfGermany/info; www.facebook.com/germanys.next.topmodel/info; www.prosieben.de/tv/germanys-next-topmodel; www.facebook.com/Galileo/info; http://www.prosieben.de/tv/galileo

ProSiebenSat.1 Digital manages social media as a third channel of communication, next to TV and online. Content is closely connected, but not restricted, to TV as the core product. Special content available on the social web only is supposed to increase TV viewers' and users' loyalty to the programmes and to allow their favourite programmes to entertain them on all available platforms.

ProSiebenSat.1 Digital supported the survey by inviting users of the Facebook pages for the programmes *The Voice of Germany*, *Germany's Next Topmodel* and *Galileo* via the pages. The invitations were posted directly by the editorial teams managing the pages (cf. Figure 4-1).

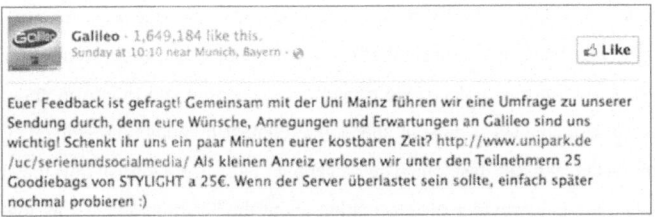

Figure 4-1: Survey invitation posted to Galileo Facebook page

Source: Original post on Galileo Facebook page http://www.facebook.com/galileo/posts/10152057139824535 [last updated 21 July 2013; last accessed 16 January 2014]; for translation cf. [46]

Additional participants were recruited via e-mailing lists and social networks. This was done in order to increase the number of respondents who did not usually use social media offerings associated with television content and to gain insight into why these offerings do not appeal to certain viewers.

4.2.2 Questionnaire

The questionnaire started out with filter questions in order to exclude unsuitable respondents from the main questionnaire and redirect them to the alternative non-user questionnaire, and to let respondents qualifying for the main questionnaire choose a programme and a social media tool to answer the questionnaire for.

Respondents were then asked questions that were later used for model testing. These questions referred to respondents' loyalty toward and relationship with their chosen programme, their attitude toward and engagement in the social media programme accompanying it, the gratifications respondents obtained from the television programme and

---

[46] "We need your feedback! Together with Mainz university, we're conducting a survey on our programme because we value your wishes, suggestions, and expectations concerning *Galileo!* Are you giving us a few minutes of you precious time?" Added are the survey link and a hint at the incentive (a "goodiebag" with products by STYLIGHT, a fashion platform ProSiebenSat.1 subsidiary SevenVentures had invested in).

its accompanying social media programme, and respondents' perceptions regarding word-of-mouth and critics' responses.[47]

After that, respondents were asked about their television consumption and social media usage: which types of television formats they usually watched, how much television they watched, and how often they used which social media tools.

Also, they were asked questions aiming at the connection between television and social media, namely whether they had ever watched a television series/serial solely because their attention had been attracted in social media, whether the conversations in social media had ever made them continue watching a television series/serial they had actually not wanted to continue, whether they made use of social media to exchange views about the programme while they watched television, how important it was for them to find their favourite series/serial on social media, and which features of the social media presence of their favourite television series/serial they considered important.

Lastly, respondents were asked to provide demographic information.

4.2.3   Data collection

Altogether, a total of 6,387 users clicked the links leading to the questionnaire. A total of 2,639 questionnaires was collected. After data cleansing, 2,357 questionnaires remained for data analysis. An additional 260 correctly completed questionnaires were collected for the non-user sample. For further description of the findings regarding the non-user sample, see section 5.5.2. All subsequent descriptions and analyses refer to the user sample only.

On the first page of the questionnaire, users were asked to decide which programme to answer the questionnaire for. They could choose between *The Voice of Germany* (TVoG), *Germany's Next Topmodel* (GNTM), and *Galileo*. In addition, they were offered the opportunity to answer the questionnaire for another programme of their choice. This option was included in order to not have respondents abandon the questionnaire because they did not feel sufficiently familiar with one of the programmes. However, this option was chosen by only 2.7 percent of respondents. 20.5 percent chose TVoG, 23.2 percent chose GNTM, and 53.5 percent chose

---

[47] Details concerning items, scales and the phrasing of questions can be found in section 4.4, which deals with the operationalisation of the constructs.

Galileo. This is due to the fact that the Galileo Facebook page has the largest follower base and that the survey invitation was posted there twice.[48]

The second page asked respondents to choose which social media tool to answer the questionnaire for, i.e. which social media tool they usually used with regard to the programme they had chosen. 95 percent chose Facebook, 1 percent chose Twitter, 0.9 percent chose Instagram, 2.7 percent chose YouTube, 0.1 percent chose Tumblr, 0.3 percent chose others. Users who indicated that they used none of the above were the ones redirected to the alternative questionnaire for non-users. Since Facebook was used as recruitment channel for the survey, it is not surprising that the vast majority chose Facebook as the social media offering to answer the questionnaire for. In fact, of the three programmes, only TVoG and GNTM had official Twitter channels, Galileo did not have any official social media offerings besides Facebook.

Age	full sample in %	TVoG sub-sample in %	GNTM sub-sample in %	Galileo sub-sample in %	free choice subsample in %
14-19	47.2	19.6	60.0	52.8	35.9
20-29	30.4	27.7	30.2	30.8	45.3
30-39	11.5	24.6	5.7	8.8	14.1
40-49	6.3	17.1	1.6	4.4	3.1
50-59	2.5	8.3	0.9	1.0	1.6
60-69	0.5	1.2	0.2	0.4	0.0
Total	98.4	98.6	98.5	98.2	100
Missing	1.6	1.4	1.5	1.8	0.0
Total	100.0	100.0	100.0	100.0	100.0

Table 4-4: Age of questionnaire respondents

Source: Own design

The sample consisted of 60.9 percent female respondents (TVoG: 82.9 percent, GNTM 95.2 percent, Galileo 36.5 percent, free choice 82.8 percent). Respondents were rather young with almost 80 percent of them under 30 years of age. The majority of respondents, i.e. almost 70 percent, had either completed or were pursuing a degree after 10 years of school ("Realschulabschluss") or A-levels (30.4 percent and 37.6 percent, respectively). Approximately 10 percent had no degree (2.7 percent) or had completed or were pursuing a degree after 9 years of school ("Hauptschulabschluss") (7.3 percent). 15.4 percent held or were pursuing a university degree. This corresponds to the fact that respondents were quite young and leads to the conclusion that a majority of them had not completed their education.

---

[48] For a detailed schedule of invitations, see Appendix B.

In fact, 52.9 percent indicated that they were students (39.4 percent high school and 13.5 percent university). 31.9 percent were employed, 1.5 percent were civil servants, 3.8 percent were homekeepers, 1.5 percent were unemployed, 0.8 percent were retired.

Hence, the majority of respondents was a female high school or university student between 14 and 29 years of age, having completed or pursuing a high or medium level of education. For a detailed overview of demographics, see Appendix C.

4.3 Structural equation modelling with PLS

This section deals with structural equation modelling with the Partial Least Squares approach (PLS). Sections 4.3.1 and 4.3.2 outline the construction of the PLS model as well as the specifics of how to operationalise the constructs, and section 4.3.3 outlines how to evaluate both the structural and the measurement model.

4.3.1   Construction and estimation of the PLS model

As indicated above, PLS can be used to test theoretical assumptions with empirical data, which allows for the subsequent acceptance or rejection of research hypotheses. Hence, it is possible "to construct a research model that represents a certain theory, simply by converting theoretical and derived concepts into unobservable (latent) variables, and empirical concepts into indicators, which are linked by a set of hypotheses" (Haenlein & Kaplan 2004, p. 286). This model can then be represented graphically by a path diagram, also called arrow scheme (Fornell & Cha 1994, p. 54).

The causal relationships between the latent variables as well as those between latent variables and their indicators are then summarised in a complete system consisting of structural as well as measurement equations. Within the overall model, the inner or structural model, which forms the core of the model, relates the constructs to each other, while the measurement or outer model relates the constructs to their measures (Fornell & Cha 1994, pp. 55ff.). Figure 4-2 provides an example of a complete PLS model.

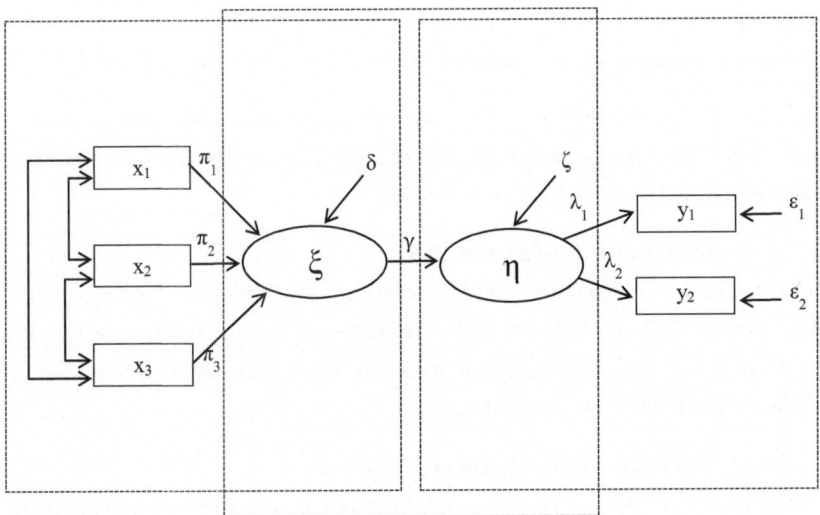

formative measurement model;   structural model   reflective measurement model;
latent exogenous variable   latent endogenous variable

Figure 4-2: PLS model with structural and measurement model

Source: Own design, adapted from Diamantopoulos and Winklhofer (2001, p. 270); Huber et al. (2007, p. 8)

η	latent endogenous variable
ξ	latent exogenous variable
y	observed measures, i.e. indicators, of η
x	observed measures, i.e. indicators, of ξ
ε	residual variables, i.e., measurement error, of y
δ	residual variable of ξ
ζ	residual variable of η
γ	path coefficient between ξ and η

The structural model

The structural model, or inner relations, depicts the relationships among the latent variables as derived from theory and plausibility considerations. It results in a set of theoretical equations which can be described as

(1) $\eta = B\eta + \Gamma\xi + \zeta$

where η is the vector of the endogenous latent variables, ξ is the vector of the exogenous latent variables, and ζ is the vector of residual variables, i.e. unexplained variance. B as well as Γ are the path coefficient matrices (Chin & Newsted, 1999, p. 321; Fornell & Cha 1994, p. 58; Haenlein & Kaplan 2004, p. 288).

The measurement model

The measurement model, or outer relations, specifies the relationships between the latent and the manifest variables. In the reflective case, these relationships are defined as

(2) $y = \Lambda_y\eta + \epsilon_y$

(3) $x = \Lambda_x\xi + \epsilon_x$

where η and ξ are, as specified in (1), the vectors of the endogenous and the exogenous latent variables respectively. y and x are the observed measures, i.e. the indicators, of η and ξ. Λ_y and Λ_x are the matrices of loadings relating the latent variables to their measures, and ϵ, or ε, stands for the associated measurement error, or noise (Chin & Newsted, 1999, p. 323; Fornell & Cha 1994, p. 59).

In the formative case, the relationships between the latent and the manifest variables can be defined as

(4) $\eta = \pi_\eta y + \delta_\eta$

(5) $\xi = \pi_\xi x + \delta_\xi$

with η, ξ, y and x as specified in (1)-(3), πs as the multiple regression coefficients and δs as the residuals from regression (Fornell & Cha 1994, p. 60).[49]

Weight relations

In addition to the inner and the outer relations, PLS also has a third component, the weight relations, which are used to estimate case values for the latent variables (Chin & Newsted 1999, pp. 321ff.; Fornell & Cha 1994, p. 57). The latent variable estimates are linear aggregates of their empirical indicators whose weights are obtained via the estimation procedure as specified by the inner and outer models, with η, ξ, ζ, B and Γ as specified in (1) (Chin & Newsted, 1999, p. 324; Fornell & Cha 1994, p. 62).

PLS starts by calculating the case values, in contrast to covariance-based SEM, which estimates the model parameters first and the case values after that (Dijkstra 1983, p. 78). An overview of the iterative estimation process of the PLS model is provided by Ringle (2004a, pp. 24ff.):

1st stage: Iterative estimation of weights and latent variable scores

The process starts with step 4; steps 1 through 4 are to be repeated until convergence is obtained.

Step 1: calculation of inner weights

Step 2: inside approximation

Step 3: calculation of outer weights

Step 4: outside approximation

2nd stage: Estimation of path loading coefficients

3rd stage: Calculation of location parameters

At stage 1, weights and latent variable scores are estimated. The estimation process starts with an outside approximation, in which case values for each latent variable are estimated. In the following step – inside approximation – improved case values are determined as a weighted

---

[49] "This should not be confused with weight relations [...] Whereas weight relations define the *estimated* latent variables as the weighted aggregates of the manifest variables, the formative specification describes the relationships between the manifest variables and the *true* latent variables." (Fornell & Cha 1994, p. 60; italics in original)

average of neighbouring latent variables (Ringle 2004a, p. 24).[50] Weight relations are modified with this second estimate and the process is repeated from the beginning and until convergence of the case values is obtained (Haenlein & Kaplan 2004, p. 291). After latent variable scores have been estimated, stage 2 of the process estimates the path loading coefficients and factor loadings with OLS regression. Stage 3 calculates the location parameters (Ringle 2004a, p. 25).

The more model indicators are included in a PLS model, the better the latent variables are explained. In PLS, due to a phenomenon called consistency at large, "better estimates cannot simply be obtained by increasing the sample size. Both more indicators and more cases are needed" (Chin & Newsted 1999, p. 329). There are no rules for the size of the sample; however, PLS allows for appropriate models at sample sizes as small as 20 (Chin & Newsted 1999, p. 335).

4.3.2 Designing the measurement model: Specifics of operationalisation

As indicated above, PLS, in contrast to covariance-based SEM, allows for formative as well as reflective indicators in the measurement model. While reflective (effect) indicators (also called scale) are assumed to be a reflection of and caused by an underlying construct, formative (cause, causal) indicators (also called index) form, or cause, a latent variable (Diamantopoulos & Winklhofer 2001, p. 269; Fornell & Cha 1994, p. 59).

This implies that eliminating an indicator from a reflective model does not alter the meaning of the construct, since the measures are expected to be correlated, while eliminating an indicator from a formative model can alter the meaning of the construct, because the measures are not expected to correlate (Jarvis et al. 2003, p. 201). Hence, reflective indicators are "essentially interchangeable", while formative indicators are not, meaning that failure to consider all facets in a formative model leads to an exclusion of relevant indicators and a misspecification of the construct (Diamantopoulos & Winklhofer 2001, p. 271). Jarvis et al. (2003, p. 203) provide a set of decision rules for determining whether a construct is formative or reflective. These differences in indicators need to be taken into consideration when the model is evaluated.

---

[50] The weights can be estimated by a centroid weighting scheme, a factor weighting scheme or a path weighting scheme (Fornell & Cha 1994, p. 65).

	formative model	reflective model
Direction of causality	from items to construct	from construct to items
Are the indicators defining characteristics or manifestations of the construct?	defining characteristics	manifestations
Would changes in the indicators cause changes in the construct?	yes	no
Would changes in the construct cause changes in the indicators?	no	yes
Interchangeability of the indicators	indicators need not be interchangeable	indicators should be interchangeable
Should the indicators have the same or similar content? Do they share a common theme?	not necessarily	yes
Would dropping one of the indicators alter the meaning of the construct?	yes (probably)	no
Covariation among the indicators	not necessarily	yes
Should a change in one of the indicators be associated with changes in the other indicators?	not necessarily	yes
Nomological net of the construct indicators	may differ	should not differ
Are the indicators expected to have the same antecedents and consequences?	not necessarily	yes

Table 4-5: Decision rules for construct operationalisation

Source: Own design, adapted from Jarvis et al. (2003, p. 203)

4.3.3   Evaluation of the structural equation model

Due to the fact that PLS makes no assumptions about distribution, many of the commonly used measures cannot be used to evaluate the model. Since there is a lack of structured approaches to evaluate PLS models, the structural model, as well as the formative and the reflective measurement models need to be validated separately.

4.3.3.1   Evaluation of the reflective measurement model

Evaluation of the measurement model starts out with the reflective measurement models before progressing to the formative measurement models.

Indicator reliability

In a first step, indicator loadings on the latent variable and their significance are evaluated. In general, at least 50 percent of the variance of an indicator should be due to the latent variable (Huber et al. 2007, p. 35). As a result, loadings should be at least 0.7 in order to be considered acceptable (Sarkar, Echambadi, Cavusgil, & Aulakh 2001, pp. 365f.). In exploratory studies, weaker indicators with loadings between 0.4 and 0.7 may also be considered acceptable (Hair, Ringle, & Sarstedt 2011, p. 146; Hair, Sarstedt, Ringle, & Mena 2012, p. 429); indicators with loadings lower than 0.4 should be removed (Huber, Meyer, & Weißhaar 2013, p. 62).

Significance of the loadings can be measured with t-tests which are calculated with the bootstrapping or the jackknifing method.[51] The loading should be significant at the 0.05 level (one-tailed t-test; t-value > 1.66) (Huber et al. 2007, p. 35; Huber et al. 2013, p. 62).

Convergent validity

Composite reliability and average variance extracted (AVE) serve to determine convergent validity (Hair et al. 2012, p. 423).

Composite reliability estimates a construct's internal consistency and ranges from 0 to 1, 0.7 being considered acceptable (Huber et al. 2007, p. 35). However, values of 0.6 are also considered acceptable in exploratory studies (Hair et al. 2011, p. 145). For PLS, composite reliability is a more suitable measure for construct reliability assessment than Cronbach's alpha, because it does not assume equal reliability of all indicators (ibid.).

Average variance extracted (AVE) is a measure first proposed by Fornell and Larcker (1981) and measures the variance captured by the indicators relative to the amount of variance due to measurement error (Fornell & Cha 1994, p. 69). It ranges from 0 to 1 and should be greater than 0.6 (Huber et al. 2007, p. 36).

Discriminant validity

Discriminant validity is estimated to assess whether the constructs differ sufficiently. To evaluate discriminant validity, the Fornell-Larcker criterion and cross-loadings can be used (Hair et al. 2011, p. 145). The Fornell-Larcker criterion is based on Fornell's and Larcker's suggestion that AVE of a reflective latent construct should be greater than any squared correlation of that construct with another latent variable (Fornell & Cha 1994, p. 69; Fornell & Larcker 1981, p. 46). Also, all indicators of a latent variable should have the highest loadings on that variable, i.e. all reflective indicators' loadings should be higher than their cross-loadings (Hair et al. 2011, p. 146).

---

[51] Both bootstrapping and jackknifing are resampling methods. Because it has a smaller standard error, bootstrapping is the preferable method (Huber et al. 2007, p. 35).

Unidimensionality

Unidimensionality means that a set of indicators share only one underlying factor, i.e. all indictors can be clearly assigned to one construct only (Anderson, Gerbing, & Hunter 1987; Segars 1997, p. 108). Hence, measures of a construct and their residuals should only correlate with each other, and cross-correlations between indicators of one construct and another construct should be low (Huber et al. 2007, p. 37; Segars 1997, pp. 117f.).

Stone-Geisser's Q^2 (Communality)

Stone-Geisser's Q^2 indicates "how well the observed values can be reconstructed by the model and its parameters" (Fornell & Cha 1994, p. 72). It compares residuals for indicators predicted by the model with the residuals of a trivial predication. A Q^2 greater than 0 indicates that the relations in the model have predictive relevance (Fornell & Cha 1994, p. 73; Huber et al. 2007, p. 37).

4.3.3.2 Evaluation of the formative measurement model

Formative indicators have a number of properties that sharply distinguish them from reflective indicators, making the procedures used to assess the validity and reliability of reflective indicators inappropriate for formative indicators.[52]

Significance of indicator weights

Indicator weights, loadings and significances can be examined; critical t-values for a two-tailed test are 1.66 (0.1 level) and 1.98 (0.05 level) (Hair et al. 2011, p. 145; Huber et al. 2007, p. 45). However, indicators may not be removed due to low significance levels because this alters the meaning of the construct (Jarvis et al. 2003, p. 202).

Discriminant validity

Huber et al. (2007, p. 38) suggest determining discriminant validity in the formative measurement model by determining correlations between latent variables, instead of comparing squared correlations to AVE, as in the reflective measurement model. Correlations should not exceed a value of 0.9.

Multicollinearity

Diamantopoulos and Winklhofer (2001) emphasize the importance of evaluating indicator multicollinearity. Multicollinearity means that one indicator can be predicted by the other

---

[52] For a detailed description of how differences in indicator properties impact evaluation, see Diamantopoulos and Winklhofer (2001, p. 271).

indicators. Since indicators in the formative measurement model are considered independent, there should be no multicollinearity.

Multicollinearity is examined by each construct's variance inflation factor (VIF), which is based on the share of variance of an indicator explained by the other indicators of that construct (Huber et al. 2007, p. 39). VIF is calculated with regression analysis and should be smaller than 5 (Hair et al. 2011, p. 145).

$$VIF = \frac{1}{1 - R^2}$$

Table 4-6 summarises all procedures used to evaluate the measurement model.

Procedure	Reflective measurement model	Formative measurement model
Weights	irrelevant	not specified
Loading	> 0.7 > 0.4 for exploratory studies	irrelevant
t-value	> 1.66 one-tailed (0.05 level) > 1.29 one-tailed (0.1 level)	> 1.98 two-tailed (0.05 level) > 1.66 two-tailed (0.1 level)
Convergent validity	composite reliability > 0.7 AVE > 0.6	not applicable
Discriminant validity	• Fornell-Larcker-criterion: AVE of a constructs should be greater than any squared correlation of that construct with another variable • Cross-loadings: all indicators of a latent variable should have the highest loadings on that variable	correlations between latent variables < 0.9
Unidimensionality	measures of a construct and their residuals should only correlate with each other	not applicable
Predictive relevance	Stone-Geisser's $Q^2 > 0$	not applicable
Multicollinearity	not applicable	VIF < 5

Table 4-6: Evaluation of the measurement model

Source: Own design, adapted from Huber et al. (2007, p. 45)

4.3.3.3   Evaluation of the structural model

Significance of path coefficients

Evaluation of the structural model serves the examination of hypotheses. Whether a hypothesis is retained or rejected is decided by examining path coefficients and their t-values. Significance of path coefficients can be evaluated with t-values obtained through bootstrapping. Chin (1998, p. 324) suggests acceptance of path coefficients starting at a value of 0.2. For significance at the 0.01 level, the t-value should be at least 2.58 (two-tailed); for significance at the 0.05 level, the t-value should be at least 1.98 (two-tailed); for significance at the 0.1 level, the t-value should be at least 1.66 (two-tailed) (Hair et al. 2011, p. 145; Huber et al. 2007, p. 45). If the t-value falls below 1.66, the hypothesis has to be rejected.

Variance explained (R^2)

In order to evaluate the structural model, R^2 can be used, which is known as the proportion of variance explained by the model within total variance. R^2 greater than 0.67 is substantial, while values around 0.33 and 0.19 are moderate and weak, respectively (Chin 1998, p. 323; Ringle 2004b, p. 15). R^2 can only be used for the evaluation of endogenous constructs; values of 0.3 and above are desirable (Huber et al. 2013, p. 64).

Stone-Geisser's Q^2 (Redundancy)

Stone-Geisser's Q^2 can be used to test predictive relevance. Q^2-values greater than 0 indicate that the relations in the model have predictive relevance, i.e. that the exogenous constructs "have predictive relevance for the endogenous construct under consideration" (Hair et al. 2011, p. 145).

Multicollinearity

In order to control for multicollinearity between the constructs influencing an endogenous construct, regression analysis can be conducted for each endogenous construct at a time. VIF values can be computed and should not exceed a value of 5 (Hair et al. 2011, p. 145; Huber et al. 2013, p. 64).

Procedure	Structural model
t-value	> 2.58 two-tailed (0.01 level)
	> 1.98 two-tailed (0.05 level)
	> 1.66 two-tailed (0.1 level)
R^2	> 0.3
Predictive relevance	Stone-Geisser's $Q^2 > 0$
Multicollinearity	VIF < 5

Table 4-7: Evaluation of the structural model

Source: Own design, adapted from Huber et al. (2007, p. 45)

4.4 Operationalisation

In order to test the causal relationships hypothesized in chapter 3, the latent variables need to be operationalised, i.e. observable variables describing them need to be identified. These indicators have to be formulated as statements suitable for a survey in order to allow respondents to evaluate them (Stichnoth 2008, p. 54).

The following sections describe the operationalisation of the latent variables, including the items used for the survey which correspond to the respective indicators. Since respondents received the questionnaire in German, German versions of the questions are provided in Appendix A.[53]

4.4.1 Brand Loyalty

For products like television programmes that are intangible and do not have a price, the willingness to pay a price premium cannot be used as an indicator for brand loyalty. Hence, loyalty cannot purely be measured by established indicators. Alternatives might be usage frequency or recommendations. Dick and Basu (1994, p. 107) suggest favourable word-of-mouth as an indicator for brand loyalty, in addition to reduced motivation to search for alternative products and a resistance to counter-persuasion. For serialised television brands in particular, two more indicators might be continued willingness to watch the series or serial even if it is moved to a less favourable slot in the schedule, or continued consumption on the respective television channel if the brand is also available on other media, allowing for timeshifted television.

---

[53] The translation was reviewed by a professional translator.

On the basis of conceptualisations in the literature, commonly used items are applied to serialised TV brands and new items that appear suitable for serialised TV brands are added. Hence, in this study, following Oliver's (1999, p. 34) definition that loyalty is a "deeply held commitment to rebuy or repatronize a preferred product/service consistently in the future", brand loyalty consists of

- the intention to watch the serialised TV brand the next time it runs on TV, based on the concepts of attitudinal loyalty and repeat purchase as derived from Oliver's definition (Chaudhuri & Holbrook 2001; Jacoby & Chestnut 1978; Oliver 1999);
- the intention to keep watching the serialised TV brand, based on the concepts of attitudinal loyalty and continued purchase as derived from Oliver's definition (Chaudhuri & Holbrook 2001; Jacoby & Chestnut 1978; Oliver 1999);
- the willingness to pay for the serialised TV brand if it was not available free of charge, based on the assumption that brand loyal consumers are willing to pay a price premium (Chaudhuri & Holbrook 2001);
- the willingness to watch the serialised TV brand even if it was moved to a less favourable programme slot, based on the assumption that brand loyal customers purchase the brand again despite situational influences and marketing (Oliver 1999);
- the willingness to recommend the serialised TV brand to friends, based on the assumption that favourable word-of-mouth is an indicator for brand loyalty (Dick & Basu 1994).

These indicators translate into the following scale used for evaluation by respondents of the questionnaire:

- Reflective indicators
- Q: How would you describe your commitment to [the serialised TV brand]?
- 7-point Likert scale (fully agree – fully disagree)

Item #	Item description	Source
BL_1	I will watch [the serialised TV brand] the next time it runs on TV.	adapted from Chaudhuri & Holbrook 2001 Jacoby & Chestnut 1978 Oliver 1999
BL_2	I intend to keep watching [the serialised TV brand].	adapted from Chaudhuri & Holbrook 2001 Jacoby & Chestnut 1978 Oliver 1999
BL_3	I would be willing to pay for [the serialised TV brand] if it was not available free of charge.	adapted from Chaudhuri & Holbrook 2001
BL_4	I would be willing to watch [the serialised TV brand] even if it was moved to a less favourable programme slot.	own design based on Oliver 1999
BL_5	I would recommend [the serialised TV brand] to my friends.	own design based on Dick & Basu 1994

Table 4-8: Operationalisation of construct BL

Source: Own design

4.4.2   Consumer-brand relationship

Probably the most well-known attempt to operationalise the consumer-brand relationship is Fournier's work (1994; 1998). With reference to Blackston (1992) and Fournier (1994; 1998), brand relationship quality can be defined as the relationship of a consumer toward a brand as a relationship partner and consisting of interdependence, temporality, and an emotional or substantive bond. According to the framework of identity-based brand management, it links the two concepts of brand identity and brand image.

However, Fournier's approach has been widely reviewed and criticized over the years: Firstly, the application of her scale is complicated and secondly, empirical validation stands to question (for a detailed description of work completed with regard to Fournier's scale, refer to Wenske 2008, pp. 102ff.). Wenske attempted to prove that Fournier's scale could be reduced to an eight item unidimensional scale and subsequently succeeded in proving the reliability of the indicators she had chosen (ibid., pp. 212ff.).

The consumer-brand relationship scale used in this study is the one developed by Wenske (2008) based on Fournier's work. Wenske proved the unidimensionality of the construct (p.

214) which consists of eight indicators (p. 212). The scale was used and proved reliable in Arnhold's dissertation (2010, p. 242) that investigates user generated brand related content with regard to consumer goods. It was slightly modified for this study in order to correspond better to a television programme so that the consumer-brand relationship in this study means

- the impression that the serialised TV brand shows an interest in the respondent's well-being,
- the respondent loving the serialised TV brand,
- fond memories attached to the serialised TV brand,
- a perceived similarity between the serialised TV brand's image and the respondent's self-image,
- familiarity with the serialised TV brand's characteristics,
- the perception that the overall relationship with the serialised TV brand is of high quality.

These indicators translate into a six-item scale[54] with the following characteristics:

- Reflective indicators
- Q: How would you describe your relationship with [the serialised TV brand]?
- 7-point Likert scale (fully agree – fully disagree)

Item #	Item description	Source
CBR_1	[The serialised TV brand] shows an interest in my well-being.	Wenske 2008
CBR_2	I love [the serialised TV brand].	Wenske 2008
CBR_3	I have lots of fond memories I attach to [the serialised TV brand].	Wenske 2008
CBR_4	[The serialised TV brand's] image and my self-image are very similar.	Wenske 2008
CBR_5	I am entirely familiar with [the serialised TV brand's] characteristics.	Wenske 2008
CBR_6	My overall relationship to [the serialised TV brand] is of high quality.	Wenske 2008

Table 4-9: Operationalisation of construct CBR

Source: Own design

---

[54] Items "I do not want to miss the brand in my life." and "I am a loyal customer of the brand." from Wenske's original scale were deleted in order to clearly distinguish the construct from brand loyalty.

4.4.3 Attitude toward the social media programme for the serialised TV brand

A social media programme attitude scale measuring attitude toward a company-sponsored programme of user generated brand related content was developed and validated by Arnhold (2010, p. 239) and is based on the works of Lee and Mason (1999), Lynch, Kent, and Srinivasan (2001), and Stichnoth (2008). In the tradition of this prior research, attitude toward the social media programme of the serialised TV brand is operationalised as

- being interested in the social media programme for the serialised TV brand,
- finding the topic of the social media programme for the serialised TV brand appealing,
- finding the social media programme for the serialised TV brand attractive,
- being able to easily identify with the social media programme for the serialised TV brand,
- thinking that the social media programme for the serialised TV brand has a good reputation,
- finding that the social media programme for the serialised TV brand lives up to its promises,
- finding the social media programme for the serialised TV brand well done,
- liking the social media programme for the serialised TV brand,
- feeling entertained by the social media programme for the serialised TV brand, an item that is added with particular reference to the TV brands under investigation in this study.

This translates into a nine-item scale with the following items and characteristics:

- Reflective indicators
- Q: How do you like the social media programme for [the serialised TV brand]?
- 7-point Likert scale (fully agree – fully disagree)

Item #	Item description	Source
SMP_1	The social media programme for [the serialised TV brand] interests me.	Arnhold 2010 Stichnoth 2008
SMP_2	The topic of the social media programme for [the serialised TV brand] is appealing to me.	Arnhold 2010 Stichnoth 2008
SMP_3	The social media programme for [the serialised TV brand] is attractive to me.	Arnhold 2010 Stichnoth 2008
SMP_4	I can easily identify with the social media programme for [the serialised TV brand].	Arnhold 2010 Stichnoth 2008
SMP_5	The social media programme for [the serialised TV brand] has a good reputation.	Arnhold 2010 Stichnoth 2008
SMP_6	The social media programme for [the serialised TV brand] lives up to its promises.	Arnhold 2010 Stichnoth 2008
SMP_7*	The social media programme for [the serialised TV brand] is poor/ in need of improvement.	Arnhold 2010 Stichnoth 2008
SMP_8*	I dislike the social media programme for [the serialised TV brand].	Arnhold 2010 Stichnoth 2008
SMP_9	The social media programme for [the serialised TV brand] is entertaining.	own design

Table 4-10: Operationalisation of construct SMP

* reverse coded

Source: Own design

4.4.4 Engagement in the social media programme for the serialised TV brand

User engagement with the social media programme is operationalised as a mixture of involvement and usage intensity. The scale is based on the work of Christodoulides et al. (2012), who developed a scale for involvement based on Zaichkowsky's (1994) reduced PII scale for involvement and a scale for community based on the works of McMillan and Chavis (1986) as well as Muniz and O'Guinn (2001). Two further items were added in order to better address the specific research question, i.e. to directly refer the scale to usage of the social media programme of a serialised TV brand. This resulted in the following five-item scale:

- Reflective indicators
- Q: How would you describe your level of engagement in social media offerings for [the serialised TV brand]?
- 7-point Likert scale (fully agree – fully disagree)

Item #	Item description	Source
SME_1	During the season, I frequently (at least once every week) engage in social media offerings for [the serialised TV brand].	own design
SME_2	I am an active user of social media offerings for [the serialised TV brand], i.e., I do usually contribute.	own design
SME_3	I engage in social media offerings for [the serialised TV brand] because of a shared interest in [the serialised TV brand].	Christodoulides et al. 2012
SME_4	The social media offerings for [the serialised TV brand] mean a lot to me.	Zaichkowsky 1994
SME_5	The social media offerings for [the serialised TV brand] interest me.	Zaichkowsky 1994

Table 4-11: Operationalisation of construct SME

Source: Own design

4.4.5 Gratifications obtained from the social media programme

For gratifications obtained from the social media programme for the serialised TV brand, an index is designed that incorporates television experience factors as well as an extension with regard to social media (cf. 3.1.5). Although television gratifications have been researched and identified in a number of studies (e.g. Haridakis 2002; Kim & Rubin 1997; Palmgreen & Lawrence 1991; Papacharissi & Mendelson 2007), index construction is based on television experience factors emotionality, orientation, balance, pastime, and social experience by Dehm and Storll (2003), because these indicators have been identified for a German viewership, which corresponds to the sample used in this study, and because these experience factors have been reviewed in a television and in an internet context (Dehm et al. 2005; 2006). The factor "emotionality" is rephrased to "entertainment" for measurement due to better fit with wording in other studies and with the particular TV brands under investigation.

An additional indicator focusing on interaction is added to account for social media specifics (e.g. Busemann et al. 2012; Foregger 2008; Nardi et al. 2004; Park et al. 2009; Quan-Haase & Young 2010; Raacke & Bonds-Raacke 2008).

The construct is operationalised with formative indicators because it is hypothesized that if these indicators, i.e. expectations, are met, consumers obtain their desired gratifications.

This results in the following index:

- Formative indicators
- Q: In how far does [the social media programme for the serialised TV brand] meet your expectations with regard to…?
- 7-point Likert scale (completely – not at all)

Item #	Item description	Source
GOS_1	interesting information	Dehm & Storll 2003
GOS_2	entertainment	e.g. Palmgreen & Lawrence 1991
GOS_3	generates ideas[55]	Dehm & Storll 2003
GOS_4	forget everyday concerns	Dehm & Storll 2003
GOS_5	enjoyable and convenient pastime	Dehm & Storll 2003
GOS_6	sense of belonging	Dehm & Storll 2003
GOS_7	be in touch with likeminded people	e.g. Quan-Haase & Young 2010; Foregger 2008

Table 4-12: Operationalisation of construct GOS
Source: Own design

4.4.6 Gratifications obtained from the serialised TV brand

For gratifications obtained from the serialised TV brand, the index developed for gratifications obtained from the social media programme for the serialised TV brand is used again, but without the seventh item, i.e. the interaction item.

- Formative indicators
- Q: In how far does [the serialised TV brand] meet your expectations with regard to…?
- 7-point Likert scale (completely – not at all)

---

[55] Original dimension referred to the providing of orientation, which does not seem suitable for this study.

Item #	Item description	Source
GO_1	interesting information	Dehm & Storll 2003
GO_2	entertainment	e.g. Palmgreen & Lawrence 1991
GO_3	generates ideas[56]	Dehm & Storll 2003
GO_4	forget everyday concerns	Dehm & Storll 2003
GO_5	enjoyable and convenient pastime	Dehm & Storll 2003
GO_6	sense of belonging	Dehm & Storll 2003

Table 4-13: Operationalisation of construct GO

Source: Own design

4.4.7   Perceived critics' response

Perceived critics' response refers to critics' reactions or reviews with regard to the serialised TV brand, as perceived by the consumers. The construction of the scale was based on the findings of what influences product success with regard to critics' reviews, as well as on media research and findings on how messages reach the audience. Relevant elements of perceived critics' response are that

- the TV brand is talked/written about (agenda-setting),
- the TV brand is discussed controversially (negative and extreme views),
- critics actively recommend the TV brand (influence effect),
- the TV brand is talked/written about in a favourable context (priming / framing).

This leads to the construction of a four-item scale with reflective indicators.
- Reflective indicators
- Q: What is your perception of critics' response to [the serialised TV brand]?
- 7-point Likert scale (fully agree – fully disagree)

---

[56] Original dimension referred to the providing of orientation, which does not seem suitable for this study.

Item #	Item description	Source
Pcr_1	From what I have heard/read, [the serialised TV brand] is talked and/or written about a lot in the media.	Iyengar & Kinder 1987
Pcr_2	I think that [the serialised TV brand] is discussed controversially by critics.	Clement, Proppe, & Rott 2007
Pcr_3	I think that critics actively recommend [the serialised TV brand].	Reinstein & Snyder 2005
Pcr_4	To my knowledge, [the serialised TV brand] is talked/written about in a favourable context.	Iyengar & Kinder 1987

Table 4-14: Operationalisation of construct PCR

Source: Own design

4.4.8 Perceived WOM response

Perceived WOM response refers to reactions from users' online and offline social network toward the serialised TV brand as registered by the user, i.e. perceived recommendations and positive comments from the online and offline social network. The scale used is based on Romaniuk's (2007) study on WOM communication referring to television programmes.

- Reflective indicators
- Q: What is your perception of other people's response to [the serialised TV brand]?
- 7-point Likert scale (fully agree – fully disagree)

Item #	Item description	Source
Pwr_1	My friends talked positively about it.	Romaniuk 2007
Pwr_2	My friends recommended it.	Romaniuk 2007
Pwr_3	Friends in my online social network talked positively about it.	adapted from Romaniuk 2007
Pwr_4	Friends in my online social network recommended it.	adapted from Romaniuk 2007

Table 4-15: Operationalisation of construct PWR

Source: Own design

5   Empirical model evaluation and hypothesis testing

Chapter 5 deals with the empirical model evaluation and the testing of hypotheses. It starts out with the evaluation of the measurement and the structural models, using the PLS algorithm. After the evaluation of the complete model, moderating effects are examined by conducting group comparisons (section 5.4.1) and by investigating interaction effects (5.4.2). After that, selected constructs are further examined by exploratory data analysis (section 5.5). To determine statistically significant differences within constructs, Kruskal-Wallis tests are used because the data is not normally distributed, as will be shown with exploratory data analysis. Sections 5.5.2 and 5.5.3 summarise the outcomes of the extended questionnaire on TV and social media usage for the user and the non-user samples, respectively. Section 5.7 concludes the chapter with an outline of the findings of empirical model evaluation and hypothesis testing.

5.1   Evaluation of the measurement model

The evaluation of the measurement model starts out by examining the reflective latent variables before continuing with the formative latent variables. T-values were obtained by executing the bootstrapping function in smartPLS[57] (5,000 bootstrap samples).

Indicators BL_3 (I would be willing to pay for [the serialised TV brand] if it was not available free of charge.), SME_5 (The social media offerings for [the serialised TV brand] interest me.), PCR_1 and PCR_2 (From what I have heard/read, [the serialised TV brand] is talked and/or written about a lot in the media. / I think that [the serialised TV brand] is discussed controversially by critics.) were eliminated from the analysis at an earlier stage of model testing because they did not meet the criteria for indicator reliability (BL_3, PCR_1 and PCR_2) or the criteria for discriminant validity (SME_5), respectively.

All other indicators remain in the model. Loadings should be at least 0.7 in order to be considered acceptable and the vast majority of indicators meets this criterion. Indicators BL_4, CBR_5, smp_7_r and smp_8_r[58] do not exceed a minimum value of 0.7 but of 0.6. They are kept in the model since this is acceptable for exploratory studies and because the

---

[57] Ringle, C. M., Wende, S., & Will, S.: SmartPLS 2.0 (M3) Beta, Hamburg 2005, http://www.smartpls.de
[58] Items for smp_7 and smp_8 were reverse coded. smp_7_r and smp_8_r are the recoded items used for model testing and evaluation.

respective constructs met all other evaluation criteria. All factor loadings are significant at the
.05 level.

latent variable	indicator	factor loading	standard deviation	t-value
Brand loyalty (BL)	BL_1	0.84**	0.011	76.52
	BL_2	0.89**	0.006	141.91
	BL_4	0.65**	0.017	38.81
	BL_5	0.86**	0.008	111.32
Consumer brand relationship (CBR)	CBR_1	0.76**	0.011	71.46
	CBR_2	0.83**	0.007	126.35
	CBR_3	0.80**	0.009	87.78
	CBR_4	0.77**	0.010	78.94
	CBR_5	0.63**	0.016	38.80
	CBR_6	0.87**	0.006	150.63
Perceived critics' response (PCR)	Pcr_3	0.93**	0.005	200.36
	Pcr_4	0.93**	0.004	214.63
Perceived WOM response (PWR)	Pwr_1	0.83**	0.008	110.23
	Pwr_2	0.86**	0.007	122.97
	Pwr_3	0.87**	0.007	133.85
	Pwr_4	0.87**	0.007	126.73
Engagement in the social media programme for the serialised TV brand (SME)	sme_1	0.77**	0.011	73.14
	sme_2	0.77**	0.011	72.68
	sme_3	0.83**	0.008	104.76
	sme_4	0.86**	0.005	168.14
Attitude toward the social media programme for the serialised TV brand (SMP)	smp_1	0.86**	0.008	110.89
	smp_2	0.84**	0.007	115.50
	smp_3	0.86**	0.007	119.13
	smp_4	0.76**	0.012	65.83
	smp_5	0.77**	0.011	70.05
	smp_6	0.80**	0.011	72.73
	smp_7_r	0.64**	0.018	35.71
	smp_8_r	0.63**	0.022	28.89
	smp_9	0.84**	0.008	111.14

Table 5-1: Evaluation of the reflective measurement model – indicator reliability

Source: Own design and computation

**   significant at the .05 level (> 1.66 one-tailed)

*   significant at the .1 level (> 1.29 one-tailed)

Criteria for convergent validity are met as well. Composite reliability exceeds the minimum value of 0.7 and AVE exceeds the minimum value of 0.6 for all constructs.

	AVE	Composite Reliability	R Square
BL	0.66	0.89	0.45
CBR	0.61	0.90	0.54
PCR	0.87	0.93	0.00
PWR	0.73	0.92	0.00
SME	0.65	0.88	0.41
SMP	0.61	0.93	0.45

Table 5-2: Evaluation of the reflective measurement model – overview of quality criteria

Source: Own design and computation

Criteria for discriminant validity are also met. The Fornell-Larcker criterion, according to which AVE of a reflective latent construct should be greater than any squared correlation of that construct with another latent variable, is met: The lowest AVE is 0.61, while the highest value for squared correlations is 0.48 (see Table 5-3 and Appendix D). All indicators had the highest loadings on "their" latent variable, i.e. there were no cross-loadings (for a full table of cross-loadings, see Appendix D).

	BL	CBR	GO	GOS	PCR	PWR	SME	SMP
BL	1	0	0	0	0	0	0	0
CBR	0.32	1	0	0	0	0	0	0
GO	0.32	0.41	1	0	0	0	0	0
GOS	0.24	0.30	0.48	1	0	0	0	0
PCR	0.12	0.15	0.13	0.11	1	0	0	0
PWR	0.27	0.28	0.27	0.21	0.26	1	0	0
SME	0.21	0.36	0.26	0.30	0.10	0.20	1	0
SMP	0.35	0.32	0.40	0.45	0.14	0.26	0.38	1

Table 5-3: Squared latent variable correlations

Source: Own design and computation

Criteria for unidimensionality are met, i.e. all indictors can be clearly assigned to one construct only as shown by factor analysis (Varimax).

Component	BL	CBR	SMP	SME	PCR	PWR
BL_1	0.79	0.17	0.18	0.17	0.00	0.16
BL_2	0.79	0.21	0.30	0.04	0.05	0.15
BL_4	0.59	0.12	0.18	0.18	0.12	0.05
BL_5	0.67	0.25	0.31	0.07	0.18	0.27
CBR_1	0.01	0.73	0.25	0.14	0.14	0.13
CBR_2	0.39	0.64	0.23	0.18	0.05	0.19
CBR_3	0.21	0.71	0.14	0.19	0.09	0.13
CBR_4	0.06	0.71	0.18	0.24	0.15	0.12
CBR_5	0.13	0.63	0.12	0.06	-0.06	0.15
CBR_6	0.25	0.75	0.22	0.17	0.14	0.16
SMP_1	0.25	0.14	0.76	0.24	0.09	0.16
SMP_2	0.26	0.23	0.67	0.30	0.05	0.17
SMP_3	0.22	0.14	0.79	0.19	0.06	0.13
SMP_4	0.16	0.25	0.60	0.28	0.11	0.16
SMP_5	0.19	0.22	0.65	0.18	0.12	0.16
SMP_6	0.18	0.19	0.73	0.16	0.02	0.15
SMP_7_r	-0.00	0.11	0.72	-0.00	0.11	0.06
SMP_8_r	0.10	0.12	0.66	0.00	0.11	0.08
SMP_9	0.20	0.13	0.75	0.27	0.02	0.15
SME_1	0.27	0.15	0.22	0.66	-0.05	0.12
SME_2	0.03	0.20	0.15	0.76	0.13	0.09
SME_3	0.14	0.21	0.25	0.72	0.04	0.15
SME_4	0.10	0.38	0.37	0.63	0.15	0.12
PCR_3	0.12	0.15	0.16	0.10	0.86	0.22
PCR_4	0.11	0.14	0.18	0.09	0.84	0.25
PWR_1	0.28	0.19	0.23	-0.05	0.27	0.70
PWR_2	0.21	0.19	0.19	0.01	0.20	0.77
PWR_3	0.11	0.20	0.19	0.27	0.10	0.78
PWR_4	0.07	0.20	0.17	0.27	0.09	0.80

Table 5-4: Rotated component matrix

Source: Own design and computation

With the blindfolding method, construct crossvalidated communality was calculated in order to examine Stone-Geisser's Q^2. All reflective latent variables meet the criteria, i.e. $Q^2 > 0$.

	Stone-Geisser's Q^2 (Communality)
BL	0.45
CBR	0.46
PCR	0.83
PWR	0.70
SME	0.66
SMP	0.61

Table 5-5: Stone-Geisser's Q^2 (Communality)

Source: Own design and computation

Hence, the reflective measurement model meets all quality criteria. The evaluation of the formative measurement model starts out by examining indicator weights and significances.

latent variable	indicator[59]	weights	standard deviation	t-value
Gratifications obtained from the social media programme for the serialised TV brand (GOS)	GOS_1_r	0.35**	0.035	9.87
	GOS_2_r	0.16**	0.037	4.33
	GOS_3_r	0.18**	0.030	5.87
	GOS_4_r	0.08**	0.028	2.82
	GOS_5_r	0.21**	0.034	6.24
	GOS_6_r	0.25**	0.032	7.74
	GOS_7_r	0.04	0.027	1.62
Gratifications obtained from the serialised TV brand (GO)	GO_1_r	0.32**	0.035	9.03
	GO_2_r	0.26**	0.039	6.77
	GO_3_r	0.11**	0.033	3.26
	GO_4_r	0.03	0.021	1.18
	GO_5_r	0.30**	0.037	8.11
	GO_6_r	0.29**	0.031	9.28

Table 5-6: Evaluation of the formative measurement model – indicator weights

Source: Own design and computation

** significant at the .05 level (> 1.98 two-tailed)

* significant at the .1 level (> 1.66 two-tailed)

The weight for indicator GOS_4 is rather low, it is, however, significant at the .05 level. The weights of indicators GOS_7 and GO_4 are not significant. However, despite their coming short of meeting the relevant quality criteria, being formative indicators, they remain in the measurement model.

Discriminant validity, in the formative measurement model, is examined by determining correlations between latent variables which should not exceed a value of 0.9. This criterion is met.

---

[59] GOS_1 is called GOS_1_r (and so forth) because of a recoding issue due to questionnaire software setup.

	BL	CBR	GO	GOS	PCR	PWR	SME	SMP
BL	1	0	0	0	0	0	0	0
CBR	0.56	1	0	0	0	0	0	0
GO	0.56	0.64	1	0	0	0	0	0
GOS	0.49	0.55	0.69	1	0	0	0	0
PCR	0.35	0.39	0.37	0.34	1	0	0	0
PWR	0.52	0.53	0.52	0.46	0.51	1	0	0
SME	0.46	0.60	0.51	0.55	0.32	0.45	1	0
SMP	0.59	0.57	0.63	0.67	0.38	0.51	0.62	1

Table 5-7: Latent variable correlations

Source: Own design and computation

Multicollinearity is examined by each construct's variance inflation factor (VIF), which is supposed to be lower than 5 and calculated via regression analyses. VIF is considerably lower than 5 for all indicators of both formative constructs GOS and GO.

formative construct GOS	adjusted R^2	VIF
dependent indicator GOS_1_r	0.60	2.50
dependent indicator GOS_2_r	0.64	2.77
dependent indicator GOS_3_r	0.45	1.82
dependent indicator GOS_4_r	0.43	1.76
dependent indicator GOS_5_r	0.64	2.75
dependent indicator GOS_6_r	0.50	2.00
dependent indicator GOS_7_r	0.40	1.66

Table 5-8: Examining multicollinearity for construct GOS

Source: Own design and computation

formative construct GO	adjusted R^2	VIF
dependent indicator GO_1_r	0.58	2.40
dependent indicator GO_2_r	0.56	2.25
dependent indicator GO_3_r	0.56	2.28
dependent indicator GO_4_r	0.38	1.61
dependent indicator GO_5_r	0.57	2.34
dependent indicator GO_6_r	0.40	1.68

Table 5-9: Examining multicollinearity for construct GO

Source: Own design and computation

Hence, measurement model evaluation leads to the conclusion that the measurement model meets the required criteria. This allows for an evaluation of the structural model and hypothesis testing.

5.2   Evaluation of the structural model

In order to evaluate the structural model, R^2 and Stone-Geisser's Q^2 are examined. To obtain Q^2 values, the blindfolding procedure in smartPLS is executed. All R^2 values are above 0.3 with the exception of R^2 of GO. However, since it exceeds the value of 0.25, it is still considered acceptable. All Q^2 values exceed 0, meaning that for all endogenous constructs under consideration, the respective exogenous constructs have predictive relevance.

	R^2	Q^2
BL	0.45	0.29
CBR	0.54	0.32
GO	0.28	0.15
SME	0.41	0.26
SMP	0.45	0.28

Table 5-10: Evaluation of the structural model – R^2 and Q^2

Source: Own design and computation

In order to control for multicollinearity between the constructs influencing an endogenous construct, regression analyses were conducted for each endogenous construct at a time. For this, standardised construct values had to be computed, based on the constructs' indicators and weights as derived from measurement model evaluation.[60] VIF values were then computed and did not exceed the required value of 5 for any of the analyses (for full tables, cf. Appendix D), meaning that there are no multicollinearity issues in the structural model.

The structural model hence meets the required quality criteria. What follows is the most important part of structural model evaluation, hypothesis testing, which is based on the examination of path coefficients and t-values. To proceed with hypothesis testing, significance of path coefficients is examined to decide whether hypotheses can be accepted. T-values are obtained through bootstrapping. If the t-value falls below 1.66, the hypothesis has to be rejected.

---

[60] For a detailed description of how to compute standardised construct values, refer to Huber et al. (2007, pp. 109ff.).

hypothesis	path	path coefficient	standard deviation	t-value	evaluation
H1	CBR -> BL	0.2527	0.026	9.93***	accept
H2	SMP -> BL	0.3242	0.032	10.30***	accept
H3	SMP -> CBR	0.0467	0.024	1.99**	accept
H4	SME -> BL	0.0101	0.015	0.69	*reject*
H5	SME -> CBR	0.2895	0.020	14.78***	accept
H6	SMP -> SME	0.4609	0.026	17.63***	accept
H7	GOS -> CBR	0.0453	0.024	1.88*	accept
H8	GOS -> SME	0.2360	0.027	8.66***	accept
H9	GOS -> SMP	0.6720	0.019	34.77***	accept
H10	GO -> BL	0.1900	0.033	5.82***	accept
H11	GO -> CBR	0.3256	0.027	12.21***	accept
H12	PCR -> CBR	0.0644	0.017	3.75***	accept
H13	PCR -> GO	0.1389	0.021	6.51***	accept
H14	PWR -> CBR	0.1528	0.023	6.62***	accept
H15	PWR -> GO	0.4498	0.022	20.36***	accept

Table 5-11: Evaluation of the structural model – hypothesis testing

Source: Own design and computation

***   significant at the .01 level (> 2.58 two-tailed)

**   significant at the .05 level (> 1.98 two-tailed)

*   significant at the .1 level (> 1.66 two-tailed)

T-values indicate that with the exception of H4, which has to be rejected, all hypotheses can be accepted. H7 is accepted at the .1 level, H3 at the .05 level; all other hypotheses are accepted at the .01 level.

Since many constructs impact the outcome variable BL via various paths, total cumulative effects can be computed with regard to BL:

input construct		total effect on BL
SMP	H2+H3*H1+H6*H5*H1	0.37
SME	H5*H1	0.07
GOS	H7*H1+H8*H5*H1+H9*H3*H1+H9*H2+H9*H6*H5*H1	0.28
PWR	H14*H1+H15*H11*H1+H15*H10	0.16
PCR	H12*H1+H13*H11*H1+H13*H10	0.05
GO	H11*H1+H10	0.27

Table 5-12: Total effects on construct BL

Source: Own design and computation

In addition to having the strongest direct influence on brand loyalty (BL), attitude toward the social media programme (SMP) also influences brand loyalty via engagement and the consumer-brand relationship, thereby creating an even stronger cumulative effect. Other important effects are these of gratifications obtained from the television (GO) and the social media programme (GOS) on brand loyalty. These paths will be discussed and interpreted in greater detail alongside the direct paths in the following section.

5.3 Summary of results of model evaluation and hypothesis testing

The evaluation of the model has shown that most hypotheses can be accepted and that operationalisation of the constructs is largely acceptable as well. The brand loyalty construct as conceptualised and operationalised in this study proved a viable concept.

BL_3, "I would be willing to pay for [the serialised TV brand] if it was not available free of charge." had to be eliminated from the scale. This is not very surprising since being willing to pay a higher price for a product, which is part of the brand loyalty concept as used in other studies, means moving away from a learned price of zero in the case of TV content. Free alternatives being available as well as (illegal) online availability cause the price to keep tending towards zero because it is difficult to introduce paid content in such an environment (Picot et al. 2009; Shapiro & Varian 1999, pp. 20ff.).

The newly developed television specific indicator BL_4 "I would be willing to watch [the serialised TV brand] even if it was moved to a less favourable programme slot." could be proven a valuable contribution to the construct. With regard to hypotheses, SMP has the strongest impact on BL, the path SMP -> BL (H2; $\beta = 0.32$; $t = 10.30$ (sig. .01)) being the strongest with regard to BL. This means that a positive attitude towards the social media programme for the respective brand strongly influences loyalty towards it, i.e. willingness to continue watching it and to recommend it to others. Summing up all direct and indirect influences of SMP on BL, a cumulative impact[61] of 0.37 can be detected.

2	Attitude toward the social media programme for the serialised TV brand positively affects brand loyalty.	accept

It could also be shown that the consumer-brand relationship (CBR) does in fact positively impact brand loyalty (H1; $\beta = 0.25$; $t = 9.93$ (sig. .01)).

1	The consumer-brand relationship positively influences brand loyalty.	accept

---

[61] Total effect SMP -> BL: H2 + H3*H1 + H6*H5*H1 = 0.32+ 0.01 + 0.03 = 0.37

GOS impacts BL via the indirect path H9*H2, i.e. SMP mediates the relationship between GOS and BL. Hence, the fulfilment of gratifications with regard to the social media programme positively impacts attitude toward the social media programme, which in turn positively impacts brand loyalty. Summing up all direct and indirect influences of GOS on BL, a cumulative effect (H9*H2 + H7*H1 + H9*H3*H1 + H9*H6*H5*H1 + H8*H5*H1) of 0.28 can be detected. This impact is stronger than the direct impact of gratifications obtained from the TV brand on brand loyalty (GO -> BL: H10; $\beta = 0.19$; $t = 5.82$ (sig. .01)), but roughly equals the impact of GO on BL, if total effects are taken into account, which adds up to 0.27 (H11*H1 + H10).

| 10 | Gratifications obtained from the serialised TV brand positively affect brand loyalty. | accept |

H4, asserting a direct influence of engagement in the social media programme for the serialised TV brand on brand loyalty, has to be rejected (SME -> BL ($\beta = 0.01$; $t = 0.69$)) due to insignificance.

| 4 | Engagement in the social media programme for the serialised TV brand positively affects brand loyalty. | *reject* |

Hence, a direct influence is not detectable. The same holds true for the indirect path via CBR, the path coefficient being too low, meaning there is no mediating effect detectable.

The operationalisation used for the consumer-brand relationship proved suitable for this study, as all indicators meet the required quality criteria. GO has the strongest individual influence on CBR (H11: GO -> CBR; $\beta = 0.33$; $t = 12.21$ (sig. .01)), meaning that gratifications obtained from the serialised TV brand have the strongest influence on the consumer-brand relationship, which in turn impacts brand loyalty. A mediating effect of CBR on the GO-BL relationship could not be detected due to a very low path coefficient,[62] but summarising direct and indirect influences adds up to a cumulative impact of GO on BL of 0.27 (H10 + H11*H1), which roughly equals the effect of GOS on BL (see above).

| 11 | Gratifications obtained from the serialised TV brand positively affect the consumer-brand relationship. | accept |

---

[62] GO -> BL via CBR: H11*H1 = 0.08

Engagement in the social media programme for the serialised TV brand has the second strongest impact on CBR (H5: SME -> CBR; β = 0.29; t = 14.78 (sig. .01)), meaning that increased usage of the social media programme strengthens users' relationship with the brand.

5	Engagement in the social media programme for the serialised TV brand positively affects the consumer-brand relationship.	accept

Users' social environment (PWR) positively impacts the consumer-brand relationship both directly (H14: PWR -> CBR; β = 0.15; t = 6.62 (sig. .01)) and indirectly via GO, which adds up to an indirect effect of 0.15.

14	Perceived WOM response to the serialised TV brand positively affects the consumer-brand relationship.	accept

This influence is stronger than that of critics (H12: PCR -> CBR; β = 0.06; t = 3.75 (sig. .01) / H13*H11: PCR -> CBR via GO (β = 0.05)), H12 and the indirect path both having a path coefficient so low as to be negligible. Since paths are significant and relevant for the computation of total effects, they are kept in the model, but require further investigation.

12	Perceived critics' response to the serialised TV brand positively affects the consumer-brand relationship.	accept

Attitude toward the social media programme (SMP) impacts the consumer-brand relationship only indirectly via SME,[63] the direct path having an unacceptably low path coefficient. Since it is significant at the .05-level (H3: SMP -> CBR; β = 0.05; t = 1.99 (sig. .05)), the path is kept in the model because it is relevant for the computation of total effects.

3	Attitude toward the social media programme for the serialised TV brand positively affects the consumer-brand relationship.	accept

The direct impact of GOS on CBR, significant at the .1-level, also proves meaningless with regard to the path coefficient (H7: GOS -> CBR; β = 0.05; t = 1.88 (sig. .10)), but is kept in the model.

The total effect including indirect paths[64] shows a stronger impact of 0.24.

---

[63] SMP -> CBR via SME: H6*H5 = 0.14
[64] Total effect GOS -> CBR: H9*H3 + H9*H6*H5 + H8*H5 + H7 = 0.03 + 0.09 + 0.07 + 0.05= 0.24

| 7 | Gratifications obtained from the social media programme for the serialised TV brand positively affect the consumer-brand relationship. | accept |
| 7_m | The impact of gratifications obtained from the social media programme for the serialised TV brand on brand loyalty is mediated by the consumer-brand relationship. | *reject* |

Attitude toward the social media programme for the serialised TV brand (SMP) was operationalised using an established scale with one additional new item that met all quality criteria. SMP is strongly influenced by GOS (H9: GOS -> SMP; $\beta = 0.67$; $t = 34.77$ (sig. .01)), GOS -> SMP being the strongest path in the model and supporting the hypothesis that the fulfilment of gratifications with regard to the social media programme positively impacts attitude toward the social media programme, which in turn positively impacts brand loyalty.

| 9 | Gratifications obtained from the social media programme for the serialised TV brand positively affect attitude toward the social media programme for the serialised TV brand. | accept |

Construct SME, engagement with the social media programme, was operationalised on the basis of scales for engagement and involvement, with the addition of items developed for this particular study. Indicator sme_5 "The social media offerings for [the serialised TV brand] interest me." had to be removed due to cross-loading issues. SME is strongly influenced by SMP (H6: SMP -> SME; $\beta = 0.46$; $t = 17.63$ (sig. .01)), supporting the hypothesis that a positive attitude toward the social media programme leads to increased engagement.

| 6 | Attitude toward the social media programme for the serialised TV brand positively affects engagement in the social media programme for the serialised TV brand. | accept |

SME is also positively influenced by GOS (H8: GOS -> SME; $\beta = 0.24$; $t = 8.66$ (sig. .01)); however, the indirect path via SMP is even stronger,[65] indicating a mediating effect.

| 8 | Gratifications obtained from the social media programme for the serialised TV brand positively affect engagement in the social media programme for the serialised TV brand. | accept |

Constructs perceived WOM response (PWR) and perceived critics' response (PCR) deal with influences by the social environment. While PWR is sound in its operationalisation, impacts CBR (H14) and has a strong influence on GO (H15), the scale PCR was measured by had to be reduced by two indicators (PCR_1 and PCR_2) that did not meet the quality criteria for

---

[65]GOS -> SME via SMP: H9*H6 = 0.31

indicator reliability. Also, the impact of PCR on CBR (H12) is so weak as to be negligible and the impact on GO (H13) is rather weak as well. Since the paths are significant, they remain in the model.

13	Perceived critics' response positively affects gratifications obtained from the serialised TV brand.	accept
15	Perceived WOM response to the serialised TV brand positively affects gratifications obtained from the serialised TV brand.	accept

GOS (gratifications obtained from social media programme) and GO (gratifications obtained from the serialised TV brand) are the only constructs with formative indicators. Both were based on scales measuring television gratifications and intentionally operationalised very similarly in order to allow for comparability of gratifications. Due to their formative operationalisation, all indicators remain in the measurement model, despite the fact that weights of indicators GOS_7 and GO_4 were not significant. This indicates that the item "forget everyday concerns" (GO_4) does not significantly contribute to viewers obtaining gratifications from the TV programme. The fact that being in touch with likeminded people (GOS_7) is not a viable gratification users obtain from the social media programme for the serialised TV brand is in line with other findings indicating that communication with other users is not very important in this study (see below). GO is weakly influenced by perceived critics' response (H13: PCR -> GO; β = 0.14; t = 6.51 (sig. .01)) and more strongly by perceived word-of-mouth response (H15: PWR -> GO; β = 0.45; t = 20.36 (sig. .01)). It is striking that while gratifications obtained from the TV brand (GO) strongly impact the consumer-brand relationship (H11), the impact of gratifications obtained from the social media programme (GOS) on CBR is so weak as to be negligible (H7). Instead, GOS strongly impacts SMP and in turn BL. Hence, gratifications with regard to TV predominantly impact the consumer-brand relationship, while gratifications with regard to social media impact brand loyalty.

Altogether, findings from model testing provide first evidence that social media do in fact support and drive television usage by positively impacting both brand loyalty and the consumer-brand relationship.

It can be shown that attitude toward the social media programme strongly impacts brand loyalty: Not only does it have the strongest direct influence on brand loyalty, it also influences it via engagement and the consumer-brand relationship, which results in an even stronger cumulative effect. Attitude toward the social media programme also has a strong positive impact on engagement in the social media programme, which in turn influences the consumer-brand relationship.

A particularly noteworthy finding is that attitude toward the social media programme directly positively affects brand loyalty, while engagement in the social media programme only impacts the consumer-brand relationship directly and therefore influences loyalty via the relationship with the brand only.

The importance of gratifications obtained also becomes apparent in the model. Gratifications obtained from the social media programme positively affect both attitude and engagement directly. Gratifications obtained from the television brand itself are, however, crucial as well: While attitude toward the social media programme has the strongest direct impact on brand loyalty, gratifications obtained from the television brand itself have the strongest direct impact on the consumer-brand relationship.

This means that while social media have a positive effect on brand loyalty, the television brand is the decisive driver for the consumer-brand relationship. However, gratifications obtained from both the social media programme and the TV brand itself impact brand loyalty approximately equally strongly: While gratifications obtained from the TV brand impact brand loyalty with a cumulative effect of 0.27, gratifications obtained from the social media programme impact brand loyalty with a cumulative effect of 0.28.

These findings will be expanded by the analysis of moderating effects in section 5.4. Further insights into selected constructs will be granted by exploratory analysis in section 5.5, and findings of the additional and the non-user questionnaires will be provided in sections 5.5.2 and 5.5.3. Table 5-13 shows an overview of the basic as well as the mediator hypotheses tested and evaluated above. The full structural model, including path coefficients, is shown in Figure 5-1. Having evaluated both the measurement and the structural models, it is now possible to further analyse the data. The following sections therefore deal with moderating effects and exploratory data analysis.

#	Hypothesis	
1	The consumer-brand relationship positively influences brand loyalty.	accept
2	Attitude toward the social media programme for the serialised TV brand positively affects brand loyalty.	accept
3	Attitude toward the social media programme for the serialised TV brand positively affects the consumer-brand relationship.	accept
4	Engagement in the social media programme for the serialised TV brand positively affects brand loyalty.	*reject*
5	Engagement in the social media programme for the serialised TV brand positively affects the consumer-brand relationship.	accept
6	Attitude toward the social media programme for the serialised TV brand positively affects engagement in the social media programme for the serialised TV brand.	accept
7	Gratifications obtained from the social media programme for the serialised TV brand positively affect the consumer-brand relationship.	accept
7_m	The impact of gratifications obtained from the social media programme for the serialised TV brand on brand loyalty is mediated by the consumer-brand relationship.	*reject*
8	Gratifications obtained from the social media programme for the serialised TV brand positively affect engagement in the social media programme for the serialised TV brand.	accept
9	Gratifications obtained from the social media programme for the serialised TV brand positively affect attitude toward the social media programme for the serialised TV brand.	accept
10	Gratifications obtained from the serialised TV brand positively affect brand loyalty.	accept
11	Gratifications obtained from the serialised TV brand positively affect the consumer-brand relationship.	accept
12	Perceived critics' response to the serialised TV brand positively affects the consumer-brand relationship.	accept
13	Perceived critics' response positively affects gratifications obtained from the serialised TV brand.	accept
14	Perceived WOM response to the serialised TV brand positively affects the consumer-brand relationship.	accept
15	Perceived WOM response to the serialised TV brand positively affects gratifications obtained from the serialised TV brand.	accept

Table 5-13: Overview of hypotheses

Source: Own design

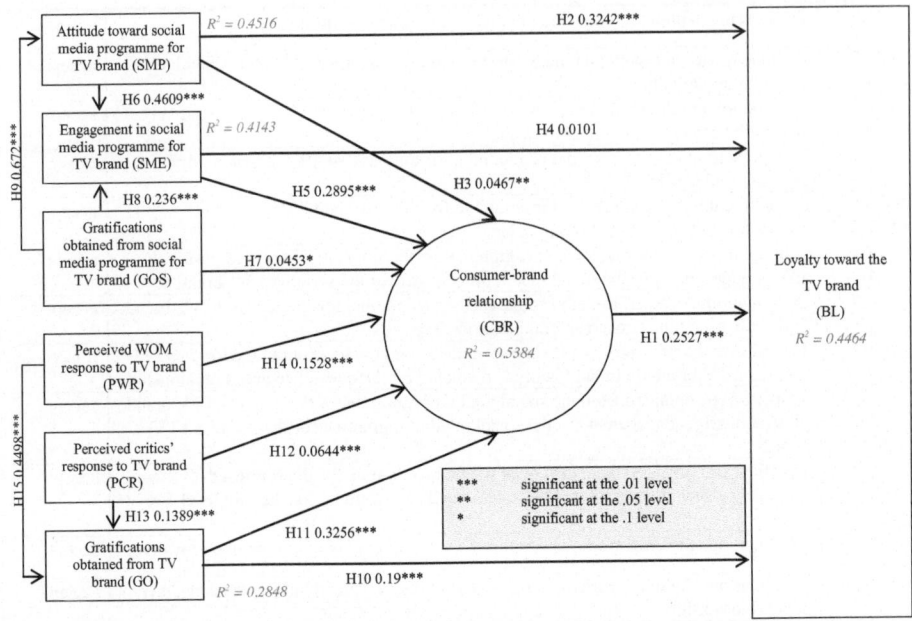

Figure 5-1: Full structural model with path coefficients

Source: Own design

5.4 Investigation of moderating effects

Having tested the comprehensive model, it is of interest if and to which extent relationships between latent variables are subject to further effects. Direct and mediating effects have been analysed above; moderating effects shall be examined next. In PLS, moderating effects can be investigated after testing of the comprehensive model is completed.

Depending on the nature of the moderating variable, different approaches can be used to investigate moderating effects. If the moderating effect is based on a categorical moderator variable like gender, multigroup comparisons can be used (Henseler & Chin 2010, p. 107; Huber et al. 2007, pp. 49f.). In multigroup comparison, the full sample is split into subsamples and the causal relationships examined for the overall model are investigated for subsamples (Nitzl 2010, p. 43), i.e. it is examined whether outcomes significantly differ between groups.

Multigroup comparisons are, however, less adequate to examine metric moderating variables; instead, an interaction term can be introduced into the model (Nitzl 2010, p. 47). Both approaches are used in this study with different objectives.

5.4.1 Group comparisons

Huber et al. (2007, pp. 48ff.; 2013, pp. 65ff.) suggest using Chin's (2000) approach to group comparisons in order to examine categorical moderator variables. While it is often argued (Chin 2000; Henseler & Chin 2010, p. 107) that the measurement models of the different groups should not statistically significantly differ ("measurement invariance"), Huber et al. (2007, p. 50; 2013, p. 66) argue that this precondition can be neglected.

In a first step, the subsamples have to be created. After that, model testing is executed separately for all subsamples (Huber 2007, p. 118). The measurement model is not evaluated again; only hypothesis testing is carried out and compared for the subsamples. If a hypothesis is statistically significant for one subsample, but not for the other, there is an obvious statistically significant difference between the groups. If it is statistically significant for both subsamples, the difference has to be examined (Huber et al. 2013, pp. 66f.).

Following Chin's (2000) suggestion, this is done with a t-test making use of the following formula (Huber et al. 2013, pp. 66ff.):

$$t = \left| \frac{p_x^1 - p_x^2}{S \cdot \sqrt{\frac{1}{m} + \frac{1}{n}}} \right|$$

with

$$S = \sqrt{\frac{(m-1)^2}{(m+n-2)} \cdot \left(\sigma(p_x^1)\right)^2 + \frac{(n-1)^2}{(m+n-2)} \cdot \left(\sigma(p_x^2)\right)^2}$$

m	size of subsample 1
n	size of subsample 2
p_x^1	path coefficient subsample 1
p_x^2	path coefficient subsample 2
$\sigma(p_x^1)$	standard error of path coefficient subsample 1
$\sigma(p_x^2)$	standard error of path coefficient subsample 2

In this study, the choice of TV programme the questionnaire was answered for ("choice") as well as gender and age were interesting as moderating variables. In a first step, the subsamples for three analyses were prepared:

1. **Choice:** Subsamples were created for TVoG, GNTM and Galileo. Since the smallest subsample is the TVoG subsample with 484 cases, random groups of cases consisting of 484 cases were selected from the other subsamples, arriving at three subsamples each consisting of 484 cases.

2. **Gender:** Subsamples were created for male and female respondents. Since the smaller subsample is the male subsample with 899 cases, a random group of cases consisting of 899 cases was selected from the female subsample, arriving at two subsamples each consisting of 899 cases.

3. **Age:** Subsamples were created for three age groups. Since the group aged 14-19 was the biggest, it was treated as a separate group labelled "Teens". The second group, labelled "Twens", consisted of respondents aged 20-29. For group three, "Adults", all remaining groups were combined; respondents who had not stated their age were excluded. Since the smallest subsample is the Adult subsample with 490 cases, random groups of cases consisting of 490 cases were selected from the other subsamples, arriving at three subsamples each consisting of 490 cases.

The analyses for choice and for age consist of more than two groups. For comparing more than two groups, pairwise comparisons are conducted for all groups (cf. Huber et al. 2013, pp. 98ff.). Analyses and interpretation of the group comparisons for moderating variables choice, gender and age are presented below. For detailed tables, full data presentation of group comparisons, and a summary overview of all group comparisons, refer to Appendix F.

5.4.1.1 Choice as moderating variable

It was hypothesized that hypotheses were not determined by TV programme choice, i.e. that there are no moderating effects.

hypo-thesis	relationship	Sig. TVoG	Sig. GNTM	Path coeff. TVoG	Path coeff. GNTM	t-value	Sig. different?
H1	CBR -> BL	yes	yes	0.24	0.36	-1.32	no
H2	SMP -> BL	yes	yes	0.24	0.31	-0.68	no
H3	SMP -> CBR	yes	yes	0.07	0.07	0.08	no
H4	SME -> BL			-0.03	-0.03		no
H5	SME -> CBR	yes	yes	0.30	0.33	-0.36	no
H6	SMP -> SME	yes	yes	0.32	0.47	-1.73	yes
H7	GOS -> CBR			-0.05	0.08		no
H8	GOS -> SME	yes	yes	0.37	0.32	0.63	no
H9	GOS -> SMP	yes	yes	0.61	0.68	-1.35	no
H10	GO -> BL		yes	0.11	0.13		yes
H11	GO -> CBR	yes	yes	0.43	0.29	1.74	yes
H12	PCR -> CBR	yes		0.06	-0.05		yes
H13	PCR -> GO		yes	0.06	0.12		yes
H14	PWR -> CBR		yes	0.04	0.21		yes
H15	PWR -> GO	yes	yes	0.35	0.45	-1.39	no

Table 5-14: Group comparisons – choice as moderating variable: TVoG–GNTM

Source: Own design and computation

Since there are three choice subsamples, three pairwise comparisons need to be conducted in order to arrive at a conclusion (cf. Table 5-15 and Table 5-16).

Taking into account all three tables, no moderating effect of choice can be detected on H1, H2, H3, H4 (not significant for all groups), H5, H7 (not significant for all groups), and H9. The other causal relationships are subject to moderating effects due to choice, which means that the hypothesis of no moderation has to be rejected.

16	TV programme choice has no moderating effect on the causal model.	*reject*

However, despite the fact that H16 has to be formally rejected, this rigid evaluation needs to be challenged by a more intuitive approach of interpretation. Although moderating effects seem to be present, there is no consistent pattern that might be explained by distinct peculiarities of the programmes. Some differences result from insignificance in either the TVoG or the GNTM subsamples. It might therefore be suspected that the differences are due to sampling issues, demographic distribution within the subsamples or other heterogeneity between subsamples.

hypo-thesis	relationship	Sig. TVoG	Sig. Galileo	Path coeff. TVoG	Path coeff. Galileo	t-value	Sig. different?
H1	CBR -> BL	yes	yes	0.24	0.26	-0.19	no
H2	SMP -> BL	yes	yes	0.24	0.28	-0.30	no
H3	SMP -> CBR	yes	yes	0.07	0.16	-1.22	no
H4	SME -> BL			-0.03	0.00		no
H5	SME -> CBR	yes	yes	0.30	0.22	1.29	no
H6	SMP -> SME	yes	yes	0.32	0.46	-1.64	no
H7	GOS -> CBR			-0.05	0.02		no
H8	GOS -> SME	yes	yes	0.37	0.23	1.72	yes
H9	GOS -> SMP	yes	yes	0.61	0.70	-1.53	no
H10	GO -> BL		yes	0.11	0.30		yes
H11	GO -> CBR	yes	yes	0.43	0.22	2.69	yes
H12	PCR -> CBR	yes	yes	0.06	0.08	-0.35	no
H13	PCR -> GO		yes	0.06	0.11		yes
H14	PWR -> CBR		yes	0.04	0.23		yes
H15	PWR -> GO	yes	yes	0.35	0.55	-2.90	yes

Table 5-15: Group comparisons – choice as moderating variable: TVoG–Galileo

Source: Own design and computation

hypo-thesis	relationship	Sig. Galileo	Sig. GNTM	Path coeff. Galileo	Path coeff. GNTM	t-value	Sig. different?
H1	CBR -> BL	yes	yes	0.26	0.36	-1.19	no
H2	SMP -> BL	yes	yes	0.28	0.31	-0.44	no
H3	SMP -> CBR	yes	yes	0.16	0.07	1.30	no
H4	SME -> BL			0.00	-0.03		no
H5	SME -> CBR	yes	yes	0.22	0.33	-1.65	no
H6	SMP -> SME	yes	yes	0.46	0.47	-0.12	no
H7	GOS -> CBR			0.02	0.08		no
H8	GOS -> SME	yes	yes	0.23	0.32	-1.04	no
H9	GOS -> SMP	yes	yes	0.70	0.68	0.33	no
H10	GO -> BL	yes	yes	0.30	0.13	1.71	yes
H11	GO -> CBR	yes	yes	0.22	0.29	-0.88	no
H12	PCR -> CBR	yes		0.08	-0.05		yes
H13	PCR -> GO	yes	yes	0.11	0.12	-0.12	no
H14	PWR -> CBR	yes	yes	0.23	0.21	0.20	no
H15	PWR -> GO	yes	yes	0.55	0.45	1.33	no

Table 5-16: Group comparisons – choice as moderating variable: Galileo–GNTM

Source: Own design and computation

5.4.1.2 Gender as moderating variable

It was hypothesized that hypotheses were not determined by gender, i.e. that there are no moderating effects.

hypo-thesis	relationship	Sig. M	Sig. F	Path coeff. M	Path coeff. F	t-value	Sig. different?
H1	CBR -> BL	yes	yes	0.26	0.34	-1.35	no
H2	SMP -> BL	yes	yes	0.34	0.23	1.59	no
H3	SMP -> CBR	yes		0.10	0.02		yes
H4	SME -> BL			0.02	-0.04		no
H5	SME -> CBR	yes	yes	0.24	0.32	-1.71	yes
H6	SMP -> SME	yes	yes	0.49	0.44	0.75	no
H7	GOS -> CBR			0.06	0.06		no
H8	GOS -> SME	yes	yes	0.20	0.28	-1.19	no
H9	GOS -> SMP	yes	yes	0.70	0.66	0.75	no
H10	GO -> BL	yes	yes	0.19	0.20	-0.09	no
H11	GO -> CBR	yes	yes	0.26	0.36	-1.53	no
H12	PCR -> CBR	yes		0.10	0.02		yes
H13	PCR -> GO	yes	yes	0.16	0.15	0.26	no
H14	PWR -> CBR	yes	yes	0.18	0.15	0.50	no
H15	PWR -> GO	yes	yes	0.47	0.43	0.66	no

Table 5-17: Group comparisons – gender as moderating variable

Source: Own design and computation

However, three of the hypotheses of moderation need to be accepted: H3 and H12 are only significant for males, not for females. This means the influences of attitude towards the social media programme as well as perceived critics' response on the consumer-brand relationship, which are very weak for the full sample, are even insignificant for females, which can hardly be interpreted as a meaningful moderating effect.

Secondly, the path coefficient for H5 is stronger for females (0.32) than for males (0.24). This finding indicates that the impact engagement in the social media programme has on the consumer-brand relationship is stronger for females, meaning that if females use the social media programme intensely, it impacts their relationship with the brand more strongly than in the case of males. Hence, the hypothesis that model relationships were not subject to moderating effects by gender has to be rejected.

17	Gender has no moderating effect on the causal model.	*reject*

5.4.1.3   Age as moderating variable

It was hypothesized that hypotheses were not determined by age, i.e. that there are no moderating effects. Since there are three subsamples for age groups, three pairwise comparisons need to be conducted in order to arrive at a conclusion.

hypo-thesis	relationship	Sig. Adults	Sig. Teens	Path coeff. Adults	Path coeff. Teens	t-value	Sig. different?
H1	CBR -> BL	yes	yes	0.21	0.32	-1.46	no
H2	SMP -> BL	yes	yes	0.30	0.35	-0.58	no
H3	SMP -> CBR			-0.02	0.05		no
H4	SME -> BL			-0.04	0.01		no
H5	SME -> CBR	yes	yes	0.33	0.25	1.33	no
H6	SMP -> SME	yes	yes	0.34	0.54	-2.21	yes
H7	GOS -> CBR	yes		0.10	0.07		yes
H8	GOS -> SME	yes	yes	0.32	0.17	1.74	yes
H9	GOS -> SMP	yes	yes	0.68	0.68	-0.04	no
H10	GO -> BL	yes	yes	0.27	0.13	1.48	no
H11	GO -> CBR	yes	yes	0.25	0.32	-0.76	no
H12	PCR -> CBR	yes	yes	0.09	0.10	-0.09	no
H13	PCR -> GO	yes	yes	0.14	0.11	0.50	no
H14	PWR -> CBR	yes	yes	0.18	0.15	0.41	no
H15	PWR -> GO	yes	yes	0.43	0.50	-1.04	no

Table 5-18: Group comparisons – age as moderating variable: Adults–Teens

Source: Own design and computation

Taking into account all three tables, no moderating effect of age can be detected on H1, H2, H3 and H4 (not significant for all groups), H9, H11, H13, H14 and H15.

18	Age has no moderating effect on the causal model.	*reject*

With regard to H7, the relationship is only significant for Adults, but not for both Twens and Teens. With regard to H12, the relationship is only significant for Adults and Teens, not for Twens; there is no significant difference between Adults and Teens. With regard to both H5 and H10, the relationship is stronger for Twens than for Teens; Adults do not differ significantly from either group.

Hence, similar to the result of group comparisons by choice, moderating effects seem to be present, but there is no consistent pattern allowing for conclusions on how age affects direction and/or strength of the causal relationships. Only with regard to H8, which is stronger for Adults (0.32) than for Teens (0.17), with Twens not differing significantly from either group, might it be stated that the older the respondents, the stronger the impact of gratifications obtained from the social media programme on engagement in the social media programme. Similarly, with regard to H6, where the relationship is stronger for Teens (0.54) than for Adults (0.34), with Twens not differing significantly from either group, it can be stated that the younger the respondents, the stronger the impact of attitude toward the social media programme on engagement in the social media programme for the TV brand. This suggests the conclusion that for younger users, attitude is more relevant for engagement than gratifications obtained, while for older users, both path coefficients are roughly equal.

hypo-thesis	relationship	Sig. Adults	Sig. Twens	Path coeff. Adults	Path coeff. Twens	t-value	Sig. different?
H1	CBR -> BL	yes	yes	0.21	0.28	-0.98	no
H2	SMP -> BL	yes	yes	0.30	0.23	0.79	no
H3	SMP -> CBR			-0.02	0.04		no
H4	SME -> BL			-0.04	-0.03		no
H5	SME -> CBR	yes	yes	0.33	0.36	-0.51	no
H6	SMP -> SME	yes	yes	0.34	0.48	-1.58	no
H7	GOS -> CBR	yes		0.10	-0.01		yes
H8	GOS -> SME	yes	yes	0.32	0.20	1.31	no
H9	GOS -> SMP	yes	yes	0.68	0.71	-0.61	no
H10	GO -> BL	yes	yes	0.27	0.31	-0.39	no
H11	GO -> CBR	yes	yes	0.25	0.36	-1.47	no
H12	PCR -> CBR	yes		0.09	0.02		yes
H13	PCR -> GO	yes	yes	0.14	0.08	0.93	no
H14	PWR -> CBR	yes	yes	0.18	0.15	0.40	no
H15	PWR -> GO	yes	yes	0.43	0.47	-0.59	no

Table 5-19: Group comparisons – age as moderating variable: Adults–Twens

Source: Own design and computation

hypo-thesis	relationship	Sig. Teens	Sig. Twens	Path coeff. Teens	Path coeff. Twens	t-value	Sig. different?
H1	CBR -> BL	yes	yes	0.32	0.28	0.45	no
H2	SMP -> BL	yes	yes	0.35	0.23	1.48	no
H3	SMP -> CBR			0.05	0.04		no
H4	SME -> BL			0.01	-0.03		no
H5	SME -> CBR	yes	yes	0.25	0.36	-1.89	yes
H6	SMP -> SME	yes	yes	0.54	0.48	0.71	no
H7	GOS -> CBR			0.07	-0.01		no
H8	GOS -> SME	yes	yes	0.17	0.20	-0.45	no
H9	GOS -> SMP	yes	yes	0.68	0.71	-0.55	no
H10	GO -> BL	yes	yes	0.13	0.31	-1.98	yes
H11	GO -> CBR	yes	yes	0.32	0.36	-0.53	no
H12	PCR -> CBR	yes		0.10	0.02		yes
H13	PCR -> GO	yes	yes	0.12	0.08	0.48	no
H14	PWR -> CBR	yes	yes	0.15	0.15	-0.05	no
H15	PWR -> GO	yes	yes	0.50	0.47	0.45	no

Table 5-20: Group comparisons – age as moderating variable: Teens–Twens

Source: Own design and computation

5.4.2   Interaction effects

Group comparisons are not suitable if moderator variables are metric in nature; instead, an interaction term should be used (Huber at al. 2007, p. 51). According to Baron and Kenny (1986, p. 1174), the moderation hypothesis can be supported if the interaction term is significant, irrespective of the main effects between the predictor and the moderator variable.

The part of the comprehensive model that is to be examined for interaction effects are the relationships of the latent variables "Gratifications obtained from the serialised TV brand" (GO) and "Gratifications obtained from the social media programme for the serialised TV brand" (GOS) with the consumer-brand relationship.

To examine the relationships between the constructs in a first step, Pearson correlations were computed. Constructs GO and GOS are strongly correlated ($r = 0.700$; correlation is significant at the .01 level (2-tailed)). To examine this further, it is to be investigated whether there are

1. interactions *between* the GO and the GOS groups, but for the same original indicators, e.g. does GO_1 moderate the relationship between GOS_1 and CBR, does GO_2 moderate the relationship between GOS_2 and CBR, and so forth;
2. interactions *within* the GO and GOS groups, e.g. does GO_1 moderate the relationship between GO_2 and CBR, does GOS_2 moderate the relationship between GOS_5 and CBR, and so forth.

Henseler and Chin (2010) present four approaches suitable to examine interaction effects in PLS:

1. the product indicator approach (Chin, Marcolin, & Newsted 1996; 2003);
2. the 2-stage approach (Chin et al. 2003; Henseler & Fassott 2010);
3. the hybrid approach (Wold 1982);
4. the orthogonalizing approach (Little, Bovaird,& Widaman 2006).

The product indicator approach

The product indicator approach as put forward by Chin et al. (1996; 2003) introduces a latent interaction term as a new latent variable into an existing PLS path model. In contrast to traditional approaches for the detection of moderating effects like ANOVA, it does not assume that the measures are free of error. The procedure requires the creation of product indicators of the predictor variable X and the moderator variable M, i.e. the pairwise multiplication of the centered indicators of the exogenous variable X and of the moderator variable M.

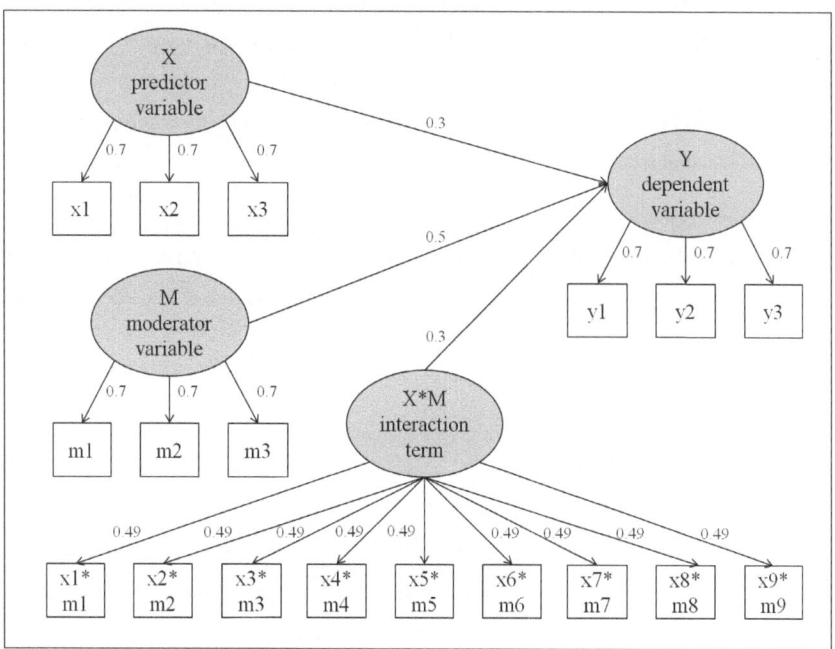

Figure 5-2: Modelling interaction effects – illustration of the product indicator approach
Source: Own design, adapted from Chin et al. (2003, p. 198)

In the example (Figure 5-2), there is an interaction effect with a path coefficient of 0.3. This implies that one standard deviation increase in M does not only impact Y by 0.5, but it would also increase the impact of X on Z from 0.3 to 0.6 (for another example, see Chin et al. 1996, p. 33). Chin et al. (2003, p. 212) recommend sample sizes of at least 100 to detect interaction effects. Although easily employable, the downside of this approach is that it is only applicable for reflective indicators, not for formative ones (Chin et al. 1996, p. 36).

The 2-stage approach

To meet the disadvantage of the product indicator approach of not being able to examine formative indicators, the 2-stage approach was put forward by Chin et al. (2003) and Henseler and Fassott (2010). The two stages are built up as follows (Henseler & Fassott 2010, p. 724):

1. The main effect PLS model is run in order to obtain estimates for the latent variable scores. The latent variable scores are calculated and saved for further analysis.

2. The interaction term $X \times M$ is calculated as the elementwise product of the latent variable scores of X and M. The interaction term as well as the latent variable scores of X and M are used as independent variables in a multiple linear regression on the latent variable scores of Y.

Henseler and Fassott (2010, p. 725) note that in PLS, latent variables with only one indicator are set equal to that indicator, regardless of the choice of measurement model. Hence, if "all formative interacting variables are measured by single indicators, the researcher can choose either the product indicator approach or the two-stage approach."

The hybrid approach

This approach, as put forward by Wold (1982), combines the two-stage approach and the product indicator approach. "Like in the two-stage approach, the element-wise product of the latent variable scores of the independent and the moderator variable serves as an interaction term; also as in the product indicator approach, the interaction term is updated during the algorithm runtime and used to estimate the latent variable scores" (Henseler & Chin 2010, p. 88). Since the hybrid approach requires a modification of the PLS algorithm which is not implemented in smartPLS, it is not appropriate for this study and will not be further considered. For a detailed description of how the hybrid approach works and should be implemented, refer to Henseler and Chin (2010, pp. 88f.).

The orthogonalizing approach

The approach put forward by Little et al. (2006) "is an extension of the use of residual centering for moderated multiple regressions" (Henseler & Chin 2010, p. 89). It is based on the idea that under ideal circumstances, "an interaction term is uncorrelated with (orthogonal to) its first-order effect terms" (Little et al. 2006, p. 499). For an overview of how to apply the approach, refer to Henseler and Chin (2010, pp. 89ff.) or the full article by Little et al. (2006).

Henseler & Chin (2010) compared all four approaches in a Monte Carlo experiment and provide an overview as to when which approach is preferable (p. 106). They recommend using either the orthogonalizing or the product indicator approach and argue that the orthogonalizing approach should be used for small sample sizes and when only few indicators per construct are used. For bigger sample sizes or if the number of indicators per construct is medium to large, they recommend using the product indicator approach. Due to the fact the sample size in this study is fairly large, it seems appropriate to use the product indicator approach. This is also in line with research efficiency requirements since it is implemented in the smartPLS software package.

It was decided to investigate interaction effects in a separate model, only consisting of the latent variables "Gratifications obtained from the serialised TV brand" (GO), "Gratifications obtained from the social media programme for the serialised TV brand" (GOS) and the consumer-brand relationship (CBR). There were three reasons for this approach:

1. It is recommended to single out the moderating effects and not test them in the complete model in smartPLS (Ringle 2005; 2006).
2. It was the aim of this part of the investigation to analyse different gratifications separately, not the complete constructs. Building a separate model allowed for the in-depth analysis of gratifications "interesting information", "entertainment", "generates ideas", "forget everyday concerns", "enjoyable and convenient pastime", and "sense of belonging".
3. Constructs GO and GOS have formative indicators. As stated above, interaction effects with formative moderators cannot be analysed with the product indicator approach. The building of single-item constructs made it possible to use the product indicator approach.

Hence, a partial model was developed that served as a starting point for the analyses of the various interaction effects to be examined. Separate parts of the model were subsequently singled out in order to test for the respective interaction effects.

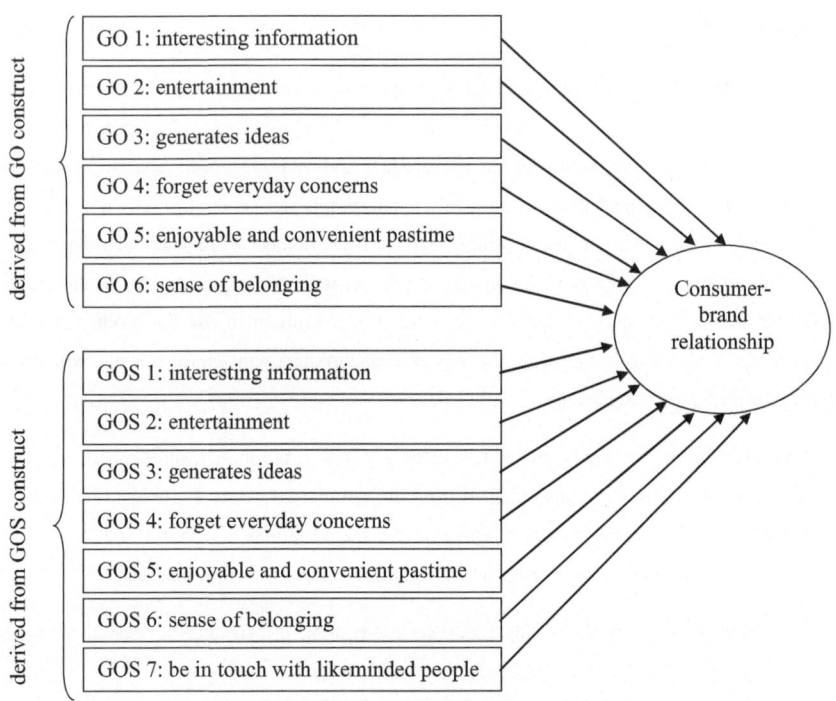

Figure 5-3: Modelling interaction effects – illustration of the partial model

Source: Own design

5.4.2.1 Interactions between GO and GOS groups

This section describes the examination of interactions between the GO and the GOS groups, but for the same original indicators, e.g. does GO_1 moderate the relationship between GOS_1 and CBR, does GO_2 moderate the relationship between GOS_2 and CBR, and so forth. This was in order to find out whether the influence of gratifications obtained from the social media programme, e.g. whether it met respondents' expectations with regard to information or entertainment, on the consumer-brand relationship was moderated by the fulfilment of corresponding gratifications obtained from the TV brand itself.

Chin et al. (1996; 2003) emphasize the importance of assessing the overall effect size for the interaction. This is done by "comparing the proportion of variance explained (as expressed by the determination coefficient R^2) of the main effect model (i.e. the model without moderating effect) with R^2 of the full model (i.e. the model including the moderating effect)" (Henseler & Fassott 2010, p. 732). Effect size f^2 can be computed using the following formula where f^2-values of 0.02, 0.15 and 0.35 denote a weak, medium, or strong impact, respectively (Cohen 1988, pp. 412ff.):[66]

$$f^2 = \frac{R^2_{included} - R^2_{excluded}}{1 - R^2_{included}} = \frac{R^2_{model\ with\ moderator} - R^2_{model\ without\ moderator}}{1 - R^2_{model\ with\ moderator}}$$

influencing dependent variable	path	path coefficient	t-value	$R^2_{included}$	$R^2_{excluded}$	f^2
interaction term	GOS_1*GO_1 -> CBR	0.04	1.94	0.3069	0.3056	0.0019
predictor	GOS_1 -> CBR	0.26	9.46			
moderator	GO_1 -> CBR	0.38	16.18			
interaction term	GOS_2*GO_2 -> CBR	0.04	1.74	0.2429	0.2417	0.0016
predictor	GOS_2 -> CBR	0.25	9.55			
moderator	GO_2 -> CBR	0.33	11.70			
interaction term	GOS_3*GO_3 -> CBR	0.05	2.38	0.2656	0.2638	0.0025
predictor	GOS_3 -> CBR	0.19	6.59			
moderator	GO_3 -> CBR	0.38	13.69			
interaction term	GOS_4*GO_4 -> CBR	0.06	2.70	0.208	0.2049	0.0039
predictor	GOS_4 -> CBR	0.23	8.57			
moderator	GO_4 -> CBR	0.28	10.54			
interaction term	GOS_5*GO_5 -> CBR	0.04	1.92	0.2803	0.2788	0.0021
predictor	GOS_5 -> CBR	0.28	11.12			
moderator	GO_5 -> CBR	0.35	13.05			
interaction term	GOS_6*GO_6 -> CBR	0.06	3.16	0.3197	0.316	0.0054
predictor	GOS_6 -> CBR	0.20	7.93			
moderator	GO_6 -> CBR	0.42	17.09			

Table 5-21: Interactions between GO and GOS groups

Source: Own design and computation

All f^2-values are visibly below the minimum value of 0.02. Hence, a moderating effect of gratifications obtained from the serialised TV brand on the influence of the corresponding gratifications obtained from the social media programme on the consumer-brand relationship could not be detected for all individual gratifications.

---

[66] This is the formula suggested by Henseler and Chin (2010, p. 105) and Henseler and Fassott (2010, p. 732). Henseler and Chin note that Chin et al. (2003, p. 211) "mistakenly labe[l]led $R^2_{excluded}$ instead of $R^2_{included}$ in the denominator of this formula, thereby provoking an underestimation of f^2" (2010, p. 105).

5.4.2.2   Interactions within GO and GOS groups

This section describes the examination of interactions between the GO and GOS groups, e.g. does GO_1 moderate the relationship between GO_2 and CBR, does GOS_2 moderate the relationship between GOS_5 and CBR, and so forth.

In order to decide which original indicators to examine for interaction effects, Pearson correlations were computed first. Since GO_1 and GO_2 as well as GOS_1 and GOS_2, gratifications "information" and "entertainment" for the serialised TV brand and the social media programme for the serialised TV brand, respectively, seemed to be of highest interest, correlations of the other gratification with those two were computed. The Pearson correlation coefficient r measures the level of linear connection between two variables. It ranges between $+1$ and -1, where a correlation coefficient of 0 means that there is no linear dependence between two variables. Correlation coefficients below 0.5, up to 0.8 and above 0.8 are regarded as indicating a weak, medium and strong correlation, respectively (Fahrmeir, Künstler, Pigeot, & Tutz 2007, p. 139).

Interactions within the GO construct are discussed first. Table 5-22 shows correlations within the GO construct.

	corr. with GO_1	corr. with GO_2
GO_1: interesting information	1	.501*
GO_2: entertainment	.501*	1
GO_3: generates ideas	.710*	.360*
GO_4: forget everyday concerns	.309*	.394*
GO_5: enjoyable and convenient pastime	.475*	.722*
GO_6: sense of belonging	.429*	.332*

Table 5-22: Correlations within GO construct

Source: Own design and computation

*   significant at the .01 level (two-tailed)

The strongest correlations of GO_1 are with GO_3 and GO_2. The strongest correlations of GO_2 are with GO_5 and GO_1. It was therefore examined whether GO_3 and GO_2 moderate the influence of GO_1 on CBR, and whether GO_5 moderates the influence of GO_2 on CBR.

influencing dependent variable	path	path coefficient	t-value	$R^2_{included}$	$R^2_{excluded}$	f^2
interaction term	GO_1*GO_2 -> CBR	0.09	3.28	0.3135	0.3085	0.0073
predictor	GO_1 -> CBR	0.39	20.01			
moderator	GO_2 -> CBR	0.29	11.82			
interaction term	GO_1*GO_3 -> CBR	0.06	2.97	0.3007	0.2981	0.0037
predictor	GO_1 -> CBR	0.37	13.50			
moderator	GO_3 -> CBR	0.25	9.38			
interaction term	GO_2*GO_5 -> CBR	0.08	2.93	0.2531	0.2488	0.0058
predictor	GO_2 -> CBR	0.26	7.82			
moderator	GO_5 -> CBR	0.33	10.61			

Table 5-23: Interactions within GO group

Source: Own design and computation

Again, all f^2-values are visibly below the minimum value of 0.02. Hence, moderating effects between the investigated gratifications within the GO group could not be detected for all individual gratifications.

The equivalent examination was then conducted for gratifications within the GOS group. At first, Pearson correlations were computed.

	corr. with GOS_1	corr. with GOS_2
GOS_1: interesting information	1	.694*
GOS_2: entertainment	.694*	1
GOS_3: generates ideas	.622*	.514*
GOS_4: forget everyday concerns	.403*	.490*
GOS_5: enjoyable and convenient pastime	.648*	.745*
GOS_6: sense of belonging	.455*	.462*
GOS_7: be in touch with likeminded people	.423*	.441*

Table 5-24: Correlations within GOS construct

Source: Own design and computation

*   significant at the .01 level (two-tailed)

The strongest correlations of GOS_1 are with GOS_2 and GOS_5. The strongest correlations of GOS_2 are with GOS_5 and GOS_1, which corresponds to correlations.

f^2-values are above the minimum value of 0.02 or only slightly below, indicating a weak and a very weak moderating effect, respectively.

influencing dependent variable	path	path coefficient	t-value	$R^2_{included}$	$R^2_{excluded}$	f^2
interaction term	GOS_2*GOS_1 -> CBR	0.18	5.97	0.2508	0.2284	0.0299
predictor	GOS_2 -> CBR	0.24	9.12			
moderator	GOS_1 -> CBR	0.38	14.52			
interaction term	GOS_1*GOS_5 -> CBR	0.16	5.60	0.2679	0.2495	0.0251
predictor	GOS_1 -> CBR	0.35	14.66			
moderator	GOS_5 -> CBR	0.28	11.27			
interaction term	GOS_2*GOS_5 -> CBR	0.14	4.78	0.2263	0.2131	0.0171
predictor	GOS_2 -> CBR	0.25	8.77			
moderator	GOS_5 -> CBR	0.33	11.55			

Table 5-25: Interactions within GOS group

Source: Own design and computation

GOS_1 (information) moderates the influence of GOS_2 (entertainment) on the consumer-brand relationship. Since the interaction effect has a path coefficient of 0.18, an increase in GOS_1 by one standard deviation does not only impact CBR by 0.38, but also increases the impact of GOS_2 on CBR from 0.24 to 0.42. This means that for respondents who indicated that the social media programme for the serialised TV brand meets their expectations of information, the impact its fulfilled entertainment gratifications have on the consumer-brand relationship is stronger.

GOS_5 (enjoyable and convenient pastime) moderates the influence of GOS_1 (information) on the consumer-brand relationship. Since the interaction effect has a path coefficient of 0.16, an increase in GOS_5 by one standard deviation does not only impact CBR by 0.28, but also increases the impact of GOS_1 on CBR from 0.35 to 0.51. This means that for respondents who indicated that the social media programme for the serialised TV brand meets their expectations of enjoyability and convenient pastime, the impact its fulfilled information gratifications has on the consumer-brand relationship is stronger.

GOS_5 (enjoyable and convenient pastime) moderates the influence of GOS_2 (entertainment) on the consumer-brand relationship. Since the interaction effect has a path coefficient of 0.14, an increase in GOS_5 by one standard deviation does not only impact CBR by 0.3253, but also increases the impact of GOS_2 on CBR from 0.25 to 0.38. This means that for respondents who indicated that the social media programme for the serialised TV brand meets their expectations of enjoyability and convenient pastime, the impact its fulfilled entertainment gratifications have on the consumer-brand relationship is stronger.

5.5 Further insights by exploratory data analysis

To gain further insight into selected constructs and the specifics of the data, additional analyses were conducted. At first, constructs brand loyalty (BL) and consumer-brand relationship (CBR) as the key outcome variables of the structural model and attitude toward the social media programme (SMP) and engagement in the social media programme (SME) as the key social media constructs were examined in greater detail. Insights from the extended questionnaire are provided, and the non-user sample is analysed.

5.5.1 Analysis of selected constructs

In this section, selected constructs are further analysed. Since the GO and GOS constructs have already been investigated in detail in section 5.4.2, this section focuses on brand loyalty, the consumer-brand relationship, as well as attitude towards and engagement in the social media programme. For exploratory data analysis,[67] construct values were used as computed during evaluation of the structural model.

standardised construct values	BL	CBR	GOS	GO	PCR	PWR	SME	SMP
Mean	5.87	4.44	4.99	5.24	4.46	4.76	3.67	5.22
N	2357	2357	2357	2357	2357	2357	2357	2357
Std. Deviation	1.157	1.408	1.185	1.115	1.507	1.476	1.525	1.139
Median	6.20	4.54	5.10	5.34	4.50	4.99	3.68	5.39

Table 5-26: Standardised construct values

Source: Own design and computation

At a first glance, construct values are rather high: On a scale from 1 to 7, construct value for brand loyalty of 5.87 indicates high brand loyalty. In contrast, engagement with a construct value of 3.67 is just slightly above the mid-point of the scale. These findings will be discussed in the following sections.

5.5.1.1 Further analysing brand loyalty

Brand loyalty (standardised construct value) is not normally distributed with a skewness of -1.720 ($SE = 0.05$) and kurtosis of 3.442 ($SE = 0.101$). Brand loyalty (construct value) shows

---

[67] Detailed tables of all data can be found in Appendix E.

negative skewness and positive kurtosis.[68] Since 7 on the measurement scale stands for "fully agree", there is a tendency toward strong brand loyalty detectable.

Histogram

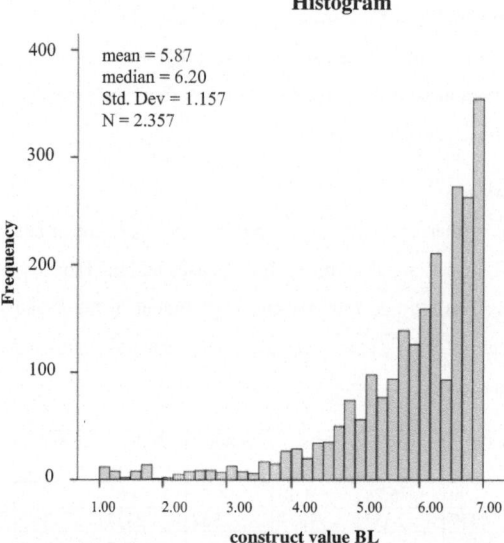

Figure 5-4: Histogram for construct value BL
Source: Own design

This distribution shows that there are a number of highly loyalty respondents in the sample, which is not very surprising since a basic level of loyalty is inherent in the sample. The mean value is quite high as well, meaning that the sample tends to be rather loyal on average; nevertheless, data are scattering across the scale. Although not many, there are respondents having a very low degree of loyalty.

In order to investigate whether the degree of loyalty depends on the format for which respondents answered the survey, group comparisons were conducted. To assess which kind of test was required, a test for normality was conducted first. Both the Kolmogorov-Smirnov test and the Shapiro-Wilk test are testing the null hypothesis that the distribution of the data is

---

[68] Skewness indicates the symmetry of the distribution, while kurtosis indicates the "peakedness", both of which have a value of 0 if the distribution is perfectly normal (Pallant 2010, p. 57). The direction of skewness and kurtosis values indicates the type of violation of normality. Skewness values > 0 indicate positive skewness, which is a clustering to the left, while skewness values < 0 indicate negative skewness and a clustering of scores to the right (ibid.). Kurtosis values > 0 indicate positive kurtosis, i.e. a peaked curve, while kurtosis values < 0 indicate negative kurtosis, i.e. a flat curve (ibid.).

equal to a normal distribution.[69] For a *p*-value of less than .05, the normality assumption is violated and has to be rejected, i.e., the test is significant at the $p < 0.05$ level (e.g. Pallant 2010, p. 63). In this case, the null hypothesis of normal distribution has to be rejected, meaning that the data for construct value BL is not normally distributed.

In order to examine differences in construct values by groups, Kruskal-Wallis tests (Kruskal & Wallis 1952) can be conducted. The Kruskal-Wallis test is used to determine whether there are any statistically significant differences between the distributions of three or more independent (unrelated) groups. It is the non-parametric alternative to the one-way ANOVA and has to be used in this study because the data is not normally distributed.

To rule out that differences are due to differences in group sizes, subsamples were created for TVoG, GNTM and Galileo. Since the smallest subsample was the TVoG subsample with 484 cases, random groups of cases consisting of 484 cases were selected from the other subsamples, arriving at three subsamples each consisting of 484 cases. Test results are presented below. For full tables and figures, refer to Appendix E.

A Kruskal-Wallis test was run to determine if there were differences in construct value BL between categories of programme choice.[70] The null and alternative hypotheses for the Kruskal-Wallis test are:

H_0:   the distribution of construct value BL is the same across categories of choice

H_A: at least two of the groups differ with respect to location (median)

Null Hypothesis	Test	Sig.	Decision
The distribution of construct value BL is the same across categories of choice.	Independent-Samples Kruskal-Wallis Test	.000	Reject the null hypothesis.

Asymptotic significances are displayed. The significance level is .05.

Table 5-27: Independent-Samples Kruskal-Wallis Test summary for BL

Source: Own design

---

[69] The null and alternative hypotheses for the Kolmogorov-Smirnov test are:
    H_0:   the distribution of the construct value under investigation is normal
    H_A: the distribution of the construct value under investigation is not normal
[70] The values indicated as "complete sample" for the further analyses differ slightly from the mean and median values indicated for construct values BL, CBR and SMP in exploratory data analysis because the complete sample (i.e. 2,357 cases) was used there for computation, while in this case the full sample consists of the three subsamples (i.e. 3*484=1,452).

Pairwise comparisons were performed using Dunn's procedure with a Bonferroni correction (Dunn 1961; 1964) for multiple comparisons. Construct value BL is statistically significantly different between the different levels of choice, $\chi^2(2) = 57.807$, $p = .000$.

Total N	1,452
Test Statistic	57.807
Degrees of Freedom	2
Asymptotic Sig. (2-sided test)	.000

The test statistic is adjusted for ties.

Table 5-28: Independent-Samples Kruskal-Wallis Test for construct value BL

Source: Own design an computation

Post-hoc analysis revealed that construct value BL is statistically significantly different between all groups: between the Galileo (median = 6.0021) and GNTM (median = 6.31) subsamples ($p = .000$), between the Galileo and TVoG (median = 6.5096) subsamples ($p = .000$), and between the GNTM and TVoG subsamples ($p = .010$). Hence, it can be stated that brand loyalty is strongest for the TVoG subsample and weakest for the Galileo subsample.

5.5.1.2 Further analysing the consumer-brand relationship

The data for construct consumer-brand relationship (standardised construct value) are not normally distributed either, with a skewness of -0.338 ($SE = 0.05$) and kurtosis of -0.431 ($SE = 0.101$). CBR shows negative skewness and negative kurtosis, i.e. clustering to the right and a rather flat curve. The histogram illustrates this finding (Figure 5-5).

The consumer-brand relationship for the sample tends to be above average, but data is highly scattered. It is striking that a noticeable number of respondents seem to have a very strong relationship with the brand. However, a lot of respondents also give their relationship with the television brands a slightly above average rating only.

CBR is strongly correlated with GO ($r = 0.634$; correlation is significant at the .01 level (2-tailed)), which is in line with the finding from model testing that GO has the strongest direct impact on CBR.

Both the Kolmogorov-Smirnov test and the Shapiro-Wilk test show that the null hypothesis of normal distribution has to be rejected. Hence, a Kruskal-Wallis test was run to determine if there were differences in construct value CBR between categories of choice. Groups were the same as used in section 5.5.1.1. Procedures corresponding to those outlined above were conducted for construct value CBR. For tables and figures, refer to Appendix E.

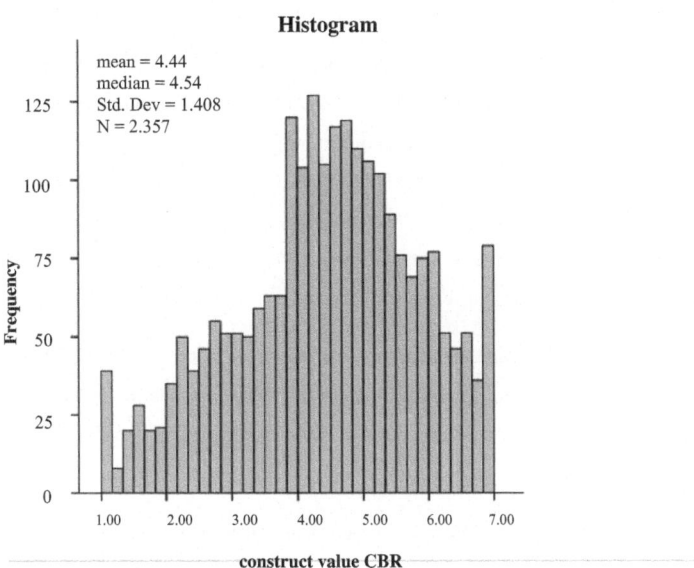

Figure 5-5: Histogram for construct value CBR

Source: Own design

Pairwise comparisons were performed using Dunn's procedure with a Bonferroni correction (Dunn 1961; 1964) for multiple comparisons. Construct value CBR is statistically significantly different between the different levels of choice, $\chi^2(2) = 28.461$, $p = .000$. Post-hoc analysis revealed that construct value CBR is statistically significantly different between the GNTM (median = 4.2080) and TVoG (median = 4.7238) subsamples ($p = .000$) and between the Galileo (median = 4.4495) and the TVoG subsamples ($p = .001$). There is no statistically significant difference between the GNTM and Galileo subsamples ($p = .266$). It can hence be stated that the consumer-brand relationship is strongest for TVoG and weakest for GNTM.

5.5.1.3 *Further analysing attitude toward the social media programme*

Construct attitude toward the social media programme (construct value) is also not normally distributed with a skewness of -0.809 ($SE = 0.05$) and kurtosis of 0.529 ($SE = 0.101$). SMP (construct value) shows negative skewness and positive kurtosis, i.e. clustering to the right and a peaked curve.

Attitude toward the social media programme is strongly correlated with GOS ($r = 0.668$) and SME ($r = 0.619$; correlations are significant at the .01 level (2-tailed)), the other social media constructs in the model. Attitude toward the social media programme is rather positive (mean = 5.22; median = 5.39). In this case, it is particularly interesting whether this depends on the format respondents were answering the survey for, because significant differences in attitude for the different formats would indicate that brand image effects impact changes in attitude and make it difficult to generalize attitude effects in this study.

Both the Kolmogorov-Smirnov test and the Shapiro-Wilk test show that the null hypothesis of normal distribution has to be rejected. Therefore, a Kruskal-Wallis test was run to determine if there were differences in the construct value of SMP between the different levels of format choice.

Groups were the same as used in section 5.5.1.1. Procedures corresponding to those outlined above were conducted for construct value SMP. For tables and figures, refer to Appendix E.

The subsamples for Galileo (median = 5.3569), GNTM (median = 5.2862) and TVoG (median = 5.4062) are not statistically significantly different, $\chi^2(2) = 5.742$, $p = .057$. Considering that the social media programmes used by the respondents – most of them use Facebook for their format brands – are very similar, this indicates that in this study, differences in attitude are not due to mere brand image effects.

5.5.1.4   Further analysing implications of engagement

In order to gain further insights into the impact active usage of the social media programme has, construct value SME as well as individual indicators of engagement are investigated.

Engagement in the social media programme is strongly correlated with SMP ($r = 0.619$) and CBR ($r = 0.599$; correlations are significant at the .01 level (2-tailed)). Engagement in the social media programme is comparatively low for the full sample (mean = 3.67; std. dev. = 1.525) and not normally distributed with a skewness of 0.069 ($SE = 0.05$) and kurtosis of -0.779 ($SE = 0.101$). Engagement in the social media programme (construct value) shows almost no skewness and negative kurtosis, i.e. slight clustering to the left and a flat curve. The histogram illustrates the fact that a high number of respondents score very low on the construct value of social media engagement.

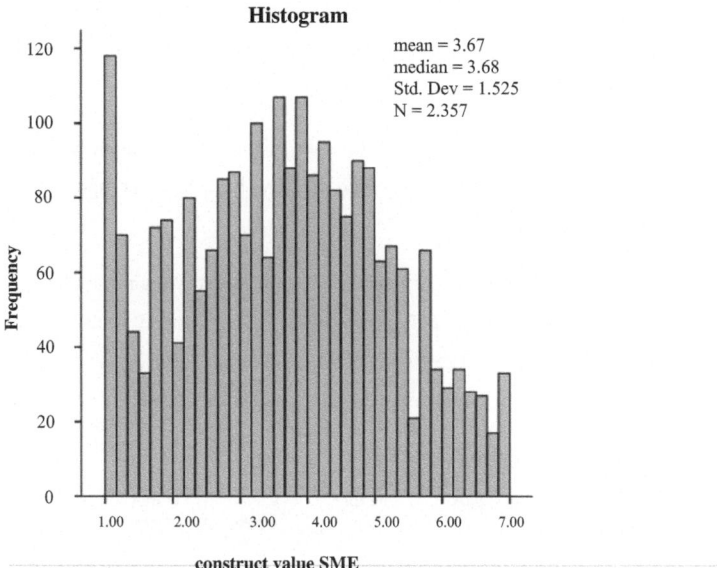

Figure 5-6: Histogram for construct value SME

Source: Own design

This leads to the assumption that the sample collected consists of users relatively weakly engaged. When investigating indicator SME_2, "I am an active user of social media offerings for [the serialised TV brand], i.e., I do usually contribute.", this becomes even more clear:

I am an active user of social media offerings for [the serialised TV brand], i.e., I do usually contribute.		
	Frequency	%
fully disagree	846	35.9
rather disagree	583	24.7
partly disagree	202	8.6
neither, nor	231	9.8
partly agree	341	14.5
rather agree	92	3.9
fully agree	62	2.6
Total	2357	100.0

Table 5-29: Distribution of SME_2

Source: Own design and computation

With regard to these results, it seems possible that the finding that communication with other fans is so much less important than (background) information is due to the fact that the sample consists of a majority of social media consumers instead of active participators. Table 5-30 shows respondents' rating of the importance of communication with other fans by activity.

Obviously, active users consider communication with other fans a lot more important than inactive users: 38.7 percent of the active users find it very important, as opposed to 4.0 percent of the inactive users.

One reason for the detected low importance of interactivity in this study might therefore be that the sample did not contain enough active users or opinion leaders. It is difficult to make assumptions on why this is the case. They may not have been reached by the survey invitation, or the TV brands investigated might attract a rather passive audience.

	I am an active user of social media offerings for [the serialised TV brand], i.e., I do usually contribute.													
	fully disagree		rather disagree		partly disagree		neither, nor		partly agree		rather agree		fully agree	
communica-tion with other fans	Σ	%	Σ	%	Σ	%	Σ	%	Σ	%	Σ	%	Σ	%
very important	34	4.0	27	4.6	18	8.9	24	10.4	52	15.2	25	27.2	24	38.7
important	48	5.7	62	10.6	39	19.3	36	15.6	68	19.9	18	19.6	11	17.7
more important than not	115	13.6	104	17.8	40	19.8	37	16.0	101	29.6	18	19.6	11	17.7
neither, nor	120	14.2	110	18.9	34	16.8	63	27.3	51	15.0	9	9.8	7	11.3
rather un-important	172	20.3	154	26.4	34	16.8	34	14.7	41	12.0	10	10.9	1	1.6
not important	139	16.4	73	12.5	20	9.9	16	6.9	16	4.7	6	6.5	6	9.7
not at all important	218	25.8	53	9.1	17	8.4	21	9.1	12	3.5	6	6.5	2	3.2
Total	846	100	583	100	202	100	231	100	341	100	92	100	62	100

Table 5-30: Importance of communication for active users of social media

Source: Own design and computation

5.5.2   Insights from extended questionnaire

In addition to the questions referring to the structural model, the survey aimed at finding out more about respondents' usage patterns of TV and social media. Complete results and full tables can be found in Appendix C; this section presents key results.

TV and social media usage

Respondents watch television mostly via the television set: 81.8 percent indicated that they did so frequently, 13.2 percent that they did from time to time – as opposed to 12.1 percent of frequent (29.9 percent occasional) watchers of television content via internet and 6.0 percent of frequent (13.6 percent occasional) watchers of television content via mobile devices. The data are very similar for the full sample and the TVoG and the Galileo subsamples; for the GNTM subsample, watching via internet seems to be more common, with 17.0 percent of frequent and 38.8 percent of occasional online watching (cf. Appendix C).

Facebook is the social media tool that is used most: 84.0 percent use it several times a day; in contrast, Twitter is never used by 70.7 percent of respondents, Pinterest by 90.1 percent, Instagram by 69.7 percent, and Tumblr by 85.3 percent (cf. Appendix C). Also, 70.2 percent indicate that they only use official social media offerings, not social media offerings managed and produced by fans, and that they do not produce, share, post or review fan fiction or fan art (cf. Appendix C). These findings are in line with the fact that the survey was conducted mainly amongst Facebook users since the invitation was posted via Facebook. Facebook is a social media tool not allowing for a high degree of creativity by individual users – fan art and similar content are more often found on platforms such as Tumblr.

38.2 percent of respondents frequently or from time to time make use of social media while a programme is running in order to engage in conversations about it. Further 21.6 percent have not done so yet, but claim that they can imagine doing so in the future (cf. Table 5-31). The TVoG subsample shows the highest percentage of second screen usage for users indicating that they make use of a second screen frequently or from time to time. This is probably due the fact that viewers of the programme are engaged by social media while the programme is running (cf. the examples for viewer interaction of TVoG described in section 2.5.3). The GNTM subsample shows the highest percentage of second screen usage for users indicating that they make use of a second screen frequently, underpinning particular social media affinity. It is striking that, in general, the numbers of viewers using social media while watching TV seem to be moderate at best. Less than 10 percent make use of a second screen frequently. This is far off from percentages often claimed in the press (cf. section 2.5.3).

Second screen usage	full sample	TVoG subsample	GNTM subsample	Galileo subsample
Yes, frequently.	5.2%	6.0%	8.6%	3.2%
Yes, from time to time.	33.0%	37.8%	34.0%	30.7%
No, never.	40.2%	37.6%	35.8%	42.9%
Not yet, but I can imagine doing it.	21.6%	18.6%	21.6%	23.1%
Total	100.0%	100.0%	100.0%	100.0%

Table 5-31: Overview of second screen usage

Source: Own design and computation

Impact of social media usage on TV usage

About half of the respondents has already watched a TV series or serial because their attention was attracted in social media. 49.5 percent (41.3 percent TVoG / 60.1 percent GNTM / 48.3 percent Galileo) indicate they have done so because social media have made them curious, and 29.0 percent (21.7 percent TVoG / 36.6 percent GNTM / 27.7 percent Galileo) because the series or serial seemed to suit their tastes. This allows for the conclusion that social media do in fact increase brand awareness.

Q: Have you ever watched a TV series/serial solely because your attention was attracted in social media?				
	No, never.	Yes, because I wanted to participate in the conversation.	Yes, because it made me curious.	Yes, because the series/serial seemed to suit my tastes.
full sample	44.2%	7.2%	49.5%	29.0%
TVoG subsample	53.9%	3.9%	41.3%	21.7%
GNTM subsample	32.5%	9.7%	60.1%	36.6%
Galileo subsample	45.8%	7.3%	48.3%	27.7%

Table 5-32: Overview of attention attracted for TV by social media

Source: Own design and computation

The fact that these values are highest for the GNTM subsample seem to be in line with prior findings indicating higher online affinity for the GNTM subsample. Also striking is the fact that less than 10 percent of respondents claimed wanting to participate in the conversation to be a reason for watching a TV series/serial to which their attention was attracted in social media (cf. Table 5-32). This is in line with various other findings of this study that indicate that discourse with other users is not a core need.

Another question aimed at loyalty toward the TV programme. Respondents were asked whether they had ever continued watching a TV series/serial they actually did not want to continue watching because of the conversations in social media. 14.8 percent have, and further 19.6 percent have not, but claim that they can imagine doing it. Again, these values are highest for the GNTM subsample (18.6 percent have already done so and 26.3 percent claim they can imagine doing it), strengthening the argument that the GNTM subsample has more affinity for social media than the other subsamples (cf. Table 5-33).

Q: Have you ever continued watching a TV series/serial you actually did not want to continue watching because of the conversations in social media?				
Social media impact	*full sample*	*TVoG subsample*	*GNTM subsample*	*Galileo subsample*
Yes.	14.8%	12.4%	18.6%	14.4%
No, never.	65.5%	70.9%	55.0%	67.4%
No, but I can imagine doing it.	19.6%	16.7%	26.3%	18.1%
Total	100%	100%	100%	100%

Table 5-33: Overview of loyalty impact of social media for TV

Source: Own design and computation

Importance of social media

When asked how important it is for them to find their favourite series or serials on social media, more than half of the respondents claim they do not think social media are very important, but a nice add-on. Respondents of the GNTM subsample attached most importance to social media.

Q: How important is it for you to find your favourite series/serial on social media?				
Social media importance	*full sample*	*TVoG subsample*	*GNTM subsample*	*Galileo subsample*
very important	13.7%	13.8%	16.8%	12.3%
more important than not	23.8%	25.0%	26.5%	22.0%
not very important, but a nice add-on	51.6%	51.7%	49.2%	52.5%
not at all important	10.9%	9.5%	7.5%	13.2%
Total	100%	100%	100%	100%

Table 5-34: Overview of social media importance

Source: Own design and computation

Social media gratifications

In another question, it was attempted to gain more insights into gratifications sought and obtained from social media. In a first step, respondents were asked what they expected from the social media programme.

	interesting information		enter-tainment		generates ideas		forget everyday concerns		enjoyable and convenient pastime		sense of belonging		be in touch with likeminded people	
	Σ	%	Σ	%	Σ	%	Σ	%	Σ	%	Σ	%	Σ	%
very important	1274	54.1	979	41.5	631	26.8	321	13.6	588	24.9	280	11.9	283	12.0
important	694	29.4	822	34.9	652	27.7	384	16.3	787	33.4	382	16.2	482	20.4
more important than not	232	9.8	342	14.5	454	19.3	442	18.8	543	23.0	399	16.9	517	21.9
neither, nor	74	3.1	97	4.1	258	10.9	452	19.2	229	9.7	488	20.7	397	16.8
rather un-important	23	1.0	47	2.0	186	7.9	345	14.6	111	4.7	338	14.3	332	14.1
not important	15	0.6	24	1.0	84	3.6	194	8.2	46	2.0	223	9.5	162	6.9
not at all important	45	1.9	46	2.0	92	3.9	219	9.3	53	2.2	247	10.5	184	7.8
Total	2357	100	2357	100	2357	100	2357	100	2357	100	2357	100	2357	100

Table 5-35: Gratifications sought from the social media programme

Source: Own design and computation

Interesting information and entertainment are considered very important or important by a large majority of respondents (83.5 percent and 76.4 percent, respectively). It is striking that only about one third of respondents (32.4 percent) find being in touch with likeminded people very important or important.

When having a look at the gratifications sought from the TV brand itself, information and entertainment are most important as well, indicating that users do not have completely dissimilar expectations from the TV brand and its social media programme.

	interesting information		enter-tainment		generates ideas		forget everyday concerns		enjoyable and convenient pastime		sense of belonging	
	Σ	%	Σ	%	Σ	%	Σ	%	Σ	%	Σ	%
very important	1273	54.0	1316	55.8	767	32.5	425	18	944	40.1	291	12.3
important	558	23.7	712	30.2	582	24.7	469	19.9	852	36.1	332	14.1
more important than not	251	10.6	194	8.2	366	15.5	487	20.7	343	14.6	367	15.6
neither, nor	118	5.0	61	2.6	241	10.2	339	14.4	107	4.5	472	20.0
rather un-important	83	3.5	28	1.2	198	8.4	263	11.2	48	2.0	367	15.6
not important	35	1.5	16	0.7	98	4.2	164	7.0	20	0.8	224	9.5
not at all important	39	1.7	30	1.3	105	4.5	210	8.9	43	1.8	304	12.9
Total	2357	100	2357	100	2357	100	2357	100	2357	100	2357	100

Table 5-36: Gratifications sought from the serialised TV brand

Source: Own design and computation

To gain more insights into the expectations with regard to the social media programme, respondents were asked which particular features of the social media presence of their favourite TV series/serial they considered important. Information about and content from the TV programme are considered most important, a direct connection to the programme is slightly less important, and again, communication with other fans is considerably less important.

	information about the TV programme (schedule, dates, etc.)	background information (look behind the scenes, exclusive content)	communication with other fans	direct link to the TV programme	content from the TV programme in case I missed it
very important	42.6%	32.8%	8.7%	19.8%	43.7%
important	34.5%	33.8%	12.0%	24.6%	30.1%
more important than not	14.7%	17.6%	18.1%	24.5%	14.9%
neither, nor	3.8%	6.7%	16.7%	14.6%	4.5%
rather un-important	1.6%	4.7%	18.9%	7.6%	2.4%
not important	1.0%	1.7%	11.7%	3.7%	1.6%
not at all important	1.9%	2.8%	14.0%	5.3%	2.8%
Total	100.0%	100.0%	100.0%	100.0%	100.0%

Table 5-37: Overview of important features of social media (full sample)

Source: Own design and computation

The GNTM subsample finds the direct connection to the programme more important than the full sample (21.8 percent very important as opposed to 19.8 percent for the full sample), while the Galileo subsample finds it only slightly more important than the full sample (20.2 percent very important) and the TVoG subsample finds it less important (14.7 percent very important; cf. Appendix C). This is in contrast to the fact that TVoG viewers do in fact have a rather direct connection to the programme (cf. the examples for viewer interaction of TVoG described in section 2.5.3).

When comparing preferred social media by age group and gender (cf. Appendix C), data do not widely differ from the full sample. Younger users in general seem to attach more importance to the features, older users being more moderate in their judgement. Males and females do not differ remarkably with regard to features like information about and content from the TV programme. With regard to communication with other fans, males find the feature more important (10.1 percent very important, 13.8 percent important) than females

(7.9 percent very important, 11 percent important), which is in contrast to common gender stereotypes. They also find having a direct connection to the programme more important (22 percent very important, 26.4 percent important) than females (18.6 percent very important, 23.7 percent important).

5.5.3 Non-user sample

Respondents who had indicated at the beginning of the questionnaire that they did not use social media for television series/serial related content were redirected to an alternative questionnaire that asked them for the reasons they did not make use of such offerings. 260 people chose this option, 64.2 percent of which were female (32.7 percent male; 3.1 percent not indicated). Respondents were slightly older than those of the user sample, but not much.

Age	full sample in %
14-19	33.5
20-29	34.6
30-39	14.6
40-49	4.6
50-59	7.7
60-69	2.3
Total	97.3
Missing (system)	2.7
Total	100.0

Table 5-38: Age structure of non-user sample

Source: Own design

Like the respondents of the user sample, the majority of respondents, i.e. over 55 percent, had either completed or were pursuing a degree after 10 years of school ("Realschulabschluss") or A-levels (23.1 percent and 33.8 percent, respectively). Less than 10 percent had no degree (1.2 percent) or had completed or were pursuing a degree after 9 years of school ("Hauptschulabschluss") (7.7 percent).

26.2 percent held or were pursuing a university degree, in contrast to 15.4 percent in the user sample. 45.4 percent indicated that they were students (26.9 percent high school students and 18.5 percent university students), as opposed to 52.9 percent in the user sample. 38.8 percent were employed, 0.4 percent were civil servants, 2.3 percent were homekeepers, 1.9 percent were unemployed, and 1.9 percent were retired. The structure of occupation is in line with the non-user sample's higher age. For a detailed overview of demographics, see Appendix C.

Reasons for not using TV series/serial related social media offerings	%
These offerings don't appeal to me.	34.2
I hardly use social media in general.	20.4
I find these offerings confusing.	6.9
I have concerns regarding data protection and privacy.	13.5
I'm content watching my favourite programmes on TV - I have no further interest in them.	61.2
I don't know anybody who is actively using such websites.	17.3
I don't have time for things like that.	21.2
To my mind, social media offerings of serialised TV brands don't offer any additional information.	23.1
These websites aren't entertaining.	30.8
I'm not interested in other people's opinion about TV series/serials.	38.5
I don't want to get in touch with other people.	4.2
I get all the information I need about the TV series/serials I watch from other media.	22.3

Table 5-39: Reasons for not using social media offerings of serialised TV brands

Source: Own design

The vast majority indicate that they do not make use of social media offerings of serialised TV brands because they are content watching their favourite programmes on TV and have no further interest in them (61.2 percent).

Other important reasons are that they are not interested in other people's opinion about TV series/serials (38.5 percent), because the offerings do not appeal to them (34.2 percent), and because they do not find them entertaining (30.8 percent).

This shows that non-usage is not mostly due to a general dislike of social media offerings, or any functional reservations (e.g. only 13.5 percent have concerns regarding data protection and privacy issues). Instead, respondents do not seem to feel that they are in need of social media offerings for serialised TV brands. They do not require additional content, and/or they do not believe that social media offerings let them obtain any gratifications sought.

This shows the difficulty in increasing the number of fans to a Facebook page: If social media offerings are not even part of users' relevant set, increasing usage might be difficult.

5.6 Importance performance analysis

To outline diagnostic value and to develop a prioritisation for managerial decisions, an importance performance analysis of the PLS estimates is conducted (Slack 1994; for examples of application cf. Martensen & Grønholdt 2003; Völckner et al. 2010).

Following the procedure as applied by Völckner et al. (2010) as post-hoc analysis of their PLS model, importance is quantified as the total effects of the estimated relationships, i.e. the path coefficients, in PLS. For performance values, the latent variable scores as obtained from smartPLS were rescaled to a 0-to-100 scale.[71]

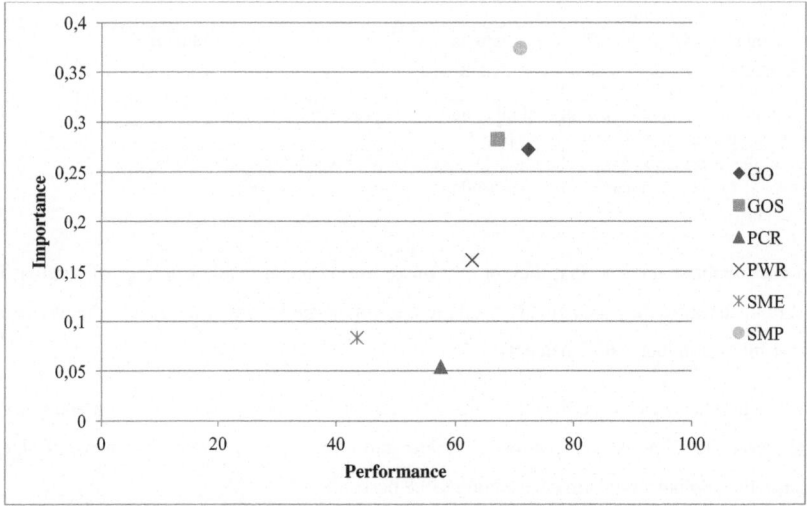

Figure 5-7: Importance-performance matrix
Source: Own design and computation

Managers should focus on and prioritise constructs that score high on the importance dimension and low on the performance dimension (Völckner et al. 2010, p. 389).

In this matrix, the constructs scoring high on the importance dimension are also the ones scoring highest on the performance dimension. Performance might be increased for the less important constructs. This applies in particular to the SME construct, i.e. users' engagement in the social media programme.

It has been shown above that the sample consisted of rather passive users, with low engagement levels, and who considered interactive participation and communication not very important. It might therefore be worthwhile to positively influence engagement.

---

[71] A sound instruction on how to obtain the relevant values from smartPLS is provided by Bido (2008).

5.7   Discussion and summary of additional analyses

After the evaluation of the structural model and the completion of hypothesis testing, additional analyses were conducted, the results of which are summarised in this section.

Multigroup comparisons were carried out in order to examine whether the causal relationships of the model were moderated by programme choice, gender, and age. While the hypothesis that TV programme choice has no moderating effect on the causal model had to be rejected, no consistent pattern in moderation effects could be detected. The hypothesis that gender has no moderating effect on the causal model also had to be rejected. The impact engagement in the social media programme has on the consumer-brand relationship is stronger for females than for males (H5), and the influences of attitude towards the social media programme as well as perceived critics' response on the consumer-brand relationship, which are very weak for the full sample, are even insignificant for females (H3 and H12). The hypothesis that age has no moderating effect on the causal model also had to be rejected. While some of the moderating effects seem to not underlie a consistent pattern, two effects can be stated: The older the respondents, the stronger the impact of gratifications obtained from the social media programme on engagement (H8), and the younger the respondents, the stronger the impact of attitude toward the social media programme on engagement (H6).

In order to further investigate gratifications obtained from the social media programme and from the TV brand, interaction effects with regard to the impact on the consumer-brand relationship were examined within the groups of individual indicators of both GO and GOS, as well as between those groups. Only for the group of GOS indicators could interaction effects be determined. These are within-group interaction effects; no across-group interactions could be detected. For respondents who indicated that the social media programme met their expectations of information, the impact its perceived entertainment had on the consumer-brand relationship was stronger. Also, for respondents who indicated that the social media programme met their expectations of enjoyability and convenient pastime, the impact its perceived information value as well as its perceived entertainment value had on the consumer-brand relationship were stronger.

The extended questionnaire that asked respondents about their usage patterns of TV and social media showed that social media features affect TV usage as well as loyalty toward the programme positively, the GNTM subsample showing particularly high affinity for social media offerings. While these results shed a positive light on social media tools in the television context, they need to be treated with care. More than half of the respondents claim that they do not think social media offerings for their favourite TV series/serials are very important, but only a nice add-on. When investigating social media gratifications with regard to TV content, interesting information and entertainment are considered very important or important by a large majority of respondents. (Background) information about and content from the TV programme in particular are considered to be most important, a direct connection to the programme is slightly less important, and communication with other fans is considerably less important. The examination of the non-user sample showed that non-usage is not due to a general dislike of social media offerings or functional reservations. Respondents feel they do not need them, i.e. they see no advantage or additional benefit.

To gain further insight into selected constructs, additional analyses were conducted, focusing on BL, CBR, SMP and SME. Brand loyalty (construct value) and SMP (construct value) show negative skewness and positive kurtosis, indicating a high degree of brand loyalty and a positive attitude toward the social media programme across the sample. Kruskal-Wallis tests showed that BL is statistically significantly different between all groups of programme choice, being strongest for the TVoG subsample and weakest for the Galileo subsample. The consumer-brand relationship is strongest for TVoG and weakest for GNTM, while SMP is not statistically significantly different for the groups. SME, i.e. engagement in the social media programme, is comparatively low for the full sample. Since active users consider communication with other fans a lot more important than inactive users, the finding that communication with other fans is considered so much less important than information might be due to the fact that the sample consists of a majority of social media consumers instead of active participators. This suggests focusing on making users more engaged with the social media programme as a management task, which is also indicated by importance-performance analysis.

6   Conclusion

6.1   Results and findings

This study has explored the employment of social media tools for brand management purposes with regard to serialised television brands and has investigated the impact of social media strategies on users' relationship with and loyalty towards these brands.

Drawing upon existing literature, a model framework was developed that assumes loyalty as the key television specific success indicator and that investigates the hypothesized causal relationships between social media related constructs, television related constructs, constructs referring to the social environment as well as brand related constructs.

Using data collected by a survey mainly targeting users of the Facebook pages of German television programmes *The Voice of Germany, Germany's Next Topmodel* and *Galileo* ($n \approx 2,300$), the model was evaluated using structural equation modelling (Partial Least Squares).

Findings from model testing as well as the empirical data gained from the additional questionnaire provide evidence that social media do in fact support and drive TV usage by positively impacting both brand loyalty and the consumer-brand relationship. This study thereby supports and enriches findings of research in neighbouring fields of study. It is in line with, for instance, brand community research, which detected positive effects on constructs such as relationship quality and loyalty by brand communities in general and social media based communities in particular (cf. 2.3.2).

A positive attitude toward the social media programme strongly impacts brand loyalty, i.e. the intention to continue consuming the content and to recommend it to others. In addition to having the strongest direct influence on loyalty, attitude toward the social media programme also influences brand loyalty via engagement and the consumer-brand relationship, which creates an even stronger cumulative effect.

Attitude toward the social media programme also has a strong positive impact on engagement in the social media programme, i.e. usage and involvement. Usage intensity in turn influences the key outcome variables: The more frequently the social media programme is used, the stronger the consumer-brand relationship. This impact is moderated by gender since the impact engagement in the social media programme has on the consumer-brand relationship is stronger for females, meaning that if females use the social media programme intensely, it impacts their relationship with the brand more strongly than in the case of males. No sound hypotheses of moderation by TV programme choice could be detected for this and the other relationships, indicating that the model is robust and applicable to other programmes as well.

The importance of social media offerings is underpinned by the fact that almost half of the respondents have watched serialised TV content in the past because they became aware of it in social media. Almost 15 percent have already continued watching serialised TV content they actually did not want to continue watching because of the conversations in social media, and further 19.6 percent have not, but claim that they can imagine doing it. In addition, almost 40 percent of respondents already make use of social media while a programme is running in order to engage in conversations about it, and further 21.6 percent have not done so yet, but claim that they can imagine doing so in the future. This means that the social media offerings surrounding their favourite TV programmes have meaning in consumers' lives and matter for their usage patterns.

It is notable that attitude toward the social media programme for the serialised TV brand directly positively affects brand loyalty, while engagement in the social media programme for the serialised TV brand impacts brand loyalty via its positive influence on the consumer-brand relationship. Hence, attitude impacts loyalty directly. Engagement, however, influences loyalty via the relationship with the brand. This fits with the strategies for employing social media in a television context elaborated on in section 2.5, which explicitly include generating viewer interaction and strengthening the relationship between consumer and brand.

To generate these positive effects, the features of the social media programme are crucial. Gratifications obtained positively affect both attitude and engagement directly. The influence of gratifications obtained from the social media programme on engagement is moderated by age: The older the respondents, the stronger the impact of gratifications obtained from the social media programme on engagement in the social media programme. Consequently, it is worth making social media programmes live up to users' needs and expectations a management task. In fact, almost 35 percent of non-users claimed they did not use social media offerings for serialised TV brands because the offerings did not appeal to them.

When investigating gratifications in detail, it becomes clear that series/serial brand related content is the most important feature for users, not communication or interaction with other users. This is particularly interesting because social media gratifications as identified in section 2.4.2 include, in addition to information organisation, seeking and sharing, and entertainment, a social interaction function. In this study, however, information about and content from the TV brand are considered most important, while communication with other fans is considerably less important. 38.5 percent of non-users claimed they did not use social media offerings for serialised TV brands because they were not interested in other people's opinion on the TV brand. Also, perceived WOM response only weakly impacts the consumer-brand relationship, while perceived critics' response impacts the consumer-brand relationship so weakly as to be negligible. Both have no direct impact on brand loyalty. Word-of-mouth response does, however, have a substantial effect on gratifications obtained from the TV brand, so that this study does at least in part support the positive effects of (e)WOM found in other studies (cf. 2.3.5).

Despite the obvious positive effects of social media, the importance of the TV programme itself must be emphasized as well. While attitude towards the social media programme has the strongest direct impact on brand loyalty, gratifications obtained from the serialised TV brand have the strongest direct impact on the consumer-brand relationship. Hence, despite social media having a positive effect on brand loyalty, the television programme is the decisive driver for the consumer-brand relationship.

This argument is supported by the fact that for more than half the respondents, serialised TV brand related social media programmes are not particularly important, but only an add-on. Also, the degree of brand loyalty seems to depend on programme choice: A Kruskal-Wallis test revealed that the construct value for brand loyalty is statistically significantly different between all programme choice subsamples, brand loyalty being strongest for the TVoG subsample (mean = 6.1817 / median = 6.5096), followed by the GNTM subsample (mean = 5.9392 / median = 6.5096), and weakest for the Galileo subsample (mean = 5.6545 / median = 6.0021). Also, consumer-brand relationship quality seems to depend on programme choice because the TVoG subsample had significantly higher values for the consumer-brand relationship than the other subsamples. This is not explained by the fact that the social media programme is perceived as being better for one or two of the subsamples because attitude toward the social media programme did not significantly differ between the three subsamples. Also, analysis of the data from the additional questionnaire indicated greater social media affinity for the GNTM subsample than for the other subsamples; nevertheless, the GNTM subsample did not yield the highest results for brand loyalty and the consumer-brand relationship.

When investigating gratifications obtained from the serialised TV brand and from its social media programme in more detail, it can be detected that they are strongly correlated. This is in line with findings of gratifications research, which identify very similar gratifications users obtain from TV and social media.

While gratifications obtained from the serialised TV brand directly affect brand loyalty, and also influence it by the indirect path via the consumer-brand relationship, adding up to a cumulative effect of 0.27, gratifications obtained from the social media programme do not directly influence brand loyalty. However, gratifications obtained from the social media programme influence brand loyalty via several indirect paths, the cumulative effect adding up to 0.28. This allows for the conclusion that gratifications obtained from both the social media programme and the serialised TV brand itself impact brand loyalty approximately equally strongly. It is important to note that this only applies to users who already use the respective social media programmes for serialised TV brands. For them, the gratifications they obtain from the brand itself and from the corresponding social media activities are comparable.

To sum up, this results in the following findings:

Social media support and drive TV usage. This refers to the attitude users have toward the social media programme, to their engagement, i.e. usage intensity and involvement, and the gratifications they obtain from it. Positive attitude toward the social media programme for the TV brand is crucial because it directly positively affects brand loyalty, i.e. the intention to continue consuming the content and to recommend it to others. Attitude toward the social media programme also has a strong positive impact on engagement in the social media programme for the TV brand, i.e. usage and involvement. Engagement, on the other hand, impacts brand loyalty via its positive influence on the consumer-brand relationship. In general, the more frequently the social media programme is used, the stronger the consumer-brand relationship.

Features of the social media programme are crucial to generate these positive effects. Gratifications obtained from the social media programme positively affect both attitude and engagement directly. This means that the fulfilment of expectations with regard to the social media programme leads to higher usage intensity and a more positive attitude, both of which positively impact the brand relationship and loyalty, respectively. This means that it is crucial to analyse users' wants and needs carefully and regularly to optimally meet them.

This study provides first insights to users' wants and needs and comes to the conclusion that **TV brand related content is the most important feature for users.** Information about and content from the TV brand are considered most important, communication with other fans is considerably less important. What users value most are information about the TV brand, background content and/or content from the TV brand in case it was missed while it was broadcast.

Despite the importance of the social media programme, **the television programme is the decisive driver for the consumer-brand relationship.** While attitude towards the social media programme has the strongest direct impact on brand loyalty, gratifications obtained from the TV brand itself have the strongest direct impact on the consumer-brand relationship.

6.2 Managerial implications

This study provides evidence that social media do in fact support and drive TV usage by positively influencing the consumer-brand relationship and loyalty toward the serialised TV brand. Key findings provided by structural equation modelling and additional analyses stress the importance of both the social media and the television programme.

It could be shown that social media support and drive TV usage, that features of the social media programme are crucial to generate these positive effects, and that the television programme is the decisive driver for the consumer-brand relationship. This results in a number of implications and recommendations for television and social media managers.

Firstly, that social media do have a positive impact on brand related key outcome variables means that it is worth investing time and money in them. Many (media) companies have by now realised that this includes employing full-time social media managers who can focus on social media as their sole task instead of performing additional tasks in marketing and/or PR.

This allows for consistent communication and wording within and across social media channels and ensures that users feel addressed by a single voice.

To ensure positive attitude toward the social media programme, it is crucial to generate and post high-quality, relevant content that makes the social media programme live up to its promises from a user perspective. It has to be appealing, for instance by including high-quality pictures and videos, and have comparable or even better quality standards than the social media programmes of comparable (media) products. This refers to look and feel, multimedia content as well as interactivity. In addition, feedback loops must be ensured: If users have questions or post comments, a reaction from the social media management team must follow.

Further positive effects of social media hinge on engagement in the social media programme. It could be shown that respondents of the survey did not have a particularly high level of engagement. In accordance with this finding, it could be shown with importance performance analysis that an increase in performance with regard to users' engagement in the social media programme might be identified as a managerial target.

Firstly, this might be achieved by short-term measures such as competitions, prizes, or goodies. This encourages users to actively take part or even share content, which might even win over new users.

Secondly, increasing engagement might be achieved by lowering the threshold for initial engagement. For instance, while and after a particularly spectacular or controversial episode of a programme is running, it is more likely that users would like to engage in the social media programme and contribute to discussions that feel relevant to them. It can then be attempted to make these contributors regular users with a high level of engagement by embedding them more deeply in the community. If users feel that they are acknowledged experts or leaders in the social media community that centres around a TV brand they love, they are more likely to further distinguish themselves as members of the community by being more active and more involved. The social media management team might therefore address promising users directly in discussions, invite them to online and/or offline events or ask them to moderate groups, events or discussions within the social media programme.

The data suggest that to generate these positive effects of social media, features of the social media programme are crucial, which directly refers to gratifications obtained from the social media programme. Hence, particular market research on social media might be conducted in order to analyse users' needs in detail. This can also mean to closely listen to the community: One advantage of social media is that users voluntarily share information on their preferences and needs. This information needs to be collected and analysed. It is important to keep in mind that these preferences can be different for the social media programmes centring around different brands. Social media managers therefore need to monitor their respective target groups closely and cater for their particularities. To pursue this in a strategically sound manner, it should be analysed which user segments the respective target groups consist of, which gratifications they obtain from using the social media programme and how to best meet their various needs.

It has already been shown that TV brand related content is the most important feature for users. This means that the features of the social media programme that lead to the most positive effects are information about the TV brand and background content and/or content from the TV brand in case it was missed while it was broadcast. This implies that TV social media managers should pay particular attention to the content they provide as opposed to engaging users with each other. Clearly, users value the social media programmes more for communicative messages from the brand, not so much for communication about the brand with others. Social media managers face the challenge of increasing engagement while at the same time giving users the impression of being in an exclusive dialogue with the brand. A way to combine both – increase engagement and meet users' needs and preferences – would be to provide the required amount of information to fulfil basic needs. It could then be attempted to pursue strategies to increase engagement while at the same time evoking the impression that users still get exclusive content by posting surprising, attractive specials that spark discussions. Special sub-groups or forums for information and discussion on certain topics might be one attempt to achieve this.

As shown above, despite the importance of the social media programme, the television programme is the decisive driver for the consumer-brand relationship. Hence, social media are a powerful tool for marketing and branding objectives, but with regard to their relationship with the brand, consumers are not distracted from the brand's features. While social media support and strengthen consumers' relationships with their TV brands, these brands' features and the gratifications users obtain from them are still at the heart of the relationship. This calls for TV managers, not social media managers, to provide interesting, relevant, entraining high-quality television content. The media product at the core of social media communication is the TV programme. If it does not live up to viewers' expectations, they will not engage in social media in the first place. Since a basic attraction to the TV brand is needed to encourage consumers to join a social media community or sign up for a social media feed at all, the obvious step to positively influence brand loyalty and the consumer-brand relationship is compelling television content that attracts users, both as viewers of the TV programme and as users of the social media programme.

6.3   Limitations

One limitation in research focusing on social media for marketing and branding is the fact that users have to show a certain degree of intrinsic motivation to engage with the brand in order to have entered into an interactive relationship with it. Users of social media programmes for brand related content undergo a two-step process: If a certain degree of brand awareness and interest in the brand are present, they start engaging in the social media programme. The second step is for them to make use of the brand related social media offerings and thereby develop positive responses with regard to the brand. For research to examine the second step, which was the objective of this study, respondents need to be selected that have already taken the first step. This issue has been addressed as being a limitation the sample used for this study is subject to, this study being an investigation into social media users' loyalty to serialised TV brands.

A limitation to the transferability of results are the aforementioned particularities of the German television market. The German television market is characterised by a broad offer of public service broadcasting and a high number of free-to-air programmes, and a relatively low willingness to pay for television content. Findings might therefore not relate to other markets where consumers are more willing to spend money on pay television, which leads to different loyalty and re-use behaviours.

Other limitations are largely sampling issues. While the size of the sample as well as that of the subsamples was sufficient, the programmes investigated were very similar. They are all entertainment programmes, with similar slots in the programme scheme, and very similar social media offerings. While this provided the necessary comparability and allowed for their treatment in the same sample, inferences for other types of programmes and social media programmes focusing on tools other than Facebook are limited. Also, respondents were very young, the sample not being representative of the population. This is justified for this study; however, in the long run, when TV related social media programmes are more wide-spread, it would be desirable to have a sample that is representative of the viewer structure.

While the operationalisation of the construct proved rather sound, the scale perceived critics' response was measured on requires improvement. Being a combination of media research dimensions rather than an established scale, this is not very surprising.

6.4   Suggestions for further research

Having answered the research questions, the findings also raise a number of further questions. Firstly, it seems viable to further investigate engagement in the social media programme. While a number of studies have examined motivating factors to produce content as well as gratifications users obtain from social media (sections 2.3.4 and 3.1.5), engagement seems to be no either-or construct. This study showed that while users were willing enough to make use of the social media offerings and to some degree engage in them (otherwise, they would not have taken part in the survey), they still indicated to be rather passive participants and attached no significant importance to interaction with other users. The study should be repeated for more active users and results should be compared.

It would also be interesting to do more detailed research on the different levels on which television brands operate. A TV programme brand is subject to influences of the channel brand, or, if applicable, the brands of actors, producers, directors, etc. While it might be difficult to single out individual effects, research could focus on the impact that actors' personal social media profiles and channels have on the programme brand.

Another particularly interesting extension of this study would be an application to fictional serials. In section 2.2.3, narrative complexity and innovations in storytelling and viewer behaviour for serialised quality TV have been outlined. Research might focus on a combination of social media research in a media management research context and parasocial interaction theory. It would be worthwhile investigating the joint effects of parasocial relationships with the main characters in fictional television serials, and social media communication with and about those characters and the actors behind them, on viewing behaviour and loyalty toward the serial brand.

6.5   Revisiting objectives of this study and evaluating results

By investigating social media branding for serialised television brands, it was stated as the intention of this study to contribute to the national and international state of the art in media branding research. With regard to the identified research deficits in the field of social media branding for serialised television brands, the key question has been formulated: How does accompanying social media content support successful management of a serialised television brand? Four research questions were formulated for this study:

1. Which drivers – social media related, TV related, and/or related to the social environment – are most important for a consumer's relationship with the serialised television brand?
2. How do social media influence the image of the serialised television brand?
3. Which conditions drive social media usage as well as attitude toward the social media programme for the serialised television brand?
4. Which aspects of the social media programme for the serialised television brand are particularly important for users?

These questions can be answered with the results from model evaluation and additional analyses. Derived from literature research, social media related input factors, TV related input factors, and social environment related input factors were identified as potential influences on the consumer-brand relationship and brand loyalty. All hypothesized influences proved viable, either directly or indirectly.

Social media influence the serialised television brand in various ways: Attitude toward the social media programme directly positively affects brand loyalty, while engagement in the social media programme impacts brand loyalty via its positive influence on the consumer-brand relationship. Social media usage as well as attitude toward the social media programme are driven by the features of the social media programme: Gratifications obtained positively affect both attitude and engagement directly. When investigating gratifications in detail and which aspects of the social media programme are particularly important for users, it becomes clear that serialised brand related content is the most important feature for users, not communication or interaction with other users.

However, despite the obvious positive effects of social media, the study also found evidence for the importance of the TV programme itself. While attitude towards the social media programme has the strongest direct impact on brand loyalty, gratifications obtained from the TV brand have the strongest direct impact on the consumer-brand relationship. This and other findings lead to the conclusion that despite social media being a powerful tool for the stimulation of brand loyalty, the television programme is the decisive driver for the consumer-brand relationship.

References

Aaker, D. A. (1991). *Managing brand equity: Capitalizing on the value of a brand name.* New York, Free Press.

Aaker, D. A. (1996). *Building strong brands.* New York, Free Press.

Aaker D., & Biel L. (1993). *Brand Equity and Advertising.* Hillsdale: Lawrence Erlbaum Associates.

Aaker, J. L. (1997). Dimensions of Brand Personality. *Journal of Marketing Research,* 34(3), 347–356.

Agarwal, M., & Rao, V. (1996). An Empirical Comparison of Consumer-Based Measures of Brand Equity. *Marketing Letters,* 7(3), 237-247.

AGF/GfK. (2014). *Marktanteile der AGF-Lizenzsender im Tagesdurchschnitt 2013* [Market shares of AGF licensed broadcasters, daily average in 2013]. Retrieved from http://www.agf.de/daten/marktdaten/marktanteile/ [Accessed: 27 February 2014].

Ailawadi, K. L., Lehmann, D. R., & Neslin, S. A. (2003). Revenue Premium as an Outcome Measure of Brand Equity. *Journal of Marketing,* 67(October), 1–17.

Allen, N. J., & Meyer, J. P. (1990). The measurement and antecedents of affective, continuance and normative commitment to the organization. *Journal of Occupational Psychology,* 63(1), 1–18.

ALM GbR / Arbeitsgemeinschaft der Landesmedienanstalten. (2013). *Jahrbuch 2012/2013: Landesmedienanstalten und privater Rundfunk in Deutschland* [Yearbook 2012/2013: State media authorities and private broadcasting]. Retrieved from http://www.die-medienanstalten.de/fileadmin/Download/Publikationen/ALM-Jahrbuch/Jahrbuch_2013/Jahrbuch_2012-13_Druckversion.pdf [Accessed: 6 March 2014].

ALM GbR / Arbeitsgemeinschaft der Landesmedienanstalten. (2014). *Jahrbuch 2013/2014: Landesmedienanstalten und privater Rundfunk in Deutschland* [Yearbook 2013/2014: State media authorities and private broadcasting]. Retrieved from http://www.die-medienanstalten.de/fileadmin/Download/Publikationen/ALM-Jahrbuch/Jahrbuch_2014/Jahrbuch_2013-14_Druckversion.pdf [Accessed: 27 January 2015].

American Marketing Association. (2014). *Definition "Brand".* Retrieved from http://www.marketingpower.com/_layouts/dictionary.aspx?dLetter=B [Accessed: 13 March 2014].

Andersen, P. H. (2005). Relationship marketing and brand involvement of professionals through web- enhanced brand communities: the case of Coloplast. *Industrial Marketing Management,* 34(1), 39–51.

Anderson, E. W. (1998). Customer Satisfaction and Word of Mouth. *Journal of Service Research,* 1(1), 5–17.

Anderson, J. C., Gerbing, D. W., & Hunter, J. E. (1987). On the Assessment of Unidimensional Measurement: Internal and External Consistency, and Overall Consistency Criteria. *Journal of Marketing Research*, 24(4), 432–437.

ARD/ZDF-Onlinestudie 2013. (2013a). *Nutzung von Web 2.0 Anwendungen nach Geschlecht, Alter und Bildung 2013* [Usage of web 2.0 applications by gender, age, and education]. Retrieved from http://www.ard-zdf-onlinestudie.de/index.php?id=397 [Accessed: 15 January 2014].

ARD/ZDF-Onlinestudie 2013. (2013b). *Nutzung von Twitter nach Geschlecht und Alter 2010 bis 2013* [Usage of Twitter by gender and age from 2010 to 2013]. Retrieved from http://www.ard-zdf-onlinestudie.de/index.php?id=436 [Accessed: 13 February 2015].

ARD/ZDF-Onlinestudie 2013. (2013c). *Nutzung von Web-2.0-Anwendungen 2007 bis 2013* [Usage of web 2.0 applications from 2007 to 2013]. Retrieved from http://www.ard-zdf-onlinestudie.de/index.php?id=397 [Accessed: 15 January 2014].

ARD-Forschungsdienst. (2011). Nutzung und Funktionen von Social Communitys [Usage and features of social communities]. *Media Perspektiven*, 2, 115–120.

Arnhold, U. (2010). *User Generated Branding: Integrating User Generated Content into Brand Management*. Wiesbaden: Gabler Verlag / Springer Fachmedien.

Assael, H. (1998). *Consumer behavior and marketing action* (6th ed.). Cincinnati, Ohio: South-Western College Pub.

Aumüller, K. (2011). "Made by RTL". In K. Förster (Ed.), *Strategien erfolgreicher TV-Marken. Eine internationale Analyse* (pp. 172–185). Wiesbaden: VS, Verl. für Sozialwiss.

Bain, J. S. (1959). *Industrial organization*. New York : Wiley.

Baldinger, A. L., Blair, E., & Echambadi, R. (2002). Why Brands Grow. *Journal of Advertising Research*, 42(1), 7–14.

Ballantine, P. W., & Martin, B. A. S. (2005). Forming Parasocial Relationships in Online Communities. *Advances in Consumer Research*, 32(1), 197–201.

Barney, J. (1991). Special Theory Forum - The Resource-Based Model of the Firm: Origins, Implications, and Prospects. *Journal of Management*, 17(1), 97–98.

Baron, R. M., & Kenny, D. A. (1986). The moderator-mediator variable distinction in social psychological research: Conceptual, strategic, and statistical consideration. *Journal of Personality and Social Psychology*, 51(6), 1173–1182.

Becker, J. U., Clement, M., & Schaedel, U. (2010). The Impact of Network Size and Financial Incentives on Adoption and Participation in New Online Communities. *Journal of Media Economics*, 23(3), 165–179.

Bens, E. de, & Smaele, H. de. (2001). The Inflow of American Television Fiction on European Broadcasting Channels Revisited. *European Journal of Communication*, 16(1), 51–76.

Berry, L. L., & Parasuraman, A. (1991). *Marketing services: Competing through quality*. New York, Toronto: Free Press.

Berthon, P., Pitt, L., & Campbell, C. (2008). Ad lib: When customers create the ad. *California Management Review*, 50(4), 6–30.

Bezjian-Avery, A., Calder, B. J., & Iacobucci, D. (1998). New media interactive advertising vs. traditional advertising. *Journal of Advertising Research*, 38(4), 23–32.

Bido, D. (2008). Importance-performance map (ECSI). *smartPLS forum article*. Retrieved from http://www.smartpls.de/forum/viewtopic.php?t=751&highlight=importance (10 July 2008) [Accessed: 20 February 2014].

Bignell, J. (2004). *An introduction to television studies*. London: Routledge.

Blackston, M. (1992). Observations: Building brand equity by managing the brand's relationships. *Journal of Advertising Research*, May/June, 79–83.

Bloemer, J. M. M., & Kasper, H. D. P. (1995). The complex relationship between consumer satisfaction and brand loyalty. *Journal of Economic Psychology*, 16, 311–329.

Blumenthal, H. J., & Goodenough, O. R. (2006). *This business of television* (3rd ed.). New York: Billboard Books.

Bock, A. (2013). *Fernsehserienrezeption: Produktion, Vermarktung und Rezeption US-amerikanischer Prime-Time-Serien* [Reception of television series: Production, commercialization, and reception of American prime time series]. Wiesbaden: Springer Fachmedien.

Bonoma, T. V. (1985). Case Research in Marketing: Opportunities, Problems, and a Process. *Journal of Marketing Research*, 22(2), 199–208.

Boyd, D. M., & Ellison, N. B. (2007). Social Network Sites: Definition, History, and Scholarship. *Journal of Computer-Mediated Communication*, 13(1), 210–230. Retrieved from http://onlinelibrary.wiley.com/doi/10.1111/j.1083-6101.2007.00393.x/full [Accessed 22 March 2012].

Boyle, E. (2007). A process model of brand cocreation: brand management and research implications. *Journal of Product & Brand Management*, 16(2), 122–131.

Brandtzæg, P. B., Lüders, M., & Skjetne, J. H. (2010). Too Many Facebook "Friends"? Content Sharing and Sociability Versus the Need for Privacy in Social Network Sites. *International Journal of Human-Computer Interaction*, 26(11), 1006–1030.

Brown, J., Broderick, A. J., & Lee, N. (2007). Word of mouth communication within online communities: Conceptualizing the online social network. *Journal of Interactive Marketing*, 21(3), 2–20.

Burmann, C. (2005). Kritische Reflektion zum Markenmanagement [Critical reflection on brand management]. In H. Meffert (Ed.), *Markenmanagement. Identitätsorientierte*

Markenführung und praktische Umsetzung; mit Best-practice-Fallstudien (2nd ed., pp. 855–860). Wiesbaden: Gabler.

Burmann, C., & Arnhold, U. (2008). *User generated branding: State of the art of research.* Berlin, Münster: Lit.

Burmann, C., Blinda, L., & Nitschke, A. (2003). *Konzeptionelle Grundlagen des identitätsbasierten Markenmanagements* [Conceptual background of identity-based brand management]. (Working Paper No. 1). Universität Bremen, Bremen. Retrieved: http://www.lim.uni-bremen.de/files/burmann/publikationen/LiM-AP-01-Identitaetsbasiertes-Markenmanagement.pdf

Burmann, C., & Meffert, H. (2005a). Theoretisches Grundkonzept der identitätsorientierten Markenführung [Theoretical background of identity-based brand management]. In H. Meffert (Ed.), *Markenmanagement. Identitätsorientierte Markenführung und praktische Umsetzung; mit Best-practice-Fallstudien* (2nd ed., pp. 37–72). Wiesbaden: Gabler.

Burmann, C., & Meffert, H. (2005b). Managementkonzept der identitätsorientierten Markenführung [Managerial concept of identity-based brand management]. In H. Meffert (Ed.), *Markenmanagement. Identitätsorientierte Markenführung und praktische Umsetzung; mit Best-practice-Fallstudien* (2nd ed., pp. 73–114). Wiesbaden: Gabler.

Burmann, C., Meffert, H., & Feddersen, C. (2007). Identitätsbasierte Markenführung [Identity-based brand management]. In A. Florack (Ed.), *Psychologie der Markenführung* (pp. 3–30). München: Vahlen.

Burmann, C., Meffert, H., & Koers, M. (2005). Stellenwert und Gegenstand des Markenmanagements [Significance and issues of brand management]. In H. Meffert (Ed.), *Markenmanagement. Identitätsorientierte Markenführung und praktische Umsetzung; mit Best-practice-Fallstudien* (2nd ed., pp. 3–17). Wiesbaden: Gabler.

Burmann, C., & Stolle, W. (2007). *Markenimage. Konzeptualisierung eines komplexen mehrdimensionalen Konstrukts* [Brand image: conceptualisation of a complex, multidimensional construct]. (Working Paper No. 28). Universität Bremen, Bremen. Retrieved: http://www.lim.uni-bremen.de/files/burmann/publikationen/LIM-AP-28-Markenimagekonzeptualisierung.pdf

Burmann, C., & Zeplin, S. (2005). Building brand commitment: A behavioural approach to internal brand management. *Journal of Brand Management, 12*(4), 279–300.

Burton, J., & Khammash, M. (2010). Why do people read reviews posted on consumer-opinion portals? *Journal of Marketing Management, 26*(3/4), 230–255.

Busemann, K., Fisch, M., & Frees, B. (2012). Dabei sein ist alles – zur Nutzung privater Communitys [Taking part is the most important thing – on usage of private communities]. *Media Perspektiven, 5*, 258–267.

Business Wire. (2013). *Activision Blizzard Announces Transformative Purchase of Shares from Vivendi and New Capital Structure.* Retrieved from http://www.businesswire.com/news/home/20130725006767/en/Activision-Blizzard-Announces-Transformative-Purchase-Shares-Vivendi#.UxXtN4VH3To (25 July 2013) [Accessed 4 March 2014].

Calder, B. J., & Malthouse, E. C. (2008). Media Brands and Consumer Experiences. In M. Ots (Ed.), *Jönköping International Business School (JIBS) Research Report 2008-1* (pp. 89-93). Jönköping, Sweden.

Calder, B. J., Malthouse, E. C., & Schaedel, U. (2009). An Experimental Study of the Relationship between Online Engagement and Advertising Effectiveness. *Journal of Interactive Marketing*, 23(4), 321–331.

Carter, M. (2009a). Brands and Twitter: Joining the chatter. *New Media Age*, (19 February 2009), 19–20.

Carter, M. (2009b). TV and Social Media: Fighting for Dominance. *New Media Age*, (16 April 2009), 16–17.

Casaló, L. V., Flavián, C., & Guinalíu, M. (2008). Promoting Consumer's Participation in Virtual Brand Communities. *Journal of Marketing Communications*, 14(1), 19–36.

Casteleyn, J., Mottart, A., & Rutten, K. (2009). How to use Facebook in your market research. *International Journal of Market Research*, 51(4), 439–447.

Cha, J., & Chan-Olmsted, S. M. (2012). Substitutability between Online Video Platforms and Television. *Journalism & Mass Communication Quarterly*, 89(2), 261-278.

Chang, B.-H., & Chan-Olmsted, S. M. (2010). Success Factors of Cable Network Brand Extension: Focusing on the Parent Network, Composition, Fit, Consumer Characteristics, and Viewing Habits. *Journal of Broadcasting & Electronic Media*, 54(4), 641-656.

Chang, B.-H., & Ki, E.-J. (2005). Devising a practical model for predicting theatrical movie success: Focusing on the experience good property. *The Journal of Media Economics*, 18(4), 247–269.

Chang, B.-H., Bae, J., and Lee, S.-E. (2004). Consumer evaluations of cable network brand extensions: A case study of the discovery channels. *Journal of Media Business Studies*, 1(2), 47–71.

Chan-Olmsted, S. M. (2006). *Competitive strategy for media firms: Strategic and brand management in changing media markets. LEA's communication series.* Mahwah, N.J. [etc.]: Lawrence Erlbaum Associates.

Chan-Olmsted, S. M. (2011). Media Branding in a Changing World: Challenges and Opportunities 2.0. *International Journal on Media Management*, 13(1), 3-19.

Chan-Olmsted, S. M., & Cha, J. (2007). Branding television news in a multichannel environment: an exploratory study of network news brand personality. *International Journal on Media Management*, 9(4), 135–150.

Chan-Olmsted, S. M., & Cha, J. (2008). Exploring the antecedents and effects of brand images for television news: An application of brand personality construct in a multichannel news environment. *International Journal on Media Management*, 10(1), 32–45.

Chan-Olmsted, S. M., Cha, J., & Oba, G. (2008). An Examination of the Host Country Factors Affecting the Export of U.S. Video Media Goods. *Journal of Media Economics*, 21(3), 191–216.

Chan-Olmsted, S. M., & Jung, J. (2001). Strategizing the net business: How the U.S. television networks diversify, brand, and compete in the age of the Internet. *International Journal on Media Management*, 3(4), 213–225.

Chan-Olmsted, S. M., & Kim, Y. (2002). The PBS Brand Versus Cable Brands: Assessing the Brand Image of Public Television in a Multichannel Environment. *Journal of Broadcasting & Electronic Media*, 46(2), 300-320.

Chaudhuri, A., & Holbrook, M. B. (2001). The Chain of Effects from Brand Trust and Brand Affect to Brand Performance: The Role of Brand Loyalty. *Journal of Marketing*, 65(April), 81–93.

Chernatony, L. de. (1999). Brand Management Through Narrowing the Gap Between Brand Identity and Brand Reputation. *Journal of Marketing Management*, 15(1-3), 157–179.

Chernatony, L. de, & Dall'Omlo Riley, F. (1998). Defining A "Brand": Beyond The Literature With Experts' Interpretations. *Journal of Marketing Management*, 14, 417–443.

Chesbrough, H. W. (2003). The Era of Open Innovation. *MIT Sloan Management Review*, 44(3), 35–41.

Cheung, M. Y., Luo, C., Sia, C. L., & Chen, H. (2009). Credibility of Electronic Word-of-Mouth: Informational and Normative Determinants of On-line Consumer Recommendations. *International Journal of Electronic Commerce*, 13(4), 9–38.

Chevalier, J. A., & Mayzlin, D. (2006). The Effect of Word of Mouth on Sales: Online Book Reviews. *Journal of Marketing Research*, 43(3), 345–354.

Chin, W. W. (1998). The partial least squares approach to structural equation modeling. In G. A. Marcoulides (Ed.), *Modern methods for business research* (pp. 295–358). Mahwah, NJ: Lawrence Erlbaum.

Chin, W. W. (2000). *Frequently Asked Questions - Partial Least Squares & PLS-Graph. Home Page. [Online]*. Retrieved from http://disc-nt.cba.uh.edu/chin/plsfaq.htm (21 December 2004) [Accessed 9 January 2014].

Chin, W. W., Marcolin, B. L., & Newsted, P. R. (1996). A partial least squares latent variable modeling approach for measuring interaction effects. Results from a monte carlo simulation study and voice mail Emotion/Adoption study. In J. I. DeGross, S. Jarvenpaa, & A. Srinivasan (Eds.), *Proceedings of the Seventeenth International Conference on Information Systems*. Cleveland, OH, 21–41.

Chin, W. W., Marcolin, B. L., & Newsted, P. R. (2003). A partial least squares latent variable modeling approach for measuring interaction effects: results from a monte carlo simulation study and an electronic-mail emotion/adoption study. *Information Systems Research*, 14(2), 189–217.

Chin, W. W., & Newsted, P. R. (1999). Structural equation modeling analysis with small samples using partial least squares. In R. H. Hoyle (Ed.), *Statistical strategies for small sample research* (pp. 307–342). Thousand Oaks, CA: Sage.

Christodoulides, G. (2009). Branding in the post-internet era. *Marketing Theory*, 9(1), 141–144.

Christodoulides, G., Jevons, C., & Blackshaw, P. (2011). The Voice of the Consumer Speaks Forcefully in Brand Identity: User-Generated Content Forces Smart Marketers to listen. *Journal of Advertising Research*, March 2011 Supplement, 101–108.

Christodoulides, G., Jevons, C., & Bonhomme, J. (2012). Memo to Marketers: Quantitative Evidence for Change: How User-Generated Content Really Affects Brands. *Journal of Advertising Research*, 52(1), 53–64.

Christophersen, T., & Grape, C. (2007). Die Erfassung latenter Konstrukte mit Hilfe formativer und reflektiver Messmodelle [Modelling of latent constructs with formative and reflective measurement models]. In S. Albers (Ed.), *Methodik der empirischen Forschung* (2nd ed., pp. 103–118). Wiesbaden: Gabler.

Chu, S.-C. (2011). Viral Advertising in Social Media: Participation in Facebook Groups and Responses Among College-Aged Users. *Journal of Interactive Advertising*, 12(1), 30–43.

Chu, S.-C., & Kim, Y. (2011). Determinants of consumer engagement in electronic word-of-mouth (eWOM) in social networking sites. *International Journal of Advertising*, 30(1), 47–75.

Clement, M., Proppe, D., & Rott, A. (2007). Do Critics Make Bestsellers? Opinion Leaders and the Success of Books. *Journal of Media Economics*, 20(2), 77–105.

Coffey, A. J., & Cleary, J. (2011). Promotional practices of cable news networks: A comparative analysis of new and traditional spaces. *International Journal on Media Management*, 13(3), 161–176.

Cohen, J. (1988). *Statistical power analysis for the behavioral sciences* (2nd ed.). Hillsdale, NJ: L. Erlbaum Associates.

Collins, N. L., & Miller, L. C. (1994). Self-Disclosure and Liking: A Meta-analytical Review. *Psychological Bulletin*, 116(3), 457–474.

Crocker, J., & Luhtanen, R. (1990). Collective self-esteem and ingroup bias. *Journal of Personality and Social Psychology*, 58(1), 60–67.

Daft, R. L., & Lengel, R. H. (1986). Organizational information requirements, media richness, and structural design. *Management Science*, 32(5), 554–571.

Dahlén, M., & Lange, F. (2006). A Disaster Is Contagious: How a Brand in Crisis Affects Other Brands. *Journal of Advertising Research*, 46(4), 388–397.

Daugherty, T., Eastin, M. S., & Bright, L. (2008). Exploring consumer motivations for creating user-generated content. *Journal of Interactive Advertising*, 8(2), 1–24.

Daugherty, T., Eastin, M. S., & Gangadharbatla, H. (2005). eCRM: Understanding Internet Confidence and Implications for Customer Relationship Management. In I. Clarke & T. Flaherty (Eds.), *Advances in electronic marketing* (pp. 67–82). Hershey, PA: Idea Group Pub.

Davies, M. B. (2007). *Doing a successful research project: Using qualitative or quantitative methods* (4th ed.). Basingstoke: Palgrave Macmillan.

Day, G. S. (1969). A Two-Dimensional Concept Of Brand Loyalty. *Journal of Advertising Research*, 9(3), 29–35.

Dehm, U., & Storll, D. (2003). TV-Erlebnisfaktoren: Ein ganzheitlicher Forschungsansatz zur Rezeption unterhaltender und informierender Fernsehangebote [TV experience factors: An integrated research approach to the reception of entertaining and informative television content]. *Media Perspektiven*, 9, 425–434.

Dehm, U., Storll, D., & Beeske, S. (2005). Die Erlebnisqualität von Fernsehsendungen: Eine Anwendung der TV-Erlebnisfaktoren [Experience quality of television programmes: An application of TV experience factors]. *Media Perspektiven*, 2, 50–60.

Dehm, U., Storll, D., & Beeske, S. (2006). Das Internet: Erlebnisweisen und Erlebnistypen: Sich ergänzende und konkurrierende Gratifikationen durch Fernsehen und Internet [The internet: Manners and types of experience: Complementing and competing gratifications from television and internet]. *Media Perspektiven*, 2, 91–101.

Deighton, J. (1996). The future of interactive marketing. *Harvard Business Review*, 74(6), 151–161.

Dekimpe, M. G., Steenkamp, J.-B. E. M., Mellens, M., & Abeele, P. V. (1997). Decline and variability in brand loyalty. *International Journal of Research in Marketing*, 14(5), 405–420.

Dellarocas, C. (2003). The Digitization of Word of Mouth: Promise and Challenges of Online Feedback Mechanisms. *Management Science*, 49(10), 1407–1424.

Denson, S. (2011). "To be continued...": Seriality and Serialization in Interdisciplinary Perspective: Conference Proceedings of: What Happens Next: The Mechanics of Serialization. Graduate Conference at the University of Amsterdam, March 25–26, 2011. *Journal of Literary Theory*, JLTonline 17 June 2011. Retrieved from http://www.jltonline.de/index.php/conferences/article/view/346/1004 [Accessed 25 January 2013].

Deshpandé, R. (1983). 'Paradigms Lost': On Theory and Method in Research in Marketing. *Journal of Marketing*, 47(4), 101–110.

Dhar, V., & Chang, E. A. (2009). Does Chatter Matter? The Impact of User-Generated Content on Music Sales. *Journal of Interactive Marketing*, 23(4), 300–307.

Diamantopoulos, A., & Winklhofer, H. M. (2001). Index construction with formative indicators: an alternative to scale development. *Journal of Marketing Research*, 38(2), 269–277.

Dichter, E. (1966). How Word-of-Mouth Advertising Works. *Harvard Business Review*, 44(6), 147–166.

Dick, A. S., & Basu, K. (1994). Customer Loyalty: Toward an Integrated Conceptual Framework. *Journal of the Academy of Marketing Science*, 22(Spring), 99–113.

Dijkstra, T. (1983). Some comments on maximum likelihood and partial least squares methods. *Journal of Econometrics*, 22(1-2), 67–90.

Dimmick, J., & Rothenbuhler, E. (1984). The Theory of the Niche: Quantifying Competition Among Media Industries. *Journal of Communication*, 34(1), 103–119.

Dimmick, J., Kline, S., & Stafford, L. (2000). The Gratification Niches of Personal E-mail and the Telephone. Competition, Displacement, and Complementarity. *Communication Research*, 27(2), 227-248.

Doyle, G. (2006). Managing Global Expansion of Media Products and Brands: A Case Study of FHM. *International Journal on Media Management*, 8(3), 105-115.

Dosi, G. (1988). The nature of the innovative process. In G. Dosi, C. Freeman, R. Nelson, G. Silverberg, & L. L. Soete (Eds.), *Technical change and economic theory* (pp. 221–238). London, New York: Pinter Publishers.

Dunn, O. J. (1961). Multiple Comparisons Among Means. *Journal of the American Statistical Association*, 56(293), 52–64.

Dunn, O. J. (1964). Multiple comparisons using rank sums. *Technometrics*, 6(3), 241–252.

Eagly, A. H., & Chaiken, S. (1998). Attitude Structure and Function. In D. T. Gilbert, S. T. Fiske, & G. Lindzey (Eds.), *The Handbook of social psychology* (4th ed., pp. 269–322). USA: Oxford University Press.

Easterby-Smith, M., Thorpe, R., & Lowe, A. (1991). *Management Research: An Introduction*. London: Sage.

Ebersbach, A., Glaser, M., Heigl, R., & Dueck, G. (2006). *Wiki: Web collaboration*. Berlin, New York: Springer.

Eick, D. (2007). *Programmplanung: Die Strategien deutscher TV-Sender* [Programme planning: Strategies of German broadcasters]. Konstanz: UVK Verlagsgesellschaft.

Elberse, A., & Eliashberg, J. (2003). Demand and Supply Dynamics for Sequentially Released Products in International Markets: The Case of Motion Pictures. *Marketing Science*, 22(3), 329–354.

Eliashberg, J., Elberse, A., & Leenders, M. A. (2006). The Motion Picture Industry: Critical Issues in Practice, Current Research, and New Research Directions. *Marketing Science*, 25(6), 638–661.

Eliashberg, J., & Shugan, S. M. (1997). Film Critics: influencers or Predictors? *Journal of Marketing*, 61(2), 68–78.

Esch, F.-R. (2005). *Strategie und Technik der Markenführung* [Strategy and technique of brand management] (3rd ed.). München: Vahlen.

European Commission. (2014). *A profile of current and future audiovisual audience.* Retrieved from: http://bookshop.europa.eu/de/a-profile-of-current-and-future-audiovisual-audience-pbNC0114077/downloads/NC-01-14-077-DE-N/NC0114077DEN_002.pdf?FileName=NC0114077DEN_002.pdf&SKU=NC0114077DE N_PDF&CatalogueNumber=NC-01-14-077-DE-N [Accessed 26 January 2015].

Evans, J. R., & Laskin, R. L. (1994). The relationship marketing process. *Industrial Marketing Management*, 23(5), 439–452.

Facebook. (2010). *Statistics, Press Room.* Retrieved from http://www.facebook.com/press/info.php?statistics [Accessed 20 August 2010].

Facebook. (2013). *Annual Report 2012.* Retrieved from https://materials.proxyvote.com/Approved/30303M/20130409/AR_166822/document.pdf [Accessed 4 March 2014].

Facebook. (2014). *About.* Retrieved from https://www.facebook.com/facebook/info [Accessed 4 March 2014].

Fahrmeir, L., Künstler, R., Pigeot, I., & Tutz, G. (2007). *Statistik: Der Weg zur Datenanalyse* [Statistics: The way to data analysis] (6th ed.). *Springer-Lehrbuch.* Berlin: Springer.

Farquhar P. (1989). Managing brand equity. *Marketing Research*, 1(September), 24–33.

Fazio, R. H., & Olson, M. A. (2003). Attitudes: Foundations, Functions, and Consequences. In M. Hogg & J. Cooper (Eds.), *The Sage Handbook of Social Psychology* (pp. 139–160). London: Sage.

Fishbein, M., & Ajzen, I. (1975). *Belief, attitude, intention, and behavior: An introduction to theory and research.* Reading, MA: Addison-Wesley Pub. Co.

Fitzsimons, G. J., & Lehmann, D. R. (2004). Reactance to Recommendations: When Unsolicited Advice Yields Contrary Responses. *Marketing Science*, 23(1), 82–94.

Foregger, S. K. (2008). *Uses and gratifications of Facebook.com.* (Unpublished doctoral dissertation). Michigan State University, East Lansing.

Fornell, C., & Bookstein, F. L. (1982). Two structural equation models: LISREL and PLS applied to consumer exit-voice theory. *Journal of Marketing Research*, 19(4), 440–452.

Fornell, C., & Cha, J. (1994). Partial Least Squares. In R. P. Bagozzi (Ed.), *Advanced methods of marketing research* (pp. 52–78). Cambridge, MA: Blackwell Business.

Fornell, C., & Larcker, D. F. (1981). Evaluating Structural Equation Models with Unobservable Variables and Measurement Error. *Journal of Marketing Research*, 18(1), 39–50.

Förster, K. (2011). TV-Markenführung: Besonderheiten, Strategien und Instrumente [Television brand management: Particularities, strategies and tools]. In K. Förster (Ed.), *Strategien erfolgreicher TV-Marken. Eine internationale Analyse* (pp. 9–30). Wiesbaden: VS, Verl. für Sozialwiss.

Fournier, S. (1994). *A consumer-brand relationship framework for strategic brand management* (Unpublished doctoral dissertation). University of Florida, Gainesville.

Fournier, S. (1998). Consumers and Their Brands: Developing Relationship Theory in Consumer Research. *Journal of Consumer Research*, 24(3), 343–373.

Fournier, S., & Yao, J. L. (1997). Reviving brand loyalty: A reconceptualization within the framework of consumer-brand relationships. *International Journal of Research in Marketing*, 14(5), 451–472.

Freeman, C. (1988). Introduction. In G. Dosi, C. Freeman, R. Nelson, G. Silverberg, & L. L. Soete (Eds.), *Technical change and economic theory* (pp. 1–8). London, New York: Pinter Publishers.

Frees, B., & Fisch, M. (2011). Veränderte Mediennutzung durch Communitys? [Changes in media consumption due to communities?]. *Media Perspektiven*, 3, 154–164.

Gangadharbatla, H. (2008). Facebook Me: Collective Self-Esteem, Need to Belong, and Internet Self-Efficacy as Predictors of the IGeneration's Attitudes Toward Social Networking Sites. *Journal of Interactive Advertising*, 8(2), 5–15.

Ganley, D., & Lampe, C. (2009). The ties that bind: Social network principles in online communities. *Decision Support Systems*, 47(3), 266–274.

Gardner, W. L., & Knowles, M. L. (2008). Love makes you real: Favorite television characters are perceived as "real" in a social facilitation paradigm. *Social Cognition*, 26(2), 156–168.

GfK. (2013). *Studie zur digitalen Content-Nutzung (DCN-Studie)* [Study on digital content usage]. Retrieved from: http://www.gvu.de/media/pdf/866.pdf [Accessed 26 January 2015].

GfK. (2014). *Twitter and GfK announce partnership*. Retrieved from http://www.gfk.com/news-and-events/press-room/press-releases/Pages/Twitter-and-GfK-announce-partnership.aspx (23 January 2014) [Accessed 6 March 2014].

Gilmore, G. W. (1919). *Animism: Or, Thought currents of primitive peoples*. Boston, MA: Marshall Jones Company.

Gitlin, T. (1980). *The whole world is watching: Mass media in the making & unmaking of the New Left*. Berkeley, CA: University of California Press.

Godes, D., & Mayzlin, D. (2004). Using Online Conversations to Study Word-of-Mouth Communication. *Management Science*, 23(4), 545–560.

Godes, D., & Mayzlin, D. (2009). Firm-Created Word-of-Mouth Communication: Evidence from a Field Test. *Marketing Science*, 28(4), 721–739.

Godwin-Jones, R. (2003). Emerging Technologies. Blogs and Wikis: Environments for Online Collaboration. *Language Learning & Technology*, 7(2), 12–16.

Goldenberg, J., Han, S., Lehmann, D. R., & Hong, J. W. (2009). The Role of Hubs in the Adoption Process. *Journal of Marketing*, 73(2), 1–13.

Grégoire, Y., Tripp, T. M., & Legoux, R. (2009). When customer love turns into lasting hate: the effects of relationship strength and time on customer revenge and avoidance. *Journal of Marketing*, 73(6), 18–32.

Grossman, R. P. (1998). Developing and managing effective consumer relationships. *Journal of Product & Brand Management*, 7(1), 27–40.

Gundlach, G. T., Achrol, R. S., & Mentzer, J. T. (1995). The Structure of Commitment in Exchange. *Journal of Marketing*, 59(January), 78-92.

Ha, C. L. (1998). The theory of reasoned action applied to brand loyalty. *Journal of Product & Brand Management*, 7(1), 51–61.

Ha, L., & Chan-Olmsted, S. M. (2004). Cross-Media Use in Electronic Media: The Role of Cable Television Web Sites in Cable Television Network Branding and Viewership. *Journal of Broadcasting & Electronic Media*, 48(4), 620-645.

Habann, F. (2003). *Innovationsmanagement in Medienunternehmen: Theoretische Grundlagen und Praxiserfahrungen* [Innovation management in media companies: Theoretical background and practical experience]. Wiesbaden: Gabler.

Habann, F., Nienstedt, H.-W., & Reinelt, J. (2008). Success factors of brand expansions in the newspaper industry. An empirical analysis. In M. Ots (Ed.), *Jönköping International Business School (JIBS) Research Report 2008-1* (pp. 25-46). Jönköping, Sweden.

Haenlein, M., & Kaplan, A. M. (2004). A Beginner's Guide to Partial Least Squares Analysis. *UNDERSTANDING STATISTICS*, 3(4), 283–297.

Hair, J. F., Ringle, C. M., & Sarstedt, M. (2011). PLS-SEM: Indeed a silver bullet. *The Journal of Marketing Theory and Practice*, 19(2), 139–152.

Hair, J. F., Sarstedt, M., Ringle, C. M., & Mena, J. A. (2012). An assessment of the use of partial least squares structural equation modeling in marketing research. *Journal of the Academy of Marketing Science*, 40(3), 414–433.

Haridakis, P. M. (2002). Viewer Characteristics, Exposure to Television Violence, and Aggression. *Media Psychology*, 4(4), 323-352.

Haridakis, P. M., & Hanson, G. (2009). Social interaction and co-viewing with YouTube: Blending mass communication reception and social connection. *Journal of Broadcasting & Electronic Media*, 53(2), 317–335.

Hauschildt, J., & Salomo, S. (2011). *Innovationsmanagement* [Innovation management] (5th ed.). München: Franz Vahlen.

Heffler, M., & Möbus, P. (2014). Der Werbemarkt 2013. Fernsehwerbung dominiert den Werbemarkt [The advertising market in 2013. Television advertising dominates the advertising market]. *Media Perspektiven*, 6, 314–324.

Hein, D. (2012a). RTL 2: Warum die Event-Programmierung von "Game of Thrones" wegweisend sein könnte [Why event programming of "Game of Thrones" might be ground-breaking]. *Horizont*. Retrieved from http://www.horizont.net/aktuell/medien/pages/protected/RTL-2-Warum-die-Event-Programmierung-von-Game-of-Thrones-wegweisend-sein-koennte_106583.html (23 March 2012) [Accessed 6 September 2012].

Hein, D. (2012b). RTL 2 trifft mit Serienevent "Game of Thrones" ins Schwarze [RTL 2 strikes home with event "Game of Thrones"]. *Horizont*. Retrieved from http://www.horizont.net/aktuell/medien/pages/protected/RTL-2-trifft-mit-Serienevent-Game-of-Thrones-ins-Schwarze-_106606.html (26 March 2012) [Accessed 6 September 2012].

Hein, D. (2014). TV-Markt 2013: ZDF behauptet Führung, RTL und Sat 1 verlieren [Television market in 2013: ZDF maintains leadership, RTL and Sat 1 lose]. *Horizont*. Retrieved from http://www.horizont.net/aktuell/medien/pages/protected/TV-Markt-2013-ZDF-behauptet-Fuehrung-RTL-und-Sat-1-verlieren_118434.html html (2 January 2014) [Accessed 27 February 2014]

Heinrich, J. (2010). *Medienökonomie: Band 2: Hörfunk und Fernsehen* [Media economics: Instalment 2: sound and television broadcasting] (2nd ed.). Wiesbaden: Westdt. Verl.

Hennig-Thurau, T., Gwinner, K. P., Walsh, G., & Gremler, D. D. (2004). Electronic Word-of-Mouth via Consumer-Opinion Platforms: What motivates consumers to articulate themselves on the internet? *Journal of Interactive Marketing*, 18(1), 38–52.

Henseler, J., & Chin, W. W. (2010). A Comparison of Approaches for the Analysis of Interaction Effects Between Latent Variables Using Partial Least Squares Path Modeling. *Structural Equation Modeling*, 17(1), 82–109. Retrieved from http://www.pls-institute.org/uploads/Henseler_Chin_2010.pdf

Henseler, J., & Fassott, G. (2010). Testing Moderating Effects in PLS Path Models: An Illustration of Available Procedures. In V. Esposito Vinzi, W. W. Chin, J. Henseler, & H. Wang (Eds.), *Handbook of Partial Least Squares: Concepts, Methods and Applications* (pp. 713–735). Berlin: Springer-Verlag. Retrieved from http://pls-institute.org/uploads/Henseler_Fassott_2010.pdf

Hesse, A. (2008). *"Terra X" als neue Dachmarke* ["Terra X" as new umbrella brand]. Retrieved from http://www.zdf-jahrbuch.de/2008/programmarbeit/hesse.php [Accessed 25 September 2012].

Hickethier, K. (1992). Die Fernsehserie – eine Kette von Verhaltenseinheiten [The television series – a chain of behavioural entities]. In F. Salow (Ed.), *Serie Kunst im Alltag* (pp. 11–18). Berlin: Vistas.

Hippel, E. von. (1986). Lead users: a source of novel product concepts. *Management Science*, 32(7), 791–805.

Hippel, E. von. (2001). Innovation by User Communities: Learning from Open-Source Software. *MIT Sloan Management Review*, 42(4), 82–86.

Hippel, E. von. (2006). *Democratizing innovation*. Cambridge, MA, London: MIT Press.

Hirsch, C., & Förster, K. (2011). ZDF – Ihr gutes öffentliches Recht? [ZDF – Public service broadcasting you deserve?]. In K. Förster (Ed.), *Strategien erfolgreicher TV-Marken. Eine internationale Analyse* (pp. 154–171). Wiesbaden: VS, Verl. für Sozialwiss.

Hirschman, E. C., & Holbrook, M. B. (1982). Hedonic Consumption: Emerging Concepts, Methods and Propositions. *Journal of Marketing*, 46(3), 92–101.

Hofstätter, E. (2011). ProSieben: Die Entertainmentwelt von Stefan Raab [ProSieben: Stefan Raab's world of entertainment]. In K. Förster (Ed.), *Strategien erfolgreicher TV-Marken. Eine internationale Analyse* (pp. 186–198). Wiesbaden: VS, Verl. für Sozialwiss.

Homburg, C., & Pflesser, C. (1999). Strukturgleichungsmodelle mit latenten Variablen: Kausalanalyse [Structural equation modelling with latent variables: causal analysis]. In A. Herrmann & C. Homburg (Eds.), *Marktforschung. Methoden, Anwendungen, Praxisbeispiele* (pp. 633–659). Wiesbaden: Gabler.

Howard, J. A., & Sheth, J. N. (1969). *The Theory of Buyer Behavior*. New York: John Wiley & Sons.

Hsu, H. Y., & Tsou, H.-T. (2011). Understanding customer experiences in online blog environments. *International Journal of Information Management*, 31(6), 510–523.

Huang, C.-Y., Shen, Y.-Z., Lin, H.-X., & Chang, S.-S. (2007). Bloggers' Motivations and Behaviors: A Model. *Journal of Advertising Research*, 47(4), 472–484.

Huber, F., Herrmann, A., Meyer, F., Vogel, J., & Vollhardt, K. (2007). *Kausalmodellierung mit Partial Least Squares: Eine anwendungsorientierte Einführung* [Causal modelling with Partial Least Squares: An application-oriented introduction]. Wiesbaden: Gabler.

Huber, F., Meyer, F., & Weißhaar, I. (2013). *Die Rolle von Markenvertrauen für die Erreichung von Konsumzielen: Eine kausalanalytische Studie am Beispiel von gesunder Ernährung mit Functional Food* [The role of brand trust for the achievement of consumption targets: A causal analysis study using the example of healthy nutrition with functional food]. *Reihe: Marketing: Vol. 68*. Lohmar, Köln: Eul.

Interbrand. (2014). *Best Global Brands – Ranking*. Retrieved from http://www.bestglobal brands.com/2014/ranking/ [Accessed 29 January 2015].

Iyengar, S., & Kinder, D. R. (1987). *News that matters: Television and American Opinion*. Chicago, London: University of Chicago Press.

Iyengar, S., & Simon, A. (1993). News Coverage of the Gulf Crisis and Public Opinion : A Study of Agenda-Setting, Priming, and Framing. *Communication Research*, 20(3), 365–383.

Iyer, R., & Muncy, J. A. (2005). The Role of Brand Parity in Developing Loyal Customers. *Journal of Advertising Research*, 45(2), 222–228.

Jaccard, J., & Turrisi, R. (2003). *Interaction effects in multiple regression* (2nd ed.). *Sage university papers series. Quantitative applications in the social sciences: no. 07-72*. Thousand Oaks, CA: Sage Publications.

Jäckel, M. (2011). *Medienwirkungen: Ein Studienbuch zur Einführung* [Media effects: An introductory textbook] (5th ed.). Wiesbaden: VS Verlag für Sozialwissenschaften.

Jacoby, J., & Chestnut, R. W. (1978). *Brand loyalty: Measurement and management.* New York: Wiley.

Jahn-Sudmann, A., & Kelleter, F., (2012). Die Dynamik serieller Überbietung: Amerikanische Fernsehserien und das Konzept des Quality TV [Dynamics of serial outbidding: American television serials and the concept of quality TV]. In F. Kelleter (Ed.), *Populäre Serialität: Narration - Evolution - Distinktion. Zum seriellen Erzählen seit dem 19. Jahrhundert* (pp. 205–224). Bielefeld: transcript.

Jansen, B. J., Zhang, M., Sobel, K., & Chowdhury, A. (2009). Twitter Power: Tweets as Electronic Word of Mouth. *Journal of the American Society for Information Science and Technology*, 60(11), 2169–2188.

Jarvis, C., MacKenzie, S. B., & Podsakoff, P. M. (2003). A Critical Review of Construct Indicators and Measurement Model Misspecifications in Marketing and Consumer Research. *Journal of Consumer Research*, 30(2), 199–218.

Java, A., Song, X., Finin, T., & Tseng, B. (2007). *Why We Twitter: Understanding Microblogging Usage and Communities.* Proceedings of the Joint 9th WEBKDD and 1st SNA-KDD Workshop 2007, 12 August 2007.

Jenkins, H. (1995). 'Do You Enjoy Making the Rest of Us Feel Stupid?' Alt.tv.twinpeaks, the Trickster Author, and Viewer Mastery. In D. Lavery (Ed.), *Full of Secrets: Critical Approaches to Twin Peaks* (pp. 51–69). Detroit: Wayne State University Press.

Joao Louro, M., & Vieira Cunha, P. (2001). Brand Management Paradigms. *Journal of Marketing Management*, 17, 849–875.

Kapferer, J.-N. (1992). *Strategic brand management: New approaches to creating and evaluating brand equity.* London, Paris: Kogan Page.

Kapferer, J.-N. (2008). *The new strategic brand management: Creating and sustaining brand equity long term* (4th ed.). London, Philadelphia: Kogan Page.

Kaplan, A. M., & Haenlein, M. (2010). Users of the world, unite! The challenges and opportunities of Social Media. *Business Horizons*, 53(1), 59–68.

Kaplan, A. M., & Haenlein, M. (2011). The early bird catches the news: Nine things you should know about micro-blogging. *Business Horizons*, 54(2), 105–113.

Karstens, E., & Schütte, J. (2010). *Praxishandbuch Fernsehen: Wie TV-Sender arbeiten* [Handbook of broadcasting. How TV broadcasters work] (2nd ed.). Wiesbaden: VS Verlag für Sozialwissenschaften (GWV).

Katz, E., Blumler, J. G., & Gurevitch, M. (1974). Utilization of Mass Communication by the Individual. In J. G. Blumler & E. Katz (Eds.), *The Uses of Mass Communications. Current Perspectives on Gratifications Research* (pp. 19–32). Beverly Hills, London: Sage Publications.

Keller, K. L. (1993). Conceptualizing, Measuring, and Managing Customer-Based Brand Equity. *Journal of Marketing*, 57(1), 1–22.

Keller, K. L. (2008). *Strategic brand management: Building, measuring, and managing brand equity* (3rd, internat. ed.). Upper Saddle River, NJ: Pearson/Prentice Hall.

Keller, K. L. (2009). Building strong brands in a modern marketing communications environment. *Journal of Marketing Communications*, 15(2-3), 139–155.

Kelleter, F. (2011). Serienhelden sehen dich an [TV series heroes are looking at you]. *Psychologie Heute*, 38(4), 70–75.

Kelleter, F. (2012a). Serien als Stresstest [Serials as stress test]. *Frankfurter Allgemeine Zeitung*. Retrieved from http://www.faz.net/frankfurter-allgemeine-zeitung/amerikanisches-fernsehen-serien-als-stresstest-11636816.html (3 February 2012) [Accessed 29 January 2013].

Kelleter, F. (2012b). Populäre Serialität: Eine Einführung [Popular seriality: An introduction]. In F. Kelleter (Ed.), *Populäre Serialität: Narration - Evolution - Distinktion. Zum seriellen Erzählen seit dem 19. Jahrhundert* (pp. 11–46). Bielefeld: transcript.

Kelleter, F. (2012c). Seinfeld. In T. Klein & C. Hißnauer (Eds.), *Klassiker der Fernsehserie* (pp. 203–209). Stuttgart: Reclam.

Kepplinger, H. M. (2009). Wirkung der Massenmedien [Mass media effect]. In E. Noelle-Neumann, W. Schulz, & J. Wilke (Eds.), *Fischer Lexikon Publizistik* (1st ed., pp. 651–702). Frankfurt am Main: Fischer, S.

Kiefer, M.-L. (2002). Kirch-Insolvenz: Ende einer ökonomischen Vision? [Kirch bankruptcy: The end of an economic vision?]. *Media Perspektiven*, 10, 491-500.

Kim, J., & Rubin, A. M. (1997). The variable influence of audience activity on media effects. *Communication Research*, 24, 107–135.

Kompare, D. (2006). Publishing Flow : DVD Box Sets and the Reconception of Television. *Television New Media*, 7(4), 335–360.

Kotler, P. (1991). *Marketing Management: Analysis, Planning, and Control* (8th ed.). Englewood Cliffs, NJ: Prentice-Hall.

Kotler, P., & Keller, K. L. (2007). *A framework for marketing management* (3rd ed.). Upper Saddle River, NJ: Prentice Hall.

Kotler, P., Keller, K. L., Brady, M., Goodman, M., & Hansen, T. (2009). *Marketing management*. Harlow, New York: Pearson/Prentice Hall.

Kozinets, R. V., de Valck, K., Wojnicki, A. C., & Wilner, S. J. (2010). Networked Narratives: Understanding Word-of-Mouth Marketing in Online Communities. *Journal of Marketing*, 74(2), 71–89.

Kressmann, F., Sirgy, M. J., Herrmann, A., Huber, F., Huber, S., & Lee, D.-J. (2006). Direct and indirect effects of self-image congruence on brand loyalty. *Journal of Business Research*, 59, 955–964.

Krishnamurthy, S., & Dou, W. (2008). Advertising with User-Generated Content: A Framework and Research Agenda. *Journal of Interactive Advertising*, 8(2), 1–4.

Kristensson, P., Matthing, J., & Johansson, N. (2008). Key strategies for the successful involvement of customers in the co-creation of new technology-based services. *International Journal of Service Industry Management*, 19(4), 474–491.

Kruskal, W. H., & Wallis, W. A. (1952). Use of ranks in one-criterion variance analysis. *Journal of the American Statistical Association*, 47(260), 583–621.

Kuhn, T. (1962). *The Structure of Scientific Revolutions*. Chicago, IL: University of Chicago Press.

Kumar, R. (2011). *Research methodology: A step-by-step guide for beginners* (3rd ed.). Los Angeles: Sage.

Kwon, E. S., & Sung, Y. (2011). Follow Me! Global marketers' Twitter use. *Journal of Interactive Advertising*, 12(1), 4–16.

Laroche, M., Habibi, M. R., & Richard, M.-O. (2013). To be or not to be in social media: How brand loyalty is affected by social media? *International Journal of Information Management*, 33(1), 76–82.

Laurel, B. (1993). *Computers as theatre*. Reading, MA: Addison-Wesley Pub. Co.

Lazarsfeld, P. F., Berelson, B., & Gaudet, H. (1948). *The People's Choice: How the Voter Makes Up His Mind in a Presidential Campaign*. New York: Columbia University Press.

Lee, Y. H., & Mason, C. (1999). Responses to Information Incongruency in Advertising: The Role of Expectancy, Relevancy, and Humor. *Journal of Consumer Research*, 26(2), 156–169.

Leitherer, E. (2001). Geschichte der Markierung und des Markenwesens [History of branding and brand management]. In M. Bruhn (Ed.), *Die Marke. Symbolkraft eines Zeichensystems* (pp. 55–74). Bern [etc.]: Haupt.

Lenhart, A. & Madden, M. (2007). *Social Networking Websites and Teens*. Retrieved from http://www.pewinternet.org/Reports/2007/Social-Networking-Websites-and-Teens.aspx (7 January 2007) [Accessed 22 March 2012].

Lento, T., Welser, H. T., Smith, M., & Gu, L. (2006). *The Ties that Blog: Examining the Relationship Between Social Ties and Continued Participation in the Wallop Weblogging System*. Retrieved from http://www.blogpulse.com/www2006-workshop/papers/Lento-Welser-Gu-Smith-TiesThatBlog.pdf

Lewin, K. (1943). Forces behind food habits and methods of change. *Bulletin of the National Research Council*, 108, 35–65.

Lin, J.-S., & Peña, J. (2011). Are you following me? A content analysis of TV networks' brand communication on Twitter. *Journal of Interactive Advertising*, 12(1), 17–29.

Linden Lab. (2013). *Celebrate a Decade of Second Life!* Retrieved from http://community. secondlife.com/t5/Featured-News/Celebrate-a-Decade-of-Second-Life/ba-p/2033461 (3 June 2013) [Accessed 4 March 2014].

Linden Lab. (2014). *Products: Second Life.* Retrieved from http://lindenlab.com/ products/second-life [Accessed 4 March 2014].

Lipsman, A., Mud, G., Rich, M., & Bruich, S. (2012). The Power of "Like": How Brands Reach (and Influence) Fans Through Social-Media Marketing. *Journal of Advertising Research*, 52(1), 40–52.

Lis, B., & Berz, J. (2011). Using Social Media for Branding in Publishing. *Online Journal of Communication and Media Technologies*, 1(4), 193–213.

Lis, B., & Post, M. (2013). What's on TV? The Impact of Brand Image and Celebrity Credibility on Television Consumption from an Ingredient Branding Perspective. *International Journal on Media Management*, 15(4), 229-244.

Little, T. D., Bovaird, J. A., & Widaman, K. F. (2006). On the merits of orthogonalizing powered and product terms: Implications for modeling interactions among latent variables. *Structural Equation Modeling*, (13(4), 497–519.

Logan, K. (2011). Hulu.com or NBC? Streaming Video versus Traditional TV A Study of an Industry in Its Infancy. *Journal of Advertising Research*, 51(1), 276-287.

Low, G. S., & Fullerton, R. A. (1994). Brands, Brand Management, and the Brand Manager System: A Critical-Historical Evaluation. *Journal of Marketing Research*, 14(May), 173–190.

Lynch, P. D., Kent, R. J., & Srinivasan, S. S. (2001). The Global Internet Shopper: Evidence from Shopping Tasks in Twelve Countries. *Journal of Advertising Research*, 41(3), 15–23.

Majica, M., Mielke, R., & Wirth, B. (2012). Prüde Amis, besoffene Russen [Prim Americans, drunken Russians]. *Frankfurter Rundschau*. Retrieved from http://www.fr-online.de/medien/sex-im-all-pruede-amis--besoffene-russen,1473342,17171572.html (5 September 2012) [Accessed 13 September 2012].

Malmelin, N., & Moisander, J. (2014). Brands and Branding in Media Management – Toward a Research Agenda. *International Journal on Media Management*, 16(1), 9-25.

Mangold, W. G., & Faulds, D. J. (2009). Social media: The new hybrid element of the promotion mix. *Business Horizons*, 52, 357–365.

Mark, S. (2011). The brighter Side? Eine Analyse der Markenführung des Senders ITV1 [The brighter side? An analysis of ITV1's brand management]. In K. Förster (Ed.), *Strategien erfolgreicher TV-Marken. Eine internationale Analyse* (pp. 97–113). Wiesbaden: VS, Verl. für Sozialwiss.

Mark, S., & Swann, A. (2011). Umfeldbedingungen [Environmental conditions]. In K. Förster (Ed.), *Strategien erfolgreicher TV-Marken. Eine internationale Analyse* (pp. 75–77). Wiesbaden: VS, Verl. für Sozialwiss.

Markenverband. (2011). *Markenwirtschaft steigert Umsatz deutlich* [Brand companies considerably increase sales]. Retrieved from http://www.markenverband.de/presse/ archiv-2011/markenwirtschaft-steigert-umsatz-deutlich (3 November 2011) [Accessed 25 September 2012].

Markenverband. (2013). *Die Markenwirtschaft 2013 – Jahresbericht des Markenverbandes* [Brand companies in 2013 – Yearbook of Markenverband]. Retrieved from http://www.markenverband.de/publikationen/Geschaeftsberichte/gbmv2013 [Accessed 25 February 2014].

Martensen, A., & Grønholdt, L. (2003). Improving library user's perceived quality, satisfactions and loyalty: an integrated measurement and management system. *The Journal of Academic Librarianship*, 29(3), 140–147.

McAlexander, J. H., Kim, S. K., & Roberts, S. D. (2003). Loyalty: The Influences of Satisfaction and Brand Community. *Journal of Marketing Theory and Practice*, 11(4), 1–11.

McAlexander, J. H., Schouten, J. W., & Koenig, H. F. (2002). Building Brand Community. *Journal of Marketing*, 66(January), 38–54.

McCracken, G. (1993). The Value of the Brand: An Anthropological Perspective. In D. A. Aaker & A. L. Biel (Eds.), *Brand equity & advertising. Advertising's role in building strong brands* (pp. 125–139). Hillsdale, NJ: Lawrence Erlbaum Associates.

McDowell, W. S. (2006a). *Broadcast television: A complete guide to the industry*. New York [etc.]: Lang.

McDowell, W. S. (2006b). Issues in Marketing and Branding. In: A. B. Albarren, S. M. Chan-Olmsted, & M. O. Wirth (Eds.), *Handbook of Media Management* (pp. 229-250), London: Lawrence Erlbaum.

McDowell, W. S., & Sutherland, J. (2000). Choice Versus Chance: Using Brand Equity Theory to Explore TV Audience Lead-in Effects, A Case Study. *Journal of Media Economics*, 13(4), 233-247.

McFedries, P. (2007). All A-Twitter. *IEEE Spectrum*. Retrieved from http://spectrum.ieee.org/computing/software/all-atwitter (1 October 2007) [Accessed 10 January 2011]

McMillan, D. W., & Chavis, D. M. (1986). Sense of Community: A Definition and Theory. *Journal of Community Psychology*, 14(1), 6–23.

Meffert, H., & Burmann, C. (1996). *Identitätsorientierte Markenführung – Grundlagen für das Management von Markenportfolios* [Identity-based brand management – Basic principles for managing brand portfolios]. (Working Paper No. 100). Wissenschaftliche Gesellschaft für Marketing und Unternehmensführung e.V., Münster.

Meffert, H., & Burmann, C. (2005). Wandel in der Markenführung – vom instrumentellen zum identitätsorientierten Markenverständnis [Changes in brand management – from an instrumental to an identity-based understanding of brands]. In H. Meffert (Ed.),

Markenmanagement. Identitätsorientierte Markenführung und praktische Umsetzung; mit Best-practice-Fallstudien (2nd ed., pp. 19–36). Wiesbaden: Gabler.

Meffert, H., Burmann, C., & Kirchgeorg, M. (2008). *Marketing: Grundlagen marktorientierter Unternehmensführung ; Konzepte, Instrumente, Praxisbeispiele* [Marketing: Basic principles of market-oriented management; concepts, tools, practical examples] (10th ed.). Wiesbaden: Betriebswirtschaftlicher Verlag Dr. Th. Gabler.

Mikos, L. (1992). Serien als Fernsehgenre: Zusammenhänge zwischen Dramaturgie und Aneignungsweisen des Publikums [Serials as television genre: Connections between dramaturgy and audience adoption]. In F. Salow (Ed.), *Serie Kunst im Alltag* (pp. 19–27). Berlin: Vistas.

Milstein, S., Chowdhury, A., Hochmuth, G., Lorica, B., & Magoulas, R. (2008). *Twitter and the micro-messaging revolution: Communication, connections, and immediacy - 140 characters at a time*. Sebastopol, CA.

Mittell, J. (2006). Narrative Complexity in Contemporary American Television. *The Velvet Light Trap*, 58(Fall), 29–40.

Mittell, J. (2009). Sites of participation: Wiki fandom and the case of Lostpedia. *Transformative Works and Cultures*, 3. Retrieved from http://journal. transformativeworks.org/index.php/twc/article/view/118/117 [Accessed 29 January 2013].

Mittell, J. (2010). *Serial Boxes: The Cultural Values of Long-Form American Television*. Retrieved from http://justtv.wordpress.com/2010/01/20/serial-boxes (20 January 2010) [Accessed 29 January 2013].

Möbus, P., & Heffler, M. (2011). Die Talfahrt ist gestoppt [The downturn has ended]. *Media Perspektiven*, 6, 321–330.

Moorman, C., Zaltman, G., & Deshpandé, R. (1992). Relationships Between Providers and Users of Market Research: The Dynamics of Trust Within and Between Organizations. *Journal of Marketing Research*, 29(August), 314–328.

Morgan, R. M., & Hunt, S. D. (1994). The Commitment-Trust Theory of Relationship Marketing. *Journal of Marketing*, 58(July), 20–38.

Muniz, A. M., & O'Guinn, T. C. (2001). Brand Community. *Journal of Consumer Research*, 27(March), 412–432.

Muniz, A. M., & Schau, H. J. (2007). Vigilante Marketing and Consumer-Created Communications. *Journal of Advertising Research*, 36(3), 35–50.

Myers, S. D. (2012). Facebook and Pharmaceutical Companies: An Industry in Need of Guidance. *Online Journal of Communication and Media Technologies*, 2(3), 48–70.

Nardi, B. A., Schiano, D. J., Gumbrecht, M., & Swartz, L. (2004). Why we blog. *Communications of the ACM*, 47(12), 41–46.

Neff, J. (2010). What happens when Facebook trumps your brand site? *Advertising Age*, 81(30), 2–22.

Nielsen. (2013). *New Nielsen Research Indicates Two-Way Causal Influence Between Twitter Activity and TV Viewership*. Retrieved from http://www.nielsen.com/us/en/press-room/2013/new-nielsen-research-indicates-two-way-causal-influence-between-.html (6 August 2013) [6 March 2014].

Nienstedt, H.-W., Huber, F., & Seelmann, C. (2012). The Influence of the Congruence Between Brand and Consumer Personality on the Loyalty to Print and Online Issues of Magazine Brands. *International Journal on Media Management*, 14(1), 3–26.

Nitzl, C. (2010). *Eine anwenderorientierte Einführung in die Partial Least Square (PLS)-Methode* [A user-oriented introduction to Partial Least Squares]. (Working Paper No. 21, Ed.: Prof. Dr. K.-W. Hansmann). Universität Hamburg, Institut für Industrielles Management, Hamburg. Retrieved: http://papers.ssrn.com/sol3/papers.cfm?abstract_id=2097324

Nysveen, H., Thorbjørnsen, H., & Pedersen, P. E. (2005). WebTV channel additions: Channel complementarity in the broadcasting industry. *International Journal on Media Management*, 7(3–4), 127–137.

O'Brien, H. L., & Toms, E. G. (2008). What is User Engagement? A Conceptual Framework for Defining User Engagement with Technology. *Journal of the American Society for Information Science and Technology*, 59(6), 938–955.

O'Brien, H. L., & Toms, E. G. (2010). The Development and Evaluation of a Survey to Measure User Engagement. *Journal of the American Society for Information Science and Technology*, 61(1), 50–69.

OECD. (2007). *Participative Web and user-created content: Web 2.0, wikis and social networking*. Paris: Organisation for Economic Co-operation and Development.

Ogilvy, D. (1951). *Speech to American marketing association annual meeting*. AMA proceedings, Chicago: American Marketing Association.

Oliver, R. L. (1999). Whence Consumer Loyalty? *Journal of Marketing*, 63(Special Issue), 33–44.

Olsen, B. (1993) Brand Loyalty and Lineage: Exploring New Dimensions for Research. *Advances in Consumer Research*, 20, 575–579.

Ots, M. (2008). Media and Brands: New Ground to Explore. In M. Ots (Ed.), *Jönköping International Business School (JIBS) Research Report 2008-1* (pp. 1-7). Jönköping, Sweden.

Ots, M., & Wolff, P.-E. (2008). Media Consumer Brand Equity: Implications for Advertising Media Planning. In M. Ots (Ed.), *Jönköping International Business School (JIBS) Research Report 2008-1* (pp. 95-112). Jönköping, Sweden.

Oyedeji, T. A. (2007). The relation between the customer-based brand equity of media outlets and their media channel credibility: An exploratory study. *International Journal on Media Management*, 9(3), 116-125.

Pagani, M., & Mirabello, A. (2011). The influence of personal and social-interactive engagement in social TV Web sites. *International Journal of Electronic Commerce*, 16(2), 41–67.

Pallant, J. (2010). *SPSS survival manual: A step by step guide to data analysis using SPSS* (4th ed.). Maidenhead, New York: McGraw Hill.

Palmgreen, P., & Lawrence, P. A. (1991). Avoidances, gratifications, and consumption of theatrical films: The rest of the story. In Austin, B. A. (Ed.), *Current research in film. Audiences, economics and law* (pp. 39-55). Norwood, N.J: Ablex Publishing Corporation.

Palmgreen, P., Wenner, L. A., & Rayburn, J. D., II. (1980). Relations Between Gratifications Sought and Obtained: A Study of Television News. *Communication Research*, 7(2), 161–192.

Palmgreen, P., Wenner, L. A., & Rayburn, J. D., II. (1981). Gratification Discrepancies and News Program Choice. *Communication Research*, 8(4), 451–478.

Papacharissi, Z., & Mendelson, A. L. (2007). An Exploratory Study of Reality Appeal: Uses and Gratifications of Reality TV Shows. *Journal of Broadcasting & Electronic Media*, 51(2), 355-370.

Paperlein, J. (2013). Seven-One Media: Parallelnutzung senkt Zapping [Seven-One Media: Parallel usage decreases zapping]. *Horizont*. Retrieved from http://www.horizont.net/ aktuell/medien/pages/protected/Seven-One-Media-Parallelnutzung-senkt-Zapping_116144.html (15 August 2013) [Accessed 4 March 2014].

Park, J.-Y. (2004). *Programm-Promotion im Fernsehen* [Programme promotion on television]. Konstanz: UVK Verlagsgesellschaft.

Park, N., Kee, K. F., & Valenzuela, S. (2009). Being Immersed in Social Networking Environment: Facebook Groups, Uses and Gratifications, and Social Outcomes. *CyberPsychology & Behavior*, 12(6), 729–733.

Pessemier, E. (1959). A New Way to Determine Buying Decisions. *Journal of Marketing*, 24(October), 41–46.

Perry, C. (1998). Processes of a Case Study Methodology for Postgraduate Research in Marketing. *European Journal of Marketing*, 32(9/10), 785–802.

Petty, R. E., & Cacioppo, J. T. (1981). *Attitudes and Persuasion: Classic and Contemporary Approaches*. Dubuque, IA: William C. Brown.

Petty, R. E., & Cacioppo, J. T. (1983). Central and Peripheral Routes to Persuasion: Application to Advertising. In L. Percy & A. Woodside (Eds.), *Advertising and Consumer Psychology* (pp. 3–23). Lexington, MA: Lexington Books.

Petty, R. E., & Cacioppo, J. T. (1984). The Effects of Involvement on Responses to Argument Quantity and Quality: Central and Peripheral Routes to Persuasion. *Journal of Personality and Social Psychology*, 46(1), 69–81.

Petty, R. E., Cacioppo, J. T., & Schumann, D. (1983). Central and Peripheral Routes to Advertising Effectiveness: The Moderating Role of Involvement. *Journal of Consumer Research*, 10(2), 135–146.

Picard, R. G. (2005). Unique Characteristics and Business Dynamics of Media Products. *Journal of Media Business Studies*, 2(2), 61-69.

Picot, A., Kooths, S., Kruse, J., & Dewenter, R. (2009). Was kostet das Internet: Zeitgespräch: Was darf das Internet kosten? [How much does the internet cost? Discussion: How much may the internet cost?]. *Wirtschaftsdienst*, 89(10), 643–659.

Plake, K. (2004). *Handbuch Fernsehforschung: Befunde und Perspektiven* [Handbook of television research: Findings and perspectives]. Wiesbaden: VS Verl. für Sozialwiss.

Porter, M. E. (1996). What Is Strategy? *Harvard Business Review*, 6(Nov/Dec), 61–78.

Porter, M. E. (1998). *Competitive Advantage: Creating and Sustaining Superior Performance*. New York London: Free Press.

Prahalad, C. K., & Ramaswamy, V. (2004). Co-creation experiences: The next practice in value creation. *Journal of Interactive Marketing*, 18(3), 5–14.

Quan-Haase, A., & Young, A. L. (2010). Uses and Gratifications of Social Media: A Comparison of Facebook and Instant Messaging. *Bulletin of Science, Technology & Society*, 30(5), 350–361.

Raacke, J., & Bonds-Raacke, J. (2008). MySpace and Facebook: Applying the Uses and Gratifications Theory to Exploring Friend-Networking Sites. *CyberPsychology & Behavior*, 11(2), 169–174.

Radtke, S. U. (2010). *Strategisches Management von etablierten Fernsehsendern im digitalen Zeitalter: Ein ressourcen- und fähigkeitsbasierter Ansatz* [Strategic management of established television channels in the digital age: A resource and capability based approach]. Wiesbaden: Gabler.

Reinstein, D. A., & Snyder, C. M. (2005). The Influence of Expert Reviews on Consumer Demand for Experience Goods: A Case Study of Movie Critics. *Journal of Industrial Economics*, 53(1), 27–51.

Richter, F. (2013). Netflix is Almost as Popular as Cable Among Young Adults. *Statista*. Retrieved from http://www.statista.com/topics/1309/pay-tv/chart/1688/pay-tv-adoption-in-the-us/ (4 December 2013) [6 March 2014].

Ringle, C. M. (2004a). *Messung von Kausalmodellen: Ein Methodenvergleich* [Measurement of causal models: A comparison of methods]. (Working Paper No. 14, Ed.: Prof. Dr. K.-W. Hansmann). Universität Hamburg, Institut für Industrielles Management, Hamburg. Retrieved: http://www.uni-hamburg.de/onTEAM/grafik/1319531056/ap14.pdf

Ringle, C. M. (2004b). *Gütemaße für den Partial Least Squares-Ansatz zur Bestimmung von Kausalmodellen* [Evaluation of causal models using the Partial Least Squares-approach]. (Working Paper No. 16, Ed.: Prof. Dr. K.-W. Hansmann). Universität Hamburg, Institut für Industrielles Management, Hamburg. Retrieved: https://www.wiwi.uni-muenster.de/mcm/studium/veranstaltungen/downloads/2011_WS/AdvancedMarketResearc h/Ringle_WP_2004_Guetemasse.pdf

Ringle, C. M. (2005). Modeling moderating effects with formative indicators. *smartPLS forum article*. Retrieved from http://www.smartpls.de/forum/viewtopic.php?t= 142&highlight= moderator+formative (30 December 2005) [Accessed 13 December 2013].

Ringle, C. M., Wende, S., & Will, S. (2005) SmartPLS 2.0 (M3) Beta, Hamburg 2005, http://www.smartpls.de

Ringle, C. M. (2006). Moderators in PLS: Which modeling approach is appropriate? *smartPLS forum article*. Retrieved from http://www.smartpls.de/forum/viewtopic.php?t= 180&highlight=moderator+formative (16 March 2006) [Accessed 13 December 2013].

Roberts, E. B. (1987). Managing Technological Innovation – A Search for Generalizations. In E. B. Roberts (Ed.), *Generating technological innovation* (pp. 3–12). New York: Oxford University Press.

Romaniuk, J. (2007). Word of Mouth and the Viewing of Television Programs. *Journal of Advertising Research*, 47(4), 462–471.

Rosenberg, M., & Hovland, C. (1960). Cognitive, Affective, and Behavioral Components of Attitudes. In M. Rosenberg & C. Hovland (Eds.), *Attitude Organization and Change: An Analysis of Consistency Among Attitude Components* (pp. 1–14). New Haven: Yale University Press.

Rotter, J. B. (1967). A new scale for the measurement of interpersonal trust. *Journal of Personality*, 35(4), 651–665.

Sarkar, M., Echambadi, R., Cavusgil, S. T., & Aulakh, P. S. (2001). The Influence of Complementarity, Compatibility, and Relationship Capital on Alliance Performance. *Journal of the Academy of Marketing Science*, (29(4), 358–373.

Schau, H. J., & Gilly, M. C. (2003). We Are What We Post? Self-Presentation in Personal Web Space. *Journal of Consumer Research*, 30(3), 385–404.

Schau, H. J., Muniz, A. M., & Arnould, E. J. (2009). How Brand Community Practices Create Value. *Journal of Marketing*, 73(5), 30–51.

Schmidt, H. (2011). Internetfirmen nehmen sich das Fernsehen vor [Internet companies take on television]. *Netzökonom - Frankfurter Allgemeine Blogs*. Retrieved from http://blogs.faz.net/netzwirtschaft-blog/2011/10/24/internetfirmen-nehmen-sich-das-fernsehen-vor-3028/ (24 October 2011) [Accessed 25 September 2012].

Schouten, J. W., & McAlexander, J. H. (1995). Subcultures of Consumption: An Ethnography of the New Bikers. *Journal of Consumer Research*, 22(1), 43–61.

Schulz, S., Mau, G., & Löffler, S. (2007). Virales Marketing im Web 2.0 [Viral marketing in web 2.0]. In: T. Kilian, B. Hass, & G. Walsh (Eds.), *Web 2.0 – Neue Perspektiven im E-Business* (pp. 249-268). Heidelberg: Springer.

Schumpeter, J. A. (1942). *Capitalism, Socialism and Democracy*. New York, London: Harper.

Schröder, J. (2014). *Deutschlands populärste Medienmarken: Bild und Apotheken Umschau* [Germany's most popular media brands: Bild and Apotheken Umschau]. Retrieved from http://meedia.de/2014/09/18/deutschlands-populaerste-medienmarken-bild-und-apotheken-umschau/ [Accessed 29 January 2015].

Schwegler, P. (2013). Second Screen boomt: Mehr als jeder zweite User surft beim Fernsehen [Second screen is booming: One in two users are surfing while watching TV]. *W&V*. Retrieved from http://www.wuv.de/medien/second_screen_boomt_mehr_als_jeder_zweite_user_surft_beim_fernsehen (5 February 2013) [Accessed 4 March 2014].

Segars, A. H. (1997). Assessing the Unidimensionality of Measurement: A Paradigm and Illustration within the Context of Information Systems Research. *Omega*, 25(1), 107–121.

Seiler, S. (2008). Vorwort [Preface]. In S. Seiler (Ed.), *Was bisher geschah. Serielles Erzählen im zeitgenössischen amerikanischen Fernsehen* (pp. 6–9). Köln: Schnitt - der Filmverl.

Shapiro, C., & Varian, H. R. (1999). *Information Rules: A Strategic Guide to the Network Economy*. Boston, Jackson: Harvard Business School Press.

Sheth, J. N. (1971). Word-of-Mouth in Low-Risk Innovations. *Journal of Advertising Research*, 11(3), 15–18.

Shoemaker, P. J., Eichholz, M., Kim, E., & Wrigley, B. (2001). Individual and routine forces in gatekeeping. *Journalism and Mass Communication Quarterly*, 78(2), 233–246.

Short, J., Williams, E., & Christie, B. (1976). *The social psychology of telecommunications*. London, New York: Wiley.

Siegert, G. (2001). *Medien Marken Management: Relevanz, Specifika und Implikationen einer medienökonomischen Profilierungsstrategie* [Media brand management: Relevance, specifics and implications of a media economic profiling strategy]. München: Verlag Reinhard-Fischer.

Siegert, G. (2002). Medienmanagement als Marketingmanagement [Media management as marketing management]. In M. Karmasin & C. Winter (Eds.), *Grundlagen des Medienmanagements* (2nd ed., pp. 173–195). München: W. Fink.

Siegert, G. (2013). Stichwort Medienmarke [Keyword media brand]. In Bentele, G., Brosius, H.-B., & Jarren, O. (Eds.), *Lexikon Kommunikations- und Medienwissenschaft* (2nd ed., pp. 215-216). Wiesbaden Springer VS.

Siegert, G., Gerth, M. A., & Rademacher, P. (2011). Brand Identity-Driven Decision Making by Journalists and Media Managers – The MBAC Model as a Theoretical Framework. *International Journal on Media Management*, 13(1), 53-70.

Simon C., & Sullivan M. (1993). The measurement and determinants of brand equity: a financial approach. *Marketing Science*, 12 (1), 28–52.

Sirgy, M. J., Johar, J. S., Samli, A. C., & Claiborne, C. B. (1991). Self-Congruity Versus Functional Congruity: Predictors of Consumer Behavior. *Journal of Academic Marketing Science*, 19(4), 363–375.

Slack, N. (1994). The Importance-Performance Matrix as a Determinant of Improvement Priority. *International Journal of Operations*, 14(5), 59–75.

Sledgianowski, D., & Kulviwat, S. (2009). Using Social Network Sites: The Effects of Playfulness, Critical Mass and Trust in a Hedonic Context. *Journal of Computer Information Systems*, 49(4), 74–83.

Smith, T. (2009). The social media revolution. *International Journal of Market Research*, 51(4), 559–561.

SocialGuide. (2014). *Nielsen Twitter TV Ratings*. Retrieved from http://www.socialguide.com/product/nielsen-twitter-tv-ratings/ [Accessed 6 March 2014].

Stichnoth, F. (2008). *Virtuelle Brand Communities zur Markenprofilierung – Der Einsatz virtueller Brand Communities zur Stärkung der Marke-Kunden-Beziehung* [Virtual brand communities for brand profiling – Using virtual communities to strengthen the consumer-brand relationship]. (Working Paper No. 35). Universität Bremen, Bremen. Retrieved: http://www.lim.uni-bremen.de/files/burmann/publikationen/LiM-AP-35-Brand-Communities.pdf

Stipp, H. (2012). The Branding of Television Networks: Lessons From Branding Strategies in the U.S. Market. *International Journal on Media Management*, 14(2), 107–119.

Sullivan, B. F. (2007). Interview: "Supernatural" Creator Eric Kripke. *The Futon Critic*. Retrieved from http://www.thefutoncritic.com/interviews/2007/10/04/interview-supernatural-creator-eric-kripke-25631/20071004_supernatural/ (4 October 2007) [Accessed 25 January 2014].

Sung, Y., & Park, N. (2011). The dimensions of cable television network personality: implications for media brand management. *International Journal on Media Management*, 13(1), 87–105.

Swann, A., & Förster, K. (2011). BBC1: A trademark of Britishness. In K. Förster (Ed.), *Strategien erfolgreicher TV-Marken. Eine internationale Analyse* (pp. 78–96). Wiesbaden: VS, Verl. für Sozialwiss.

Taylor, D. G., Lewin, J. E., & Strutton, D. (2011) Do Ads Work on Social Networks? How Gender and Age Shape Receptivity. *Journal of Advertising Research*, 51(1), 258-275.

Thompson, R. J. (1996). *Television's second golden age: From Hill Street blues to ER: Hill Street blues, St. Elsewhere, Cagney & Lacey, Moonlighting, L.A. law, thirtysomething, China Beach, Twin peaks, Northern exposure, Picket fences, with brief reflections on Homicide, NYPD blue, ER, Chicago hope, and other quality dramas*. New York: Continuum.

Thorbjørnsen, H., Supphellen, M., Nysveen, H., & Pedersen, P. E. (2002). Building brand relationships online: a comparison of two interactive applications. *Journal of Interactive Marketing*, 16(3), 17–34.

Thorson, K. S., & Rodgers, S. (2006). Relationships between blogs as eWOM and interactivity, perceived interactivity, and parasocial interaction. *Journal of Interactive Advertising*, 6(2), 34–44.

Trommsdorff, V. (2009). *Konsumentenverhalten* [Consumer behaviour] (7th ed.). *Kohlhammer Edition Marketing*. Stuttgart: Kohlhammer.

Trusov, M., Bodapati, A. V., & Bucklin, R. E. (2010). Determining Influential Users in Internet Social Networks. *Journal of Marketing Research*, 47(4), 643–658.

Trusov, M., Bucklin, R. E., & Pauwels, K. (2009). Effects of Word-of-Mouth Versus Traditional Marketing: Findings from an Internet Social Networking Site. *Journal of Marketing*, 73(September), 90–102.

Tucker, W. (1964). The Development of Brand Loyalty. *Journal of Marketing Research*, 1(August), 32–35.

Twitter. (2009). *What's Happening?* Retrieved from https://blog.twitter.com/2009/whats-happening (19 November 2009) [Accessed 4 March 2014].

Twitter. (2014). *About: Company*. Retrieved from https://about.twitter.com/company [Accessed 4 March 2014].

Uncles, M. D., East, R., & Lomax, W. (2010). Market share is correlated with word-of-mouth volume. *Australasian Marketing Journal*, 18(3), 145–150.

Uncles, M. D., Ehrenberg, A., & Hammond, K. (1995). Patterns of Buyer Behavior: Regularities, Models, and Extensions. *Marketing Science*, 14(3 Part 2), G71-G78.

Upshaw, L. B. (1995). *Creating brand identity: The strategy for success in a cluttered and confused marketplace*. New York: John Wiley.

Valkenburg, P. M., Peter, J., & Schouten, A. P. (2006). Friend Networking Sites and Their Relationship to Adolescents' Well- Being and Social Self-Esteem. *CyberPsychology & Behavior*, 9(5), 584–590.

Verspohl, L. (2008). *Die strategische TV-Programmplanung und das Bild des Zuschauers: Eine Analyse anhand der Sender NBC, RTL und Das Erste* [Strategic programme planning and the viewer: An analysis using the example of channels NBC, RTL and Das Erste]. Saarbrücken: VDM Verlag Dr. Müller Aktiengesellschaft & Co. KG.

Völckner, F., & Sattler, H. (2006). Drivers of Brand Extension Success. *Journal of Marketing*, 70(2), 18–34.

Völckner, F., Sattler, H., Hennig-Thurau, T., & Ringle, C. M. (2010). The role of parent brand quality for service brand extension success. *Journal of Service Research*, 13(4), 379–396.

Vries, L. de, Gensler, S., & Leeflang, P. S. (2012). Popularity of Brand Posts on Brand Fan Pages: An Investigation of the Effects of Social Media Marketing. *Journal of Interactive Marketing*, 26(2), 83–91.

Weber, S. (2011). Warum "The Voice of Germany" auch digital so gut funktioniert [Why "The Voice of Germany" is working so well in a digital environment]. *Horizont*. Retrieved from http://www.horizont.net/aktuell/digital/pages/protected/printall.php?id=104422 (9 December 2011) [Accessed 6 September 2012].

Weber, T., & Junklewitz, C. (2008). Das Gesetz der Serie – Ansätze zur Definition und Analyse [The Law of the Series – Approaches for definition and analysis]. *MEDIENwissenschaft*, 1, 13–31.

Webster, F. E. (1992). The Changing Role of Marketing in the Corporation. *Journal of Marketing*, 56(4), 1–17.

Weil, S. (2011). *Strategisches TV-Management. Erlösdiversifizierung privater deutscher Free-TV-Unternehmen* [Strategic TV management: Revenue diversification of private German free TV companies]. (Unpublished doctoral dissertation). Johannes Gutenberg-Universität, Mainz.

Wenske, A. V. (2008). *Management und Wirkungen von Marke-Kunden-Beziehungen im Konsumgüterbereich: Eine Analyse unter besonderer Berücksichtigung des Beschwerdemanagements und der Markenkommunikation* [Management and effect of consumer-brand relationships for consumer goods: An analysis with particular attention to complaint management and brand communication]. Wiesbaden: Gabler Verlag / GWV Fachverlage.

Wheeler, S., Yeomans, P., & Wheeler, D. (2008). The good, the bad and the wiki: Evaluating student-generated content for collaborative learning. *British Journal of Educational Technology*, 39(6), 987–995.

White, D. M. (1950). The "gate keeper": A case study in the selection of news. *Journalism Quarterly*, 27, 383–390.

Williams, R. (2003). *Television: Technology and Cultural Form* (3rd ed.). London: Routledge.

Wirtz, B. W. (2006). *Medien- und Internetmanagement* [Media and internet management] (5th ed.). Wiesbaden: Gabler.

Wold, H. (1982). Soft modeling: The basic design and some extensions. In K. G. Jöreskog & H. Wold (Eds.), *Systems under indirect observation: Causality, structure, prediction, Vol. 2* (pp. 1–54). Amsterdam: North-Holland.

YouTube. (2014a). *About YouTube*. Retrieved from http://www.youtube.com/yt/about/ [Accessed 4 March 2014].

YouTube. (2014b). *Statistics: Viewership*. Retrieved from http://www.youtube.com/yt/press/statistics.html [Accessed 4 March 2014].

ZAW Zentralverband der deutschen Werbewirtschaft e.V. (2014). *Netto-Werbeeinnahmen erfassbarer Werbeträger in Deutschland* [Net advertising revenues of measurable advertising media]. Retrieved from http://www.zaw.de/index.php?menuid=33 [Accessed 26 January 2015].

Zaichkowsky, J. L. (1986). Conceptualizing Involvement. *Journal of Advertising Research*, 15(2), 4–34.

Zaichkowsky, J. L. (1994). The Personal Involvement Inventory: Reduction, Revision, and Application to Advertising. *Journal of Advertising Research*, 23(4), 59–70.

Zeng, F., Huang, L., & Dou, W. (2009). Social factors in user perceptions and responses to advertising in online social networking communities. *Journal of Interactive Advertising*, 10(1), 1–13.

Zubayr, C., & Gerhard, H. (2011). Tendenzen im Zuschauerverhalten: Fernsehgewohnheiten und Fernsehreichweiten im Jahr 2010 [Tendecies in viewer behaviours: Television habits and television reach in 2010]. *Media Perspektiven*, 3, 126–138.

Appendices

If not otherwise indicated, all tables and figures in this chapter are of own design and/or computation.

Appendix A   Questionnaire: Questions for model testing

This section contains the questions asked in the questionnaire which were necessary for model testing. Respondents answered the questionnaire in German; therefore, this section is bilingual. The translation was reviewed by a professional translator. In the following sections, #Format# is a proxy for "the serialised TV brand" and #sma# is a proxy for "selected social media programme for the serialised TV brand".

Brand loyalty

- Reflective indicators
- Q: How would you describe your commitment to [the serialised TV brand]?
  Wie würden Sie ihre Bindung an #Format# beschreiben?
- 7-point Likert scale (fully agree – fully disagree) [stimme überhaupt nicht zu –stimme voll und ganz zu][72]

Item #	Item description	Source
BL_1	I will watch [the serialised TV brand] the next time it runs on TV. *Ich werde #Format# schauen, wenn es das nächste Mal im TV läuft.*	adapted from Chaudhuri & Holbrook 2001; Jacoby & Chestnut 1978; Oliver 1999
BL_2	I intend to keep watching [the serialised TV brand]. *Ich werde #Format# weiterhin schauen.*	adapted from Chaudhuri & Holbrook 2001; Jacoby & Chestnut 1978; Oliver 1999
BL_3	I would be willing to pay for [the serialised TV brand] if it was not available free of charge. *Ich würde für #Format# bezahlen, wenn es nicht kostenlos verfügbar wäre.*	adapted from Chaudhuri & Holbrook 2001
BL_4	I would be willing to watch [the serialised TV brand] even if it was moved to a less favourable programme slot. *Ich würde #Format# auch dann schauen, wenn es auf einen weniger günstigen Programmplatz verschoben würde.*	own design based on Oliver 1999
BL_5	I would recommend [the serialised TV brand] to my friends. *Ich würde #Format# meinen Freunden empfehlen.*	own design based on Dick & Basu 1994

App. Table 1: Operationalisation and indicators for construct BL

---

[72] If not otherwise indicated, the same scale was used for all other items.

Consumer-brand relationship

- Reflective indicators
- Q: How would you describe your relationship with [the serialised TV brand]?
  Wie würden Sie Ihre Beziehung zu #Format# beschreiben?
- 7-point Likert scale (fully agree – fully disagree)

Item #	Item description[73]	Source
CBR_1	[The serialised TV brand] shows an interest in my well-being. *#Format# ist an meinem Wohlbefinden interessiert.*	Wenske 2008
CBR_2	I love [the serialised TV brand]. *Ich liebe #Format#.*	Wenske 2008
CBR_3	I have lots of fond memories I attach to [the serialised TV brand]. *Mit #Format# verbinde ich viele schöne Erinnerungen.*	Wenske 2008
CBR_4	[The serialised TV brand's] image and my self-image are very similar. *Es besteht eine große Ähnlichkeit zwischen dem Bild, das ich von #Format# habe und dem Bild, das ich von mir selbst habe.[74]*	Wenske 2008
CBR_5	I am entirely familiar with [the serialised TV brand's] characteristics. *Die Eigenschaften von #Format# sind mir voll und ganz bekannt.*	Wenske 2008
CBR_6	My overall relationship to [the serialised TV brand] is of high quality *Alles in allem hat meine Beziehung zu #Format# eine hohe Qualität.*	Wenske 2008

App. Table 2: Operationalisation and indicators for CBR

Attitude toward the social media programme for the serialised TV brand

- Reflective indicators
- Q: How do you like the social media programme for [the serialised TV brand]?
  Wie gefällt Ihnen die #sma#-Seite von #Format#?
- 7-point Likert scale (fully agree – fully disagree)

Item #	Item description	Source
SMP_1	The social media programme for [the serialised TV brand] interests me. *Die #sma#-Seite von #Format# ist interessant.*	Arnhold 2010 Stichnoth 2008
SMP_2	The topic of the social media programme for [the serialised TV brand] is appealing to me. *Die Inhalte der #sma#-Seite von #Format# treffen genau meine Interessen.*	Arnhold 2010 Stichnoth 2008
SMP_3	The social media programme for [the serialised TV brand] is attractive to me. *Die #sma#-Seite von #Format# ist ansprechend.[75]*	Arnhold 2010 Stichnoth 2008
SMP_4	I can easily identify with the social media programme for [the serialised TV brand]. *Ich kann mich mit der #sma#-Seite von #Format# identifizieren.*	Arnhold 2010 Stichnoth 2008

---

[73] Items "I do not want to miss the brand in my life." and "I am a loyal customer of the brand." from Wenske's original scale were deleted in order to clearly distinguish the construct from brand loyalty.

[74] Wording slightly changed. Original: "Es besteht eine enge Verbindung zwischen der Marke und dem Bild, was ich von mir selbst habe."

[75] Wording changed; original: "verlockend"

SMP_5	The social media programme for [the serialised TV brand] has a good reputation. *Die #sma#-Seite von #Format# hat einen guten Ruf.[76]*	Arnhold 2010 Stichnoth 2008
SMP_6	The social media programme for [the serialised TV brand] lives up to its promises. *Die #sma#-Seite von #Format# hält was sie verspricht.*	Arnhold 2010 Stichnoth 2008
SMP_7*	The social media programme for [the serialised TV brand] is poor/ in need of improvement. *Die #sma#-Seite von #Format# ist schlecht gemacht / verbesserungswürdig.*	Arnhold 2010 Stichnoth 2008
SMP_8*	I dislike the social media programme for [the serialised TV brand]. *Ich mag die #sma#-Seite von #Format# nicht.*	Arnhold 2010 Stichnoth 2008
SMP_9	The social media programme for [the serialised TV brand] is entertaining. *Ich fühle mich von der #sma#-Seite von #Format# unterhalten.*	own design

App. Table 3: Operationalisation and indicators for construct SMP
* reverse coded

Engagement in the social media programme for the serialised TV brand

- Reflective indicators
- Q: How would you describe your level of engagement in social media offerings for [the serialised TV brand]?
  Wie stark interagieren Sie mit der #sma#-Seite von #Format#?
- 7-point Likert scale (fully agree – fully disagree)

Item #	Item description	Source
SME_1	During the season, I frequently (at least once every week) engage in social media offerings for [the serialised TV brand]. *Ich beschäftige mich während der Staffel häufig (mindestens einmal pro Woche) mit der #sma#-Seite von #Format#.*	own design
SME_2	I am an active user of social media offerings for [the serialised TV brand], i.e., I do usually contribute. *Ich bin ein aktiver Nutzer der #sma#-Seite von #Format#, d.h. ich trage meistens selbst etwas bei.*	own design
SME_3	I engage in social media offerings for [the serialised TV brand] because of a shared interest in [the serialised TV brand]. *Ich beschäftige mich mit der #sma#-Seite von #Format#, weil andere Nutzer und ich ein gemeinsames Interesse an #Format# haben.*	Christodoulides et al. 2012
SME_4	The social media offerings for [the serialised TV brand] mean a lot to me. *Die #sma#-Seite von #Format# bedeutet mir viel.*	Zaichkowsky 1994
SME_5	The social media offerings for [the serialised TV brand] interest me. *Ich finde die #sma#-Seite von #Format# interessant.*	Zaichkowsky 1994

App. Table 4: Operationalisation and indicators for construct SME

---

[76] German wording originally "*hat eine gute Reputation*". Pretest comments suggested that this sounded too complicated.

Gratifications obtained from the social media programme for the serialised TV brand

- Formative indicators
- Q: In how far does [the social media programme for the serialised TV brand]
  meet your expectations with regard to...?
  Inwieweit entspricht die #sma#-Seite von #Format# Ihren Erwartungen?
- 7-point Likert scale (completely – not at all) [voll und ganz –überhaupt nicht]

Item #	Item description	Source
GOS_1	interesting information *interessante Informationen*	Dehm & Storll 2003
GOS_2	entertainment *Unterhaltsamkeit*	e.g. Palmgreen & Lawrence 1991
GOS_3	generates ideas[77] *Anregungen und Stoff zum Nachdenken*	Dehm & Storll 2003
GOS_4	forget everyday concerns *Ablenkung von den Alltagssorgen*	Dehm & Storll 2003
GOS_5	enjoyable and convenient pastime *gelungener und angenehmer Zeitvertreib*	Dehm & Storll 2003
GOS_6	sense of belonging *Vermittlung des Gefühls, dazuzugehören*	Dehm & Storll 2003
GOS_7	be in touch with likeminded people *Möglichkeit, sich mit Gleichgesinnten auszutauschen*	e.g. Quan-Haase & Young 2010; Foregger 2008

App. Table 5: Operationalisation and indicators for construct GOS

Gratifications obtained from the serialised TV brand

- Formative indicators
- Q: In how far does [the serialised TV brand] meet your expectations with regard
  to...?
  Inwieweit entspricht #Format# Ihren Erwartungen?
- 7-point Likert scale (completely – not at all) [voll und ganz –überhaupt nicht]

Item #	Item description	Source
GO_1	interesting information *interessante Informationen*	Dehm & Storll 2003
GO_2	entertainment *Unterhaltsamkeit*	e.g. Palmgreen & Lawrence 1991
GO_3	generates ideas *Anregungen und Stoff zum Nachdenken*	Dehm & Storll 2003
GO_4	forget everyday concerns *Ablenkung von den Alltagssorgen*	Dehm & Storll 2003
GO_5	enjoyable and convenient pastime *gelungener und angenehmer Zeitvertreib*	Dehm & Storll 2003
GO_6	sense of belonging *Vermittlung des Gefühls, dazuzugehören*	Dehm & Storll 2003

App. Table 6: Operationalisation and indicators for construct GO

---

[77] Original dimension referred to the providing of orientation, which does not seem suitable for this study.

Perceived critics' response

- Reflective indicators
- Q: What is your perception of critics' response to [the serialised TV brand]?
  In Zeitungen, Zeitschriften oder auch im Internet wird von Journalisten und Kritikern über TV-Serien berichtet, in Fernsehzeitungen werden Sendungen empfohlen oder als wenig sehenswert beschrieben. Wie ist Ihre Wahrnehmung der Kritikermeinung zu #Format#?
- 7-point Likert scale (fully agree – fully disagree)

Item #	Item description	Source
Pcr_1	From what I have heard/read, [the serialised TV brand] is talked and/or written about a lot in the media. *Meiner Meinung nach wird in den Medien viel über #Format# gesprochen/geschrieben.*	Iyengar & Kinder 1987 (agenda setting)
Pcr_2	I think that [the serialised TV brand] is discussed controversially by critics. *Meiner Meinung nach wird #Format# von Kritikern kontrovers diskutiert.*	Clement, Proppe, & Rott 2007
Pcr_3	I think that critics actively recommend [the serialised TV brand]. *Meiner Meinung nach wird #Format# von Kritikern empfohlen.*	Reinstein & Snyder 2005 (influence effect)
Pcr_4	To my knowledge, [the serialised TV brand] is talked/written about in a favourable context. *Meiner Meinung nach wird #Format# in den Medien positiv besprochen.*	Iyengar & Kinder 1987 (priming / framing)

App. Table 7: Operationalisation and indicators for construct PCR

Perceived WOM response

- Reflective indicators
- Q: What is your perception of other people's response to [the serialised TV brand]?
  Wie nehmen Ihrer Meinung nach andere Personen #Format# wahr?
- 7-point Likert scale (fully agree – fully disagree)

Item #	Item description	Source
Pwr_1	My friends talked positively about it. *Meine Bekannten/Freunde haben sich positiv über #Format# geäußert.*	Romaniuk 2007
Pwr_2	My friends recommended it. *Meine Bekannten/Freunde haben #Format# empfohlen.*	Romaniuk 2007
Pwr_3	Friends in my online social network talked positively about it. *Freunde aus meinem Online-Netzwerk haben sich positiv über #Format# geäußert.*	adapted from Romaniuk 2007
Pwr_4	Friends in my online social network recommended it. *Freunde aus meinem Online-Netzwerk haben #Format# empfohlen.*	adapted from Romaniuk 2007

App. Table 8: Operationalisation and indicators for construct PWR

Appendix B   Survey logistics

Day	Date	Activity	Total (ca.)	Cumulative
Mon	08/07/13	Facebook The Voice of Germany	400	400
Tue	09/07/13	private Facebook & Twitter accounts	100	500
Wed	10/07/13	E-Mailing list	50	550
Thu	11/07/13	Facebook Galileo private Twitter accounts	550	1100
Fri	12/07/13	private Twitter accounts	100	1200
Sat	13/07/13	private Twitter accounts	20	1220
Sun	14/07/13		5	1225
Mon	15/07/13	Facebook (private)	5	1230
Tue	16/07/13	Facebook sixx	230	1460
Wed	17/07/13	Facebook Germany's Next Topmodel	385	1845
Thu	18/07/13		15	1860
Fri	19/07/13		10	1870
Sat	20/07/13		5	1875
Sun	21/07/13	Facebook Galileo	700	2575
Mon	22/07/13		25	2600
Tue	23/07/13		20	2620
Wed	24/07/13		5	2625
Thu	25/07/13		5	2630
Fri	26/07/13		4	2634
Sat	27/07/13		1	2635
Sun	28/07/13		1	2636
Mon	29/07/13		1	2637
Tue	30/07/13	8:00 downloading of file	2	2639

App. Table 9: Questionnaire invitation posting schedule

Appendix C   Survey results

Programme and social media choice

Programme choice	Frequency	Percent
The Voice of Germany	484	20.5
Germany's Next Topmodel	547	23.2
Galileo	1262	53.5
Free choice	64	2.7
Total	2357	100

App. Table 10: Programme choice of questionnaire respondents

Social media choice	Frequency	Percent
Facebook	2240	95.0
Twitter	23	1.0
Instagram	21	0.9
YouTube	63	2.7
Tumblr	3	0.1
Free choice	7	0.3
Total	2357	100

App. Table 11: Social media choice of questionnaire respondents

Demographics of the user sample

Gender	full sample		TVoG subsample		GNTM subsample		Galileo subsample		Free choice subsample	
	Fre-quency	Per-cent	Fre-quency	Per-cent	Fre-quency	Per-cent	Fre-quency	Per-cent	Fre-quency	Per-cent
female	1436	60.9	401	82.9	521	95.2	461	36.5	53	82.8
male	899	38.1	78	16.1	20	3.7	791	62.7	10	15.6
Total	2335	99.1	479	99.0	541	98.9	1252	99.2	63	98.4
Missing (system)	22	0.9	5	1.0	6	1.1	10	0.8	1	1.6
Total	2357	100	484	100	547	100	1262	100	64	100

App. Table 12: Gender of questionnaire respondents

Age	full sample		TVoG subsample		GNTM subsample		Galileo subsample		Free choice subsample	
	Fre-quency	Per-cent	Fre-quency	Per-cent	Fre-quency	Per-cent	Fre-quency	Per-cent	Fre-quency	Per-cent
14-19	1112	47.2	95	19.6	328	60.0	666	52.8	23	35.9
20-29	717	30.4	134	27.7	165	30.2	389	30.8	29	45.3
30-39	270	11.5	119	24.6	31	5.7	111	8.8	9	14.1
40-49	149	6.3	83	17.1	9	1.6	55	4.4	2	3.1
50-59	59	2.5	40	8.3	5	0.9	13	1	1	1.6
60-69	12	0.5	6	1.2	1	0.2	5	0.4	0	0
Total	2319	98.4	477	98.6	539	98.5	1239	98.2	64	100
Missing (system)	38	1.6	7	1.4	8	1.5	23	1.8	0	0
Total	2357	100	484	100	547	100	1262	100	64	100

App. Table 13: Age of questionnaire respondents

Education	full sample		TVoG subsample		GNTM subsample		Galileo subsample		Free choice subsample	
	Fre-quency	Per-cent	Fre-quency	Per-cent	Fre-quency	Per-cent	Fre-quency	Per-cent	Fre-quency	Per-cent
no degree	63	2.7	5	1.0	12	2.2	45	3.6	1	1.6
9 years of school ("Hauptschul-abschluss")	172	7.3	39	8.1	19	3.5	112	8.9	2	3.1
10 years of school ("Realschul-abschluss")	716	30.4	159	32.9	112	20.5	419	33.2	26	40.6
A-levels ("Abitur")	886	37.6	148	30.6	264	48.3	458	36.3	16	25
university degree	362	15.4	106	21.9	100	18.3	143	11.3	13	20.3
Total	2199	93.3	457	94.4	507	92.7	1177	93.3	58	90.6
Missing (system)	158	6.7	27	5.6	40	7.3	85	6.7	6	9.4
Total	2357	100	484	100	547	100	1262	100	64	100

App. Table 14: Education of questionnaire respondents

Occupation	full sample		TVoG subsample		GNTM subsample		Galileo subsample		Free choice subsample	
	Fre-quency	Per-cent	Fre-quency	Per-cent	Fre-quency	Per-cent	Fre-quency	Per-cent	Fre-quency	Per-cent
high school student	929	39.4	73	15.1	270	49.4	566	44.8	20	31.3
university student	319	13.5	56	11.6	101	18.5	156	12.4	6	9.4
employed	752	31.9	225	46.5	119	21.8	381	30.2	27	42.2
civil servant	35	1.5	9	1.9	5	0.9	21	1.7	0	0
home-keeper	90	3.8	45	9.3	14	2.6	29	2.3	2	3.1
unem-ployed	35	1.5	11	2.3	6	1.1	18	1.4	0	0
retired	18	0.8	9	1.9	1	0.2	7	0.6	1	1.6
Total	2178	92.4	428	88.4	516	94.3	1178	93.3	56	87.5
Missing (system)	179	7.6	56	11.6	31	5.7	84	6.7	8	12.5
Total	2357	100	484	100	547	100	1262	100	64	100

App. Table 15: Occupation of questionnaire respondents

Demographics of the non-user sample

Gender	full sample	
	Frequency	Percent
female	167	64.2
male	85	32.7
Total	252	96.9
Missing (system)	8	3.1
Total	260	100

App. Table 16: Gender of respondents of non-user sample

Age	full sample	
	Frequency	Percent
14-19	87	33.5
20-29	90	34.6
30-39	38	14.6
40-49	12	4.6
50-59	20	7.7
60-69	6	2.3
Total	253	97.3
Missing (system)	7	2.7
Total	260	100

App. Table 17: Age of respondents of non-user sample

Education	full sample	
	Frequency	Percent
no degree	3	1.2
9 years of school ("Hauptschulabschluss")	20	7.7
10 years of school ("Realschulabschluss")	60	23.1
A-levels ("Abitur")	88	33.8
university degree	68	26.2
Total	239	91.9
Missing (system)	21	8.1
Total	260	100.0

App. Table 18: Education of respondents of non-user sample

Occupation	*full sample*	
	Frequency	Percent
high school student	70	26.9
university student	48	18.5
employed	101	38.8
civil servant	1	0.4
homekeeper	6	2.3
unemployed	5	1.9
retired	5	1.9
Total	236	90.8
Missing (system)	24	9.2
Total	260	100

App. Table 19: Occupation of respondents of non-user sample

TV usage (kind)

Q: How do you usually watch TV? / *Auf welche Art sehen Sie meistens fern?*

full sample	with a television set		via internet		via mobile devices	
	Frequency	Percent	Frequency	Percent	Frequency	Percent
frequently	1927	81.8	286	12.1	142	6.0
from time to time	310	13.2	705	29.9	320	13.6
rarely	92	3.9	772	32.8	543	23
never	28	1.2	594	25.2	1352	57.4
Total	2357	100	2357	100	2357	100

App. Table 20: TV usage (kind) of full sample

TVoG subsample	with a television set		via internet		via mobile devices	
	Frequency	Percent	Frequency	Percent	Frequency	Percent
frequently	413	85.3	53	11.0	15	3.1
from time to time	50	10.3	158	32.6	35	7.2
rarely	16	3.3	165	34.1	101	20.9
never	5	1.0	108	22.3	333	68.8
Total	484	100	484	100	484	100

App. Table 21: TV usage (kind) of TVoG subsample

GNTM subsample	with a television set		via internet		via mobile devices	
	Frequency	Percent	Frequency	Percent	Frequency	Percent
frequently	420	76.8	93	17.0	29	5.3
from time to time	86	15.7	212	38.8	87	15.9
rarely	33	6.0	162	29.6	137	25.0
never	8	1.5	80	14.6	294	53.7
Total	547	100	547	100	547	100

App. Table 22: TV usage (kind) of GNTM subsample

Galileo subsample	with a television set		via internet		via mobile devices	
	Frequency	Percent	Frequency	Percent	Frequency	Percent
frequently	1039	82.3	128	10.1	96	7.6
from time to time	167	13.2	312	24.7	190	15.1
rarely	42	3.3	427	33.8	296	23.5
never	14	1.1	395	31.3	680	53.9
Total	1262	100	1262	100	1262	100

App. Table 23: TV usage (kind) of Galileo subsample

Free choice subsample	with a television set		via internet		via mobile devices	
	Frequency	Percent	Frequency	Percent	Frequency	Percent
frequently	55	85.9	12	18.8	2	3.1
from time to time	7	10.9	23	35.9	8	12.5
rarely	1	1.6	18	28.1	9	14.1
never	1	1.6	11	17.2	45	70.3
Total	64	100	64	100	64	100

App. Table 24: TV usage (kind) of Free choice subsample

Social media usage (frequency)

Q: How frequently do you use which social media offerings? / *Wie häufig nutzen Sie welche Social Media-Angebote?*

Total	Facebook		Twitter		Pinterest		Instagram		Tumblr	
	Σ	%	Σ	%	Σ	%	Σ	%	Σ	%
several times a day	1981	84.0	112	4.8	14	0.6	254	10.8	42	1.8
once a day	240	10.2	66	2.8	17	0.7	90	3.8	28	1.2
several times a week	89	3.8	82	3.5	23	1.0	59	2.5	40	1.7
at least once a week	25	1.1	58	2.5	19	0.8	57	2.4	30	1.3
at least once a month	8	0.3	117	5.0	27	1.1	72	3.1	49	2.1
less frequently than once a month	8	0.3	183	7.8	48	2.0	103	4.4	71	3.0
never	3	0.1	1666	70.7	2123	90.1	1643	69.7	2011	85.3
not quoted	3	0.1	73	3.1	86	3.6	79	3.4	86	3.6
Total	2357	100	2357	100	2357	100	2357	100	2357	100

App. Table 25: Social media usage (frequency)

Other social media offerings used: Google+, Skype, WhatsApp, YouTube.

Social media usage (kind)

Q: Apart from official social media offerings, do you use social media offerings managed and produced by fans, and do you produce, share, post or review fan fiction or fan art regularly? / *Nutzen Sie außer offiziellen Social Media-Angeboten auch von Fans betriebene Seiten bzw. produzieren, teilen, posten oder bewerten Sie regelmäßig Fan-Fiction oder Fan-Art?*

	Frequency	Percent
yes	702	29.8
no	1655	70.2
Total	2357	100

App. Table 26: Social media usage (kind)

Social media usage – attention for TV

Q: Have you ever watched a TV series/serial solely because your attention was attracted in social media? / *Haben Sie schon einmal eine TV-Serie nur deshalb geschaut, weil Sie in Social Media darauf aufmerksam geworden sind?*

(multiple selection)

full sample	No, never. / *Nein, noch nie.*		Yes, because I wanted to participate in the conversation. / *Ja, weil ich mitreden wollte.*		Yes, because it made me curious. / *Ja, weil ich neugierig geworden bin.*		Yes, because it seemed to suit my tastes. / *Ja, weil die Serie genau meinem Geschmack zu entsprechen schien.*		Yes, for another reason. / *Ja, aus einem anderen Grund.*	
	Fre-quency	Percent	Fre-quency	Percent	Fre-quency	Percent	Fre-quency	Percent	Fre-quency	Percent
not quoted	1315	55.8	2187	92.8	1190	50.5	1674	71.0	2319	98.4
quoted	1042	44.2	170	7.2	1167	49.5	683	29.0	38	1.6
Total	2357	100	2357	100	2357	100	2357	100	2357	100

App. Table 27: Social media usage (attention) of full sample

TVoG sub-sample	No, never. / Nein, noch nie.		Yes, because I wanted to participate in the conversation. / Ja, weil ich mitreden wollte.		Yes, because it made me curious. / Ja, weil ich neugierig geworden bin.		Yes, because it seemed to suit my tastes. / Ja, weil die Serie genau meinem Geschmack zu entsprechen schien.		Yes, for another reason. / Ja, aus einem anderen Grund.	
	Fre-quency	Percent	Fre-quency	Percent	Fre-quency	Percent	Fre-quency	Percent	Fre-quency	Percent
not quoted	223	46.1	465	96.1	284	58.7	379	78.3	480	99.2
quoted	261	53.9	19	3.9	200	41.3	105	21.7	4	0.8
Total	484	100	484	100	484	100	484	100	484	100

App. Table 28: Social media usage (attention) of TVoG subsample

GNTM sub-sample	No, never. / Nein, noch nie.		Yes, because I wanted to participate in the conversation. / Ja, weil ich mitreden wollte.		Yes, because it made me curious. / Ja, weil ich neugierig geworden bin.		Yes, because it seemed to suit my tastes. / Ja, weil die Serie genau meinem Geschmack zu entsprechen schien.		Yes, for another reason. / Ja, aus einem anderen Grund.	
	Fre-quency	Percent	Fre-quency	Percent	Fre-quency	Percent	Fre-quency	Percent	Fre-quency	Percent
not quoted	369	67.5	494	90.3	218	39.9	347	63.4	539	98.5
quoted	178	32.5	53	9.7	329	60.1	200	36.6	8	1.5
Total	547	100	547	100	547	100	547	100	547	100

App. Table 29: Social media usage (attention) of GNTM subsample

Galileo Sub-sample	No, never. / Nein, noch nie.		Yes, because I wanted to participate in the conversation. / Ja, weil ich mitreden wollte.		Yes, because it made me curious. / Ja, weil ich neugierig geworden bin.		Yes, because it seemed to suit my tastes. / Ja, weil die Serie genau meinem Geschmack zu entsprechen schien.		Yes, for another reason. / Ja, aus einem anderen Grund.	
	Fre-quency	Percent	Fre-quency	Percent	Fre-quency	Percent	Fre-quency	Percent	Fre-quency	Percent
not quoted	684	54.2	1170	92.7	653	51.7	913	72.3	1239	98.2
quoted	578	45.8	92	7.3	609	48.3	349	27.7	23	1.8
Total	1262	100	1262	100	1262	100	1262	100	1262	100

App. Table 30: Social media usage (attention) of Galileo subsample

Free choice sub-sample	No, never. / Nein, noch nie.		Yes, because I wanted to participate in the conversation. / Ja, weil ich mitreden wollte.		Yes, because it made me curious. / Ja, weil ich neugierig geworden bin.		Yes, because it seemed to suit my tastes. / Ja, weil die Serie genau meinem Geschmack zu entsprechen schien.		Yes, for another reason. / Ja, aus einem anderen Grund.	
	Fre-quency	Percent	Fre-quency	Percent	Fre-quency	Percent	Fre-quency	Percent	Fre-quency	Percent
not quoted	39	60.9	58	90.6	35	54.7	35	54.7	61	95.3
quoted	25	39.1	6	9.4	29	45.3	29	45.3	3	4.7
Total	64	100	64	100	64	100	64	100	64	100

App. Table 31: Social media usage (attention) of Free choice subsample

Social media usage – loyalty for TV

Q: Have you ever continued watching a TV series/serial you actually did not want to continue watching because of the conversations in social media? / *Haben Sie schon einmal eine TV-Serie, die Sie eigentlich nicht weiter schauen wollten, auf Grund der Gespräche in Social Media doch weiterhin geschaut?*

social media impact	full sample		TVoG subsample		GNTM subsample		Galileo subsample		Free choice subsample	
	Fre-quency	Percent	Fre-quency	Percent	Fre-quency	Percent	Fre-quency	Percent	Fre-quency	Percent
Yes.	350	14.8	60	12.4	102	18.6	182	14.4	6	9.4
No, never.	1544	65.5	343	70.9	301	55.0	851	67.4	49	76.6
No, but I can imagine doing it.	463	19.6	81	16.7	144	26.3	229	18.1	9	14.1
Total	2357	100	484	100	547	100	1262	100	64	100

App. Table 32: Social media usage (loyalty)

Second screen

Q: Do you make use of social media to exchange views about the programme while you watch TV? / *Nutzen Sie Social Media, um sich über die Sendung auszutauschen, während Sie fernsehen?*

Second Screen	full sample		TVoG subsample		GNTM subsample		Galileo subsample		Free choice subsample	
	Fre-quency	Percent	Fre-quency	Percent	Fre-quency	Percent	Fre-quency	Percent	Fre-quency	Percent
Yes, frequently.	122	5.2	29	6.0	47	8.6	41	3.2	5	7.8
Yes, from time to time.	778	33.0	183	37.8	186	34.0	388	30.7	21	32.8
No, never.	948	40.2	182	37.6	196	35.8	542	42.9	28	43.8
Not yet, but I can imagine doing it.	509	21.6	90	18.6	118	21.6	291	23.1	10	15.6
Total	2357	100	484	100	547	100	1262	100	64	100

App. Table 33: Social media usage (second screen)

Social media importance

Q: How important is it for you to find your favourite series/serial on social media? / *Wie wichtig ist Ihnen, dass Ihre Lieblingsserien auf Social Media präsent sind?*

Social media importance	full sample		TVoG subsample		GNTM subsample		Galileo subsample		Free choice subsample	
	Fre-quency	Percent	Fre-quency	Percent	Fre-quency	Percent	Fre-quency	Percent	Fre-quency	Percent
very important	323	13.7	67	13.8	92	16.8	155	12.3	9	14.1
more important than not	560	23.8	121	25.0	145	26.5	278	22.0	16	25.0
not very important, but a nice add-on	1217	51.6	250	51.7	269	49.2	663	52.5	35	54.7
not at all important	257	10.9	46	9.5	41	7.5	166	13.2	4	6.3
Total	2357	100	484	100	547	100	1262	100	64	100

App. Table 34: Social media importance

Social media – important features

Q: Which features of the social media presence of your favourite TV series/serial do you consider important? / *Was ist Ihnen bei der Social Media-Präsenz Ihrer Lieblingsserien wichtig?*

full sample	smf_1 information about the TV programme (schedule, dates, etc.)		smf_2 background information (look behind the scenes, exclusive content)		smf_3 communi-cation with other fans		smf_4 direct link to the TV programme		smf_5 content from the TV programme in case I missed it		smf_6 other	
	Σ	%	Σ	%	Σ	%	Σ	%	Σ	%	Σ	%
very important	1003	42.6	772	32.8	204	8.7	466	19.8	1030	43.7	46	2.0
important	813	34.5	796	33.8	282	12.0	580	24.6	710	30.1	38	1.6
more important than not	347	14.7	416	17.6	426	18.1	577	24.5	352	14.9	20	0.8
neither nor	89	3.8	158	6.7	394	16.7	343	14.6	106	4.5	66	2.8
rather un-important	37	1.6	111	4.7	446	18.9	180	7.6	56	2.4	10	0.4
not important	24	1.0	39	1.7	276	11.7	87	3.7	37	1.6	17	0.7
not at all important	44	1.9	65	2.8	329	14.0	124	5.3	66	2.8	136	5.8
not selected											2024	85.9
Total	2357	100	2357	100	2357	100	2357	100	2357	100	2357	100

App. Table 35: Social media – important features (full sample)

TVoG subsample	smf_1 information about the TV programme (schedule, dates, etc.)		smf_2 background information (look behind the scenes, exclusive content)		smf_3 communi- cation with other fans		smf_4 direct link to the TV programme		smf_5 content from the TV programme in case I missed it		smf_6 other	
	Σ	%	Σ	%	Σ	%	Σ	%	Σ	%	Σ	%
very important	182	37.6	141	29.1	30	6.2	71	14.7	200	41.3	7	1.4
important	176	36.4	171	35.3	55	11.4	130	26.9	155	32	5	1
more important than not	83	17.1	96	19.8	102	21.1	117	24.2	84	17.4	1	0.2
neither nor	19	3.9	34	7	96	19.8	80	16.5	19	3.9	19	3.9
rather un- important	7	1.4	17	3.5	96	19.8	34	7	10	2.1	4	0.8
not important	7	1.4	9	1.9	46	9.5	19	3.9	3	0.6	2	0.4
not at all important	10	2.1	16	3.3	59	12.2	33	6.8	13	2.7	38	7.9
not selected											408	84.3
Total	484	100	484	100	484	100	484	100	484	100	484	100

App. Table 36: Social media – important features (TVoG subsample)

GNTM subsample	smf_1 information about the TV programme (schedule, dates, etc.)		smf_2 background information (look behind the scenes, exclusive content)		smf_3 communi- cation with other fans		smf_4 direct link to the TV programme		smf_5 content from the TV programme in case I missed it		smf_6 other	
	Σ	%	Σ	%	Σ	%	Σ	%	Σ	%	Σ	%
very important	251	45.9	218	39.9	48	8.8	119	21.8	259	47.3	11	2.0
important	186	34.0	193	35.3	57	10.4	128	23.4	165	30.2	13	2.4
more important than not	78	14.3	77	14.1	98	17.9	140	25.6	77	14.1	5	0.9
neither nor	11	2.0	25	4.6	74	13.5	61	11.2	16	2.9	10	1.8
rather un- important	13	2.4	20	3.7	124	22.7	54	9.9	7	1.3	1	0.2
not important	2	0.4	8	1.5	69	12.6	22	4.0	9	1.6	4	0.7
not at all important	6	1.1	6	1.1	77	14.1	23	4.2	14	2.6	23	4.2
not selected											480	87.8
Total	547	100	547	100	547	100	547	100	547	100	547	100

App. Table 37: Social media – important features (GNTM subsample)

Galileo subsample	smf_1 information about the TV programme (schedule, dates, etc.)		smf_2 background information (look behind the scenes, exclusive content)		smf_3 communi-cation with other fans		smf_4 direct link to the TV programme		smf_5 content from the TV programme in case I missed it		smf_6 other	
	Σ	%	Σ	%	Σ	%	Σ	%	Σ	%	Σ	%
very important	537	42.6	393	31.1	116	9.2	255	20.2	534	42.3	27	2.1
important	430	34.1	408	32.3	164	13	305	24.2	375	29.7	20	1.6
more important than not	179	14.2	228	18.1	212	16.8	309	24.5	182	14.4	14	1.1
neither nor	58	4.6	95	7.5	213	16.9	194	15.4	68	5.4	35	2.8
rather un-important	15	1.2	73	5.8	213	16.9	89	7.1	39	3.1	5	0.4
not important	15	1.2	22	1.7	157	12.4	43	3.4	25	2	11	0.9
not at all important	28	2.2	43	3.4	187	14.8	67	5.3	39	3.1	71	5.6
not selected											1079	85.5
Total	1262	100	1262	100	1262	100	1262	100	1262	100	1262	100

App. Table 38: Social media – important features (Galileo subsample)

Free choice subsample	smf_1 information about the TV programme (schedule, dates, etc.)		smf_2 background information (look behind the scenes, exclusive content)		smf_3 communi-cation with other fans		smf_4 direct link to the TV programme		smf_5 content from the TV programme in case I missed it		smf_6 other	
	Σ	%	Σ	%	Σ	%	Σ	%	Σ	%	Σ	%
very important	33	51.6	20	31.3	10	15.6	21	32.8	37	57.8	1	1.6
important	21	32.8	24	37.5	6	9.4	17	26.6	15	23.4	0	0
more important than not	7	10.9	15	23.4	14	21.9	11	17.2	9	14.1	0	0
neither nor	1	1.6	4	6.3	11	17.2	8	12.5	3	4.7	2	3.1
rather un-important	2	3.1	1	1.6	13	20.3	3	4.7	0	0	0	0
not important	0	0	0	0	4	6.3	3	4.7	0	0	0	0
not at all important	0	0	0	0	6	9.4	1	1.6	0	0	4	6.3
not selected											57	89.1
Total	64	100	64	100	64	100	64	100	64	100	64	100

App. Table 39: Social media – important features (Free choice subsample)

Social media – important features (by age group)

smf_1: information about the TV programme (schedule, dates, etc.)

	14-19		20-29		30-39		40-49		50-59		60-69		not indicated	
	Σ	%	Σ	%	Σ	%	Σ	%	Σ	%	Σ	%	Σ	%
very important	506	45.5	303	42.3	107	39.6	55	36.9	14	23.7	3	25	15	39.5
important	385	34.6	254	35.4	93	34.4	47	31.5	18	30.5	4	33.3	12	31.6
more important than not	148	13.3	105	14.6	44	16.3	28	18.8	14	23.7	2	16.7	6	15.8
neither nor	34	3.1	25	3.5	14	5.2	7	4.7	5	8.5	1	8.3	3	7.9
rather un- important	22	2	7	1	5	1.9	2	1.3	1	1.7				
not important	6	0.5	9	1.3	2	0.7	3	2	4	6.8				
not at all important	11	1	14	2	5	1.9	7	4.7	3	5.1	2	16.7	2	5.3
Total	1112	100	717	100	270	100	149	100	59	100	12	100	38	100

App. Table 40: Social media – important features (smf_1 by age group)

smf_2: background information (look behind the scenes, exclusive content)

	14-19		20-29		30-39		40-49		50-59		60-69		not indicated	
	Σ	%	Σ	%	Σ	%	Σ	%	Σ	%	Σ	%	Σ	%
very important	405	36.4	215	30	82	30.4	47	31.5	12	20.3	1	8.3	10	26.3
important	359	32.3	259	36.1	104	38.5	45	30.2	15	25.4	3	25	11	28.9
more important than not	180	16.2	145	20.2	39	14.4	30	20.1	13	22	4	33.3	5	13.2
neither nor	69	6.2	39	5.4	26	9.6	10	6.7	7	11.9	1	8.3	6	15.8
rather un- important	62	5.6	28	3.9	10	3.7	6	4	3	5.1	1	8.3	1	2.6
not important	12	1.1	14	2	3	1.1	2	1.3	5	8.5	1	8.3	2	5.3
not at all important	25	2.2	17	2.4	6	2.2	9	6	4	6.8	1	8.3	3	7.9
Total	1112	100	717	100	270	100	149	100	59	100	12	100	38	100

App. Table 41: Social media – important features (smf_2 by age group)

smf_3: communication with other fans

	14-19		20-29		30-39		40-49		50-59		60-69		not indicated	
	Σ	%	Σ	%	Σ	%	Σ	%	Σ	%	Σ	%	Σ	%
very important	115	10.3	53	7.4	23	8.5	8	5.4	1	1.7			4	10.5
important	151	13.6	75	10.5	26	9.6	20	13.4	4	6.8	2	16.7	4	10.5
more important than not	189	17	135	18.8	56	20.7	25	16.8	13	22	3	25	5	13.2
neither nor	181	16.3	108	15.1	56	20.7	32	21.5	10	16.9	1	8.3	6	15.8
rather un- important	206	18.5	146	20.4	53	19.6	23	15.4	9	15.3			9	23.7
not important	132	11.9	86	12	27	10	14	9.4	10	16.9	4	33.3	3	7.9
not at all important	138	12.4	114	15.9	29	10.7	27	18.1	12	20.3	2	16.7	7	18.4
Total	1112	100	717	100	270	100	149	100	59	100	12	100	38	100

App. Table 42: Social media – important features (smf_3 by age group)

smf_4: direct link to the TV programme

	14-19		20-29		30-39		40-49		50-59		60-69		not indicated	
	Σ	%	Σ	%	Σ	%	Σ	%	Σ	%	Σ	%	Σ	%
very important	275	24.7	118	16.5	42	15.6	18	12.1	2	3.4	1	8.3	10	26.3
important	304	27.3	165	23	62	23	28	18.8	12	20.3	2	16.7	7	18.4
more important than not	260	23.4	201	28	64	23.7	32	21.5	11	18.6	1	8.3	8	21.1
neither nor	131	11.8	109	15.2	47	17.4	31	20.8	15	25.4	3	25	7	18.4
rather un-important	73	6.6	62	8.6	23	8.5	14	9.4	6	10.2	1	8.3	1	2.6
not important	31	2.8	22	3.1	15	5.6	8	5.4	8	13.6	2	16.7	1	2.6
not at all important	38	3.4	40	5.6	17	6.3	18	12.1	5	8.5	2	16.7	4	10.5
Total	1112	100	717	100	270	100	149	100	59	100	12	100	38	100

App. Table 43: Social media – important features (smf_4 by age group)

smf_5: content from the TV programme in case I missed it

	14-19		20-29		30-39		40-49		50-59		60-69		not indicated	
	Σ	%	Σ	%	Σ	%	Σ	%	Σ	%	Σ	%	Σ	%
very important	534	48	304	42.4	108	40	52	34.9	16	27.1	1	8.3	15	39.5
important	338	30.4	217	30.3	79	29.3	45	30.2	17	28.8	3	25	11	28.9
more important than not	138	12.4	112	15.6	54	20	27	18.1	14	23.7	3	25	4	10.5
neither nor	39	3.5	36	5	12	4.4	11	7.4	4	6.8	1	8.3	3	7.9
rather un- important	27	2.4	15	2.1	5	1.9	6	4	2	3.4	1	8.3		
not important	18	1.6	10	1.4	3	1.1	1	0.7	3	5.1	1	8.3	1	2.6
not at all important	18	1.6	23	3.2	9	3.3	7	4.7	3	5.1	2	16.7	4	10.5
Total	1112	100	717	100	270	100	149	100	59	100	12	100	38	100

App. Table 44: Social media – important features (smf_5 by age group)

Social media – important features (by gender)

smf_1: information about the TV programme (schedule, dates, etc.)

	female		male		not indicated	
	Σ	%	Σ	%	Σ	%
very important	627	43.7	369	41	7	31.8
important	487	33.9	319	35.5	7	31.8
more important than not	216	15	128	14.2	3	13.6
neither nor	46	3.2	40	4.4	3	13.6
rather unimportant	28	1.9	9	1		
not important	10	0.7	14	1.6		
not at all important	22	1.5	20	2.2	2	9.1
Total	1436	100	899	100	22	100

App. Table 45: Social media – important features (smf_1 by gender)

smf_2: background information (look behind the scenes, exclusive content)

	female		male		not indicated	
	Σ	%	Σ	%	Σ	%
very important	474	33	294	32.7	4	18.2
important	507	35.3	282	31.4	7	31.8
more important than not	250	17.4	165	18.4	1	4.5
neither nor	91	6.3	61	6.8	6	27.3
rather unimportant	62	4.3	47	5.2	2	9.1
not important	20	1.4	18	2	1	4.5
not at all important	32	2.2	32	3.6	1	4.5
Total	1436	100	899	100	22	100

App. Table 46: Social media – important features (smf_2 by gender)

smf_3: communication with other fans

	female		male		not indicated	
	Σ	%	Σ	%	Σ	%
very important	113	7.9	91	10.1		
important	158	11	124	13.8		
more important than not	275	19.2	147	16.4	4	18.2
neither nor	218	15.2	172	19.1	4	18.2
rather unimportant	309	21.5	130	14.5	7	31.8
not important	169	11.8	106	11.8	1	4.5
not at all important	194	13.5	129	14.3	6	27.3
Total	1436	100	899	100	22	100

App. Table 47: Social media – important features (smf_3 by gender)

smf_4: direct link to the TV programme

	female		male		not indicated	
	Σ	%	Σ	%	Σ	%
very important	267	18.6	198	22	1	4.5
important	340	23.7	237	26.4	3	13.6
more important than not	366	25.5	207	23	4	18.2
neither nor	215	15	122	13.6	6	27.3
rather unimportant	121	8.4	55	6.1	4	18.2
not important	55	3.8	32	3.6		
not at all important	72	5	48	5.3	4	18.2
Total	1436	100	899	100	22	100

App. Table 48: Social media – important features (smf_4 by gender)

smf_5: content from the TV programme in case I missed it

	female		male		not indicated	
	Σ	%	Σ	%	Σ	%
very important	643	44.8	380	42.3	7	31.8
important	435	30.3	267	29.7	8	36.4
more important than not	220	15.3	130	14.5	2	9.1
neither nor	58	4	46	5.1	2	9.1
rather unimportant	25	1.7	30	3.3	1	4.5
not important	19	1.3	18	2		
not at all important	36	2.5	28	3.1	2	9.1
Total	1436	100	899	100	22	100

App. Table 49: Social media – important features (smf_5 by gender)

Non-user sample: Reasons for not using TV series/serial related social media offerings

	Reason	quoted	not quoted
nng_1	These offerings don't appeal to me.	89	171
% nng_1	*Ich fühle mich von den Angeboten nicht angesprochen.*	34.2%	65.8%
nng_2	I hardly use social media in general.	53	207
% nng_2	*Ich nutze generell kaum Social Media.*	20.4%	79.6%
nng_3	I find these offerings confusing.	18	242
% nng_3	*Ich finde die Angebote verwirrend/ unübersichtlich.*	6.9%	93.1%
nng_4	I have concerns regarding data protection and privacy.	35	225
% nng_4	*Ich habe Bedenken in Bezug auf Datenschutz und Privatsphäre.*	13.5%	86.5%
nng_5	I'm content watching my favourite programmes on TV - I have no further	159	101
% nng_5	interest in them.		
	Es reicht mir, meine Lieblingssendungen im TV zu schauen –		
	darüberhinaus habe ich kein Interesse daran.	61.2%	38.8%
nng_6	I don't know anybody who is actively using such websites.	45	215
% nng_6	*Ich kenne niemanden, der auf solchen Seiten aktiv ist.*	17.3%	82.7%
nng_7	I don't have time for things like that.	55	205
% nng_7	*Für so etwas habe ich keine Zeit.*	21.2%	78.8%
nng_8	To my mind, social media offerings of serialised TV brands don't offer	60	200
% nng_8	any additional information.		
	Die Social Media-Angebote von TV-Serien enthalten meiner Meinung		
	nach keine zusätzlichen Information.	23.1%	76.9%
nng_9	These websites aren't entertaining.	80	180
% nng_9	*Ich fühle mich von solchen Seiten nicht unterhalten.*	30.8%	69.2%
nng_10	I'm not interested in other people's opinion about TV series/serials.	100	160
% nng_10	*Es interessiert mich nicht, was andere Leute über TV-Serien denken.*	38.5%	61.5%
nng_11	I don't want to get in touch with other people.	11	249
% nng_11	*Ich möchte nicht mit anderen Leuten in Kontakt treten.*	4.2%	95.8%
nng_12	I get all the information I need about the TV series/serials I watch from	58	202
% nng_12	other media.		
	Alles, was ich über die TV-Serien, die ich schaue, wissen möchte, erfahre		
	ich aus anderen Medien.	22.3%	77.7%

App. Table 50: Reasons for not using TV series/serial related social media offerings

Appendix D Data for evaluation of the model

Complete data for evaluation of the measurement model

latent variable	indicator	factor loading	sample mean	standard deviation	standard error	t-value
Brand loyalty (BL)	BL_1	0.8351**	0.8349	0.0109	0.0109	76.5186
	BL_2	0.8897**	0.8896	0.0063	0.0063	141.9058
	BL_4	0.6511**	0.6509	0.0168	0.0168	38.8056
	BL_5	0.8589**	0.8589	0.0077	0.0077	111.318
Consumer brand relationship	CBR_1	0.7645**	0.7641	0.0107	0.0107	71.4559
(CBR)	CBR_2	0.8299**	0.83	0.0066	0.0066	126.3471
	CBR_3	0.7964**	0.7962	0.0091	0.0091	87.778
	CBR_4	0.7711**	0.771	0.0098	0.0098	78.94
	CBR_5	0.6326**	0.6326	0.0163	0.0163	38.7988
	CBR_6	0.872**	0.872	0.0058	0.0058	150.6343
Perceived critics' response	Pcr_3	0.9329**	0.9328	0.0047	0.0047	200.3584
(PCR)	Pcr_4	0.9331**	0.9331	0.0043	0.0043	214.6317
Perceived WOM response	Pwr_1	0.8328**	0.8326	0.0076	0.0076	110.2324
(PWR)	Pwr_2	0.8604**	0.8602	0.007	0.007	122.9684
	Pwr_3	0.8658**	0.8657	0.0065	0.0065	133.8474
	Pwr_4	0.8664**	0.8663	0.0068	0.0068	126.7313
Engagement in the social	sme_1	0.7672**	0.7671	0.0105	0.0105	73.1413
media programme for the	sme_2	0.7655**	0.7654	0.0105	0.0105	72.6796
serialised TV brand (SME)	sme_3	0.8295**	0.8294	0.0079	0.0079	104.7601
	sme_4	0.8648**	0.8648	0.0051	0.0051	168.1373
Attitude toward the social	smp_1	0.8635**	0.8634	0.0078	0.0078	110.8869
media programme for the	smp_2	0.8367**	0.8366	0.0072	0.0072	115.4975
serialised TV brand (SMP)	smp_3	0.8607**	0.8606	0.0072	0.0072	119.131
	smp_4	0.7577**	0.7579	0.0115	0.0115	65.832
	smp_5	0.7661**	0.7661	0.0109	0.0109	70.052
	smp_6	0.8045**	0.8044	0.0111	0.0111	72.7275
	smp_7_r	0.6447**	0.6447	0.0181	0.0181	35.7113
	smp_8_r	0.6321**	0.6322	0.0219	0.0219	28.8937
	smp_9	0.8429**	0.843	0.0076	0.0076	111.137

App. Table 51: Indicator reliability
**	significant at the .05 level (> 1.66 one-tailed)
*	significant at the .1 level (> 1.29 one-tailed)

	AVE	Composite Reliability	R Square	Cronbach's Alpha	Communality	Redundancy
BL	0.6627	0.8858	0.4464	0.8258	0.6627	0.1457
CBR	0.6105	0.9031	0.5384	0.8706	0.6105	0.1877
GO	0	0	0.2848	0	0.5346	0.0435
GOS	0	0	0	0	0.5713	0
PCR	0.8705	0.9307	0	0.8512	0.8705	0
PWR	0.7335	0.9167	0	0.8788	0.7335	0
SME	0.6526	0.8823	0.4143	0.823	0.6526	0.1301
SMP	0.6134	0.9339	0.4516	0.9196	0.6134	0.2763

App. Table 52: PLS Quality criteria

	BL	CBR	GO	GOS	PCR	PWR	SME	SMP
BL_1	0.8351	0.4449	0.4379	0.3605	0.2354	0.3962	0.3898	0.4493
BL_2	0.8897	0.4798	0.4906	0.416	0.2731	0.4199	0.3587	0.5256
BL_4	0.6511	0.3581	0.3609	0.3339	0.2255	0.3069	0.3319	0.3836
BL_5	0.8589	0.5309	0.5212	0.4649	0.3855	0.5288	0.4138	0.5538
CBR_1	0.3557	0.7645	0.5119	0.4539	0.3065	0.3922	0.4527	0.4475
CBR_2	0.5874	0.8299	0.5748	0.4708	0.3109	0.4801	0.5161	0.5173
CBR_3	0.4331	0.7964	0.4634	0.4157	0.3	0.4027	0.4685	0.4121
CBR_4	0.3731	0.7711	0.4801	0.4459	0.3124	0.3931	0.4888	0.4288
CBR_5	0.3144	0.6326	0.3639	0.2919	0.196	0.3164	0.3344	0.315
CBR_6	0.5155	0.872	0.5601	0.4817	0.3625	0.4719	0.5203	0.4957
GOS_1_r	0.4584	0.4596	0.5984	0.8667	0.3095	0.4151	0.4478	0.6183
GOS_2_r	0.4406	0.4125	0.5805	0.8209	0.2529	0.3812	0.4348	0.5957
GOS_3_r	0.2989	0.4261	0.5287	0.7458	0.2746	0.3303	0.4021	0.4933
GOS_4_r	0.2864	0.3973	0.4559	0.6507	0.1903	0.2661	0.3691	0.3947
GOS_5_r	0.4272	0.4465	0.5727	0.8387	0.2635	0.3829	0.4535	0.5805
GOS_6_r	0.3241	0.4504	0.5051	0.7339	0.2475	0.3229	0.4391	0.4246
GOS_7_r	0.2946	0.3177	0.4014	0.5935	0.1887	0.2635	0.3665	0.3723
GO_1_r	0.4493	0.5097	0.8038	0.5697	0.3179	0.4176	0.4148	0.5568
GO_2_r	0.5156	0.4419	0.7876	0.5004	0.2666	0.4106	0.3435	0.501
GO_3_r	0.3409	0.4791	0.6965	0.5496	0.2814	0.3676	0.3857	0.4749
GO_4_r	0.2797	0.4129	0.5642	0.4447	0.1701	0.2761	0.3054	0.3175
GO_5_r	0.5046	0.4715	0.8066	0.5154	0.2623	0.4263	0.3346	0.4701
GO_6_r	0.2968	0.5303	0.698	0.5285	0.2775	0.3546	0.474	0.4248
Pcr_3	0.3292	0.3606	0.3407	0.3083	0.9329	0.4597	0.2959	0.3493
Pcr_4	0.3242	0.3599	0.3427	0.3196	0.9331	0.4833	0.2986	0.3602
Pwr_1	0.495	0.4432	0.4522	0.3828	0.4807	0.8328	0.3095	0.4398
Pwr_2	0.4543	0.4357	0.4404	0.3718	0.4322	0.8604	0.3312	0.4166
Pwr_3	0.426	0.4763	0.4487	0.4084	0.4173	0.8658	0.4619	0.4545
Pwr_4	0.3936	0.4595	0.4398	0.4004	0.4016	0.8664	0.4425	0.4349
sme_1	0.394	0.427	0.3746	0.384	0.1907	0.3321	0.7672	0.4637
sme_2	0.269	0.407	0.3364	0.3599	0.2406	0.3079	0.7655	0.3952
sme_3	0.3784	0.4649	0.4031	0.4546	0.2443	0.3764	0.8295	0.4967
sme_4	0.4221	0.6035	0.5079	0.5352	0.3353	0.4265	0.8648	0.6107
smp_1	0.5356	0.4693	0.5568	0.5927	0.3346	0.4452	0.5397	0.8635
smp_2	0.5432	0.5271	0.567	0.5873	0.3194	0.4587	0.5763	0.8367
smp_3	0.5057	0.4503	0.5157	0.5701	0.3108	0.4098	0.5077	0.8607
smp_4	0.4634	0.4996	0.5039	0.5063	0.3215	0.4249	0.5274	0.7577
smp_5	0.4821	0.4705	0.4956	0.505	0.336	0.4257	0.4809	0.7661
smp_6	0.4639	0.4509	0.5011	0.5173	0.2786	0.4001	0.4717	0.8045
smp_7_r	0.2947	0.2974	0.3922	0.4182	0.2376	0.2758	0.3222	0.6447
smp_8_r	0.3498	0.324	0.3695	0.4076	0.2547	0.2968	0.3333	0.6321
smp_9	0.4819	0.4408	0.5263	0.5897	0.2748	0.4097	0.5327	0.8429

App. Table 53: Cross loadings

Component	1	2	3	4	5	6
BL_1	0.176	0.166	0.16	0.791	0.167	0
BL_2	0.295	0.211	0.153	0.788	0.036	0.051
BL_4	0.178	0.119	0.051	0.589	0.18	0.119
BL_5	0.305	0.25	0.27	0.665	0.067	0.177
CBR_1	0.252	0.727	0.126	0.012	0.14	0.141
CBR_2	0.23	0.64	0.191	0.394	0.179	0.046
CBR_3	0.135	0.713	0.129	0.212	0.194	0.09
CBR_4	0.184	0.708	0.12	0.057	0.243	0.146
CBR_5	0.12	0.629	0.151	0.132	0.059	-0.055
CBR_6	0.215	0.749	0.162	0.253	0.17	0.142
SMP_1	0.755	0.142	0.158	0.251	0.236	0.085
SMP_2	0.669	0.226	0.173	0.26	0.298	0.051
SMP_3	0.786	0.143	0.128	0.221	0.19	0.061
SMP_4	0.598	0.254	0.155	0.163	0.279	0.107
SMP_5	0.646	0.219	0.164	0.191	0.18	0.121
SMP_6	0.73	0.188	0.152	0.175	0.16	0.021
SMP_7_r	0.72	0.108	0.058	-0.002	-0.002	0.107
SMP_8_r	0.661	0.117	0.076	0.104	0.003	0.107
SMP_9	0.75	0.127	0.145	0.2	0.266	0.016
SME_1	0.224	0.153	0.119	0.271	0.656	-0.046
SME_2	0.149	0.195	0.085	0.028	0.764	0.131
SME_3	0.25	0.207	0.147	0.144	0.72	0.041
SME_4	0.374	0.378	0.117	0.098	0.625	0.148
PCR_3	0.161	0.146	0.216	0.12	0.101	0.855
PCR_4	0.176	0.142	0.249	0.113	0.088	0.842
PWR_1	0.227	0.193	0.698	0.281	-0.049	0.266
PWR_2	0.194	0.191	0.769	0.212	0.011	0.198
PWR_3	0.193	0.204	0.779	0.111	0.272	0.103
PWR_4	0.174	0.202	0.803	0.067	0.273	0.092

App. Table 54: Rotated component matrix

	BL	CBR	GO	GOS	PCR	PWR	SME	SMP
BL	1	0	0	0	0	0	0	0
CBR	0.5633	1	0	0	0	0	0	0
GO	0.562	0.6376	1	0	0	0	0	0
GOS	0.4883	0.552	0.6934	1	0	0	0	0
PCR	0.3501	0.3861	0.3662	0.3365	1	0	0	0
PWR	0.5161	0.5301	0.52	0.4567	0.5054	1	0	0
SME	0.4595	0.5992	0.5108	0.5457	0.3186	0.4522	1	0
SMP	0.594	0.5655	0.6345	0.672	0.3802	0.5099	0.6195	1

App. Table 55: Latent variable correlations

	BL	CBR	GO	GOS	PCR	PWR	SME	SMP
BL	1	0	0	0	0	0	0	0
CBR	0.31730689	1	0	0	0	0	0	0
GO	0.315844	0.40653376	1	0	0	0	0	0
GOS	0.23843689	0.304704	0.48080356	1	0	0	0	0
PCR	0.12257001	0.14907321	0.13410244	0.11323225	1	0	0	0
PWR	0.26635921	0.28100601	0.2704	0.20857489	0.25542916	1	0	0
SME	0.21114025	0.35904064	0.26091664	0.29778849	0.10150596	0.20448484	1	0
SMP	0.352836	0.31979025	0.40259025	0.451584	0.14455204	0.25999801	0.38378025	1

App. Table 56: Squared latent variable correlations

	Stone-Geisser's Q² (Communality)
BL	0.4461
CBR	0.4596
PCR	0.8279
PWR	0.7014
SME	0.6646
SMP	0.6101

App. Table 57: Stone-Geisser's Q² (Communality)

latent variable	indicator	weights	sample mean	standard deviation	standard error	t-value
Gratifications obtained from the social media programme for the serialised TV brand (GOS)	GOS_1_r	0.3455**	0.3457	0.035	0.035	9.8656
	GOS_2_r	0.1587**	0.1579	0.0366	0.0366	4.3309
	GOS_3_r	0.175**	0.1741	0.0298	0.0298	5.8652
	GOS_4_r	0.0784**	0.0791	0.0278	0.0278	2.8182
	GOS_5_r	0.214**	0.2136	0.0343	0.0343	6.2393
	GOS_6_r	0.2502**	0.2501	0.0323	0.0323	7.7398
	GOS_7_r	0.0431	0.0448	0.0266	0.0266	1.6222
Gratifications obtained from the serialised TV brand (GO)	GO_1_r	0.3193**	0.319	0.0354	0.0354	9.0299
	GO_2_r	0.2643**	0.2632	0.0391	0.0391	6.765
	GO_3_r	0.1079**	0.1078	0.0331	0.0331	3.2596
	GO_4_r	0.0251	0.0303	0.0213	0.0213	1.1794
	GO_5_r	0.3026**	0.3029	0.0373	0.0373	8.1124
	GO_6_r	0.289**	0.2887	0.0312	0.0312	9.276

App. Table 58: Indicator weights
**   significant at the .05 level (> 1.98 two-tailed)
*   significant at the .1 level (> 1.66 two-tailed)

formative construct GOS	adjusted R²	VIF
dependent indicator GOS_1_r	0.6	2.5
dependent indicator GOS_2_r	0.639	2.770083102
dependent indicator GOS_3_r	0.45	1.818181818
dependent indicator GOS_4_r	0.432	1.76056338
dependent indicator GOS_5_r	0.637	2.754820937
dependent indicator GOS_6_r	0.5	2
dependent indicator GOS_7_r	0.399	1.663893511

App. Table 59: Examining multicollinearity for construct GOS

formative construct GO	adjusted R²	VIF
dependent indicator GO_1_r	0.583	2.398081535
dependent indicator GO_2_r	0.555	2.247191011
dependent indicator GO_3_r	0.561	2.277904328
dependent indicator GO_4_r	0.377	1.605136437
dependent indicator GO_5_r	0.573	2.341920375
dependent indicator GO_6_r	0.404	1.677852349

App. Table 60: Examining multicollinearity for construct GO

Complete data for evaluation of the structural model

hypo-thesis	path	path coefficient	evaluation path coefficient	sample mean	standard deviation	standard error	t-value	evaluation t-value
H1	CBR -> BL	0.2527	accept	0.2527	0.0255	0.0255	9.9283***	accept
H2	SMP -> BL	0.3242	accept	0.3234	0.0315	0.0315	10.3045***	accept
H3	SMP -> CBR	0.0467	very low	0.0465	0.0235	0.0235	1.9879**	accept
H4	SME -> BL	0.0101	reject	0.0194	0.0147	0.0147	0.687	reject
H5	SME -> CBR	0.2895	accept	0.2894	0.0196	0.0196	14.7815***	accept
H6	SMP -> SME	0.4609	accept	0.4597	0.0261	0.0261	17.6341***	accept
H7	GOS -> CBR	0.0453	very low	0.0469	0.0242	0.0242	1.8754*	accept
H8	GOS -> SME	0.236	accept	0.2375	0.0273	0.0273	8.6566***	accept
H9	GOS -> SMP	0.672	accept	0.6728	0.0193	0.0193	34.7675***	accept
H10	GO -> BL	0.19	accept	0.1919	0.0327	0.0327	5.8181***	accept
H11	GO -> CBR	0.3256	accept	0.3264	0.0267	0.0267	12.2138***	accept
H12	PCR -> CBR	0.0644	very low	0.0642	0.0172	0.0172	3.7461***	accept
H13	PCR -> GO	0.1389	accept	0.139	0.0213	0.0213	6.5081***	accept
H14	PWR -> CBR	0.1528	accept	0.1521	0.0231	0.0231	6.6213***	accept
H15	PWR -> GO	0.4498	accept	0.4507	0.0221	0.0221	20.3593***	accept

App. Table 61: Hypothesis testing
*** significant at the .01 level (>2.58 two-tailed)
** significant at the .05 level (>1.98 two-tailed)
* significant at the .1 level (> 1.66 two-tailed)

	R^2	Q^2
BL	0.4464	0.2896
CBR	0.5384	0.3211
GO	0.2848	0.1457
SME	0.4143	0.2617
SMP	0.4516	0.275

App. Table 62: Evaluation of the structural model – R^2 and Q^2

construct BL	adjusted R²	VIF
dependent variable SMP	0.522072	2.092365377
dependent variable SME	0.474091	1.901469646
dependent variable GO	0.524349	2.102381788
dependent variable CBR	0.517971	2.074563979

App. Table 63: Testing for multicollinearity, construct BL

construct CBR	adjusted R²	VIF
dependent variable SMP	0.581317	2.388441852
dependent variable SME	0.43479	1.769253906
dependent variable GOS	0.583078	2.398530181
dependent variable GO	0.569679	2.323846617
dependent variable PCR	0.278242	1.385505945
dependent variable PWR	0.419388	1.722320586

App. Table 64: Testing for multicollinearity, construct CBR

construct SME	adjusted R²	VIF
dependent variable SMP	0.446439	1.806485645
dependent variable GOS	0.446439	1.806485645

App. Table 65: Testing for multicollinearity, construct SME

construct GO	adjusted R²	VIF
dependent variable PWR	0.254081	1.340628138
dependent variable PCR	0.254081	1.340628138

App. Table 66: Testing for multicollinearity, construct GO

Appendix E Exploratory data analysis

Correlations between constructs

	BL	CBR	SMP	SME	GOS	PWR	PCR	GO
BL	1							
CBR	.564**	1						
SMP	.591**	.567**	1					
SME	.466**	.599**	.619**	1				
GOS	.486**	.556**	.668**	.546**	1			
PWR	.514**	.530**	.509**	.453**	.455**	1		
PCR	.352**	.387**	.381**	.316**	.337**	.504**	1	
GO	.547**	.647**	.634**	.521**	.700**	.517**	.369**	1

App. Table 67: Pearson correlations between construct values (standardised)
** Correlation is significant at the .01 level (2-tailed).

Exploratory data analysis for construct value BL

Descriptives			Statistic	Std. Error
construct value BL (std)	Mean		5.8652	.02383
	95% Confidence Interval for mean	Lower Bound	7.095202	
		Upper Bound	7.209178	
	5% Trimmed Mean		5.9985	
	Median		6.1995	
	Variance		1.338	
	Std. Deviation		1.15680	
	Minimum		1.00	
	Maximum		7.00	
	Range		6.00	
	Interquartile Range		1.31	
	Skewness		-1.720	.050
	Kurtosis		3.442	.101

App. Table 68: Descriptives for construct value BL

Tests of Normality						
	Kolmogorov-Smirnov[a]			Shapiro-Wilk		
	Statistic	df	Sig.	Statistic	df	Sig.
Construct value BL (std)	.163	2357	.000	.832	2357	.000

a. Lilliefors Significance Correction
App. Table 69: Tests of Normality for construct value BL

Exploratory data analysis for construct value CBR

Descriptives			Statistic	Std. Error
construct value CBR (std)	Mean		4.4376	.02899
	95% Confidence Interval for mean	Lower Bound	4.3808	
		Upper Bound	4.4945	
	5% Trimmed Mean		4.4714	
	Median		4.5403	
	Variance		1.981	
	Std. Deviation		1.40765	
	Minimum		1.00	
	Maximum		7.00	
	Range		6.00	
	Interquartile Range		1.92	
	Skewness		-.338	.050
	Kurtosis		-.431	.101

App. Table 70: Descriptives for construct value CBR

Tests of Normality	Kolmogorov-Smirnov[a]			Shapiro-Wilk		
	Statistic	df	Sig.	Statistic	df	Sig.
Construct value CBR (std)	.052	2357	.000	.981	2357	.000

a. Lilliefors Significance Correction

App. Table 71: Tests of Normality for construct value CBR

Exploratory data analysis for construct value SMP

Descriptives			Statistic	Std. Error
construct value SMP (std)	Mean		5.2221	.02347
	95% Confidence Interval for mean	Lower Bound	5.1761	
		Upper Bound	5.2681	
	5% Trimmed Mean		5.2863	
	Median		5.3906	
	Variance		1.298	
	Std. Deviation		1.13933	
	Minimum		1.00	
	Maximum		7.00	
	Range		6.00	
	Interquartile Range		1.47	
	Skewness		-.809	.050
	Kurtosis		.529	.101

App. Table 72: Descriptives for construct value SMP

Tests of Normality						
	Kolmogorov-Smirnov[a]			Shapiro-Wilk		
	Statistic	df	Sig.	Statistic	df	Sig.
Construct value SMP (std)	.064	2357	.000	.955	2357	.000

a. Lilliefors Significance Correction

App. Table 73: Tests of Normality for construct value SMP

Exploratory data analysis for construct value SME

Descriptives			Statistic	Std. Error
construct value SME (std)	Mean		3.6746	.03141
	95% Confidence Interval for mean	Lower Bound	3.6130	
		Upper Bound	3.7361	
	5% Trimmed Mean		3.6579	
	Median		3.6825	
	Variance		2.326	
	Std. Deviation		1.52500	
	Minimum		1.00	
	Maximum		7.00	
	Range		6.00	
	Interquartile Range		2.29	
	Skewness		.069	.050
	Kurtosis		-.779	.101

App. Table 74: Descriptives for construct value SME

Testing for normality

One-Sample Kolmogorov-Smirnov Test

standardised construct values		BL	CBR	GOS	GO	PCR	PWR	SME	SMP
N		2357	2357	2357	2357	2357	2357	2357	2357
Normal Parameters[a,b]	Mean	5.8652	4.4376	4.9896	5.2413	4.4552	4.7612	3.6746	5.2221
	Std. Deviation	1.15680	1.40765	1.18498	1.11523	1.50662	1.47612	1.52500	1.13933
Most Extreme Differences	Absolute	.163	.052	.045	.057	.112	.071	.040	.064
	Positive	.163	.034	.045	.057	.066	.065	.040	.059
	Negative	-.142	-.052	-.042	-.050	-.112	-.071	-.040	-.064
Kolmogorov-Smirnov Z		7.928	2.504	2.179	2.787	5.451	3.446	1.929	3.091
Asymp. Sig. (2-tailed)		0.000	.000	.000	.000	0.000	0.000	.001	.000

a Test distribution is normal. / b Calculated from data.
App. Table 75: One-Sample Kolmogorov-Smirnov Test

One-Sample Kolmogorov-Smirnov Test (TVoG-subsample)

standardised construct values		BL	CBR	GOS	GO	PCR	PWR	SME	SMP
N		484	484	484	484	484	484	484	484
Normal Parameters[a,b]	Mean	6.1820	4.6859	4.9936	5.3218	5.3039	5.2631	3.9440	5.3477
	Std. Deviation	0.95133	1.25996	1.02456	0.92791	1.18902	1.18308	1.40477	0.93970
Most Extreme Differences	Absolute	.195	.068	.035	.038	.173	.095	.044	.059
	Positive	.195	.043	.025	.035	.128	.071	.044	.039
	Negative	-.139	-.068	-.035	-.038	-.173	-.095	-.042	-.059
Kolmogorov-Smirnov Z		4.289	1.494	.768	.835	3.808	2.088	.959	1.296
Asymp. Sig. (2-tailed)		0.000	.023	.597	.488	0.000	.000	.317	.069

a Test distribution is normal. / b Calculated from data.
App. Table 76: One-Sample Kolmogorov-Smirnov Test (TVoG-subsample)

One-Sample Kolmogorov-Smirnov Test (GNTM-subsample)

standardised construct values		BL	CBR	GOS	GO	PCR	PWR	SME	SMP
N		547	547	547	547	547	547	547	547
Normal Parameters[a,b]	Mean	5.9186	4.1978	4.8823	5.0550	3.6108	4.5033	3.6747	5.0976
	Std. Deviation	1.21331	1.50863	1.20095	1.16320	1.45137	1.46958	1.59613	1.21953
Most Extreme Differences	Absolute	.186	.038	.047	.047	.105	.060	.047	.059
	Positive	.186	.038	.039	.047	.105	.045	.042	.059
	Negative	-.164	-.036	-.047	-.040	-.077	-.060	-.047	-.059
Kolmogorov-Smirnov Z		4.359	.877	1.101	1.105	2.455	1.399	1.097	1.389
Asymp. Sig. (2-tailed)		0.000	.425	.177	.174	.000	.040	.180	.042

a Test distribution is normal. / b Calculated from data.
App. Table 77: One-Sample Kolmogorov-Smirnov Test (GNTM-subsample)

One-Sample Kolmogorov-Smirnov Test (Galileo-subsample)

standardised construct values		BL	CBR	GOS	GO	PCR	PWR	SME	SMP
N		1262	1262	1262	1262	1262	1262	1262	1262
Normal Parameters[a,b]	Mean	5.6869	4.4074	5.0163	5.2738	4.4820	4.6535	3.5409	5.2044
	Std. Deviation	1.18137	1.39862	1.23201	1.15511	1.44696	1.53803	1.51552	1.16979
Most Extreme Differences	Absolute	.133	.057	.060	.068	.141	.073	.047	.078
	Positive	.133	.032	.054	.068	.097	.064	.043	.062
	Negative	-.125	-.057	-.060	-.066	-.141	-.073	-.047	-.078
Kolmogorov-Smirnov Z		4.731	2.034	2.128	2.399	5.005	2.592	1.663	2.774
Asymp. Sig. (2-tailed)		0.000	.001	.000	.000	0.000	.000	.008	.000

a Test distribution is normal. / b Calculated from data.
App. Table 78: One-Sample Kolmogorov-Smirnov Test (Galileo-subsample)

Kruskal-Wallis tests

Kruskal-Wallis tests for standardised construct value BL

The null and alternative hypotheses for the Kruskal-Wallis test are:

H_0:   the distribution of construct value BL is the same across categories of choice

H_A: at least two of the groups differ with respect to location (median)

Hypothesis Test Summary

Null Hypothesis	Test	Sig.	Decision
The distribution of construct value BL is the same across categories of choice.	Independent-Samples Kruskal-Wallis Test	.000	Reject the null hypothesis.

Asymptotic significances are displayed. The significance level is .05.

App. Table 79: Hypothesis Test Summary – Independent-Samples Kruskal-Wallis Test for BL

Total N	1,452
Test Statistic	57.807
Degrees of Freedom	2
Asymptotic Sig. (2-sided test)	.000

1. The test statistic is adjusted for ties.

App. Table 80: SPSS output – Independent-Samples Kruskal-Wallis Test for BL

Construct value BL is statistically significantly different between the different levels of choice, $\chi^2(2) = 57.807$, $p = .000$.

Mean and median values

Choice		BL
The Voice of Germany	Mean	6.1817
	N	484
	Standard Deviation	.95142
	Median	6.5096
Germany's Next Topmodel	Mean	5.9392
	N	484
	Standard Deviation	1.19757
	Median	6.3100
Galileo	Mean	5.6545
	N	484
	Standard Deviation	1.24610
	Median	6.0021
Complete Sample	Mean	5.9251
	N	1452
	Standard Deviation	1.15847
	Median	6.2398

App. Table 81: SPSS output – Mean and median values for standardised construct value BL[78]

---

[78] The values indicated as "complete sample" differ from the mean and median values indicated for construct values BL, CBR and SMP in exploratory data analysis because the full complete sample (i.e. 2,357 cases) was

Pairwise comparisons

Pairwise comparisons were performed using Dunn's procedure with a Bonferroni correction (Dunn 1961; 1964) for multiple comparisons.

Sample1-Sample2	Test Statistic	Std. Error	Std. Test Statistic	Sig.	Adj. Sig.
Galileo-Germany's Next Topmodel	123.941	26.871	4.613	.000	.000
Galileo-The Voice of Germany	202.622	26.871	7.541	.000	.000
Germany's Next Topmodel- The Voice of Germany	78.681	26.871	2.928	.003	.010

Each row tests the null hypothesis that the Sample 1 and Sample 2 distributions are the same. Asymptotic significances (2-sided tests) are displayed. The significance level is .05.
App. Table 82: SPSS output – Pairwise Comparison of choice

Construct value BL is statistically significantly different between all groups (p = .000 between the Galileo and GNTM subsamples, p = .000 between the Galileo and the TVoG subsamples, p = .010 between the GNTM and the TVoG subsamples).

Kruskal-Wallis tests for standardised construct value CBR

The null and alternative hypotheses for the Kruskal-Wallis test are:

H_0:   the distribution of construct value CBR is the same across categories of choice

H_A: at least two of the groups differ with respect to location (median)

Hypothesis Test Summary

Null Hypothesis	Test	Sig.	Decision
The distribution of construct value CBR is the same across categories of choice.	Independent-Samples Kruskal-Wallis Test	.000	Reject the null hypothesis.

Asymptotic significances are displayed. The significance level is .05.
App. Table 83: Hypothesis test summary – Independent-Samples Kruskal-Wallis Test for CBR

Total N	1,452
Test Statistic	28.461
Degrees of Freedom	2
Asymptotic Sig. (2-sided test)	.000

1. The test statistic is adjusted for ties.
App. Table 84: SPSS output – Independent-Samples Kruskal-Wallis Test for CBR

Construct value CBR is statistically significantly different between the different levels of choice, $\chi^2(2) = 28.461, p = .000$.

---

used there for computation, while in this case the full sample consists of the three subsamples (i.e. 3*484=1,452).

Mean and median values

Choice		CBR
The Voice of Germany	Mean	4.6786
	N	484
	Standard Deviation	1.26081
	Median	4.7238
Germany's Next Topmodel	Mean	4.2016
	N	484
	Standard Deviation	1.49372
	Median	4.2080
Galileo	Mean	4.3433
	N	484
	Standard Deviation	1.43160
	Median	4.4495
Complete Sample	Mean	4.4079
	N	1452
	Standard Deviation	1.41213
	Median	4.5103

App. Table 85: SPSS output – Mean and median values for construct value CBR

Pairwise comparisons

Pairwise comparisons were performed using Dunn's procedure with a Bonferroni correction (Dunn 1961; 1964) for multiple comparisons.

Sample1-Sample2	Test Statistic	Std. Error	Std. Test Statistic	Sig.	Adj. Sig.
Germany's Next Topmodel- Galileo	-45.899	26.953	-1.703	.089	.266
Germany's Next Topmodel- The Voice of Germany	104.963	26.953	5.230	.000	.000
Galileo-The Voice of Germany	95.064	26.953	3.527	.000	.001

Each row tests the null hypothesis that the Sample 1 and Sample 2 distributions are the same. Asymptotic significances (2-sided tests) are displayed. The significance level is .05.

App. Table 86: SPSS output – Pairwise Comparison of choice

Construct value CBR is statistically significantly different between the GNTM and TVoG subsample ($p = .000$) and between the Galileo and the TVoG subsample ($p = .001$).

Kruskal-Wallis tests for standardised construct value SMP

The null and alternative hypotheses for the Kruskal-Wallis test are:

H_0:   the distribution of construct value SMP is the same across categories of choice

H_A: at least two of the groups differ with respect to location (median)

Hypothesis Test Summary

Null Hypothesis	Test	Sig.	Decision
The distribution of construct value SMP is the same across categories of choice.	Independent-Samples Kruskal-Wallis Test	.057	Retain the null hypothesis.

Asymptotic significances are displayed. The significance level is .05.

App. Table 87: Hypothesis test summary – Independent-Samples Kruskal-Wallis Test for SMP

Kruskal-Wallis test result

Total N	1,452
Test Statistic	5.742
Degrees of Freedom	2
Asymptotic Sig. (2-sided test)	.057

1. The test statistic is adjusted for ties.
2. Multiple comparisons are not performed because the overall test retained the null hypothesis of no differences.

App. Table 88: SPSS output – Independent-Samples Kruskal-Wallis Test for SMP

Construct value SMP is not statistically significantly different between the different levels of Choice, $\chi^2(2) = 5.742, p = .057$.

Mean and median values

Choice		SMP
The Voice of Germany	Mean	5.3481
	N	484
	Standard Deviation	.93979
	Median	5.4062
Germany's Next Topmodel	Mean	5.1134
	N	484
	Standard Deviation	1.20712
	Median	5.2862
Galileo	Mean	5.1528
	N	484
	Standard Deviation	1.22803
	Median	5.3569
Complete Sample	Mean	5.2048
	N	1452
	Standard Deviation	1.13647
	Median	5.3536

App. Table 89: SPSS output – Mean and median values for construct value SMP

Pairwise comparisons

Pairwise comparisons were not performed because there was no statistically significant difference between the different levels of choice.

Appendix F Moderating effects – group comparisons

Summary overview of results of group comparisons

hypo-thesis	path	path coefficient full sample	t-value full sample	Group comparison "choice"	Group comparison "gender"	Group comparison "age"
H1	CBR -> BL	0.2527	9.93	No moderating effect of choice on H1.	No moderating effect of gender on H1.	No moderating effect of age on H1.
H2	SMP -> BL	0.3242	10.30	No moderating effect of choice on H2.	No moderating effect of gender on H2.	No moderating effect of age on H2.
H3	SMP -> CBR	0.0467	1.99	No moderating effect of choice on H3.	H3 only significant for males, not for females.	No moderating effect of age on H3 (not significant for all groups).
H4	SME -> BL	0.0101	0.69	No moderating effect of choice on H4 (not significant for all groups).	No moderating effect of gender on H4 (not significant for all groups).	No moderating effect of age on H4 (not significant for all groups).
H5	SME -> CBR	0.2895	14.78	No moderating effect of choice on H5.	H5 is stronger for females (0.317) than for males (0.2407).	H5 is stronger for Twens (0.3587) than for Teens (0.2479). Adults do not differ significantly from either group.
H6	SMP -> SME	0.4609	17.63	H6 is stronger for GNTM (0.469) than for TVoG (0.3237). Galileo does not differ sig. from either group.	No moderating effect of gender on H6.	H6 is stronger for Teens (0.538) than for Adults (0.337). Twens do not differ sig. from either group.
H7	GOS -> CBR	0.0453	1.88	No moderating effect of choice on H7 (not significant for all groups).	No moderating effect of gender on H7 (not significant for all groups).	H7 is only significant for Adults, but not for both Twens and Teens.
H8	GOS -> SME	0.2360	8.66	H8 is stronger for TVoG (0.3719) than for Galileo (0.2327). GNTM does not differ sig. from either group.	No moderating effect of gender on H8.	H8 is stronger for Adults (0.3243) than for Teens (0.1651). Twens do not differ sig. from either group.

H9	GOS -> SMP	0.672	34.77	No moderating effect of choice on H9.	No moderating effect of gender on H9.	No moderating effect of age on H9.
H10	GO -> BL	0.1900	5.82	H10 is stronger for Galileo (0.295) than for GNTM (0.1305). H10 is not significant for TVoG.	No moderating effect of gender on H10.	H10 is stronger for Twens (0.3073) than for Teens (0.1289). Adults do not differ sig. from either group.
H11	GO -> CBR	0.3256	12.21	H11 is stronger for TVoG than for GNTM or Galileo. No sig. difference between GNTM and Galileo.	No moderating effect of gender on H11.	No moderating effect of age on H11.
H12	PCR -> CBR	0.0644	3.75	H12 only sig. for TVoG and Galileo, not for GNTM. No sig. difference between TVoG and Galileo.	H12 only significant for males, not for females.	H12 only sig. for Adults and Teens, not for Twens. No sig. difference between Adults and Teens.
H13	PCR -> GO	0.1389	6.51	H13 only sig. for GNTM and Galileo, not for TVoG. No sig. difference between GNTM and Galileo.	No moderating effect of gender on H13.	No moderating effect of age on H13.
H14	PWR -> CBR	0.1528	6.62	H14 only sig. for GNTM and Galileo, not for TVoG. No sig. difference between GNTM and Galileo.	No moderating effect of gender on H14.	No moderating effect of age on H14.
H15	PWR -> GO	0.4498	20.36	H15 is stronger for Galileo (0.5448) than for TVoG (0.3525). GNTM does not differ sig. from either group.	No moderating effect of gender on H15.	No moderating effect of age on H15.

App. Table 90: Group comparisons – overview

Choice as moderator

Group comparison TVoG – GNTM

Hypothesis	H1	H10	H11	H7	H8	H9	H12	H13	H14	H15	H4	H5	H2	H3	H6
Relationship	CBR -> BL	GO -> BL	GO -> CBR	GOS -> CBR	GOS -> SME	GOS -> SMP	PCR -> CBR	PCR -> GO	PWR -> CBR	PWR -> GO	SME -> BL	SME -> CBR	SMP -> BL	SMP -> CBR	SMP -> SME
Sig. TVoG	yes		yes		yes	yes	yes			yes		yes	yes	yes	yes
Sig. GNTM	yes	yes	yes		yes	yes		yes	yes	yes		yes	yes	yes	yes
Sample size TVoG	484	484	484	484	484	484	484	484	484	484	484	484	484	484	484
Sample size GNTM	484	484	484	484	484	484	484	484	484	484	484	484	484	484	484
Standard Error (STERR) TVoG	0.06	0.07	0.05	0.04	0.06	0.04	0.04	0.05	0.03	0.05	0.04	0.05	0.09	0.04	0.06
Standard Error (STERR) GNTM	0.06	0.07	0.06	0.05	0.06	0.03	0.03	0.05	0.04	0.05	0.04	0.05	0.06	0.04	0.06
Path coefficient TVoG	0.24	0.11	0.43	-0.05	0.37	0.61	0.06	0.062	0.04	0.35	-0.03	0.30	0.24	0.07	0.32
Path coefficient GNTM	0.36	0.13	0.29	0.08	0.32	0.68	-0.05	0.12	0.21	0.45	-0.03	0.33	0.31	0.07	0.47
S	1.33		1.23		1.27	0.81				1.11		1.01	1.58	0.89	1.31
t-value	-1.32		1.74		0.63	-1.35				-1.39		-0.36	-0.68	0.08	-1.73
Sig. different?	no		yes		no	no				no		no	no	no	yes

App. Table 91: Group comparisons – choice as moderating variable: TVoG vs. GNTM

Group comparison TVoG – Galileo

Hypothesis	H1	H10	H11	H7	H8	H9	H12	H13	H14	H15	H4	H5	H2	H3	H6
Relationship	CBR -> BL	GO -> BL	GO -> CBR	GOS -> CBR	GOS -> SME	GOS -> SMP	PCR -> CBR	PCR -> GO	PWR -> CBR	PWR -> GO	SME -> BL	SME -> CBR	SMP -> BL	SMP -> CBR	SMP -> SME
Sig. TVoG	yes		yes		yes	yes	yes			yes		yes	yes	yes	yes
Sig. Galileo	yes	yes	yes		yes	yes	yes	yes	yes	yes		yes	yes	yes	yes
Sample size TVoG	484	484	484	484	484	484	484	484	484	484	484	484	484	484	484
Sample size Galileo	484	484	484	484	484	484	484	484	484	484	484	484	484	484	484
Standard Error (STERR) TVoG	0.06	0.07	0.05	0.04	0.06	0.04	0.04	0.05	0.03	0.05	0.04	0.05	0.09	0.04	0.06
Standard Error (STERR) Galileo	0.05	0.06	0.06	0.04	0.06	0.04	0.04	0.05	0.06	0.05	0.02	0.04	0.06	0.06	0.06
Path coefficient TVoG	0.24	0.11	0.43	-0.05	0.37	0.61	0.06	0.06	0.04	0.35	-0.03	0.30	0.24	0.07	0.32
Path coefficient Galileo	0.26	0.30	0.22	0.02	0.23	0.70	0.08	0.11	0.23	0.54	0.00	0.22	0.28	0.16	0.46
S	1.23		1.23		1.26	0.90	0.80			1.03		0.98	1.64	1.11	1.29
t-value	-0.19		2.69		1.71	-1.53	-0.35			-2.90		1.29	-0.30	-1.22	-1.64
Sig. different?	no		yes		yes	no	no			yes		no	no	no	no

App. Table 92: Group comparisons – choice as moderating variable: TVoG vs. Galileo

Group comparison Galileo – GNTM

Hypothesis	H1	H10	H11	H7	H8	H9	H12	H13	H14	H15	H4	H5	H2	H3	H6
Relationship	CBR -> BL	GO -> BL	GO -> CBR	GOS -> CBR	GOS -> SME	GOS -> SMP	PCR -> CBR	PCR -> GO	PWR -> CBR	PWR -> GO	SME -> BL	SME -> CBR	SMP -> BL	SMP -> CBR	SMP -> SME
Sig. Galileo	yes	yes	yes		yes	yes	yes	yes	yes	yes		yes	yes	yes	yes
Sig. GNTM	yes	yes	yes		yes	yes		yes	yes	yes		yes	yes	yes	yes
Sample size Galileo	484	484	484	484	484	484	484	484	484	484	484	484	484	484	484
Sample size GNTM	484	484	484	484	484	484	484	484	484	484	484	484	484	484	484
Standard Error (STERR) Galileo	0.05	0.06	0.06	0.04	0.06	0.04	0.04	0.05	0.06	0.05	0.02	0.04	0.06	0.06	0.06
Standard Error (STERR) GNTM	0.06	0.07	0.06	0.05	0.06	0.03	0.03	0.05	0.04	0.05	0.04	0.05	0.06	0.04	0.06
Path coefficient Galileo	0.26	0.30	0.22	0.02	0.23	0.70	0.08	0.11	0.23	0.54	0.00	0.22	0.28	0.16	0.46
Path coefficient GNTM	0.36	0.13	0.29	0.08	0.32	0.68	-0.05	0.12	0.21	0.45	-0.03	0.33	0.31	0.07	0.47
S	1.28	1.49	1.32		1.32	0.82		1.07	1.14	1.09		0.99	1.29	1.10	1.25
t-value	-1.19	1.71	-0.88		-1.03	0.33		-0.12	0.20	1.33		-1.65	-0.44	1.30	-0.12
Sig. different?	no	yes	no		no	no		no	no	no		no	no	no	no

App. Table 93: Group comparisons – choice as moderating variable: Galileo vs. GNTM

Gender as moderator

Hypothesis	H1	H10	H11	H7	H8	H9	H12	H13	H14	H15	H4	H5	H2	H3	H6
Relationship	CBR -> BL	GO -> BL	GO -> CBR	GOS -> CBR	GOS -> SME	GOS -> SMP	PCR -> CBR	PCR -> GO	PWR -> CBR	PWR -> GO	SME -> BL	SME -> CBR	SMP -> BL	SMP -> CBR	SMP -> SME
Sig. M	yes	yes	yes		yes	yes	yes	yes	yes	yes		yes	yes	yes	yes
Sig. F	yes	yes	yes		yes	yes		yes	yes	yes		yes	yes		yes
Sample size M	899	899	899	899	899	899	899	899	899	899	899	899	899	899	899
Sample size F	899	899	899	899	899	899	899	899	899	899	899	899	899	899	899
Standard Error (STERR) M	0.04	0.05	0.04	0.04	0.04	0.03	0.03	0.03	0.04	0.03	0.02	0.03	0.05	0.05	0.04
Standard Error (STERR) F	0.04	0.05	0.04	0.04	0.05	0.03	0.02	0.04	0.03	0.04	0.03	0.03	0.04	0.02	0.05
Path coefficient M	0.26	0.19	0.26	0.06	0.20	0.70	0.10	0.16	0.18	0.47	0.02	0.24	0.34	0.10	0.49
Path coefficient F	0.34	0.20	0.36	0.06	0.28	0.67	0.01	0.14	0.15	0.43	-0.04	0.32	0.23	0.02	0.44
S	1.22	1.48	1.28		1.43	0.94		1.02	1.12	1.09		0.9	1.46		1.38
t-value	-1.35	-0.09	-1.53		-1.19	0.75		0.26	0.50	0.66		-1.71	1.59		0.75
Sig. different?	no	no	no		no	no		no	no	no		yes	no		no

App. Table 94: Group comparisons – gender as moderating variable

Age as moderator

Group comparison Adults – Teens

Hypothesis	H1	H10	H11	H7	H8	H9	H12	H13	H14	H15	H4	H5	H2	H3	H6
Relationship	CBR -> BL	GO -> BL	GO -> CBR	GOS -> CBR	GOS -> SME	GOS -> SMP	PCR -> CBR	PCR -> GO	PWR -> CBR	PWR -> GO	SME -> BL	SME -> CBR	SMP -> BL	SMP -> CBR	SMP -> SME
Sig. Adults	yes	yes	yes	yes	yes	yes	yes	yes	yes	yes		yes	yes		yes
Sig. Teens	yes	yes	yes		yes	yes	yes	yes	yes	yes		yes	yes		yes
Sample size Adults	490	490	490	490	490	490	490	490	490	490	490	490	490	490	490
Sample size Teens	490	490	490	490	490	490	490	490	490	490	490	490	490	490	490
Standard Error (STERR) Adults	0.05	0.07	0.06	0.05	0.07	0.04	0.04	0.05	0.06	0.05	0.04	0.04	0.07	0.03	0.07
Standard Error (STERR) Teens	0.06	0.07	0.07	0.05	0.06	0.04	0.04	0.04	0.05	0.05	0.03	0.04	0.06	0.04	0.05
Path coefficient Adults	0.21	0.27	0.25	0.10	0.32	0.68	0.09	0.14	0.18	0.43	-0.04	0.33	0.30	-0.02	0.34
Path coefficient Teens	0.32	0.13	0.32	0.07	0.17	0.68	0.09	0.11	0.15	0.50	0.01	0.25	0.35	0.05	0.54
S	1.19	1.53	1.35		1.43	0.94	0.85	1.03	1.24	1.09		0.96	1.46		1.42
t-value	-1.46	1.48	-0.76		1.74	-0.04	-0.09	0.50	0.41	-1.04		1.33	-0.58		-2.21
Sig. different?	no	no	no		yes	no	no	no	no	no		no	no		yes

App. Table 95: Group comparisons – age as moderating variable: Adults vs. Teens

Group comparison Adults – Twens

Hypothesis	H1	H10	H11	H7	H8	H9	H12	H13	H14	H15	H4	H5	H2	H3	H6
Relationship	CBR -> BL	GO -> BL	GO -> CBR	GOS -> CBR	GOS -> SME	GOS -> SMP	PCR -> CBR	PCR -> GO	PWR -> CBR	PWR -> GO	SME -> BL	SME -> CBR	SMP -> BL	SMP -> CBR	SMP -> SME
Sig. Adults	yes	yes	yes	yes	yes	yes	yes	yes	yes	yes		yes	yes		yes
Sig. Twens	yes	yes	yes		yes	yes	yes	yes	yes		yes	yes	yes	yes	yes
Sample size Adults	490	490	490	490	490	490	490	490	490	490	490	490	490	490	490
Sample size Twens	490	490	490	490	490	490	490	490	490	490	490	490	490	490	490
Standard Error (STERR) Adults	0.05	0.07	0.06	0.05	0.07	0.04	0.04	0.05	0.06	0.05	0.04	0.04	0.07	0.03	0.07
Standard Error (STERR) Twens	0.06	0.05	0.05	0.03	0.06	0.04	0.02	0.05	0.04	0.05	0.03	0.04	0.05	0.04	0.06
Path coefficient Adults	0.21	0.27	0.25	0.10	0.32	0.68	0.09	0.14	0.18	0.43	-0.04	0.33	0.30	-0.02	0.34
Path coefficient Twens	0.28	0.31	0.36	-0.01	0.20	0.71	0.02	0.08	0.15	0.47	-0.03	0.36	0.23	0.04	0.48
S	1.20	1.35	1.16		1.45	0.85	1.06	1.12	1.11			0.89	1.31		1.44
t-value	-0.98	-0.39	-1.47		1.31	-0.61	0.93	0.40	-0.59			-0.51	0.79		-1.58
Sig. different?	no	no	no		no	no	no	no	no			no	no		no

App. Table 96: Group comparisons – age as moderating variable: Adults vs. Twens

Group comparison Teens – Twens

Hypothesis	H1	H10	H11	H7	H8	H9	H12	H13	H14	H15	H4	H5	H2	H3	H6
Relationship	CBR -> BL	GO -> BL	GO -> CBR	GOS -> CBR	GOS -> SME	GOS -> SMP	PCR -> CBR	PCR -> GO	PWR -> CBR	PWR -> GO	SME -> BL	SME -> CBR	SMP -> BL	SMP -> CBR	SMP -> SME
Sig. Teens	yes	yes	yes		yes	yes	yes	yes	yes	yes		yes	yes		yes
Sig. Twens	yes	yes	yes		yes	yes		yes	yes	yes		yes	yes		yes
Sample size Teens	490	490	490	490	490	490	490	490	490	490	490	490	490	490	490
Sample size Twens	490	490	490	490	490	490	490	490	490	490	490	490	490	490	490
Standard Error (STERR) Teens	0.06	0.07	0.07	0.05	0.06	0.04	0.04	0.04	0.05	0.05	0.03	0.04	0.06	0.04	0.05
Standard Error (STERR) Twens	0.06	0.05	0.05	0.03	0.06	0.04	0.02	0.05	0.04	0.05	0.03	0.04	0.05	0.04	0.06
Path coefficient Teens	0.32	0.13	0.32	0.07	0.17	0.68	0.10	0.11	0.15	0.50	0.01	0.25	0.35	0.05	0.54
Path coefficient Twens	0.28	0.31	0.36	-0.01	0.20	0.71	0.02	0.08	0.15	0.47	-0.03	0.36	0.23	0.04	0.48
S	1.26	1.41	1.30		1.31	0.87		1.00	1.07	1.067		0.92	1.26		1.21
t-value	0.45	-1.98	-0.53		-0.45	-0.55		0.48	-0.05	0.45		-1.89	1.48		0.71
Sig. different?	no	yes	no		no	no		no	no	no		yes	no		no

App. Table 97: Group comparisons – age as moderating variable: Teens vs. Twens

Appendix G   Moderating effects – interactions

Interactions between GO and GOS groups

GO1/GOS1

path	loading	sample mean	standard deviation	standard error	t-value
CBR_1 <- CBR	0.7851	0.7855	0.0092	0.0092	85.0371
CBR_2 <- CBR	0.8234	0.8235	0.0074	0.0074	111.863
CBR_3 <- CBR	0.7823	0.7824	0.0104	0.0104	75.4366
CBR_4 <- CBR	0.7805	0.7804	0.0094	0.0094	83.0286
CBR_5 <- CBR	0.6202	0.62	0.0174	0.0174	35.6176
CBR_6 <- CBR	0.8711	0.8711	0.006	0.006	145.3249
GOS_1_r <- GOS_1	1	1	0	0	0
GOS_1_r*GO_1_r <- GOS_1*GO_1	1	1	0	0	0
GO_1_r <- GO_1	1	1	0	0	0

App. Table 98: Interactions between GO and GOS groups - GO1/GOS1 - outer loadings

path	path coefficient	sample mean	standard deviation	standard error	t-value
GOS_1*GO_1 -> CBR	0.0413	0.0426	0.0213	0.0213	1.9383
GOS_1 -> CBR	0.2567	0.2577	0.0271	0.0271	9.4614
GO_1 -> CBR	0.3826	0.383	0.0236	0.0236	16.1795

App. Table 99: Interactions between GO and GOS groups - GO1/GOS1 - path coefficients

	AVE	Composite Reliability	R Square	Cronbach's Alpha	Communality	Redundancy
CBR	0.6098	0.9028	0.3069	0.8706	0.6098	-0.0114
GOS_1*GO_1	1	1	0	1	1	0
GOS_1	1	1	0	1	1	0
GO_1	1	1	0	1	1	0

App. Table 100: Interactions between GO and GOS groups - GO1/GOS1 - PLS-Quality criteria interaction model

	AVE	Composite Reliability	R Square	Cronbach's Alpha	Communality	Redundancy
CBR	0.6098	0.9028	0.3056	0.8706	0.6098	0.1005
GOS_1	1	1	0	1	1	0
GO_1	1	1	0	1	1	0

App. Table 101: Interactions between GO and GOS groups - GO1/GOS1 - PLS-Quality criteria main effects model

GO2/GOS2

path	loading	sample mean	standard deviation	standard error	t-value
CBR_1 <- CBR	0.7513	0.7516	0.0118	0.0118	63.5613
CBR_2 <- CBR	0.8358	0.836	0.0066	0.0066	125.7184
CBR_3 <- CBR	0.7961	0.796	0.0094	0.0094	84.827
CBR_4 <- CBR	0.7611	0.761	0.0104	0.0104	73.0541
CBR_5 <- CBR	0.6534	0.6534	0.0161	0.0161	40.5775
CBR_6 <- CBR	0.8697	0.8696	0.006	0.006	145.1983
GOS_2_r <- GOS_2	1	1	0	0	0
GOS_2_r*GO_2_r <- GOS_2*GO_2	1	1	0	0	0
GO_2_r <- GO_2	1	1	0	0	0

App. Table 102: Interactions between GO and GOS groups - GO2/GOS2 - outer loadings

path	path coefficient	sample mean	standard deviation	standard error	t-value
GOS_2*GO_2 -> CBR	0.0404	0.0419	0.0232	0.0232	1.7411
GOS_2 -> CBR	0.2489	0.249	0.0261	0.0261	9.5487
GO_2 -> CBR	0.3332	0.3343	0.0285	0.0285	11.6964

App. Table 103: Interactions between GO and GOS groups - GO2/GOS2 - path coefficients

	AVE	Composite Reliability	R Square	Cronbach's Alpha	Communality	Redundancy
CBR	0.6099	0.903	0.2429	0.8706	0.6099	-0.0112
GOS_2*GO_2	1	1	0	1	1	0
GOS_2	1	1	0	1	1	0
GO_2	1	1	0	1	1	0

App. Table 104: Interactions between GO and GOS groups - GO2/GOS2 - PLS-Quality criteria interaction model

	AVE	Composite Reliability	R Square	Cronbach's Alpha	Communality	Redundancy
CBR	0.6099	0.903	0.2417	0.8706	0.6099	0.086
GOS_2	1	1	0	1	1	0
GO_2	1	1	0	1	1	0

App. Table 105: Interactions between GO and GOS groups - GO2/GOS2 - PLS-Quality criteria main effects model

GO3/GOS3

path	loading	sample mean	standard deviation	standard error	t-value
CBR_1 <- CBR	0.8075	0.8073	0.0078	0.0078	102.9317
CBR_2 <- CBR	0.8027	0.8028	0.0089	0.0089	89.7763
CBR_3 <- CBR	0.7778	0.7776	0.0104	0.0104	74.5375
CBR_4 <- CBR	0.791	0.791	0.0091	0.0091	87.0224
CBR_5 <- CBR	0.606	0.6055	0.018	0.018	33.6525
CBR_6 <- CBR	0.8685	0.8683	0.006	0.006	144.5137
GOS_3_r <- GOS_3	1	1	0	0	0
GOS_3_r*GO_3_r <- GOS_3*GO_3	1	1	0	0	0
GO_3_r <- GO_3	1	1	0	0	0

App. Table 106: Interactions between GO and GOS groups - GO3/GOS3 - outer loadings

path	path coefficient	sample mean	standard deviation	standard error	t-value
GOS_3*GO_3 -> CBR	0.0499	0.0496	0.0209	0.0209	2.3817
GOS_3 -> CBR	0.1875	0.1881	0.0285	0.0285	6.5894
GO_3 -> CBR	0.3812	0.3811	0.0279	0.0279	13.6863

App. Table 107: Interactions between GO and GOS groups - GO3/GOS3 - path coefficients

	AVE	Composite Reliability	R Square	Cronbach's Alpha	Communality	Redundancy
CBR	0.6081	0.902	0.2656	0.8706	0.6081	-0.0079
GOS_3*GO_3	1	1	0	1	1	0
GOS_3	1	1	0	1	1	0
GO_3	1	1	0	1	1	0

App. Table 108: Interactions between GO and GOS groups - GO3/GOS3 - PLS-Quality criteria interaction model

	AVE	Composite Reliability	R Square	Cronbach's Alpha	Communality	Redundancy
CBR	0.6079	0.902	0.2638	0.8706	0.6079	0.0773
GOS_3	1	1	0	1	1	0
GO_3	1	1	0	1	1	0

App. Table 109: Interactions between GO and GOS groups - GO3/GOS3 - PLS-Quality criteria main effects model

GO4/GOS4

path	loading	sample mean	standard deviation	standard error	t-value
CBR_1 <- CBR	0.7828	0.7825	0.0099	0.0099	79.2273
CBR_2 <- CBR	0.8096	0.8094	0.0083	0.0083	97.6057
CBR_3 <- CBR	0.7997	0.7995	0.0089	0.0089	89.5273
CBR_4 <- CBR	0.7886	0.7885	0.0093	0.0093	85.0028
CBR_5 <- CBR	0.6229	0.6232	0.0175	0.0175	35.6812
CBR_6 <- CBR	0.8629	0.8628	0.0067	0.0067	129.0933
GOS_4_r <- GOS_4	1	1	0	0	0
GOS_4_r*GO_4_r <- GOS_4*GO_4	1	1	0	0	0
GO_4_r <- GO_4	1	1	0	0	0

App. Table 110: Interactions between GO and GOS groups - GO4/GOS4 - outer loadings

path	path coefficient	sample mean	standard deviation	standard error	t-value
GOS_4*GO_4 -> CBR	0.0585	0.0585	0.0217	0.0217	2.6976
GOS_4 -> CBR	0.2298	0.2303	0.0268	0.0268	8.5727
GO_4 -> CBR	0.2843	0.2845	0.027	0.027	10.5449

App. Table 111: Interactions between GO and GOS groups - GO4/GOS4 - path coefficients

	AVE	Composite Reliability	R Square	Cronbach's Alpha	Communality	Redundancy
CBR	0.6104	0.9031	0.208	0.8706	0.6104	-0.0048
GOS_4*GO_4	1	1	0	1	1	0
GOS_4	1	1	0	1	1	0
GO_4	1	1	0	1	1	0

App. Table 112: Interactions between GO and GOS groups - GO4/GOS4 - PLS-Quality criteria interaction model

	AVE	Composite Reliability	R Square	Cronbach's Alpha	Communality	Redundancy
CBR	0.6103	0.903	0.2049	0.8706	0.6103	0.0805
GOS_4	1	1	0	1	1	0
GO_4	1	1	0	1	1	0

App. Table 113: Interactions between GO and GOS groups - GO4/GOS4 - PLS-Quality criteria main effects model

GO5/GOS5

path	loading	sample mean	standard deviation	standard error	t-value
CBR_1 <- CBR	0.759	0.759	0.0112	0.0112	67.6229
CBR_2 <- CBR	0.8305	0.8304	0.0068	0.0068	122.0145
CBR_3 <- CBR	0.8008	0.8006	0.009	0.009	89.0195
CBR_4 <- CBR	0.765	0.7649	0.0106	0.0106	72.2369
CBR_5 <- CBR	0.6426	0.6428	0.0166	0.0166	38.6598
CBR_6 <- CBR	0.8703	0.8702	0.0061	0.0061	143.1597
GOS_5_r <- GOS_5	1	1	0	0	0
GOS_5_r*GO_5_r <- GOS_5*GO_5	1	1	0	0	0
GO_5_r <- GO_5	1	1	0	0	0

App. Table 114: Interactions between GO and GOS groups - GO5/GOS5 - outer loadings

path	path coefficient	sample mean	standard deviation	standard error	t-value
GOS_5*GO_5 -> CBR	0.0446	0.0461	0.0232	0.0232	1.9221
GOS_5 -> CBR	0.2798	0.2801	0.0252	0.0252	11.1232
GO_5 -> CBR	0.3482	0.3489	0.0267	0.0267	13.0451

App. Table 115: Interactions between GO and GOS groups - GO5/GOS5 - path coefficients

	AVE	Composite Reliability	R Square	Cronbach's Alpha	Communality	Redundancy
CBR	0.6104	0.9031	0.2803	0.8706	0.6104	-0.0121
GOS_5*GO_5	1	1	0	1	1	0
GOS_5	1	1	0	1	1	0
GO_5	1	1	0	1	1	0

App. Table 116: Interactions between GO and GOS groups - GO5/GOS5 - PLS-Quality criteria interaction model

	AVE	Composite Reliability	R Square	Cronbach's Alpha	Communality	Redundancy
CBR	0.6104	0.9031	0.2788	0.8706	0.6104	0.1034
GOS_5	1	1	0	1	1	0
GO_5	1	1	0	1	1	0

App. Table 117: Interactions between GO and GOS groups - GO5/GOS5 - PLS-Quality criteria main effects model

GO6/GOS6

path	loading	sample mean	standard deviation	standard error	t-value
CBR_1 <- CBR	0.7915	0.7912	0.0092	0.0092	86.31
CBR_2 <- CBR	0.8025	0.8026	0.0086	0.0086	92.8986
CBR_3 <- CBR	0.7939	0.7937	0.009	0.009	88.1649
CBR_4 <- CBR	0.7932	0.793	0.0086	0.0086	92.0906
CBR_5 <- CBR	0.6184	0.6183	0.0172	0.0172	36.0535
CBR_6 <- CBR	0.8639	0.8639	0.0062	0.0062	139.7975
GOS_6_r <- GOS_6	1	1	0	0	0
GOS_6_r*GO_6_r <- GOS_6*GO_6	1	1	0	0	0
GO_6_r <- GO_6	1	1	0	0	0

App. Table 118: Interactions between GO and GOS groups - GO6/GOS6 - outer loadings

path	path coefficient	sample mean	standard deviation	standard error	t-value
GOS_6*GO_6 -> CBR	0.0609	0.0606	0.0193	0.0193	3.1571
GOS_6 -> CBR	0.2022	0.2023	0.0255	0.0255	7.9315
GO_6 -> CBR	0.4194	0.4192	0.0245	0.0245	17.0894

App. Table 119: Interactions between GO and GOS groups - GO6/GOS6 - path coefficients

	AVE	Composite Reliability	R Square	Cronbach's Alpha	Communality	Redundancy
CBR	0.6098	0.9028	0.3197	0.8706	0.6098	-0.0002
GOS_6*GO_6	1	1	0	1	1	0
GOS_6	1	1	0	1	1	0
GO_6	1	1	0	1	1	0

App. Table 120: Interactions between GO and GOS groups - GO6/GOS6 - PLS-Quality criteria interaction model

	AVE	Composite Reliability	R Square	Cronbach's Alpha	Communality	Redundancy
CBR	0.6098	0.9028	0.316	0.8706	0.6098	0.0859
GOS_6	1	1	0	1	1	0
GO_6	1	1	0	1	1	0

App. Table 121: Interactions between GO and GOS groups - GO6/GOS6 - PLS-Quality criteria main effects model

Interactions within GO and GOS groups

GO1/GO2

path	loading	sample mean	standard deviation	standard error	t-value
CBR_1 <- CBR	0.7738	0.7737	0.0101	0.0101	76.4633
CBR_2 <- CBR	0.8298	0.8296	0.0069	0.0069	121.1114
CBR_3 <- CBR	0.785	0.7851	0.0103	0.0103	76.0717
CBR_4 <- CBR	0.7723	0.7722	0.0099	0.0099	77.7997
CBR_5 <- CBR	0.6351	0.6348	0.0169	0.0169	37.5532
CBR_6 <- CBR	0.8709	0.8708	0.0059	0.0059	148.5359
GO_1_r <- GO_1	1	1	0	0	0
GO_1_r*GO_2_r <- GO_1*GO_2	1	1	0	0	0
GO_2_r <- GO_2	1	1	0	0	0

App. Table 122: Interactions within GO group - GO1/GO2 - outer loadings

path	path coefficient	sample mean	standard deviation	standard error	t-value
GO_1*GO_2 -> CBR	0.0851	0.0851	0.0259	0.0259	3.2796
GO_1 -> CBR	0.3911	0.3914	0.0195	0.0195	20.0052
GO_2 -> CBR	0.2914	0.2916	0.0247	0.0247	11.8226

App. Table 123: Interactions within GO group - GO1/GO2 - path coefficients

	AVE	Composite Reliability	R Square	Cronbach's Alpha	Communality	Redundancy
CBR	0.6103	0.903	0.3135	0.8706	0.6103	-0.0234
GO_1*GO_2	1	1	0	1	1	0
GO_1	1	1	0	1	1	0
GO_2	1	1	0	1	1	0

App. Table 124: Interactions within GO group - GO1/GO2 - PLS-Quality criteria interaction model

	AVE	Composite Reliability	R Square	Cronbach's Alpha	Communality	Redundancy
CBR	0.6102	0.903	0.3085	0.8706	0.6102	0.1485
GO_1	1	1	0	1	1	0
GO_2	1	1	0	1	1	0

App. Table 125: Interactions within GO group - GO1/GO2 - PLS-Quality criteria main effects model

GO1/GO3

path	loading	sample mean	standard deviation	standard error	t-value
CBR_1 <- CBR	0.7965	0.7961	0.0086	0.0086	92.9181
CBR_2 <- CBR	0.8152	0.8149	0.0082	0.0082	99.8541
CBR_3 <- CBR	0.7773	0.7771	0.0105	0.0105	74.0175
CBR_4 <- CBR	0.7851	0.7848	0.0094	0.0094	83.5957
CBR_5 <- CBR	0.6155	0.615	0.0176	0.0176	34.9198
CBR_6 <- CBR	0.8698	0.8698	0.006	0.006	145.1831
GO_1_r <- GO_1	1	1	0	0	0
GO_1_r*GO_3_r <- GO_1*GO_3	1	1	0	0	0
GO_3_r <- GO_3	1	1	0	0	0

App. Table 126: Interactions within GO group - GO1/GO3 - outer loadings

path	path coefficient	sample mean	standard deviation	standard error	t-value
GO_1*GO_3 -> CBR	0.0622	0.0622	0.021	0.021	2.9666
GO_1 -> CBR	0.3712	0.3719	0.0275	0.0275	13.5034
GO_3 -> CBR	0.2463	0.246	0.0263	0.0263	9.3825

App. Table 127: Interactions within GO group - GO1/GO3 - path coefficients

	AVE	Composite Reliability	R Square	Cronbach's Alpha	Communality	Redundancy
CBR	0.6092	0.9025	0.3007	0.8706	0.6092	-0.0165
GO_1*GO_3	1	1	0	1	1	0
GO_1	1	1	0	1	1	0
GO_3	1	1	0	1	1	0

App. Table 128: Interactions within GO group - GO1/GO3 - PLS-Quality criteria interaction model

	AVE	Composite Reliability	R Square	Cronbach's Alpha	Communality	Redundancy
CBR	0.6091	0.9025	0.2981	0.8706	0.6091	0.1396
GO_1	1	1	0	1	1	0
GO_3	1	1	0	1	1	0

App. Table 129: Interactions within GO group - GO1/GO3 - PLS-Quality criteria main effects model

GO2/GO5

path	loading	sample mean	standard deviation	standard error	t-value
CBR_1 <- CBR	0.747	0.7465	0.0123	0.0123	60.8853
CBR_2 <- CBR	0.839	0.8389	0.0064	0.0064	130.3816
CBR_3 <- CBR	0.7992	0.7991	0.0092	0.0092	86.5356
CBR_4 <- CBR	0.7541	0.7539	0.0113	0.0113	66.7912
CBR_5 <- CBR	0.6544	0.6541	0.0161	0.0161	40.6385
CBR_6 <- CBR	0.8709	0.8709	0.006	0.006	144.6523
GO_2_r <- GO_2	1	1	0	0	0
GO_2_r*GO_5_r <- GO_2*GO_5	1	1	0	0	0
GO_5_r <- GO_5	1	1	0	0	0

App. Table 130: Interactions within GO group - GO2/GO5 - outer loadings

path	path coefficient	sample mean	standard deviation	standard error	t-value
GO_2*GO_5 -> CBR	0.082	0.0834	0.028	0.028	2.9314
GO_2 -> CBR	0.2602	0.2613	0.0333	0.0333	7.8161
GO_5 -> CBR	0.3284	0.3286	0.031	0.031	10.6091

App. Table 131: Interactions within GO group - GO2/GO5 - path coefficients

	AVE	Composite Reliability	R Square	Cronbach's Alpha	Communality	Redundancy
CBR	0.6094	0.9028	0.2531	0.8706	0.6094	-0.0276
GO_2*GO_5	1	1	0	1	1	0
GO_2	1	1	0	1	1	0
GO_5	1	1	0	1	1	0

App. Table 132: Interactions within GO group - GO2/GO5 - PLS-Quality criteria interaction model

	AVE	Composite Reliability	R Square	Cronbach's Alpha	Communality	Redundancy
CBR	0.6094	0.9028	0.2488	0.8706	0.6094	0.0878
GO_2	1	1	0	1	1	0
GO_5	1	1	0	1	1	0

App. Table 133: Interactions within GO group - GO2/GO5 - PLS-Quality criteria main effects model

GOS1/GOS2

path	loading	sample mean	standard deviation	standard error	t-value
CBR_1 <- CBR	0.7762	0.776	0.0101	0.0101	76.6976
CBR_2 <- CBR	0.824	0.8238	0.0074	0.0074	111.5421
CBR_3 <- CBR	0.7903	0.79	0.0098	0.0098	80.474
CBR_4 <- CBR	0.7773	0.7769	0.0098	0.0098	79.3899
CBR_5 <- CBR	0.63	0.6299	0.0168	0.0168	37.4699
CBR_6 <- CBR	0.8697	0.8695	0.0061	0.0061	143.2189
GOS_1_r <- GOS_1	1	1	0	0	0
GOS_2_r <- GOS_2	1	1	0	0	0
GOS_2_r*GOS_1_r <- GOS_2*GOS_1	1	1	0	0	0

App. Table 134: Interactions within GOS group - GOS1/GOS2 - outer loadings

path	path coefficient	sample mean	standard deviation	standard error	t-value
GOS_1 -> CBR	0.3771	0.3771	0.026	0.026	14.5222
GOS_2*GOS_1 -> CBR	0.1781	0.1786	0.0298	0.0298	5.9734
GOS_2 -> CBR	0.2407	0.2409	0.0264	0.0264	9.1237

App. Table 135: Interactions within GOS group - GOS1/GOS2 - path coefficients

	AVE	Composite Reliability	R Square	Cronbach's Alpha	Communality	Redundancy
CBR	0.6106	0.9031	0.2508	0.8706	0.6106	0.1237
GOS_1	1	1	0	1	1	0
GOS_2*GOS_1	1	1	0	1	1	0
GOS_2	1	1	0	1	1	0

App. Table 136: Interactions within GOS group - GOS1/GOS2 - PLS-Quality criteria interaction model

	AVE	Composite Reliability	R Square	Cronbach's Alpha	Communality	Redundancy
CBR	0.6105	0.9031	0.2284	0.8706	0.6105	0.1188
GOS_1	1	1	0	1	1	0
GOS_2	1	1	0	1	1	0

App. Table 137: Interactions within GOS group - GOS1/GOS2 - PLS-Quality criteria main effects model

GOS1/GOS5

path	loading	sample mean	standard deviation	standard error	t-value
CBR_1 <- CBR	0.777	0.7768	0.0101	0.0101	76.8372
CBR_2 <- CBR	0.8209	0.821	0.0076	0.0076	108.1727
CBR_3 <- CBR	0.7935	0.7933	0.0095	0.0095	83.1926
CBR_4 <- CBR	0.7779	0.7778	0.0098	0.0098	78.9868
CBR_5 <- CBR	0.6292	0.6293	0.0167	0.0167	37.7398
CBR_6 <- CBR	0.8694	0.8692	0.0062	0.0062	141.2459
GOS_1_r <- GOS_1	1	1	0	0	0
GOS_1_r*GOS_5_r <- GOS_1*GOS_5	1	1	0	0	0
GOS_5_r <- GOS_5	1	1	0	0	0

App. Table 138: Interactions within GOS group - GOS1/GOS5 - outer loadings

path	path coefficient	sample mean	standard deviation	standard error	t-value
GOS_1*GOS_5 -> CBR	0.1572	0.157	0.0281	0.0281	5.602
GOS_1 -> CBR	0.3544	0.3542	0.0242	0.0242	14.6596
GOS_5 -> CBR	0.2785	0.2789	0.0247	0.0247	11.2729

App. Table 139: Interactions within GOS group - GOS1/GOS5 - path coefficients

	AVE	Composite Reliability	R Square	Cronbach's Alpha	Communality	Redundancy
CBR	0.6107	0.9032	0.2679	0.8706	0.6107	-0.0382
GOS_1*GOS_5	1	1	0	1	1	0
GOS_1	1	1	0	1	1	0
GOS_5	1	1	0	1	1	0

App. Table 140: Interactions within GOS group - GOS1/GOS5 - PLS-Quality criteria interaction model

	AVE	Composite Reliability	R Square	Cronbach's Alpha	Communality	Redundancy
CBR	0.6105	0.9031	0.2495	0.8706	0.6105	0.1114
GOS_1	1	1	0	1	1	0
GOS_5	1	1	0	1	1	0

App. Table 141: Interactions within GOS group - GOS1/GOS5 - PLS-Quality criteria main effects model

GOS2/GOS5

path	loading	sample mean	standard deviation	standard error	t-value
CBR_1 <- CBR	0.7677	0.7679	0.011	0.011	69.8045
CBR_2 <- CBR	0.823	0.8231	0.0075	0.0075	109.4419
CBR_3 <- CBR	0.7975	0.7974	0.0091	0.0091	87.7477
CBR_4 <- CBR	0.7753	0.7753	0.0098	0.0098	78.7454
CBR_5 <- CBR	0.6393	0.6398	0.0162	0.0162	39.5451
CBR_6 <- CBR	0.8674	0.8675	0.0063	0.0063	136.9437
GOS_2_r <- GOS_2	1	1	0	0	0
GOS_2_r*GOS_5_r <- GOS_2*GOS_5	1	1	0	0	0
GOS_5_r <- GOS_5	1	1	0	0	0

App. Table 142: Interactions within GOS group - GOS2/GOS5 - outer loadings

path	path coefficient	sample mean	standard deviation	standard error	t-value
GOS_2*GOS_5 -> CBR	0.139	0.1388	0.0291	0.0291	4.7828
GOS_2 -> CBR	0.2457	0.2466	0.028	0.028	8.7665
GOS_5 -> CBR	0.3253	0.3251	0.0282	0.0282	11.5515

App. Table 143: Interactions within GOS group - GOS2/GOS5 - path coefficients

	AVE	Composite Reliability	R Square	Cronbach's Alpha	Communality	Redundancy
CBR	0.6109	0.9033	0.2263	0.8706	0.6109	-0.0359
GOS_2*GOS_5	1	1	0	1	1	0
GOS_2	1	1	0	1	1	0
GOS_5	1	1	0	1	1	0

App. Table 144: Interactions within GOS group - GOS2/GOS5 - PLS-Quality criteria interaction model

	AVE	Composite Reliability	R Square	Cronbach's Alpha	Communality	Redundancy
CBR	0.6108	0.9032	0.2131	0.8706	0.6108	0.0699
GOS_2	1	1	0	1	1	0
GOS_5	1	1	0	1	1	0

App. Table 145: Interactions within GOS group - GOS2/GOS5 - PLS-Quality criteria main effects model